D0445215

Freedom's Ordeal

Pennsylvania Studies in Human Rights

Bert B. Lockwood, Jr., Series Editor

A complete list of books in the series is available from the publisher.

Freedom's Ordeal

The Struggle for Human Rights and
Democracy in Post-Soviet States

Peter Juviler

PENN

University of Pennsylvania Press

Philadelphia

To Anne Carol Stephens

10 9 8 7 6 5 4 3 2 1

Published by
University of Pennsylvania Press
Philadelphia, Pennsylvania 19104-4011

Library of Congress Cataloging-in-Publication Data
Juviler, Peter H.
  Freedom's ordeal : the struggle for human rights and democracy in post-Soviet states /
Peter Juviler.
     p.   cm. — (Pennsylvania studies in human rights)
  Includes bibliographical references and index.
  ISBN 0-8122-3418-9 (alk. paper)
  1. Human rights—Former Soviet republics—History.   2. Former Soviet republics—
Politics and government.   I. Title.   II. Series.
JC599.F6J88   1997
323'.0947'09049—dc21   97-22400
                                                                              CIP

Contents

Introduction

Three interests of mine have shaped this book: the fulfillment of human rights under the rule of law, the democratization associated with human rights, and Soviet communism as system and legacy. Together, progress and regress in human rights and democratization have shaped the ordeal of freedom in the post-Soviet states. That ordeal means a difficult time for freedom there and for their inhabitants. The "universality" of human rights is more sorely tested in post-Soviet states, generally, than it is in the post-communist states of Eastern Europe.

The rise of Nazism and Soviet communism raised questions as to whether totalitarian regimes did not reflect a human yearning to "escape from freedom" in times of economic crisis and personal insecurity, such as those that again beset most post-Soviet states. Totalitarianism prompted warnings of a possible future without freedom in such negative utopias as Eugene Zamyatin's *We* and George Orwell's *1984*. But then, as now, the outcome of the crisis has been disputed. Before Orwell published his grim scenario of total nonfreedom in 1948, George Kennan wrote back from Moscow that communism, if contained by a cordon of recovered capitalist democracies, was doomed to mellow or collapse under the weight of its own repression of human creativity and initiative. Walter Rostow in 1961 dismissed communist totalitarianism as a passing "sickness of the transition" of industrialization, even while Stalin's successor, Nikita Khrushchev, asserted that the future belonged to communism. The military defeat of Germany and Japan had cleared the way for freedom and democracy in Western Europe and parts of Asia. The emergence of new non-Western, "third world" countries, and their difficulties, prompted debate that continues to this day about the universality of human rights and democracy in our culturally diverse world of sovereign states. The debate gained a new lease on life when "democracy's third wave" swept into Spain and Portugal, Latin America, Asia, and Eastern Europe during the 1970s and 1980s.[1]

The collapse of Soviet communism and the breakup of the USSR added a new dimension to the debate and prompted the writing of this book. Do the cultural and institutional legacies of communism and prior despotism in post-Soviet countries—the dominant state and the absence of a legal market economy—make them especially unwelcoming to the survival of freedom after the Soviet breakup? Are they not culturally unwelcoming to freedom's prerequisite, democracy, and human rights under the rule of law?

The pessimists have reasons for wondering whether the long-repressed peoples of post-Soviet states might not prefer to escape their new and difficult freedom. They can point to the limit in the reach of "democracy's third wave." Only about a fifth of the world's population has lived in countries that Freedom House calls "free."[2] Internal political crises threaten democracy and international security.[3] In this "century of megadeath," whole societies have seemed to lose their moral bearings.[4] Internal wars, some of them breaking out in post-Soviet states and their neighbors, have added to the toll.[5] Threats to life, health, and well-being assume transnational dimensions in aspects of international corporate activity, terrorism, arms sales, and nuclear hazards.[6]

Pessimists point to the post-Communist legacy of venal leaders and administrators, their incompetence and authoritarian habits of rule. Alexander Motyl sees Russia headed toward a form of fascism, followed possibly by Russia's eventual breakup. Barbara Applebaum notes that the corrupt former Communist governmental insiders turned businessmen have profited from their inside track on the bargain-rate privatization of state enterprises.[7]

The pessimists point also to flaws in the new democracies, the persistent violations of civil rights, the reach of organized crime, the ethnic tensions, the tearing of the social safety net. Moscow's Red Square area is the site for gatherings of various anti-democratic demonstrators carrying red banners with hammers and sickles, portraits of Stalin, swastikas, and monarchist flags. Most of the post-Soviet countries have mortality rates at third-world levels. Women fall short on civil, economic, and social rights. Cruel wars break out. Constitutional bills of rights remain unrealized. The eradication of the experience of democratic and legal reform during Communist social cleansing remains a lingering obstacle to the formation of a democratic political community.[8]

The comedown from the euphoria at the time of the fall of the Berlin Wall in 1989 has prompted comparisons between Russia and Weimar Germany before its "escape from freedom" to tyranny in 1933. But Russia and the other post-Soviet states are not Weimar Germany all over again. Russia, for all the embedded prejudices that surface against dark-skinned people from the Caucasus and Central Asia, Jews, and so forth, lacks Weimar Germany's core of militant "volkisch" nationalism associated with late unity, its international status of a "pariah state," and its voting patterns of growing support for right-wing parties in the face of economic decline.[9]

The pessimists see the glass of freedom and democracy as half empty in

Russia and the other newly independent states—the twelve countries that knew no prior internationally recognized independence. I join with the cautious optimists about the future of freedom in the post-Soviet democratic states. We give more weight than do the pessimists to freedom's gains, to its survival since 1985, and to the contradictions of nondemocracy as a path of economic development. I specifically refute the stereotype of Russia as somehow culturally and historically doomed to despotism for reasons I lay out in Chapter 2.

Before going off to observe the December 1995 elections in Russia and to talk with human rights advocates there, I heard a gripping panel discussion on the Russian elections with participants Stephen Cohen, the distinguished expert on the USSR and Russia at Princeton University, and former U.S. ambassador to the USSR Jack Matlock. Cohen based his pessimistic appraisal of trends in Russia on Russia's erring leadership, economic shocks, irrational factors of cultural legacy, and the obsessive question of "who is guilty?" Matlock, as Cohen proposed, was more empirical. He saw the transition as a process with many factors that would determine the outcome of the present grim situation, including the need for openness as a setting for essential reforms.[10] A few days after this discussion in New York, I observed with surprise the high and peaceful turnout at the polling places around and outside the city of Moscow. The presidential election rounds of June–July 1996—for all their other faults, including unequal media access—also featured high and peaceful turnouts and an absence of significant fraud and intimidation.

I share with cautious pragmatists like Ambassador Matlock and Lilia Shevtsova a sense of an ongoing, step-by-step struggle and conflict over reform, rather than simply a stagnation under the grip of vested conservative, bureaucratic interests. And I share Robert Sharlet's sense that Russia shows some signs of movement toward a stable constitutional definition of governmental powers and processes.[11] It seems more apt to see the glass of freedom in the post-Soviet states as half full rather than half empty—after all, the glass started empty when Stalin died on March 5, 1953. True, as a skeptical student of mine noted, the contents of the glass of freedom continually evaporate, and in some post-Soviet countries, quite visibly. But in others, it is continually replenished as well, while, as I note in Chapter 10, "the struggle continues."

The course of despotism and freedom in Imperial Russia, the USSR, and the post-Soviet states convinces me that those states are not necessarily captives to their despotic past. Nikita Khrushchev rashly promised in 1961 that "the present generation of Soviet people will live under communism," an ideal system of equality and prosperity. I think I am less rash in concluding that a majority of the younger generation of former Soviet citizens may well live in significantly freer and more democratic states than their parents and grandparents did, though far from an egalitarian ideal.

Ken Jowitt, prophet of "new world disorder," points to "a distinct and unfavorable Leninist legacy" of totalitarian state collectivism, inexperienced leadership, alienated society, and emergent threats of local separatism and ethnic conflict. "We must think in terms of a 'long march' rather than a simple transition to democracy."[12] The "long march" is an apt metaphor for freedom's ordeal in post-Soviet countries.

One must expect a diversity of outcomes. We are talking not about one people, but about a former empire of many peoples who live over a vast territory, spanning eleven time zones, from Scandinavia and Eastern Europe to the Asian-Pacific region, almost to Alaska. The universality of democratic freedoms and human rights is severely tested by diversity of culture and setting among and within the mainly non-Western post-Soviet states and their roughly 300 million inhabitants.

Frederic Fleron and Erik Hoffmann call upon observers of the post-Soviet scene to "more than ever try to benefit from and contribute to the social sciences."[13] As I recount in Chapter 1, I have benefited from recent research on democratization, as well as ongoing research on law and social change in communist and post-communist states. If I am contributing to the work of others, and to the reader's understanding of freedom's ordeal in the post-Soviet countries, it is by bringing human rights and a longer than usual historical perspective into the exploration of political development in those countries.

My basic assumption, spelled out in Chapter 1, is that democracy, human rights, and the rule of law are inseparable companions to the building and consolidation of stable, inclusive, democratic communities. An emphasis on human rights as the companion to democratization has begun to shape new research on political development, as it has shaped mine. I "import" that emphasis into this study of freedom's post-Soviet ordeal.[14] Freedom's ordeal centers on the struggle to build a new political community out of the shambles of the old one, and on making that community democratic and inclusive. Human rights provide both a measure and a prerequisite of the inclusiveness of political communities of shared legitimate institutions and bearers of mutual rights and obligations. Freedom, human rights, and democracy are the central political cluster of our story. Chapter 1 presents the arguments of cultural relativists and makes an opposing case for a qualified universalist approach. It cautions that democracy and human rights must be adapted to suit countries with distinctive cultures and experiences, rather than simply being transplanted from existing democracies, East or West. The chapter cautions, too, that the stability and extent of the democratic political community depend, in turn, on choices regarding the realization of political, civil, economic, and social rights, and the equality of rights and inclusiveness of a shared, multicultural identity.

The subsequent chapters of this book review the alternatives of freedom and despotism as they took hold before and after the Bolshevik takeover in 1917. Each chapter reflects this book's special approach: to explore freedom's ordeal, demise, and rebirth in the context of human rights and democratization as proclaimed, realized, lost, and affirmed.

Chapter 2 presents reasons for doubting that Russia and its empire of old were—or are now—doomed to despotism as their cultural and historic fate. Tsarist Russia was by World War I no longer the autocratic, isolated state one might assume if one tunes into Russian history, as many books do, only *after* the Bolshevik revolution. Legal and political reforms were taking hold there by 1917. The fatal rigidities of tsarist autocracy brought it into deepening conflict with the modernizing changes in the society, the economy initiated by the regime's efforts to catch up with the West, and Russia's rapid industrialization. Russians lived in ever less isolation from the West, and the West, from Russia, until World War I brought the collapse of tsarism and, later the pro-reform Provisional Government. The Bolshevik takeover meant that growing interchanges with the West would be transformed into confrontation.

Chapter 3 further develops my argument about alternatives to despotism. The ordeal of freedom in post-Soviet countries has been made more difficult by the shared legacy of Communist political and social cleansing. It erased the experience, even the memory, of the democratic freedoms that appeared before 1917 in the Russian Empire and its short-lived successor, the Provisional Government. After Joseph Stalin's death in March 1953, the rapidity of the thaw under Nikita Khrushchev confirmed that freedom of thought and creativity had somehow survived the Leninist and Stalinist terrors. Reaction set in under Leonid Brezhnev and his successors, Yury Andropov and Konstantin Chernenko, before Mikhail Gorbachev (1964–1985). But rationality and freedom continued to clash with despotism in the Communists' would-be "scientific and technological revolution." A "creeping openness" of growing professional autonomy, rationality, and participation in decision making had begun during the thaw. It continued despite the cultural reaction and increased persecution of dissidents under Brezhnev and his successors. Bureaucratic despotism, as it existed in tsarist Russia and the former Soviet Union, appeared doomed because of its choke hold on individual initiative and creativity, just as George Kennan predicted.[15]

Chapter 4 treats the crucial test of readiness for freedom that began under Mikhail Gorbachev (1985–1991). Freedom developed out of Gorbachev's adoption of some of the dissidents' "new thinking" on human rights and democracy—for which previous leaders had sent dissidents to prison, mental institutions, and exile. As Soviet communism opened up, so did the talk of law and human rights. The constitution came to express new principles and new content compatible with a shared, multicultural recognition of universal human rights. The new principles and the new freedom informed the brightest—and originally, least central part—of Gorbachev's political bequest. At the same time, the ordeal of freedom brought growing material hardships, mounting ethnic conflicts, and incomplete decommunization to a society—and by a leadership—ill-prepared for it.

The Soviet breakup in 1991 left some newly independent states in the position of partial democracies, as I discuss in Chapter 5 and in Chapters 8, 9, and 10, which are devoted mainly to Russia. They struggled to make up for the loss of long-existing political authority and a shared national, Soviet identity in the "new historical community of hope" of the "Soviet peoples"[16]—albeit one resented by some minorities. The institution of *perestroika*, the Soviet breakup, and independence disrupted established patterns of rights and responsibilities, however limited they had been, and ended comprehensive economic planning and the minimal security of livelihood it provided. Change left even would-be reformers trapped in the dilemmas of reconciling old collectivist outlooks with demands of an unfamiliar economic and political pluralism.

The diversity and range of democratization alongside persistent authoritarianism sometimes gets lost in the selective media coverage of the post-Soviet countries. But new freedom poses difficult challenges to the brightest of leaders everywhere, and capable leaders are in short supply.

Mancur Olson says of autocracies that they do a much poorer job than democracies in "preventing leaders from carrying off large shares of the 'social surplus.'" Autocracies lack democracy's emphasis on individual rights, which is necessary also "for secure rights to both property and the enforcement of contracts."[17] Post-communist, new, and still quite incomplete democracies inherited venal and hardly accountable political elites as carryovers from communist autocracy. "Many of the formerly Communist societies," says Robert Putnam, "had weak civic traditions before the advent of Communism and totalitarian rule abused even that limited stock of social capital." Civil society—autonomous and civically active—has only just begun to reemerge in countries cleansed of civic spontaneity by the Communists. Putnam sees in southern Italy's "amoral familism, clientilism, lawlessness, ineffective government, and economic stagnation" the possible "future of Moscow"—unless, that is, "a more moderate, pragmatic, tolerant elite political culture [provides] the key to making democracy work."[18]

Such a favorable political culture had begun to emerge by the late 1990s in states that contain the vast majority of the post-Soviet population.[19] Even without the difficult Soviet communist legacy, successor states to collapsed empires have rarely achieved stable democracy on their first try. But as these states enter the twenty-first century, international supports and pressures for democratization and human rights observance have created a more favorable international context for development in the Eurasian space than existed in much of the twentieth century.

Chapter 6 recounts that a pro-democratic elite culture was eroded in authoritarian post-Soviet states and driven virtually underground in the

Central Asian dictatorships. The loss of union stirred new regional cross currents in the "near abroad" and posed new questions about Russia's growing hegemonic position there, and about the mix of cooperation and discord with the "farther abroad."

Freedom survived its ordeal best in the once again independent Baltic states, as I suggest in Chapter 7. Even so, the Soviet legacy in these states presented grave dilemmas. Years after attaining independence, Estonia and Latvia had yet to reconcile the rights of their indigenous dwellers to nationhood and cultural survival with the rights of the large immigrant minorities to citizenship and equality. The dispute over citizenship and language brings home the potential conflicts between human rights and the limits of human rights as international legal standards. Yet the human rights of minorities continued to be significant indicators of inclusiveness of membership in the political communities of the Baltic countries.

Russia, the core of two empires, is by far the biggest and most influential of the newly independent states. Chapter 8 analyzes the advent and nature of Russia's semi-democracy and its lapse into a new authoritarianism, with its poison fruit of the Chechnya war. Embattled upholders of political and religious freedoms and a range of surviving political human rights confront elements of lawlessness inside and outside the government. For all their weaknesses, the 1996 presidential elections introduced a modicum of accountability, in contrast to the rigged procedures in post-communist authoritarian countries; they played a part, along with a strong-willed general, in the latest ceasefire in a bitter history of Russian-Chechen relations.

The legal and social contexts of freedom in Russia in the late 1990s left it dangerously exposed, as I recount in Chapter 9. Civil rights of the person—the restraints on governmental abuses and the right to due process—lagged behind the progress in political freedom. Economic and social rights lagged no less dangerously. Russia could maintain its unity largely because it had become a federal state in practice as well as theory, whatever the wishes of the center. Threats to peace and unity remain, beyond Chechnya, in other regions of the Caucasus, particularly in the territorial dispute between Northern Ossetians and Ingush.

In a departure from other post-Soviet political studies, this book devotes attention to the *new* human rights movement. In Chapter 10, I convey something of the movement's day-to-day activities, as advocates network and help defend human rights in Russia. The chapter notes also the heavy dependence on foreign funding thus far, and the crucial importance of that funding. It closes by summing up the implications of the history, diverse outcomes, and agenda for the struggle for human rights and democracy in post-Soviet states.

Over most of the former Soviet region, people face a uniquely difficult task of democratization. Yet there are positive sides to the legacy, including gains in freedom and democratic political experience, civilian rule, relatively high literacy, and growing movements for human rights and freedoms. One should not speak of transplanting democracy and human rights, but of adapting them, by local efforts, with encouragement from abroad. This goal lies at the heart of freedom's ordeal and freedom's opportunity.

Acknowledgments

Grateful thanks go to the organizations and individuals who have helped to make possible the research, interchanges, and human rights dialogues that led up to the writing of this book. Many of them are listed here. The responsibility for the book's accuracy and analysis is mine alone.

Among the organizations that significantly furthered my work with grants, fellowships, or other forms of support and encouragement, I want to thank the American Council of Learned Societies, Barnard College, the Columbia University Center for the Study of Human Rights, the Citizen Exchange Council, the Ford Foundation, Hunter College, the International Research and Exchanges Board (IREX) (as funded in part by the Andrew W. Mellon Foundation, the National Endowment for the Humanities, and the U.S. Department of State), IREX's predecessor, the Inter-University Committee on Travel Grants, the Lawyers Committee for Human Rights, the Social Science Research Council, and the University of California (Berkeley).

Persons in the United States to whom thanks are owed include the late Bertram Gross, cocoordinator of the U.S.–Soviet (later International) Dialogue on Human Rights, and the late John Hazard, my graduate mentor at the Russian (now Harriman) Institute, Columbia University. I owe thanks also to many others for their insight, information, valuable scholarly cooperation, comments on my work, and research assistance: Nicholas Arena, Esq., Dorothy Atkinson, Donald Barry, Mara Bolis, Richard Buxbaum, Kelly Cannard, Walter Connor, Margaret Crahan, Alexander Dallin, Elena Daly, Esq., Rachel Denber, Jack Donnelly, Katherine Drobesh, F. J. M. Feldbrugge, Charles Fenwick, Wesley Fisher, David Forsythe, George Ginsburgs, Abbot Gleason, Alex Grigorievs, Hurst Hannum, Kathryn Hendley, Charles Henry, Susan Heuman, Erik Hoffmann, Mary Holland, Esq., Scott Horton, Esq., Kenneth Hunter, Tony Jones, Stanley Katz, Mariana Katzarova, Nadia Kavrus-Hoffmann, Edward Kline, Antti Korkeakivi, Gail Lapidus, Joan Levinson, Pavel Litvinov, Joan Lofgren, Peter B. Maggs, Rita Maran, James Millar, Henry Morton, Agnes Nagpal, Deborah Ng, Vello Pettai, Alexander Rabinowitch, Albert Schmidt, Robert Sharlet, George Sherman, Henry Shue, William Simmons, Tanya Smith, Esq., Richard Stites, Ludmilla Thorne, Rudolph Tokes, Nils Wessel, Sharon Wolchik, and numerous challenging students.

Thanks go overseas to many, including Joan Dawson (Newfoundland Legal Aid Commission); Hiroshi Kimura (Japan); Priit Jarve and colleagues (Institute of Philosophy, Sociology and Law, Tallinn), Aleksei Semyonov and Hanon Barabaner (cochairmen of the Russian Democratic Movement, Estonia), Tiiu Pohl (Tallinn Pedagogical University), and Peter Vares (Estonia); Maris Grinblats, Iuris Prikulis, and Visvaldis Latsis (Latvia); Rimguadas K. Malisauskas and Deputies Zbigniew Baltsievic, Czieslaw Okinczyc, and Riomualdas Ozalas (Lithuania); Estonian and Latvian Missions to the United Nations, Galina Kulikova, and other members of the Society for Russian Culture (Yerevan). In Russia thanks go to Valery Abramkin (Center for Prison Reform); Ludmilla Alexeeva (Moscow Helsinki Group, AFL-CIO, et al.); Justice Ernest Ametistov (Russian Constitutional Court); Anatoly Azarov (Project on "Human Rights Education in Russia"); the late Georgy and Nina Barabashev; Yelena Bonner; Yury Dzhibladze (Anti-War Organizing Committee); Vladimir Ilyushenko (Society for Russian Cultural Rebirth); Vladimir Kartashkin and Elena Lukasheva (Institute of State and Law, Russian Academy of Sciences); Viktor Kogan-Yasny ("For Human Dignity"); Dmitry Leonov, Yan Rachinsky, Arseny Roginsky, Lena Rusakova, and Aleksandr Sokolov (Moscow "Memorial" Society); Georgii Mirskii (Institute of World Economics and International Relations, et al.); the late Avgust Mishin; Irina Paikacheva (Murmansk Mothers of Russian Soldiers, Murmansk Women's Crisis Center, Kola Peninsular Congress of Women, et al.); Alexander Radygin (Department on Privatization and Ownership Structures, Institute on the Economy in Transition); the late Andrei Sakharov; Natalia Taubina, Vladimir Raskin, and Aleksei Smirnov (Moscow Research Center for Research on Human Rights); Vladimir Rudnev (Institute for Legislation and Comparative Law and Center for Prison Reform); and Lev Timofeyev (Moscow Helsinki Group).

I am grateful also for the confidence and encouragement of Bert Lockwood, Jr., series editor of Pennsylvania Studies in Human Rights, Timothy Clancy, editorial director of the University of Pennsylvania Press, and his meticulous colleagues, Mindy Brown, project editor, and Kym Silvasy, acquisitions assistant.

Chapter 1
Getting to Democracy

> Law in general is human reason inasmuch as it governs all the inhabitants of the earth; the political and civil laws of each nation ought to be only the particular cases in which human reason is applied. They should be adapted . . . to the people for whom they are framed.
> —Baron de Montesquieu[1]

Escape from Freedom?

Humans' capacity for dealing with the burden of choice that is freedom has been questioned from Plato to Freud and beyond. Should choice rest with a small elite or can it be entrusted to the community as a whole? Dostoyevsky's doubting Ivan Karamazov dreamed of a cynical Grand Inquisitor in Spain who captured Christ one night and told Him that He was offering humans a dangerous freedom of choice. Human beings, the Inquisitor told Christ, prefer others to make their choices, gladly surrendering freedom for bread. They clamor, "Make us your slaves but feed us." The ending of Ivan's dream is often ignored. After Christ had sat silently through the Inquisitor's monologue, He kissed the old man on his bloodless lips. The Inquisitor then released Christ into the Seville night. Christ always remains to challenge the devil of human subjection (for whom the Inquisitor worked) with the option of free choice.

Human rights advocates around the world today have a more positive faith than Ivan did in the reasonable side of humans and their capacity to make free choices and to realize their unalienable rights in community with others.[2] This belief has been neither refuted nor positively upheld in the post-Soviet states. But three-quarters of their population live in democracies which, however imperfect, are a quantum leap away from the restraints on public life and expression under communism.

Freedom and Democratic Choices

A stable democratic community that enjoys freedom and a broad range of human rights does not just appear through some predetermined evolution. The type of government and the responsibilities for rights that frame the democratic community take form and disappear in response to *choices* made by leaders, officials, other powerful interests and persons, expert consultants, and the involved segments of society. Choices about development and inclusivity combine with political choices to shape the democratic community or some nondemocratic alternative.[3]

As for political choices, we may observe examples of great leaps in our spheres of interest, such as the 1864 judicial reforms, the 1905 Revolution and establishment of the State Duma (parliament), the Bolshevik Revolution, and Gorbachev's *glasnost'* (lit. "openness") and "new thinking." We may also look ahead to incremental choices with cumulative effects, such as professional participation in Russia's new local governments after 1864 and the start of the liberal movement; a citizen's decision to vote in a post-Communist election or form or join pressure groups or movements, or to pay off or confront the mobsters; or the parliamentary bargaining over a budget.

The term "democracy" has not yet been defined. As used here, "democracy" means, ideally, rule by the people, either directly or through elected representatives. The distinguishing essence of representative democracy is government by *consent*, through the government's *accountability* to society.[4] Authoritarian governments are unaccountable, lacking meaningful processes of consent. Totalitarian governments hold society accountable to *them*. The Soviet government before *perestroika* (lit. "restructuring") could be said to have acted as an essentially totalitarian government. Even when it had lost its ideological fervor and slipped into conservative stagnation under Brezhnev, the government continued to hold society accountable to it through a network of censors and informers, maintaining the power to hire and fire throughout much of the economy, and exerting administrative controls over residence, travel—even the definition of one's nationality.

Pro-democratic and competent elites inside and outside government, including a reforming leadership, are essential to successful, relatively complete, and stable democratization.[5] Often the first generation of democratizing leadership comes out of the political elite of the prior regime; for example, Prince, then King, Don Juan Carlos of post-Franco Spain, and Presidents Mikhail Gorbachev of the USSR, Boris Yeltsin of Russia, and Algirdas Brazauskas of Lithuania. Juan Carlos grew up in an already quite pluralized, nontotalitarian Spain, a country relatively open to outside democratic influences. Gorbachev as leader retained the collectivist ethos of the system in which he was raised.

Democratization requires not only pro-democratic leadership but also an active, autonomous, and essentially pro-democratic "civil society." A civil society is, ideally, autonomous, active, and politically empowered. It is the source of public input and the foundation of a democratic community.[6] Political parties link civil society to government as avenues of recruitment and drafters of programmatic alternatives for the people's choice.[7] By and large, its members share a consensus on the political game and on the role and rule of law. The hallmark of a democratic civil society is a democratic political culture, "the fundamental values and beliefs, the foci of identification and loyalty, and the political knowledge and expectations which are the product of the specific experience of nations and groups." Archie Brown and most students of post-Soviet politics conceive of political culture not as rigidly bound by tradition but as changing with time and circumstances.[8]

Elements of a growing autonomy and activism are emerging in post-Soviet democracies. In the old days the Soviet public's political participation, or "inputs" to the political system, to use David Easton's term,[9] were mainly through what Easton calls "supports": taxes, military service, mobilized participation, and acquiescence. The appearance of "demand" inputs on the system began even under communism, when decision making on policy spread into the cultural and professional elites during the party-monitored "creeping openness" under Khrushchev and Brezhnev.

Perestroika and subsequent democratization have given the general public the chance to make demands through demonstrations, strikes, new parties, the media, new businesses, and various groups and movements—environmental, antiwar, women's, miners', pro-Communist, monarchist, extreme racist nationalist, and, practically speaking, criminal as well. A part-civil society has been emerging in the more democratic post-Soviet states.

One should not idealize a democratic public's opportunities or zest for participation when seeking comparisons by which to judge freedom's progress and regress in post-Soviet states. Certainly there is some truth to the ideal of a rational policy process in the United States. It begins with an electoral mandate, goes on to policy making that features hearings, lobbying, compromises, and public input, and is followed by renewed electoral accountability for policy and its results. But debates continue in the United States as to whether public participation is declining in communities and in national politics, whether media hype obscures issues while fixated on ill-informed poll results, whether the public is interacting less effectively with Congress and the executive branch as they shape national policy.[10] Voting participation of around 50–60 percent of eligible voters in presidential elections and under 40 percent in congressional elections suggests departures from an ideal "civil society"; the more so when we compare U.S. levels of participation with the over 70–80 percent participation in other advanced democracies.

Civil society is also an ideal regarding the distribution of power. Conglomerations of money and resources in media, business, and other spheres wield great power. A small percentage of the public engages in the policy process, as E. E. Schattschneider found in *The Semi-Sovereign People.*[11]

Freedom's dependence on democracy and guaranteed rights under rule of law leaves it vulnerable to the flaws in democracy everywhere. "As long as people are people," President Vaclav Havel told the U.S. Congress, "democracy in the full sense of the word will always be no more than an ideal; one may approach it as one would approach a horizon, in ways that may be better or worse, but it can never be fully attained."[12]

Without compromising on standards of democracy and human rights, we should realize, then, that even vaunted exemplars of democracy leave the glass of freedom less than full. We should keep in mind the imperfections and departures from the ideal in established democracies when assessing the extent of democratization in the post-Soviet states, as in other countries. But we should also apply the highest standards of human rights as a measure of freedom's progress.

Human Rights and Democracy

Human rights are the rights to which all people are entitled as human beings.[13] Democracy is essential to the accountability of government that is necessary for protecting human rights. Recognizing this, the drafters of the Universal Declaration of Human Rights (UDHR) included, through Article 21, the affirmation of everyone's right to participation, "directly or through freely chosen representatives," to "equal access to public service" and to government resting its authority on the will of the people as expressed in periodic, free, and fair elections.[14] Human rights, conversely, define the obligations that cement the democratic political community.[15]

UN Secretary-General Boutros Boutros-Ghali reminded us that "Human rights are both absolute and historically defined."[16] Enduring through all generations of human rights is the goal of humans' self-determination and self-fulfillment, as individuals and in community with others.[17] The specific list of recognized human rights has grown over time. The democratic community rests on guarantees of two "generations" of rights, political and economic. A growing number of advocates also argue for a third generation of "solidarity rights," so called because they affect human beings as a whole.[18] They include the human right to peace,[19] the right to a healthy environment,[20] and the right to development, a topic to be discussed shortly.

The first generation of civil and political human rights was recognized philosophically in seventeenth-century England and proclaimed politically in the eighteenth-century American colonies and France. Free elections, the immediate touchstone of democracy, form only a facade unless they are accompanied by other political rights of participation—rights to freedom of thought, conscience, expression, and information, assembly, association, and office holding, as well as the electoral franchise.[21] This ideal is approximated among the post-Soviet states only for the citizens of Estonia, Latvia, and Lithuania. However, over 70 percent of the post-Soviet population lives in partly free democracies where they exercise at least part of the range of nonelectoral political rights; they still lack a comprehensive rule of law, civil rights to due process and personal inviolability, adequate economic and social rights, and many solidarity rights (see Chapter 5).

The protection of people's rights requires an effective rule of law. Political rights can be snuffed out in the absence of firm guarantees of civil rights to personal equality, due process, and inviolability. Citizens remain vulnerable to abuse or harm by either the state or other members of society.[22] Millennia of thought and practice convey Aristotle's ancient message, "It is more proper that the law should govern than any one of its citizens." Juan Linz is joined by other scholars, by public figures, and by human rights theorist Jack Donnelly in his finding that democracy "cannot be considered fully established" until it produces constitutional rule of law to define and limit governmental authority and to protect the rights of those subject to that authority, be they in the majority or the minority.[23]

The rule of law has two levels: legality and constitutionalism. Legality means obedience to the laws by officials and the public. That in itself is an essential part of responsible government and individual security.[24] Constitutionalism embraces legality but goes beyond it: It is the spirit and practice of a government that is accountable to a higher law, as well as to its citizens.[25] During its journey toward constitutionalism, a political community replaces the dependency principle of law and rights with the supremacy principle. The community moves away from laws dependent only on the will of the majority or power elites, toward the supremacy of the higher law of the constitution over those who make and administer the laws.

Choices of Development and Inclusiveness

The stability and membership of a democratic community depend not only on choices to protect and exercise civil and political rights but also on choices shaping economic and social development and human rights. John Hazard applied to the Soviet case the old adage that property is the key to power.[26] Another key to power is legitimacy, and it rests in part on how public and private wealth is shared among the populace. To what extent do the managers of the economy make it both productive and socially equitable?

Economic and social rights obtained recognition in the nineteenth and twentieth centuries as inseparable complements to political and civil rights, and as standards of social equity and empowerment.[27] People must have all three—freedom, democracy, and human rights, imperfect though they are in life—if they are to enjoy any one of them permanently. Freedom, democracy, and human rights are interdependent. In the words of the United

Nations World Conference on Human Rights, "Democracy, development and respect for human rights and fundamental freedoms are interdependent and mutually reinforcing."[28]

The UN Development Program has measured the human well-being associated with such rights by using a human development index, HDI, based on gross national product, along with such indices of human development as literacy and longevity. The fulfillment of these human rights gives people the material and cultural basis for their participation in the life of the democratic community. Larry Diamond and other researchers conclude that democracy correlates not simply with economic growth and national income alone, but with human development and the human development index.[29]

The right to development has gained wider recognition in recent years. It is seen as being bound up with the rights of democratic participation and human development (in education, health, etc.) and with the equal rights of women as vital participants in development.[30] In most post-Soviet states, human development has been seriously compromised by the loss of basic incomes and safety nets.

Democratic community also depends on choices about the inclusiveness of identity and rights. It thrives when the government, individuals, and groups decide to share a national identity, equality of rights, and allegiance to their country's political institutions. This promotes unity across lines of distinctive identity and interests, be they ethnic, class, gender, religious, or regional. To deny inclusiveness in human rights is to undermine unity and stability.[31]

Coerced Soviet unity is being replaced by a range of choices, from Ukraine's inclusiveness to Estonia's and Latvia's exclusionary citizenship laws; nationalism ranges from an inclusive patriotism to an exclusive interethnic hostility.[32] In Russia, nation building means that we are all *rossiiane*—that is, members of the civic community of the Russian nation-state—as well as ethnic Russians (*russkie*)—Tatars, Jews, Buryats, and so forth. This has not averted the terrible war in Chechnya, intergroup conflict, and discrimination against "persons with a Caucasian complexion."

The experience of twentieth-century democracy suggests that recruits to democracy embarked on a democratic course because of a combination of committed and able leadership; relatively autonomous societies linked with market economies; a shared national identity that transcended ethnic, regional, and cultural differences; and preexisting market economies.[33] Post-Soviet states started out more or less lacking in these respects.

Adapting Democracy

The UN General Assembly approved the UDHR on December 10, 1948, by a vote of 48 to 0 with eight abstentions. In so doing, the General Assembly affirmed the universal validity of human rights. It proclaimed the UDHR "a common standard of achievement for all peoples and all nations." Universality rests on the concept that all humans are suitable bearers of rights at birth, that "All human beings are born free and equal in dignity and rights. They are endowed with reason and conscience and should act towards one another in a spirit of brotherhood."[34] The "should" in this sentence evokes countless histories of humans' accepting or rejecting that spirit of kinship.

The noneuphoric realities of freedom's ordeal recall Robert Putnam's deepening "despair about public institutions" globally. The prospects do not brighten, he says, when one considers the post-Soviet states of Eurasia, which "find themselves having to build democratic systems of governance from scratch." Putnam asks, "If we transplant democratic institutions, will they grow in the new setting as they did in the old?"[35] Of course not. Witness transplanted democracy's demise in many postcolonial emerging nations. Democracy and human rights must be not simply transplanted but adapted. As Montesquieu cautioned, in the epigraph to this chapter, the laws of each nation should reflect common human reason, its laws "should be adapted . . . to the people for [whom] they are framed."

Members of a private U.S. human rights delegation to Moscow in 1989 enthused about the U.S. Bill of Rights. They then listened to a Russian prosecutor tell them that, when it comes to rights such as the distinguished visitors from the United States described, "We live on two different planets." An attempt to transplant U.S. legal institutions in the USSR "would be like an agrarian project on Mars."[36]

Democratic institutions and the rule of law must be adapted to local cultures and conditions. This applies within the West as well as outside it.[37] Constitutional historians and lawyers have affirmed this over and again.[38] Democratic transplants have taken hold only in the case of war-defeated foes, such as Japan and Germany. Yet even there tradition and context shaped the results, as in the retention of Japan's emperor and the restoration of democratic institutions resembling the pre-Nazi parliament, the Reichstag, and German federalism.

"Relativists" deny that human rights are universally valid in this culturally diverse world. They maintain that human rights are imperialist impositions on third-world nations. They also point out that human rights stress the individual over community, whereas in many cultures, the reverse is true.[39] But the struggle for human rights has found numerous illustrious and grass-roots champions outside the West.[40] Relativism is the non-Western dictators' cloak for concealing their own abuses and discrediting their critics.[41] Also, human rights do in fact imply a responsibility of individuals to the community and to other individuals.[42] The balance between rights and responsibilities is something for each country to work out, in an eternal debate that lies at the heart of politics.

Cultural relativists argue that different cultures give such diverse meanings to words like "rights" that no common understanding of them is possible. Adda Bozeman, for example, has maintained that "it is important in today's multicultural world to combat . . . the tendency to assume, without supporting evidence, that one of *our* morally preferred words and convictions carries a universally accepted truth. In the dictionary of terms relating to foreign affairs, this is particularly true of 'peace,' 'law,' and, in more recent years, of 'human rights.'"[43]

Relativism does not explain why and how democracy and the human rights struggle have spread into non-Western countries. Moreover, the debate and struggle over the validity of human rights has also riven Western thought and politics.[44] The human rights movement, as well as the concept of human rights, originated in the West. But they have accelerated democratization and helped freedom through its struggles around the world.

The human rights movement dates back to the antislavery and women's rights movements that emerged in the first half of the nineteenth century, followed by the humanitarian work of the Red Cross in the 1860s. Labor rights received international recognition with the founding and work of the International Labor Organization (ILO), beginning in 1919. This century also brought a mixed record of self-determination and minority rights protection under the League of Nations between the two world wars.[45]

During World War II, Franklin Delano Roosevelt and Winston Churchill anticipated the codification of an international bill of rights in the Atlantic Charter they signed at sea in August 1941. Their vision of a "better future for the world" expressed respect for "the right of all peoples to choose the government under which they will live" in a world collaborating to secure "for all, improved labor standards, economic advancement, and social security." They expressed hope for a peace "after the destruction of Nazi tyranny . . . which will afford assurance that all the men in all the lands may live out their lives in freedom from fear and want."[46] President Roosevelt's 1944 State of the Union message contained an "Economic Bill of Rights" and the proposition that "necessitous men are not free men."

Eleanor Roosevelt then presided over the drafting of the UDHR. It was passed by the General Assembly on December 10, 1948. South Africa, Saudi Arabia, and the communist countries abstained. Two days earlier the General Assembly had passed the Genocide Convention for future ratification.[47] To validate human rights in this culturally diverse world, their champions added to reasons of religion and natural law the argument that, after all, human rights are a core component of international law and the constitutions of many new states.[48] The framers of the UDHR included other bases of validation: (1) Human rights benefit human beings: their recognition is a prerequisite for "freedom, justice, and peace in the world," and for human dignity as security, respect, and self-fulfillment; (2) They protect humans: disregard for human rights has resulted in outrageous barbarities; and (3) Human beings are reasonable and have a conscience.[49]

The human rights movement grew in response to industrialization in the West. As modernization spread beyond the West, so too did advocacy of human rights protections against the powerful state. The UDHR spawned the rest of the so-called International Bill of Rights—the two covenants springing from the UDHR—in 1966. Along with the ILO agreements, these grew into a corpus of about sixty global and regional international pacts, accords, and resolutions subscribed to by countries with a wide variety of cultures and traditions but sharing the experience of modernization, and the issues of human rights it opens up.[50] In the words of The UN World Conference on Human Rights (1993):

All human rights are universal, indivisible, and interdependent and interrelated. The international community must treat human rights globally in a fair and equal manner, on the same footing, and with the same emphasis. While the significance of national and regional particularities and various historical, cultural, and religious backgrounds must be borne in mind, it is the duty of States, regardless of their political, economic, and cultural systems, to promote and protect all human rights and fundamental freedoms.[51]

Human rights principles provided a framework for democracy's "third wave" in the 1970s and 1980s.[52] The human rights movement broke ground for the Helsinki Final Act of 1975, the first East–West agreement containing at least a formal consensus on human rights. The Helsinki accord inspired the East European groundswell of movements against communism in the late 1980s.

The failings of governments as guardians of human rights place a heavier responsibility than ever on the work of NGO (nongovernmental organizations) advocacy, monitoring, and humanitarian aid.[53] Home-grown NGO activism within post-Soviet states forms a crucial part of the democratic choice.[54] As human rights advocate Ludmilla Alexeyeva told an audience of Russian pedagogues, progress in human rights and democratization is not someone else's task: "it depends on each one of us."[55]

Conclusions

Research on democratization and human rights suggests a close interdependency among democracy, human rights, and the freedoms associated with them. Their realization in unfree, authoritarian countries appears to depend on factors of economic and social development and leadership committed to making formally democratic institutions democratic in content as well. The more inclusive a democratic community is, the more stable it is likely to be: hence the importance of a rule of law that protects the rights of both majorities and minorities. The essential observance of political, civil, and economic human rights cannot be simply transplanted from stable and relatively full democracies to nondemocratic countries.

Nevertheless, the spread of democracy outside the West has demonstrated that human rights and democracy can be adapted, if not transplanted, across cultures. When we attempt to gauge progress and regress in that adaptation we should, as I suggested above, keep in mind the imperfections and departures from the ideal in established democracies; but we should also apply the highest standards of human rights as a measure of freedom's progress.

The lack of time-tested conditions for democratic development in most post-Soviet states warns us not to underestimate the difficulties of freedom's ordeal there. But, as the following chapters suggest, neither should we lapse into a resigned cultural determinism or a cultural relativism that denies the importance and feasibility of post-Soviet efforts to incorporate human rights standards into law and practice.

Chapter 2
Changing Russia

> There exist two Russias, one quite different from the other, and what
> pleases one is quite sure to displease the other. . . . One is the Russia
> of the future, as dreamed of by members of the liberal professions; the
> other is an anachronism, deeply rooted in the past, and defended in
> the present by an omnipotent bureaucracy. The one spells liberty, the
> other, despotism.
>
> —Paul Milyukov, 1903[1]

Captive of History?

Why plunge back into the past of Imperial Russia in the attempt to understand the post-Soviet present? Because as Russia wavers between past and
future, in its third try for democracy, we once again confront the ambi-
guity between cultural determinism and democratic universalism, between
a liberal Russia of the future that draws on its own prerevolutionary liberal
reforms and the despotic Russia of the past.

"The political culture approach," writes Richard Sakwa, "might suggest
that the recurrent pattern of autocracy, tsarist and communist, means that
democracy and civil society are somehow alien to Russia."[2] Despotic Russia
peers out of an often distorted history of the tsarist empire, as the "patriots" don old uniforms and glorify the last tsar-martyr—sometimes carrying
Stalin's portrait in the same demonstration, while neo-Nazi heirs of the
Black Hundreds flaunt their supernationalism. Cartoonists often draw a
furry crown on the Russian president's head, and we are back, they say, to
"Tsar Boris." I suggest, rather, that linking Russia with some inevitable despotism has two flaws: It overestimates the rigidity of political culture and
it underestimates the contradictions and changes that accompanied modernization under the autocracy. Both Russia's emerging liberal reform and
absolutism's fatal rigidity and contradictions point to this problem with
cultural determinism.

By 1917 the great break with prerevolutionary Russia was represented not by democratic reformism but by despotic Bolshevism. I share the view of Theodore Taranovski and other like-minded researchers on reforms in Russia that "to discount the liberal tradition in Russian culture and public life [is] to minimize the significance of those evolutionary processes that were leading toward the formation of a civil society and constitutional government in the Russian empire."[3]

Arkady Vaksberg, a prominent commentator on reform, deplores the ignorance that exists about achievements of liberal thought and reforms in prerevolutionary Russia:

Legal nihilism also springs from our lack of memory. Today we are starting with a blank slate when we argue whether or not a jury system is democratic, although this question was resolved in our country more than a hundred years ago! We, however, do not understand our own history. We have forgotten to celebrate the centennial of the abolition of serfdom and the great reforms following, especially judicial reform.[4]

Liberal thought and reforms in Russia favored the rule of law to protect individual rights and the democratic politics of accountable government. In the human rights dialogue with Soviet scholars during the years of *perestroika* and later, U.S. scholars introduced the topic of a liberal, rights-oriented legal profession and political movement in prerevolutionary Russia. This became an important subject of research for the dialogue.[5]

A second problem with cultural determinism is that it ignores or underestimates the rigidity of Russian despotism, as revealed in the contradictions of tsarist and Communist quests for advanced modern economic and social development under a regime of extensive control over economic, intellectual, and social life more fitting to the Mongol Golden Horde than to latter-day Russia.[6]

This chapter reviews the contradictions of tsarism, the tensions between reform of local and central government, the constraints on their representativeness and freedom, the reforms under the Provisional Government in 1917, and the Bolshevik takeover.

The Contradictions of Tsarism

When Russia had expanded into a Eurasian land power in the seventeenth century, it remained culturally apart from the West and the West's growing emphasis on individual rights. The need for a large standing land army in Russia fostered dependence on an autocratic and centralized rule to extract the necessary taxes and cannon fodder for Russian expansion and defense. At the same time, Russia remained vulnerable to defeat because of the West's superior technology and economies.[7]

The contradictions developed as a result of Russia's efforts to modernize its administration, military, technology, and industry while leaving the autocracy intact. For seven briefly interrupted centuries after Moscow's founding in 1147, autocrats held almost all the rights, and the people most of the obligations. Their ministers believed, or at least claimed, that they and the tsar were acting in the people's best interests. According to Neil Weissman, "The Tsar and his bureaucratic agents had historically acted as the primary guarantors of Russian culture and popular well-being. These themes of internal order, external prestige, and general prosperity were interwoven as motivations for most major governmental acts of industrialization, reform, and taxation."[8]

The autocracy resorted to serfdom from the seventeenth century until 1861. After the emancipation of the serfs, Russia continued to draw on village communes to feed the nobility and supply money and soldiers for the tsars' campaigns. Industry, largely a state enterprise, clothed and armed and later moved the troops. "What the Bolsheviks took over in 1917," wrote Bertram Wolfe (a believer in the continuity of despotism), "even before they had nationalized a single industry on their own, was the largest state economic machine in the world"[9]—and the world's largest country. The empire, Nicholas I conceded, was "too colossal for one man."[10]

Russia suffered an identity crisis when Peter the Great (1689–1725), a giant in energy and stature, opened his "window on the West" with the building of St. Petersburg.[11] It became the imperial capital from 1703 to 1918 (renamed Petrograd in 1914 and Leningrad from 1924 to 1991). Through that window Peter imported Western modes of war, science, administration, arts (including church paintings), architecture, and dress. He forced those foreign ways upon a reluctant populace, in the belief that, in order to stand up to the West as a great power, Russia needed to adopt Western technology and skills.

The selective westernization of Peter's heirs eventually became a futile effort to import the West's methods of production, war making, high style, and administration without also importing its liberties. Time and again, efforts to catch up failed: in the disastrous Crimean War in the 1850s (which triggered the great reforms of the 1860s), the humiliation by Japan in the Far East in 1904–5, the defeat by the Central Powers in the trenches of World War I, and the Cold War. Selective westernization failed owing to the rigidities of absolutism.[12]

These failures to cope, despite high costs in taxes, services, and hardships exacted from the populace, nurtured a growing opposition. Absolutism paid the price of greater subversion when it relaxed its controls and the price of greater stagnation when it asserted them. Torn between their realization of the need for constitutional reform and their fear of it, the tsars tended to undo past reforms through subsequent reactionary measures.

Catherine the Great (1762–96) was one in a long line of German princesses wed by the tsars. After the murder of her unpopular husband, Peter III, by a group of officers from the guards' regiments, Catherine became an empress who matched Peter in energy, imperial grandeur (witness the Winter Palace in St. Petersburg and the Catherine Palace in Pushkino), and expansion west and south. Catherine's flirtation with the French Enlightenment vanished with the eruption of the French Revolution. The only charter of liberation she issued was to the nobility: it relieved them of the obligation to serve in civil or military ranks as a condition for holding on to their estates.[13]

Catherine confronted Russia's first social dissident. Out of the Russian enlightenment in the late eighteenth century, which Catherine had encouraged, came Aleksandr Nikolaevich Radishchev (1749–1802). He remained truer to the ideas of the French Encyclopedists than did his empress. Radishchev recorded Russia's departure from those ideas in its treatment of peasants and the general lack of freedom he encountered during his travels.

Open the pages of *Journey from Petersburg to Moscow* (1790) and you will encounter a peasant who works six days for his master and one for himself and must supply sheep, hens, linen, and butter to his master and pay a head tax to boot: "On his fields there are a hundred hands for one mouth, while I have two for seven mouths." A young landowner rapes the daughter of a woman whose peasant family have long been loyal and tender servants to his. To pay for a new carriage a landlord sells his young male serfs into "freedom," but in reality to crown peasant communes which send them off in a military levy rather than lose their own serfs. Military service meant a living death and separation from one's family.

Censorship, an integral part of the autocracy, Radishchev wrote, produced mental cripples:

The censorship has become the nursemaid of reason, wit, imagination, of everything great and enlightened. But where there are nurses, there are babies and leading strings, which often lead to crooked legs; where there are guardians, there are minors and immature minds unable to take care of themselves. If there are always to be nurses and guardians, the child will walk with leading strings for a long time and will grow up to be a cripple.[14]

Catherine interpreted the book as a threat rather than a revelation of injustice and crippling censorship. She noted, "Its author, infected and full of the French madness, is trying in every possible way to break down respect for authority and for the authorities, to stir up in the people indignation against the superiors and against the government." She had the book confiscated. Radishchev received a sentence of death, commuted to ten years in exile, from which he was allowed to return under Emperor Paul I in 1796. He committed suicide out of despair six years later.[15]

Alexander I (1801–25) turned away from the constitutional project proposed in 1809 by the great administrative and legal reformer Mikhail Speransky (1772–1839). The project included the separation of powers delegated under the emperor, judicial reforms including a jury system, and a four-tiered system of dumas (representative assemblies) topped by the Imperial Duma, indirectly elected by class-weighted franchise. Conservative as that proposal might now appear, it proved far too radical for Alexander.[16]

Alexander's death sparked the mutiny of the Decembrists, groups of pro-reform military officers in northern and southern Russia, veterans of the war of 1812 and thus contacts with a freer Europe. Many must have joined the victory march of Russian troops into Paris after Napoleon's defeat. The Decembrists gathered on Senate Square in St. Petersburg on December 14, 1825 (December 26, new-style calendar) in a mutinous assembly that demanded a constitution. Lacking rank-and-file support and a clear plan of action, they were shot down or arrested. Five leaders were executed, and three hundred exiled to Siberia. Their brief stand later inspired authoritarian revolutionaries and nonviolent liberals alike. Speakers at the moving memorial gatherings for Andrei Sakharov which I attended in December 1989 extolled him as a continuator of the cause of the Decembrists. He died on December 14, the anniversary of their revolt.

Noting in the Russia of Nicholas I (1825–55) the "discipline of the armed camp," the Marquis de Custine surmised that "the political system of Russia could not survive twenty years' free communication with the rest of Europe."[17] Nicholas had the distinction of producing Russia's first psychiatric patient of conscience, Pyotr Chaadaev. Chaadaev deplored Russia's intellectual isolation; he depicted Russian culture and religion as inferior to that of the West. Nicholas I had Chaadaev declared insane; for a year he had to endure daily visits by a physician and a policeman.[18]

The "golden age" of Russian literature was in stark contrast with the narrow conservatism of the bureaucracy, which worked walled off from contemporary problems by mountains of paperwork. Through its education minister, Count Uvarov, it propounded a doctrine of official nationality and its watchwords: orthodoxy, autocracy, and nationality. Nationality signified the shared, special nature of the Russian people, loyal to the autocracy and the government.[19] This stultifying bureaucracy tended to overshadow a small group of enlightened officials.[20]

Russia's defeat in the Crimean War (1855) unveiled the weaknesses of Nicholas's system and its need for change. Alexander II (1855–81) permitted a comprehensive process of reform from above, which drew portions of the bureaucracy, the nobility, and the small, educated elite into framing the emancipation of the serfs in 1861 and reforming the courts, the military, and local government (the rural zemstvo and city duma) in 1864.[21] Even when measures taken to increase autocratic strength through industrialization succeeded, Arthur Mendel wrote, they had "precisely the reverse effect." They heightened instability through social displacement of the gentry, heavy tax burdens on the peasantry, new pockets of urban poverty, and growing discontent.[22]

Between 1885 and 1914, the proportion of the population attending school increased nine times over. Secondary-school enrollments showed an even greater increase. Substantial progress toward universal elementary education had been made by 1914. The percentage of children of peasants, craftsmen, and workers in universities more than doubled, from 15.7 to 38.8, between 1880 and 1914. Non-nobles formed a growing part of the army officer corps. During the crucial decade of advance and repression before World War I, domestic capital and more self-sufficient local entrepreneurship had been shedding its "unhealthy dependence on foreign investment and government control."[23]

Pyotr Stolypin, the able and ruthless prime minister from early 1906 until his assassination in 1911, aimed to pacify the land-hungry and rebellious peasants both by force and by the inducement of radical land reform. In 1906 Stolypin placed his "wager on the strong and the free" by permitting peasants to separate from peasant communes. Each separating household took a share of its land into private farming.

By 1916, peasant communes were rapidly breaking up. It is estimated that, as a result of the decree of 1906 and Duma enactments of 1910 and 1911, the peasant communes lost over half the peasant households in Russia.[24] Rural cooperatives spread rapidly. Statistics of the time registered increases in rural savings and consumer spending power. Diverse rural development programs were sponsored by various public and official bodies. The government eliminated, one by one, discriminatory taxes and juridical procedures that had long isolated the peasants as third-class citizens. But peasant alienation continued because of land-hunger and the hardships they endured during World War I.[25]

Democrats and Authoritarians

Part of the opposition followed the path of revolutionary struggle. Members of the educated and active segment of society, revolutionaries had become disillusioned by the unresponsiveness, even hostility, of the peasants when, as enthusiasts for change, they joined the "Land and Freedom" movement and "went to the people" in the early 1870s. In 1879, Land and Freedom split into two movements, People's Will and Black Redistribution. The former, an authoritarian group on which Lenin later modeled his disciplined party core, substituted itself for the people, assassinating in their name. The Black Redistribution took up, nonviolently, the cause of land-hungry peasants who had felt cheated ever since the emancipation had left them less land to farm than before. It united agrarian socialist forerunners of the moderate Socialist Revolutionary Party.

The first Russian Marxists abandoned agrarian socialism and the uncooperative peasants and turned instead to workers in their search for a revolutionary class. Under the leadership of Georgy Plekhanov, they formed, from exile in Switzerland, the Emancipation of Labor in 1883. The first congress of the Russian Social Democratic Labor Party (RSDLP)—a handful of Marxists—met in Minsk in 1898. A recruit of theirs, Vladimir Ilyich Ulyanov (a.k.a. Lenin, 1870–1924), the son of an ennobled provincial school inspector in Simbirsk Province, became a revolutionary after the execution of his revered brother, Alexander, a People's Will terrorist, in 1887. Lenin drew from his late brother's revolutionary literature and in foreign exile developed the ideal of a disciplined, centralized, and dedicated revolutionary vanguard. His thinking blended Marxist doctrine of the class struggle and historical materialism with Russian revolutionary elitism. Russian revolutionary terrorists, Marx and Lenin shared the moral outlook that ends justify means.

Lenin caused a split within the RSDLP in 1903 over his insistence on a narrow, centralized party of professional revolutionaries modeled on the People's Will.[26] The schism in Russian Marxism later deepened when it became clear that Lenin held nothing but contempt for "bourgeois democracy" and, unlike orthodox Marxists, rejected it as a necessary stage on the way to socialism and communism (see Chapter 3). Unlike the earlier, isolated People's Will organization, the party Lenin conceptualized in the period 1900–1902 was to lead a broad-based workers' movement and to control it through front organizations, as depicted in his organizational credo, *What Is To Be Done* (1902). The new type of "vanguard" party would bring to the workers, from above, the revolutionary consciousness they lacked when left to their own "spontaneous" trade unionism.[27]

Lenin's revolutionary movement of centralized, vanguard party leadership was to take over Russia's government in 1917 as its new autocracy. One of Lenin's later closest collaborators, Leon Trotsky, opposed Lenin's model almost up until the Bolshevik Revolution itself. In 1904 Trotsky, then a champion of "permanent revolution on an international scale," predicted that Leninism would bring socialism, but without democracy. Trotsky at that time preferred the Mensheviks' plan for a broadly based party. This, he wrote, would avoid the "substitutism" of a party acting in the name of the working class. Trotsky made an uncannily accurate prediction, which years later he either ignored or discounted: "Lenin's methods lead to this: the party organization at first substitutes itself for the party as a whole; then the Central Committee substitutes itself for the organization; and finally a single 'dictator' substitutes himself for the Central Committee."[28] Lenin and his tiny circle formed a minority within the Marxist minority of the time.

Slavophile thinkers rejected Russia's westernization and the constitutional and legal regulation of collective life. But they too wanted change—in the form of closer consultative relations between monarch and people. Liberal westernizers advocated individual rights under law in a constitutional monarchy (Octobrists) or a republic (Constitutional Democrats).

The largely democratic Socialist Revolutionaries (agrarian socialists supported by peasants and intellectuals) and Marxist democratic socialists sought to combine programs for social justice with further democratization and reform.[29]

Civilly active society turned away from revolutionary activity in the later 1880s and 1890s. Its members gave humanitarian aid in the famine of 1891 and the cholera epidemic of 1892. Some activists engaged in commerce and industrialization. W. Bruce Lincoln sums up the new volunteer initiatives of *obshchestvo*—society—in public health, medicine, and education through local government and voluntary associations: "Nowhere was the emergence of Russia's new citizen society more evident than in the growth of voluntary associations, as members of *obshchestvo* organized themselves into societies for professional, occupational, philanthropic, and cultural purposes during the 1890s and the early twentieth century." [30]

Civic opinion in the 1890s turned away from social and political radicalism or, at least, sympathy with it. The converts to civic action polemicized against radicalism as irrational and self-defeating as compared to legal and political reform and sober and constructive social activity. "If I were offered a choice between the ideals of the celebrated sixties and today's poorest zemstvo hospital," the writer and physician Anton Chekhov wrote, "I'd take the latter without the least hesitation." [31]

By 1904 Russia presented a striking contrast between the Decembrist soldiers assembled on Senate Square in St. Petersburg until dispersed by a few whiffs of grapeshot in 1825 and the constituency for reform eighty years later. Industrialization had nurtured articulate new groups ready to express their dissatisfaction with the status quo as well as to do good works. "In 1905," Arthur Mendel writes, "there existed a powerful urban working class, able by its general strike to cripple the urban society (and implicitly thereby, the administrative system); a large, audacious, and embittered student body; a well-organized, united, and effective stratum of urban intellectuals—businessmen, engineers, accountants, university professors, and the like; and a generation of liberal-minded, practical men of affairs trained in the judicial and self-government institutions established by the great reforms." [32]

Representation Denied

Segments of Russian imperial society, including high administrators, favored representative government and the rule of law.[33] The autocrats weren't so sure. People's Will terrorists bombed Alexander II (1855–81) to death when he was about to approve the first consultative assembly. In response to that tragic derailment of reform, the last two tsars became downright hostile to sharing their power with anyone, in any form. Alexander III (1883–94) and Nicholas II (1894–1917) hobbled local government and parliamentary reform.

The congratulatory messages on the marriage of Nicholas II to the German princess Alexandra (1895) included a plea by the zemstvo of Tver' for consultation and rule of law, so "that the voice of the people and the expression of its desires could be listened to," and that "the law would henceforth be respected and obeyed not only by the nation but also by the representatives of the authority that rules it" and would stand "above the changing views of the individual instruments of supreme power." In his reply, written by his adviser, Konstantin Pobiedonostsev, Nicholas dismissed this plea as "senseless dreams" and affirmed his intention "to safeguard the principles of autocracy as firmly and unwaveringly as did my . . . father."[34]

Despite "the unfavorable political environment," recent researchers Olga Crisp, Linda Edmondson, and their colleagues have found that "concern for civil rights was rather more apparent than historians have been inclined to believe."[35] Individual rights and the need for a law-governed state—*pravovoe gosudarstvo*—entered increasingly into political discourse.[36] Thus, a congress of representatives of zemstvos in 1904 declared their commitment to individual rights as essential for the protection of the people and for the common good:

To avoid the possibility of administrative abuse, it is necessary to establish and maintain the principle of inviolability of person and home. No one should be subjected to search or restriction in his movements except by order of a court, independent in its authority. To achieve the above ends, it is necessary to provide for . . . civil and criminal prosecution of officials who violate the law.

In order to make possible the complete development of the spiritual resources of the people, the full expression of public needs, and the free expression of public opinion, the following are indispensable: freedom of conscience and religion, freedom of speech and press, freedom of assembly and association.

All citizens of the Russian Empire should have equal personal (civil and political) rights. . . .[37]

The liberal movement (the Union of Liberation),[38] and later liberal parliamentary parties, notably the Constitutional Democratic Party or Kadets, recruited heavily from zemstvo and municipal duma activists, lacking a strong entrepreneurial class from which to draw.[39]

Zemstvos and the town dumas became more than mere convenient appendages of the central bureaucracy in their conduct of local taxation, education, health care, and other socially oriented programs.[40] Country zemstvos and municipal dumas contained fervent supporters of democratization and public involvement,[41] but they found themselves hampered by the tight surveillance of a suspicious government and domination by the conservative gentry. The weighted electoral law of 1890 gave the gentry preferential representation in zemstvo assemblies. In 1899 Count Sergei

Witte, finance minister in 1899–1903 and prime minister in 1903–5, wrote, "The zemstvo institutions are now deprived of almost all independence, and placed under strict wardship. . . . Our local government finds itself in the most abnormal, most pitiful condition."[42] These constraints, rather than some "prepolitical mentality" of the people, were what contributed to their alienation from the zemstvos.[43] Peasants continued to be limited also by the segmentation of society into separate and stratified "estates" (theirs being the least privileged and most burdened) as a means of social control.[44]

Democracy Constrained

Some of the advisers of Alexander I and Alexander II, Terence Emmons reminds us, had come to assume earlier in the previous century "that, sooner or later, representative institutions would be introduced in Russia as part of the country's general advancement toward the status of a modern European polity. . . . And a long series of reform plans was generated within the government bureaucracy," involving indirect elections from the local assemblies up.[45] By 1905, visions of a democratic Russia advanced among the active public required thinking beyond the merely consultative assembly spurned by Nicholas in 1895.[46] A new middle class of lawyers, administrators, scholars, doctors, journalists, and entrepreneurs sought a larger part in the political process.[47]

Russia's defeat by Japan in the war of 1904–5 brought revolution, and with it demands for a democratic parliament from liberals and democratic socialists in the new local "soviets" or councils.[48] A concession to these demands took the form of the Imperial Manifesto of October 17, 1905. The Constitution of 1906 established an elected parliament, the State Duma.

By 1906, the reforms, the excellent training of the government's functionaries, and the emergence of a high-quality legal profession made the end of absolutism and guarantees of individual rights seem possible.[49] But quickly the tsar used his decree and budgetary authority to negate the Constitution's bill of rights and to curb the deputies' powers. "Why should you argue with them," said Nicholas to a new minister, "you are my minister. . . . I created the Duma not to have it instruct me, but to have it advise me." In that spirit the government curbed the flow of legitimate information and witnesses to Duma committees, monitoring and controlling the meetings of deputies with their constituents.[50]

Forty-eight percent of the budget remained in the tsar's control in 1912.[51] The monarch enjoyed the rights of absolute veto, full control over foreign policy, and near to full control over national defense; extensive powers to rule by decrees having the force of temporary law; and the handy authority to proclaim "exceptional measures," which held much of his realm under forms of martial law and suspended most rights by 1912. The tsar belonged to the ultranationalist and anti-Semitic Union of the Russian People. In 1907 he sent them a telegram expressive of his sentiments: "Let the Union of the Russian People be my support, serving in the eyes of all and in everything as an example of legality and of order."[52] The tsar's power over the Duma also extended through the upper house, the State Council, a body implacably hostile even to the relatively conservative Third and Fourth Dumas. It regularly blocked laws expanding the authority of the Duma or the representative aspects of the zemstvos.[53]

The tsar's concessions in 1905 tended to divide the opposition into moderates and extremists. Taking advantage of the ebbing protests, the government speeded their demise with a new wave of crackdowns on opposition organizations. It sent thousands into administrative exile and filled the jails of St. Petersburg with political prisoners, some of whom got to windows from which they could wave at the deputies on their way to the short-lived First Duma. The numbers of these political prisoners would be dwarfed, and their suffering far exceeded, under the Bolsheviks, as Aleksandr Solzhenitsyn pointed out in his *Gulag Archipelago*.

The First Duma, "The Duma of National Hopes," pitted an impatient parliament against a suspicious, reactionary, and unyielding tsar; Nicholas dissolved it after seventy-two days. The Second Duma, known as "The Duma of Popular Anger," lasted little longer, just over three months from its convening in the spring of 1907 until its dissolution, before it could pass any bills.[54] Then, Prime Minister Pyotr Stolypin used the tsar's power of decree to pass the unconstitutional electoral law of June 3, 1907. This law allotted one-third of the Duma seats to those holding the top third of property, one-third to a larger group holding the next third, and one-third to the overwhelming majority holding the lowest third of property. The law also favored Russian representation against that of national minorities.[55]

This Third Duma, "The Masters' Duma," did not entirely fail the people. Especially in the sphere of education, it legislated rapid progress, despite opposition from the ministers of education. The Duma quadrupled the education allocation, more than doubling its share of the budget between 1907 and 1913. It established the Moscow Shaniavsky Popular University. That institution served as a haven for victims of repression in the established universities. The Duma also passed a series of other progressive social measures, from employer-mandated workers' insurance to equal rights of male and female teachers. It extended zemstvos to nine additional provinces.

The 1907 electoral law had drastically cut the Third Duma's non-Russian minority. Although progressive socially, the Third Duma reflected the chauvinism of its government. It passed a series of Russifying and discriminatory measures curtailing freedoms of the hitherto loyal and autonomous Finns, stepping up Russification in border areas, and increasing discrimination against Jews, Poles, and other groups.

Despite all their drawbacks, the Third and Fourth Dumas acquired elec-toral and procedural experience and gained respect eclipsing that which had been accorded the bureaucracy. More reasonable bureaucrats con-cluded from their consultations with Duma committees that their real ally was not the royal court but the Duma.

The Fourth Duma (1912–17), though still elected under the skewed fran-chise favoring the rich and supposedly pro-autocratic strata, voted in 1913 to express the need for an expanded suffrage free of administrative inter-ference. In the strongest motion on record, the Fourth Duma targeted the Ministry of the Interior for systematically scorning public opinion, abusing martial law, and ignoring "the repeated wishes of the legislature." It warned of discontent among a hitherto peaceful segment of the "broad masses" and of "untold dangers" ahead.[56]

A majority of the Duma rallied behind the government in the patriotic fervor following the outbreak of World War I. But the war proved even more disruptive and alienating than had the Russo-Japanese War. By 1916, a united front of opposition had formed to counter the court camarilla's mishandling of the war effort. The opposition included government min-isters and it called for a ministry having the confidence of the people.

The quality of leadership at the top told once again. The hemophilia of their son and heir, Tsarevich Alexis, left Nicholas and Alexandra sus-ceptible to the influence of the reactionary monk Rasputin: he seemed to have miraculous powers of prolonging Alexis's life. The weak and stubborn tsar, "the tragic Tsarina, and the nightmare of madness and mediocrity that dominated the inner Court" stifled the war effort "to such an extent that it appeared in the public mind as out and out treason."[57] If one good potential for real democracy had come out of the years since 1905, it was the growing public involvement in and attention to the work of the State Duma. Its growing influence, despite the manipulations of its makeup, owed a great deal to the beginnings of a new civil society in Russia and its borderlands during the reign of Nicholas II.[58]

Nicholas made only a play of voluntarily opening up the system to the new social forces created by economic modernization. The tsar and sup-porters like the Ministry of the Interior, the State Council, the Union of the Russian People, and diehards among the gentry attempted to censor the press, limit rights of association, and deny the ever more literate pub-lic[59] a part in the making of decisions, which it found hard to endure.[60] Thus did the old regime produce not His Majesty's loyal Opposition, but opposition to His Majesty.[61]

Russia's political changes reflected contradictions that pitted choices for democracy from below, and even within, the government against choices against it by the autocrat; freedoms associated with economic modern-ization against crippling reaction; legality against arbitrariness; grievances against available remedies; legality sought by reformers against arbitrariness (*proizvol*) of government officials. Lincoln writes that the reformers serving the tsars "had not really faced squarely the hard fact that autocracy was itself an institutionalization of *proizvol*." [62]

Lacking both efficiency and democratic legitimacy, the Imperial Russian regime collapsed under the strains of participation in World War I.[63] Defeats at the front and hunger at home compounded discontent. Nicholas abdicated after a week of revolutionary disturbances in Petrograd during the days of March 8–15, 1917. Formal authority now lay with the Provisional Government, elected from a committee set up by the dissolved Duma. It had to compete for power with the obstreperous Petrograd Soviet (council of workers' and soldiers' deputies). While the government inched toward democracy and carried on the unpopular war, the soviets and other grassroots organizations clamored for a faster pace of land reform. After Lenin's return in April 1917, with German connivance in this obviously subversive event, the Bolsheviks followed his lead and demanded the end of the war and the overthrow of the Provisional Government.[64]

Under these chaotic conditions of "dual power," the Provisional Government set about completing legal reform from above. The government had a good starting point. Nicholas Riasanovsky writes that the judicial reform of 1864 "proved to be the most successful of the 'great reforms.' Almost overnight it transformed the Russian judiciary from one of the worst to one of the best." [65]

To remove later distortions of the 1864 reforms and to complete them, the Provisional Government formed an eminent commission under the renowned jurist A. F. Koni.[66] In a flurry of decrees between March and June 1917, the commission began restoring such principles of the 1864 reforms as independence of the judiciary, equality of all before the law, public trials, and jury trials for all felonies, including politically sensitive crimes. It abolished special political courts, released political prisoners, ended capital punishment (it was restored at the front in July), restored untrammeled rights to trial by jury in felony cases, and brought back elected local district justice-of-the-peace courts.

Among other reforms, the government made choices for greater inclusiveness by ending discrimination against Jews and other non-Christians in the law profession and admitting women to the bar.[67] Belatedly, after decades of tsarist "Russification," nationality issues began to be resolved by legal reform, ending other forms of discrimination that had been especially serious against the Jews.[68]

Perhaps unwisely for its own good, the government abolished the notorious tsarist secret police (*Okhrana*) and the gendarmerie (public security force). It replaced all police with a single state militia shorn of repressive powers such as extrajudicial arrest and administrative exile. Lenin had reason in April 1917 to call Russia "the freest of all belligerent countries in the world." [69] The thinking of many Russian criminologists, such as M. N.

Gernet, and penologists, such as P. I. Lyublinsky, an expert with close ties to the international penological community, shaped the decrees of March and April 1917 intended to end prison brutality and Siberian exile.[70]

Unfortunately, the people at large felt not the government's legal reforms but its delay in dealing with economic questions such as land ownership, to be resolved by the future Constituent Assembly, and in making political choices such as speeding up elections and quitting the war. By the time the government decreed free and equal elections to local government in mid-1917, it was too late for salvation through the zemstvos and dumas. Terence Emmons writes: "the possibility that the zemstvos, however constituted, could assume the primary role in local administration assigned them by the Provisional Government had vanished in the great wave of anarchy that swept away the social and institutional foundations of the old regime."[71]

The Bolshevik Takeover

The coming of world war had stirred a newfound patriotism that briefly obliterated memories of repression. But the war soon upset the balance between reform and reliance on despotic government to tide Russia over chaotic times.[72] War created opportunities for the Bolsheviks. From his exile, Lenin condemned social democrats for supporting their respective governments' declarations of war in 1914. Always the alert tactician, he transformed defeat for socialist pacifism into a wartime opportunity. Lenin saw the chance to "turn world war into civil war" and wasted no time upon his return in April 1917 in persuading his party to oppose the Provisional Government and the war.[73]

Amid growing public alienation under that government, the Bolshevik promises of "Peace, Bread, Land, and Freedom" appealed to increasing numbers of workers and peasants.[74] The Bolsheviks had only a minority of support in the country at large. By September 1917, though, they had majorities in key local soviets (councils of workers' and soldiers' representatives). This tilted the "dual power" to their advantage. Under Leon Trotsky's skilled advocacy, the Bolsheviks used the Petrograd Soviet's influence over local armed units and the Bolshevik-controlled Red Guard militias in the capital area to take over Petrograd in an armed coup on the night of November 7–8, 1917. Storming the Winter Palace (defended by a hapless detachment of women cadets), the revolutionaries arrested the government ministers who were meeting there. Meanwhile, Prime Minister Alexander Kerensky fled into eternal exile. The war had provided the context for both his elevation and his defeat.

The Bolsheviks had a majority in the Second All-Russian Congress of Soviets, the assembly of representatives from the local and hitherto unofficial soviets, when it met on November 8. The Congress appointed a group of Bolsheviks headed by Lenin to be the Council of People's Commissars, Russia's "temporary government" until "the convocation of the Constituent Assembly." They put through the Congress decrees calling for peace and ending private property in land, though not private farming of it.[75] For the next seventy years this "temporary" communist government imposed its absolutist vision of individual rights in the service of the cause rather than of individuals and their civil society.

The Bolsheviks won only 24 percent of the votes in the November Constituent Assembly elections they permitted to be held and which had been chartered under the Provisional Government to frame a new democratic polity. The other three-quarters of the votes went to mostly democratic socialist candidates who stood for parliamentary democracy and individual rights. When the assembly refused to vote them power, the Bolsheviks had their troops turn the delegates away and close it down on the morning of January 19, 1918.[76] Raphael Abramovitz, a leader of the Menshevik Party, wrote: "Russia on the eve of the war was well advanced on the path of evolution toward a modern democratic state."[77] War, and the brilliant opportunism of Lenin and Trotsky, had forestalled Russia's democratization.

Conclusions

Russian democrats bequeathed to the Bolsheviks a society ever more engaged in resolving the contradictions of tsarism democratically and under the rule of law. By the time of the Bolshevik takeover, Russia had undergone a half-century of urbanizing, organizing, educating, volunteering, and participating politically, at quickening tempos. Pro-democratic socialists and liberals won the majority of votes in free elections. After seven decades of the Communist "legal nihilism" of Arkady Vaksberg, it may take seven more to rebuild a legal profession of a quality comparable to the free one that was emerging in pre-Bolshevik Russia.

It seems reasonable to conclude that it was the reactionary politics of the autocrat and his entourage, not some predestined Russian distaste for democracy, which destroyed chances for evolution to a parliamentary constitutional monarchy. Contradictions between absolutism and modernization are not resolved automatically, in some predestined way. History is fate in the sense that it provides a range of choices of means and ends; it is up to leaders inside and outside of government to make those choices. The court circle (not all ministers or all officials) despised democracy no less than did Lenin. This was demonstrated in the efforts of the court and the Interior Ministry to limit and negate the representative principle in the zemstvos, city dumas, and four State Dumas of 1906–17.

The revolution of March 1917 came about not through any coup but through the literal collapse of the autocracy in the face of an urban popular uprising in Petrograd. The eight-month Provisional Government brought an interval of accelerated reform, including projects for parliamentary democracy. But by mid-1917, the masses of people in town and country-side had become alienated from government, whether local or national. Playing on this alienation, the Bolsheviks used the war, and their armed supporters, to lever themselves into power.

Obviously, I agree with historian Arthur Mendel that "these last decades of Imperial Russia display a potential, if trying, evolution toward something like a Western parliamentary government and open society, an evolution cut short by a convergence of many factors and events that was by no means ineluctable."[78]

Neither functionally nor culturally is despotism, rather than freedom, Russia's fate. History supports the view of Bolshevism, expressed by the Russian historians Mikhail Heller and Aleksandr Nekrich, as not a continuation of but a destructive break from Russia's development by 1917. Bolshevism transformed Russia, "a country no better or worse than any other, one with its own peculiarities to be sure, but a country comparable in all respects to the other countries of Europe—into a phenomenon such as humanity has never known."[79] The despotic Russia of the past had won, cloaked in promises of a bright Russia of the future. Democratic Russia lost in proceedings rigged by force, where the jury was locked out.

Chapter 3
The Contradictions of Communism

> Without general elections, without unrestricted freedom of press and assembly, without a free struggle of opinion, life dies out in every public institution, becomes a mere semblance of life, in which only the bureaucracy remains as the active element.
> —Rosa Luxemburg, 1918[1]

Russia abandoned World War I through the separate peace of the Treaty of Brest Litovsk, concluded with Germany, Austria-Hungary, and a puppet Ukraine on March 3, 1918. For safety's sake, the government moved itself and the capital from Petrograd (St. Petersburg) to Moscow. After 215 years, the window on the West was closing. During the civil war and costly victory against various Russian and foreign interventionists, the new Soviet regime shut the window all but completely.

As a first step in the expected worldwide proletarian revolution, the Soviet regime carried out a political and social *chistka*—purge or, literally, cleansing—wherever it could reach. No more powerful and intrusive autocracy had ever held Russia in its grip. Under Lenin and Stalin, it eradicated all possible political and ideological competition, including the initiatives and institutions associated with more than a half-century of Russian legal and political reforms. Ideas of freedom persisted underground, however, and the contradictions of absolutism reemerged over time; hence the rapidity of the post-Stalin thaw under Khrushchev, the creeping openness under the culturally more repressive Brezhnev, and the portents of a new civil society to come.

Political and Social Cleansing

Soviet Russia's unified war effort under Lenin's government and the five-million-strong Red Army under Leon Trotsky brought victory against the disunited White Russian and interventionist forces by the end of 1921. Soviet Russia emerged as the diminished successor to Imperial Russia.[2]

The Bolsheviks held the multiethnic empire together through a combination of police surveillance, military force, a core of loyal adherents, a compliant legal system, economic controls, and an increasingly corrupt and privileged *nomenklatura* of strategic officeholders.[3] Uniting all these arms of dictatorship was the vanguard Communist Party, ever more monolithic and always infallible.[4]

Lenin lost no sleep over political and social cleansing. He despised "bourgeois democracy" as the tool of the ruling capitalist class: "the *more highly* democracy is developed, the *more* the bourgeois parliament is subjected by the stock exchange and the bankers."[5] His dismissal of democracy recalls Holy Synod Procurator Konstantin Pobiedonostsev's contempt for democracy, distrust of the public's wisdom, and belief in rule by an enlightened minority.[6] Suspicious of democracy within his party, Lenin had passed a resolution against factions in 1921, though he tolerated them during the few years left to him. In this spirit of "democratic centralism," during the succession struggle spurred by Lenin's death on January 24, 1924, Trotsky told the Party Congress, "One cannot be right against the party."[7]

Lenin suffered a series of strokes beginning in December 1922. From his wheelchair, he dictated a warning to the Central Committee, not against Trotsky, but against Stalin and his "crudeness" and "excessive power" as General Secretary of the Central Committee. Fearing Trotsky more than Stalin, the Central Committee preferred to dismiss as "groundless" Lenin's warning about the man who later liquidated most of them.[8] Lenin, in turn, never heeded Rosa Luxemburg's warnings against repressing democracy.

Communist Law and Rights

Rosa Luxemburg, a revolutionary democrat and leader of the German Spartacist communist movement, was born in 1870 in the Polish part of the Russian Empire. From her prison cell in Germany in 1918, the year before her assassination by right-wing officers, Luxemburg wrote a letter acknowledging the Bolsheviks' lofty revolutionary goals and dedication but warning against a deadening repression of political rights as the means of achieving those goals: "With the repression of political life in the land as a whole, life in the soviets must also become more crippled"[9]—shades of Radishchev's plea against repression after his troubling journey from St. Petersburg to Moscow! (see Chapter 2). By the time Luxemburg wrote her futile plea for democracy in Russia, the Bolsheviks had forcibly disbanded the Constituent Assembly, after a 75 percent pro-democratic and anti-Bolshevik majority refused to yield power to them. Political and social cleansing destroyed older reforms as well, including the reformed Russian legal system.

John Hazard's lectures and writings on Marxist-Leninist Communist law revealed the "common core" of a secular "holy writ" of revolutionary ideology. The Communists, in the name of the working class, used law as a political instrument of social change.[10] According to what one might call their dependency principle of law and rights, they framed and interpreted them to serve the cause as they defined it. "The will of the ruler had the force of law" not by divine right but by the rightness of the revolutionary cause. The Bolsheviks obliterated the Russian beginnings of a constitutional, "rule-of-law state," and thereby thoroughly eliminated from theory and practice a supremacy principle of law and rights.

The first Soviet Constitution, the 1918 Constitution of the Russian Soviet Federated Socialist Republic (RSFSR) embodied the dependency principle. After spelling out the rights of conscience, expression, assembly and association, and voting, and the rights to work, education, equality under the law, and asylum (for ideological kin), the Constitution added, in Article 23, this qualification: "Guided by the *interests of the working class as a whole,* the Russian Socialist Federated Soviet Republic *shall deprive individuals and groups of rights used to the detriment of interests of the socialist revolution* [emphasis added]." The Union of Soviet Socialist Republics (1922) kept this principle.[11]

To enforce the dependency principle, Lenin, as head of the RSFSR government, along with leading officials of justice, destroyed the old court system and procedural guarantees, including jury trials. This they replaced with a supposedly more accessible, and certainly more compliant and tightly controlled, hierarchy of district, city and provincial, and republic and USSR supreme courts, where compliant lay judges replaced juries. Political oversight outweighed elements of popular participation, though cheap legal services did increase access to the courts.[12] The powerful centralized Procuracy (prosecutor's office) was reminiscent of that in prerevolutionary Russia. What withered away after the revolution was not the state and law but the nascent rule of law.[13]

Just before the Bolshevik Revolution, Lenin had signaled his readiness to finesse, if necessary, the withering away of the state and law in favor of "strong state power and centralism."[14] The Soviet government restored censorship as one of its instruments of revolutionary struggle. In December 1917 it also restored the secret police, known by its Russian acronym, Cheka. Under the fanatical Felix Dzerzhinsky, an expatriate Polish aristocrat with a reputation as a martyr of the Bolshevik underground, the Cheka became the main instrument of social cleansing. A deputy of Dzerzhinsky, Martin Latsis, told his agents not to seek proof of an individual's rebellion. "You must ask him, first, what class he belongs to, what his social origin is, what his education was and his profession. The answers must determine the fate of the accused. That is the meaning of Red Terror."[15] In the same ruthless defense of their power, the Bolsheviks crossed the ice of Petrograd's Finnish Gulf in March 1921 to massacre and silence their former allies, the radical sailors of the Kronstadt garrison, who were demanding "soviets without the communists." Soviet power was, as Kronstadt proclaimed, far more cruel and oppressive than that of the tsars.[16]

On the side of social rights, the Soviet government legislated, in 1917–18 and later, the formal equality and emancipation of women in the family and the economy.[17] As with humane correctional policy for juveniles,[18] family policy too failed, owing to the general harsh times of dire scarcities and unemployment.[19] Unscrupulous "husbands exploited the legal easing of marriage and divorce."[20] Rather than replacing "strongholds of feudalism" like the family with communes of the future, the terrible chaos, economic collapse, and famine that followed in the wake of war Communism destroyed families without providing any substitute, thus forcing as many as seven million homeless waifs onto the streets in the early 1920s.[21]

As for nationality rights, "proletarian internationalism" was to supersede narrow "bourgeois nationalism" and chauvinism. Under Lenin, the Soviet government reincorporated by force, wherever it could, the border regions of the Caucasus, the Ukraine, and Central Asia. Faced with disaffection about nationality, Lenin favored autonomy for all national minorities. He advocated a much more inclusive and less centrist path to unity than did Stalin, the People's Commissar for Nationalities. By the late 1920s, Stalin was reducing minority self-determination to the shell of culture — "national in form, socialist in content."[22]

Revolution from Above

Stalin proved a master at bureaucratic manipulation and "salami tactics" of divide and prevail.[23] Already by late 1924 he had set himself apart from the internationalist Trotsky by advocating the nationalist goal of "building socialism in one country."[24] But where to get the capital for this? On the issue of how to industrialize, Stalin first sided with the moderates on economic policy. After defeating the "left opposition" champions of peasant collectivization, including Trotsky, Stalin then turned on erstwhile allies against the "left opposition." The "right opposition" included the popular party theorist Nikolai Bukharin and others who favored a gentler and economically more pluralistic communism that supported the peasants' right to individual farming. Stephen Cohen has said that the revolution could and should have stopped right there, had Bukharin prevailed, despite the "grain crisis and peasants' withholding of produce from the industrializing towns."[25]

Impatient with the evolutionary approach of NEP, Stalin launched a new "revolution from above" or "great breakthrough" (*veliki perelom*) as his choice for development.[26] By 1930, he was calling for the "highest development of state power"[27] to serve the new nationalist goal of building "socialism in one country" without awaiting the world revolution. The peasants bore the economic brunt of industrialization. At least ten million peasants died in the violence, famine, labor-camp confinements, and deportations of collectivization. One-third of the agricultural inventory was destroyed.[28] Bukharin described the social cleansing of the farmer class as the "mass annihilation of completely defenseless men, together with their wives and children." Lady Astor asked Stalin, in the summer of 1931, "How long are you going to continue killing people?" He shot back, "As long as it is necessary." [29]

Stalin proclaimed that socialism was built in 1935 and endorsed a new, class-inclusive constitution in 1936. The single-party system enshrined therein he justified on the basis of the elimination of "antagonistic classes" —capitalists, landowners, and rich peasants—leaving only the friendly classes of "workers and peasants" and a "stratum" of intellectuals; hence the need for only one party, "the Communist Party . . . which boldly defends the interests of workers and peasants to the end." Stalin's projected images of class harmony and a new "stability of laws" [30] veiled the realities of mass purges in the later 1930s. They claimed millions of more victims— Old Bolsheviks and other alleged "enemies of the people."

The purges were begun on the pretext of the mysterious assassination of the popular party boss of Leningrad, Sergei Kirov, on December 1, 1934. Stalin used that convenient elimination of a potential rival to justify summary trial procedures for political offenders. However, the police themselves sent most suspects to execution or labor camps. The police arrested many random victims to fill quotas for slave laborers, who produced one-tenth of the national plan. Deaths due to Stalin's social cleansing and forced labor system totaled at least as many as those caused by the German invaders in World War II, and perhaps twice that.[31] Among others, the purges claimed Eugene Pashukanis, the former doyen of Soviet jurisprudence, who had propounded the once politically correct theory of the withering away of law under socialism. He was arrested and executed in 1937 as a "legal nihilist" and enemy of the people. (Khrushchev's thaw brought his rehabilitation and the reappearance of his writing.) [32]

During the war, Stalin ordered the deportation of various nationalities for alleged (and unproven) collective disloyalty, notably, the Volga Germans (1941), Karachai and Kalmyks (1943), Chechens, Ingushi, Balkars, Crimean Tatars, and Meskhetians (1944). Without warning, security forces shipped them in cattle cars to bleak settlements in Central Asia and Siberia, causing about half the deportees to die in the process.[33]

The New Legitimacy

Stalin put an end to any remaining legal commerce, save for collective farm markets and a few artisans and scattered individual farms. Inequality grew. Five levels of dining areas at the new steelmaking Ural city of Magnitogorsk in the early 1930s ranged from plush tables for VIPs to canteens serving bread and thin gruel to convict laborers. The reintroduction of internal passports in 1932 (excluding peasants, virtual serfs who had to have permission to leave their villages) completed the state regimentation of much of the populace.[34]

Stalin ruled over a juggernaut of control and political cleansing, including the Communist Party and its apparatus (cells in factories and offices, the government bureaucracy, the central and local government councils, the docile trade unions, the youth and children's organizations, the censors, and the regime's media monopoly) and the secret police working directly under him, with its network of informers keeping watch on all the other arms of control.[35]

The dictator rested his power on legitimacy as well as coercion. The purging of the old intelligentsia and officialdom cleared the way for a new generation of ambitious and relatively uncultured technical and administrative elites eager to benefit from careers open to new talent.[36] Nationalism played a part in the appeal of the "great breakthrough." Soviet newsreels depicted Stalin telling the new industrial managers, in 1931, "There are no fortresses Bolsheviks cannot storm." Reviewing a history of Russia's defeats, he told the managers: "We are fifty or a hundred years behind the advanced countries. We must make good this distance in ten years. Either we do it, or we shall go under."[37] Ten years later, in fact, the Nazi German forces attacked.

By the early 1950s, Stalin could depend on a larger than ever state-service class. The professionals raised in comfort included such future dissidents as human rights champion and physicist Andrei Sakharov and defense attorney Dina Kaminskaya.[38] Stalin's record of social and economic rights seemed impressive by non-Western standards, if one ignored the serfs on the farms and the slave laborers. He ended unemployment, sent a nation to school, and opened up professional opportunities for millions of the poor and less-educated groups. He even inspired a genuine mass movement of youthful patriots and beneficiaries devoted to building "socialism in one country."[39]

In the context of public puritanism, however, women suffered as the equality proclaimed in the Constitution of 1936 went unrealized. Stalin's campaign to encourage births through stable families began with a ban on abortions and increases in divorce fees in 1936. An edict of July 8, 1944 (written by Nikita Khrushchev, I was told) established a very difficult and expensive divorce procedure in two courts, with obligatory publication of notice. It banned paternity suits and even recognition of any voluntary paternity outside of registered marriage. Unwed mothers had a choice: accept a monthly state pittance of child support or give the child to a state children's home. Mothers of large families received bonus grants; mothers of ten living children received medals of "mother heroine" in addition.[40]

Behind women's equality of employment lurked their "double burden" of work and motherhood. This caused many to resort to the risks of illegal abortions.[41]

Stalin fostered a "cult of Lenin" and of himself, the "great leader and teacher." By 1934, he was mobilizing writers and artists to be "engineers of the human soul." Through "socialist realism" they depicted a heroic present and an even "brighter future."[42] In an era of Stalinist doublespeak, Vladimir Voinovich notes, "the betrayal of a close friend or parent, for instance, began to be considered an act of courage; . . . cruelty became humanitarianism. Countries without the slightest trace of democracy are called 'people's democracies,' and one of the most lying newspapers in the world is called *Pravda* [truth]."[43]

The victory march across Red Square on May 9, 1945, marked the high point of Soviet legitimation and Stalin's glory, as the troops tossed Nazi banners at the base of the Lenin mausoleum on which he stood, amid cheers of glory to Stalin. The Georgian's special praise of the "great Russian people" and its elevation to the status of "elder brother" followed on years of increased reliance on nationalism as legitimizer. Stalin had recreated guard regiments and made history once again glorify tsarist Russian expansion. He restored the Orthodox patriarchate in 1943, 220 years after Peter had abolished it.

Victory in the Great Fatherland War meant no surcease. The Cold War broke out in 1946 as Stalin's command economy relentlessly ground out an ever-increasing proportion of heavy industrial and military goods.[44] In 1946–48 the regime launched a campaign of denunciations and arrests of writers, composers, and other creative intelligentsia. By 1948, the wave of postwar purges engulfed "rootless cosmopolitans," a code name for Jews. The purge destroyed the Jewish theater. The secret police killed its head, Solomon Mikhoels, whom Stalin had often invited to act Shakespearean roles before him. In his history of Stalinism Roy Medvedev recounts that "Beria's agents had Mikhoels killed in Minsk, then made up the story that he had died in an automobile accident. A few years later he was posthumously labelled a spy for Anglo-American intelligence."[45] The anticosmopolitan campaign culminated in the execution of twenty-four Jewish poets in the basement of Lubyanka, on August 12, 1952, and the Doctor's Plot.[46] *Pravda* reported on January 13, 1953, the arrests of leading physicians, mostly Jewish, who the newspaper accused of the murder or attempted murder of Soviet leaders. Apparently, until death took him on March 5, 1953,[47] Stalin was planning the transport of all Jews to camps in Siberia and Kazakhstan, and the removal of leading Communist Party officials.

Two years later, at the Leningrad airport in early 1955, I observed a weary mother resting after our bumpy flight from Kiev through a blizzard in a small twin-prop plane. To calm her screaming infant, the mother opened *Ogonyok* magazine, pointed to a full-page commemorative photo in it, and cooed, "Hush! See, Uncle Stalin!" Uncle Stalin soon vanished from print altogether. The next two decades brought a series of changes, from above and below, related to the inherent contradictions in Communism and its legacy of political and social cleansing: (1) the end of mass terror and the thaw under Nikita Khrushchev, party leader from 1953 to 1964; (2) diverse movements of dissent in response to the repressiveness under Leonid Brezhnev (1964–82), Yury Andropov (1982–84), and Konstantin Chernenko (1984–85); (3) simultaneously, a creeping openness that began to replace ideology with rational choices regarding issues of economic and social development; and (4) the emergence of a nascent civil society.

The "Thaw" and Its Limits

At Stalin's funeral service on March 9, a stunned and panic-stricken public heard the bloody-handed police chief Lavrenty Beria assure them, "You can work calmly and confidently, knowing that the Soviet government will solicitously and untiringly guard your rights, which are recorded in the Stalin Constitution."[48] Stalin's cult faded rapidly. On April 4, *Pravda* and *Izvestiia* carried announcements that the "Doctor's Plot" accusations against a group of mainly Jewish Kremlin doctors had been falsified, their confessions extracted under torture, and that they had been released. A *Pravda* editorial two days later referred to citizens' rights under the "U.S.S.R. Constitution," no longer the "Stalin Constitution."[49] Beria was arrested in July 1953 and shot along with six associates for attempting to "put the MVD [his combined police ministry] above the party and the government." Trials and executions of other secret police associates of Beria for abuse of power and false accusations followed in Russia and other republics in 1954 and 1955.[50]

Khrushchev, the new General Secretary of the party, abolished in September 1953 the secret police ("troikas") purge tribunals, the separate water and railroad transportation courts, and the 1934 summary procedures in criminal cases. A sweeping amnesty of March 27 called for an end to the heavy sentences set by Stalin for petty offenses. By 1955–56, Khrushchev had begun the rehabilitation of Stalin's purge victims.[51]

The delegates to the Twentieth Congress in 1956 stirred with surprise upon hearing Politburo member Anastasias Mikoyan discuss the harm done by the "cult of personality of Stalin." Then they sat, stunned, through Khrushchev's denunciation of "the cult of Stalin and its consequences, such as the purges," in his speech to a closed session of the Congress on February 25. Grown "sickly suspicious" by the 1930s, Khrushchev said, Stalin had victimized "honest party members" and deported nationalities in World War II on unproven grounds of their disloyalty. Khrushchev obscured the full extent of the purges, downplayed the horror of collectivization, and exempted Leninism and the Soviet one-party system from any blame. But he did reject Stalin's theory of 1937 on "the intensification of the class struggle" during the completion of socialist construction. Khrushchev's open report to the same congress made it clear that he intended, if anything, to step up the ideological competition with the West in non-aligned countries.[52]

Khrushchev's attempt to revitalize Communism actually began Communism's delegitimation.[53] In 1961, at the 22d Party Congress, he clashed with Chinese delegates sent by Mao Tse-tung to criticize his attack on the Stalin personality cult. Undeterred, Khrushchev had Dora Abramovna Lazurkina, a party member since 1902, comrade in exile of Lenin, and rehabilitated purge victim of Stalin, tell the congress: "Yesterday I turned to Lenin for guidance; he stood before me as if alive and said: 'it is unpleasant for me to be alongside Stalin who did so much harm to the party' (*stormy, prolonged applause*)."[54] Stalin received a discreet reburial under a memorial slab behind the Red Square mausoleum. Still, troubled by the thaw's uncertainty, the poet Yevgeny Yevtushenko appealed to the government to "Double, triple the guard over this slab/So that Stalin will never rise again."[55]

Khrushchev enlisted intellectuals against pro-Stalinist rivals in his limited anti-Stalin campaign and neo-Leninist program for Soviet revitalization through greater openness and less inequality.[56] Nevertheless, the thaw stopped short of any substantial democratization. The rapidity of the cultural thaw's onset, and the open-mindedness of students I knew at Moscow University in 1958–59, suggested a considerable survival of independent thought and morality despite Stalin's social cleansing.[57] No sooner was Stalin laid out beside Lenin in the mausoleum on Red Square than fiction and commentary poured out, affirming human truths over a Party Truth.[58] This period of cultural revival shared its name with *The Thaw* (1954), a novel by Ilya Ehrenburg, a consummate survivor who outlived the purge of Jewish intellectuals and, under Stalin, had lent himself to the anti-Zionism campaign directed against other Jews. The novel is mediocre as fiction but offers voice to hitherto forbidden themes—anti-Semitism, bureaucratized conformity, and artistic integrity.

The thaw reached beyond literature. Already by 1954 articles demanded reform of Stalinist family law, which was seen as "patriarchal" and "un-Leninist." Khrushchev lifted the 1936 abortion ban in 1955 in response to arguments about the harm done to women by illegal abortions. However, in 1964 he barred the expected liberalization of the Stalinist divorce and paternity laws of 1944; Khrushchev himself, it seems, had proposed those measures to Stalin as ways to raise the birth rate.[59]

Although Khrushchev curbed mass terror, released and rehabilitated purge victims, and entered into dialogue with writers and artists, political prisoners remained confined in still inhumane, strictly run labor camps and prisons.[60] Khrushchev maintained a selective repression of ideological deviance. Moscow University expelled and dismissed students and faculty accused of posting news bulletins and protest leaflets about the Hungarian Revolution of October–November 1956.[61]

The contradictions between an autocratic regime and a program of rapid economic development haunted the new ruler. In the words of James Billington, Khrushchev "soon confronted the classic problem which had perplexed Catherine and the two Alexanders. *How can one introduce reforms without jeopardizing the despotic basis of control? How can one revive initiative without stimulating insubordination?* [emphasis added]."[62]

The constitution allowed freedom of religion and *antireligious* propaganda, and decreed the separation of church from school. Until Gorbachev's reforms, this was taken to mean that organized religious instruction by parents or in churches and social outreach by churches was not allowed, on pain of the loss of parental rights and possible imprisonment.[63] Khrushchev began to promote secular "civic rituals," including civil wedding ceremonies, and opened "wedding palaces" in competition with the churches and sects.[64] He ended Stalin's relative tolerance of the Orthodox Church, closed many churches, and stepped up antireligious campaigns for "scientific atheism." Religious worshipers among students faced possible expulsion for going to church.[65]

Jewish culture and the Hebrew language continued in eclipse. Jews figured prominently in the application of the new draconian penalties for "economic crimes," receiving the illegal, retroactive application of the death penalty even as non-Jewish "culprits" got away.[66]

Criminal law reforms removed the draconian penalties for petty theft and the principle of "analogy," whereby one could be punished for a crime not listed in the criminal code. The lifting of terror encouraged a debate on issues of legal reform, some of which I sat through as a visiting graduate student, in 1958.[67] The courts dispensed accessible, and generally equitable, justice in everyday civil cases.[68] A good defense lawyer could occasionally clear the accused in criminal cases.[69] But legal reform ran up against entrenched opposition in the criminal justice and party apparatuses. The drafters of the codes of criminal law and procedure rejected a clause on the presumption of innocence, the formation of a lawyers' bar association (although writers, artists, architects, and composers had their associations), and the right to counsel from the time of arrest, except for minors and the mentally and physically handicapped. Suspects could be held for months during the important pretrial investigation without communication with a lawyer. The concept of appointing a criminal investigator free of control by the Procuracy was rejected into post-Soviet times.[70]

Popular participation in justice through "comrades' courts," "people's police," and "antiparasite proceedings" did not create independent public initiatives but rather party-mobilized efforts at social control and crime prevention, and new opportunities for abuses of the rights to due process.[71]

Among those sentenced to exile in the social cleansing of "parasites"—persons "who evade socially useful work and lead an antisocial and parasitic life"—was the Leningrad poet (later Nobel Prize winner) Joseph Brodsky, who died in the United States in 1996. Brodsky's five-year court sentence in 1963 was reduced to two years after an outcry at home (unthinkable under Stalin) and abroad.[72]

Ludmilla Alexeyeva, eminent chronicler of Soviet dissent, recalls the thaw days of intense exchanges among intellectuals far into the night. She portrays Khrushchev as a leader of contrasts—the boorish, shoe-banging, futilely boastful, semiliberator, with his "illiterate pronouncements on art . . . and his shameful mistreatment of Boris Pasternak."[73] After Pasternak's death from stomach cancer on May 30, 1960, over a thousand people attended his funeral in open defiance of the authorities.[74]

Alexeyeva notes that the thaw left the Party in "total control over the distribution of ideas and information" and forbade any criticism of Lenin, of the Party that had itself implemented the Stalin "cult" for decades, or of "the socioeconomic system that had made it possible."[75] Alexeyeva could have mentioned such brutality as the shooting in 1962, in Novocherkassk and other cities, of demonstrators protesting price rises in meat and dairy products; the harassment, beatings, and arrests of participants in public poetry readings; the jailing of Alexander Ginzberg for editing an unofficial poetry magazine; and the commital of Vladimir Bukovsky to a mental hospital after a series of brushes with the regime, including his copying Milovan Djilas's *New Class.*[76]

Khrushchev nonetheless remains a basically positive, if flawed, figure for the "thaw generation":

In his uneven and boorish way, Khrushchev was one of the greatest leaders Russia ever had. He released millions of political prisoners; personally allowed the publication of some very fine literature, including [the labor-camp novel] *One Day in the Life of Alexander Denisovich*; opened dialogue about the future of the Soviet economy; increased pensions for retirees; ended the Korean War; improved relations with the United States and Yugoslavia; even made an attempt to curtail central planning in light industry.[77]

As Khrushchev failed in his promises to begin to surpass the West in living standards, liquor sales were restricted, store shelves emptied, and far-fetched plans to grow corn withered on the stalk; one could see "Nikita kukuruznik" (Nikita Khrushchev the Corn Man) losing popularity between 1958 and 1964. Khrushchev had tried to break the economic hold of the central bureaucracy and to revitalize the economy through political and administrative decentralization. He split the politically commanding local party committees and the local government councils (soviets) into urban and rural branches.[78]

Under Khrushchev, the Communist Party of the Soviet Union (CPSU) became once again the focus of supreme power over the government and its ministries. Within the CPSU, the Politburo called the shots.[79] In the absence of mass terror, the disgruntled majority within the Politburo and the Central Committee—which formally elected both the Politburo and Central Committee secretaries—ousted Khrushchev from leadership on October 13–14, 1964. His fall marked the first time the party's top leader was voted out. Khrushchev lived in peaceful retirement until his death in 1971. Gorbachev's recognition in 1987 of Khrushchev's contribution to de-Stalinization ended Khrushchev's twenty-three years as a historical nonperson. A leader of striking contradictions, both liberalizer and bigot, he wavered on the issue of freedom, exhibiting a contradictory mix of cultural openness and neo-Leninist ideological and social dictatorship. Khrushchev's family commissioned the sculptor Ernst Neizvestny, a critic of Khrushchev's inconsistent liberalization, to carve his headstone for the cemetery of Novodevichy Monastery. The artist created a striking, symbolically expressive marble memorial in black and white, evoking the contradictions of Khrushchev and the uncertain thaw.[80]

Dissent and Repression

The arrest of the writers Andrei Sinyavksy and Yuly Daniel' in September 1965 for publishing satirical works abroad sparked the first Soviet demonstration for the rule of law on Constitution Day, December 5, 1965. The protest featured demands to abide by the 1936 constitution—hardly a promising document. Its bill of rights, Chapter 10, echoed the old Article 23 of the 1918 constitution. It conditioned civil and political rights by granting them "in conformity with the interests of the toilers, and in order to strengthen the socialist system." The interests of citizens and system, Article 126 implied, would be determined by the Communist Party, "which is the vanguard of the toilers in their struggle to strengthen and develop the socialist system and the leading core of all organizations of the toilers, both social and state."[81]

On February 10, 1966, the Moscow City Court sentenced Sinyavsky to seven years in strict-regime camp and, on February 12, Yuly Daniel' to five years. Their crime was "anti-Soviet agitation and propaganda" under Article 70 of the Russian Republic criminal code. At times the authorities found it more convenient to try dissidents on a newly defined lesser crime of "falsely slandering the Soviet system" or "organizing and participating in public disorders" or even hooliganism, or to find them insane and pack them off to ordinary or "special" (KGB) psychiatric hospitals.[82] The Sinyavsky-Daniel' trial began a cycle of prosecutions, protests, and then prosecutions of the protestors.[83] In such an atmosphere, the 1968 Prague Spring of liberalization under Czechoslovak Party First Secretary Alexander Dubček stood no chance, and was put down by the Soviet-led Warsaw

Pact invasion. (My law professor friends in Moscow, by then staunch pro-democrats, were, like many others, devastated. They did not join the small group, including Pavel Litvinov and Larissa Bogaraz, who were arrested on Red Square for protesting the invasion, but they hoped that Prague would set a precedent for Moscow.)

Meanwhile, the Committee for State Security, KGB (as the secret police were renamed under Khrushchev), and compliant courts carried out a new round of political cleansing in widening circles of dissidence that encompassed dissident writers; human rights activists in various republics; seekers of religious freedom, including the Council of Relatives of Evangelical Christian and Baptist Prisoners, formed in 1964 during Khrushchev's anti-religion campaign;[84] would-be emigrant "refuseniks"; and, later, unofficial peace groups such as the Group to Establish Trust between the USSR and the USA, and advocates of free trade unions.[85] In 1980 the KGB disbanded the small first feminist group in Leningrad and exiled their leaders abroad.[86]

The persecuted dissidents included advocates of national self-determination for the Ukraine, the Baltic republics, Georgia, Armenia, and so on, as well as advocates of the rights of deported nationalities, including the Tatars' champion, Major General Petro Grigorenko. Following his arrest in May 1969 and his commital to a psychiatric hospital, fellow champions of human rights formed the Action Group for the Defense of Civil Rights. Most of them the government quickly exiled or incarcerated in labor camps or psychiatric hospitals.[87]

Among its targets, the government singled out *samizdat* (underground publications), particularly *The Chronicle of Current Events*. The devoted *samizdat* teams posted at "Erika" typewriters from East Germany pounded out multiple carbon copies of monitoring and other uncensored commentary, and broke the regime's monopoly on information. Writers who published abroad and foreign broadcasts that reached the USSR accomplished the same purpose. The arrested *Chronicle* staff included the distinguished biologist Sergei Kovalyov (later deputy and Human Rights Commissioner and, later still, a dissenter under Yeltsin). The KGB arrested Kovalyov in 1974. Tried in 1976 in Vilnius, Lithuania, he received a total sentence of ten years' confinement and exile for "anti-Soviet agitation and propaganda."[88]

Although the government packed trials like Kovalyov's with their own agents, they did not torture their prisoners into pleading guilty as Stalin had, nor did they shoot them in secret police dungeons. Stalin would have given short shrift to protestors outside the trial courts, such as the Vilnius court that sentenced Kovalyov, but demonstrators there included Andrei Sakharov (1921–89), whose father was a successful teacher and popularizer of physics and whose mother came from the gentry.

Under Stalin, Sakharov had become a renowned theoretical and fusion-reaction physicist and a developer of the Soviet hydrogen bomb; he was a recipient of the Order of Lenin, a three-time hero of Soviet Labor, and a full member of the USSR Academy of Sciences. During the late 1950s, Sakharov turned away from weapons work and tried to get Khrushchev to end nuclear weapons tests because they were environmental hazards. In the late 1960s he turned to the advocacy of democratization and the defense of human rights. He wrote four memoranda to an unheeding Brezhnev between 1968 and 1972. Sakharov urged the leadership to build a democratic and decentralized USSR with equal human rights for all individuals and national minorities, fight hunger, amnesty political prisoners, fully expose Stalin's crimes, launch deep and just economic reform, and end environmental pollution. This, he wrote, was the only way to end the arms race, to achieve peace and general well-being.[89] By the late 1960s, Sakharov had become the spiritual leader of the human rights movement. On November 4, 1970, he joined with Valery Chalidze and Andrei Tverdokhlebov to form the Committee on Human Rights.

Sakharov and the human rights movement received recognition for their work through his receipt of the Nobel Peace Prize in October 1975. Another kind of recognition of Sakharov's importance in the movement came with his illegal internal exile along with his wife, Dr. Yelena Bonner, under tight surveillance, to Gorky (Nizhny Novgorod) in 1980. There they suffered increasingly abusive treatment, apparently at grave cost to Sakharov's health.[90]

After the Six-Day War in 1967, the Soviet regime had kept up a drumfire of anti-Semitic propaganda under the guise of anti-Zionism. This intensified after the 1975 Helsinki Final Accord (discussed below), despite the accord's human rights provisions.[91] Anatoly Sharansky—now an Israeli politician, then an active supporter of both human rights and Jewish emigration to Israel—was a founding member of the Moscow Helsinki group. On June 14, 1978, Sharansky received a particularly severe sentence of thirteen years in prison and labor camps, on treason charges of spying for the United States. By then, hounded Helsinki Watch groups had sprung up in Moscow (May 12, 1976) and in Ukraine, Georgia, Lithuania, and Armenia, in response to the human rights commitment stipulated in the 1975 Helsinki Accord.[92]

The denial of democratic channels for protest and rule of law in emigration matters drove a group of nine Jews, a Russian, and a Ukrainian, to plan to hijack an Aeroflot jet from Leningrad to Sweden. Sentences in their trial (December 15–24, 1970) ranged from four to fifteen years, to death for two of the group. The death sentences were commuted to fifteen years after an international outcry. Their act drew attention to the plight of Jews and other would-be emigrants, notably Armenians and Germans, who sought a freer and better life abroad.

Once Leonid Brezhnev had unseated Khrushchev in 1964, Alexander Solzhenitsyn became an unpublished intellectual dissident.[93] He received the Nobel Prize for Literature in October 1970, eleven months after his expulsion from the Union of Soviet Writers. In 1973, on the eve of his exile the next year, he wrote to urge the Soviet leaders to abandon Communism, separate Russia from the rest of the USSR, and turn it into a moderately authoritarian but culturally free country that harmonized with his vision of its past. Solzhenitsyn has been called a latter-day Slavophile, and Andrei Sakharov, a latter-day "westernizer." For publishing *Gulag Archipelago* abroad, Solzhenitsyn was stripped of his citizenship and sent into a twenty-year exile on February 12, 1974.[94]

Dissidents gained attention abroad as well as at home. "One of the major achievements of the human rights movement," writes Joshua Rubenstein, "was the organizing of groups whose members were publicly known. The Helsinki Watch groups, the Working Commission Against the Abuse of Psychiatry for Political Purposes, the Moscow chapter of Amnesty International, the Christian Committee for the Defense of Believers' Rights were vivid examples of the dissidents' ability to attract attention inside the country and in the West."[95]

Detente and Debate

Within the framework of old thinking on individual rights and the Cold War, changes of Soviet leadership and foreign policy took the country through three stages after World War II. During the first stage, the period of isolationism in a world of "two camps" under Stalin, the Soviet Union closed off all debate on human rights and abstained from voting for the Universal Declaration of Human Rights in 1948, along with other communist countries, Saudi Arabia, and South Africa.[96]

During the second stage after Stalin, Malenkov, and then his successful rival, Khrushchev, promoted "peaceful coexistence" with its dual policy of (1) "national liberation" in the third world and (2) expanded conventional diplomatic and trade relations and arms-control negotiations with other countries, which opened the USSR up to visitors and cultural exchanges.[97] During stage 2, internal isolation quickly diminished, as I can testify, having co-organized in 1954–55 the first graduate-student group from the United States to visit the USSR after Stalin's death, and having participated in the first academic research exchange in 1958–59 and again in 1964. From above, below, and outside, society began to open up to East–West contacts as a result of exchanges, communications leaks via foreign broadcasts, *samizdat*, and the publication of dissident works abroad.[98]

Stage 3 was the period of detente engineered by Brezhnev, his prime minister, Alexei Kosygin, and President Lyndon B. Johnson. Detente showed strains over human rights issues during the Warsaw Pact invasion of Czechoslovakia in 1968. Then, in 1974, the U.S. Congress, aroused on human rights issues, including Jewish emigration from the USSR, passed the Jackson-Vanik amendment to the U.S. Trade Act, over the objections of Secretary of State Henry Kissinger. The amendment directed the president to deny most-favored-nation treatment (lowest tariff rates) to countries that restricted emigration. The accompanying Stephenson amendment, in turn, limited credits. By then Brezhnev's internal crackdown had provoked East–West debate on human rights.

Human rights meetings across the Iron Curtain began under the auspices of the Commission for Security and Cooperation in Europe pursuant to the 1975 Helsinki Final Act, which was signed after two years of negotiations by thirty-five countries (all European states—except for Canada and the United States). Conservative critics labeled the accord a sellout because it exchanged recognition of existing borders (such as those of East Germany) in exchange for clauses on freedom of information and movement, humanitarian reunions, and human rights.[99]

In fact, the Helsinki agreement provided a valuable international forum for debating human rights issues. Common pledges to respect human rights inspired the formation of Helsinki monitoring groups and human rights movements in Eastern Europe, the USSR, and the West. Human rights and emigration became regular subjects of U.S.–Soviet summits, alongside arms control, third-world conflict, and cooperation.[100] The East–West dispute escaped the controlled press and spilled over into foreign broadcasts of the BBC, Radio Liberty, and Voice of America, to which many listened avidly.

Discussing the new Constitution of 1977, Brezhnev, on the defensive, derided the "shameless falsifications [of] imperialist propaganda." The new Soviet constitution, he claimed, "inscribes the economic, social and cultural rights and freedoms of citizens and concrete guarantees of these rights more broadly, clearly and completely than this has been done at any other time, anywhere else."[101] Article 29 included among the principles of interstate relations the Helsinki Accord's principle of "the respect for human rights and fundamental freedoms." The article reflected the dualism of Soviet policy: It juxtaposed the aim of aiding "national liberation movements" with the aim of realizing principles of "peaceful coexistence."

Brezhnev's detente with the United States and the USSR's vital cheap grain purchases in 1972 did not deter him from continuing the Soviet dualism or, as Zbigniew Brzezinski put it, "breaking the rules of the game."[102] It was not clear whose "national liberation struggle" the USSR helped by sending troops into Afghanistan in 1979.[103] The war, with its setbacks, casualties, slaughter of civilians, and drain on resources, contributed to the delegitimation and downfall of the Soviet regime. It aggravated existing contradictions. In a quest for stability, General Secretary Brezhnev and his colleagues halted the thaw and attempted Stalin's partial rehabilitation. In a symbolic gesture, they had a bust placed at the slab marking Stalin's grave and praised his role in World War II.[104]

The contradictions deepened between ideology and the desired rationality of the "scientific and technological revolution," between "internationalism" and ethnic nationalism, between a corrupt and self-serving bureaucracy and the creative innovators whom it stifled.[105] These contradictions were evident at the time. On a flight out of the USSR in 1974, I noted down impressions of the contradictions between Brezhnev's "scientific and technical revolution and arbitrary pricing, . . . alienation at work and excessive centralization and red tape," and between "economic, intellectual, scientific rationalism and honesty in the arts and cultural obscurantism and conservatism."[106] Four years later, it seemed already that these were constraints on Soviet government: "tensions between nationalities, especially between Russians and certain other national minorities [and] . . . [d]isparities between economic needs and current forms of economic controls in the USSR raise the possibility of domestic tensions, even of a crisis over policy, bound up with the post-Brezhnev succession struggle."[107]

Creeping Openness

Although Brezhnev's freeze left dissenters and freethinkers on slippery slopes, he built on Khrushchev's revival of social research, which had been halted under Stalin since the 1930s. The creeping openness continued. Sandwiched between obligatory ideological citations, Soviet readers were introduced to foreign research methods and theories, from comparative behavioral political system study to the sociological problems of work and urban life.[108] Social research took up an expanding range of social issues, such as social and health problems of urbanization,[109] youth socialization,[110] family instability,[111] worker morale, labor turnover, causes of crime and delinquency,[112] time budgets and women's double burden,[113] and birthrate declines among European ethnic groups. Demographers introduced a book on urban population with the note that "Unfortunately, after a short development of demographic research in the USSR after the Great October socialist revolution, this research was almost stopped already in the early 1930s, and numerous carefully gathered demographic statistics remained secrets or were published in unexplained snippets."[114]

Debate touched on a variety of issues and interests, such as the would-be Siberian river diversion project,[115] the causes and prevention of crime, family law (reformed at last in 1965 and 1968), economic reform, foreign policy,[116] and military policy. Specialists communicated through informal networks and through their professional and political meetings and the press.[117] As the adverse health effects of environmental pollution grew, Soviet censors banned mortality figures from published statistics. By then, concern about pollution appeared in print,[118] including the effects of nuclear radiation.[119] Champions of conservation began to discuss environmental protection, officially a problem only in capitalist countries but documented in secret government reports and brought up in a 1963 article about the pollution of mighty Lake Baikal by a paper mill.[120]

Brezhnev's successor as General Secretary, Yury Andropov, former KGB head, initiated a new economic openness, with frank discussion of the drop in economic growth and productivity. Konstantin Chernenko (1984–85) brought the tottering closed system toward its last gasp with his failed attempt at ideological resuscitation.[121]

Like Alexander II in 1881, some of the party leadership, including Mikhail Gorbachev, had by the early 1980s begun to look to greater openness of public participation and other basic reforms as indispensable companions of development. Internal stagnation and external ideological expansionism proved ever more incompatible.[122]

Pre-Civil Society

Human rights groups and their members, mainly from the natural sciences, had been all but eliminated from free society in 1982.[123] The dissidents carried on their moral and political discourse in labor camps and, later, in freedom under Gorbachev. The ferment of ideas and dissent signaled, for Moshe Lewin, the beginning of the emergence of a civil society in the USSR. Under Gorbachev, this incipient civil society "instigated changes 'from below,' in the social, economic, and political structures of the country." Under Brezhnev, the economic system approached its limits. Politically, the government, "structured so as to exclude citizens from political participation, was incapable of accommodating the new social reality and the corresponding new attitudes of the citizenry."[124] This contradiction of Communism, between control and spontaneous thinking and action, grew over the decades. As George Kennan predicted in 1947, Communism broke down because of the contradictions created by tensions between regime controls and the need for greater openness and creative initiatives.[125]

Frederick Starr sees Gorbachev and his *perestroika* in 1988 as "not so much creating change as uncorking it in a forming civil society."[126] But it was a society only just beginning to form, one should add, because, as Rosa Luxemburg foresaw, the regime barred autonomous civic action. Moshe Lewin notes that "Throughout the postwar period, the old-style bureaucracy seriously hindered the creation and maturing of communal city-wide and intercity identities and solidarities, the development of shared cultural, ideological, and moral values. Depoliticization, one of the hallmarks of party rule, only added to the trouble by depriving citizens of the practice of politics."[127] The dissident intelligentsia had developed a culture of opposition rather than of political participation.[128] In addition, the country lacked the independent economic base for an autonomous civil society.

Society also lacked the experience of constitutionalism to sustain its civility. The 1977 constitution upheld the long-standing dependency principle of law. It granted rights "in accordance with the goals of building Communism," and provided that they not be exercised "to harm the interests of society or the state." The Communist Party, as "the leading and directing force of Soviet society," had the last word on the limits and meaning of rights.[129] Ethnic tensions and the repression of minority rights advocates left a legacy of unresolved and divisive grievances. As Alexander Solzhenitsyn predicted, ethnic separatism would contribute to the breakup of the USSR.[130]

Benefiting from hindsight, we can agree with Geoffrey Hosking that free thinking does not instantly translate into effective politics: "A sophisticated society is a necessary condition for sophisticated politics, but it is by no means a sufficient one."[131] Dissenting thought about rights marked a big step toward a civil society and a triumph of the idea of freedom and international communication and solidarity, despite decades of political and social cleansing; it did not yet mark the advent of a civil society. To think otherwise is to underestimate the difficulties of democratization in the former Soviet Union.

Conclusions

Theodore Von Laue argues that the "rapid industrialization of Russia," tsarist and Soviet, needed to catch up with the power of the West and also "required the effective substitution of compulsion for a lacking spontaneity."[132] Yet the history of official and unofficial choices made about freedom and development in both Soviet and tsarist Russia suggests that there is no such thing as a durable "effective substitution of compulsion for a lacking spontaneity," much as both the official Pobiedonostsev and the revolutionary Lenin despised that spontaneity.

Brezhnev found himself caught up in an international debate over human rights, sparked by human rights movements at home and abroad. Amid the confrontations and debates, the dikes of censorship against free international and domestic communication developed all sorts of leaks, ranging from cultural exchanges and foreign broadcasts to a creeping openness within the political and professional establishment.

In attempting to deal with the contradictions of Communism, post-Stalin leaders dispensed with mass terror and tried to introduce effective reforms without losing central control of the economy and society. This proved impossible. Despite its power, the Communist regime eventually ran aground on its own inner contradictions, as was foreseen by Sakharov.

Historian Roy Medvedev wrote in the mid-1970s: "An enormous contradiction now exists in our society: rapid scientific, technical and economic progress is being blocked by an excessively centralized bureaucratic system." Later, despairing of a mass movement to force democratization, Medvedev looked for it to start "from above."[133] It did, with Gorbachev. But the entrenched bureaucracy and the chilling thoroughness of Communist political and social cleansing had bequeathed a difficult ordeal for freedom, for the Soviet people, and for Gorbachev's *perestroika*.

Chapter 4
Restructuring Rights

> This is the question of today: Either Soviet society will press on with
> the deep transformations already begun—in which case . . . a worthy
> future awaits our great multinational state, or anti-restructuring forces
> will come out on top, and then . . . grim times await the country and
> the people.
>
> —Mikhail Gorbachev, July 1990[1]

Failure and Progress

Alexander Guchkov told his liberal conservative Octobrist Party during
an earlier crisis of absolutism, in November 1913, "the attempt made by
the Russian public . . . to effect a peaceful, painless transition from the
old, condemned system, to a new order—has failed."[2] Three-quarters of a
century later, Russia's successor leadership under Mikhail Gorbachev attempted a new peaceful transition from autocracy to freedom, through a
vaguely defined program of *perestroika* (restructuring). As a member of the
ruling Politburo of the Communist Party of the Soviet Union (CPSU), Gorbachev kept in touch with an informal network of leaders and professional
people seeking to reform the corrupt and stagnant Communist system.
Did they also fail?

On March 11, 1985, the Central Committee of the CPSU elected Gorbachev, the Politburo's choice, to be General Secretary. At the age of fifty-
four, he was a youth by Politburo standards,[3] especially compared to his
predecessor, the emphysemic "living corpse" Konstantin Chernenko. In
a joke circulating at the time, Brezhnev, General Secretary from 1964 to
1982, asks from the next world, "Who is leading the USSR?" He is told it
is Gorbachev. Brezhnev then asks, "Does he have support?" "No, Leonid
Ilyich," is the answer. "He can walk on his own."[4]

Appearing to live up to expectations, the energetic Gorbachev launched
a *perestroika* to revitalize the economy, with the help of *glasnost'* (openness), a new freedom to criticize and expose defects in the Soviet system.

"Once we undertake a radical, comprehensive restructuring," he wrote in 1987, "we must also develop democracy to its full potential."[5] Students at Moscow University responded enthusiastically when visiting U.S. President Ronald Reagan extolled freedom and the peaceful world to come: "In this Moscow Spring, this May 1988, we may be allowed that hope—that freedom like the green sapling planted on Tolstoy's grave, will blossom forth at last in the rich fertile soil of your people and culture . . . leading to a new world of reconciliation, friendship and peace."[6] Earlier in the week people had cheered a smiling and waving President Reagan as his cortege drove in from the airport.

Freedom *was* blossoming as President Reagan said. The Soviet war in Afghanistan ended the following year. But the "new world of reconciliation, friendship and peace" soon vanished within the USSR. Rather than being revitalized by *perestroika*, the Union collapsed altogether in another three and a half years. In late 1991, a bitter Mikhail Gorbachev tendered his resignation from the post of USSR president, which he had held since March 1990. Within three more years, beginning in late 1994, the children of the joyous mothers weeping as they greeted the U.S. president in 1988 could have been fighting, and possibly dying, in Russia's internal "Afghan war," the disaster in Chechnya. That republic inside Russia had declared its independence in November 1991, even before the final Soviet collapse.

Why did *perestroika* fail to achieve its goal of a revitalized and democratized Soviet Union? Ultranationalists and hard-line Communists have faulted the new freedoms and have maintained that authoritarian rule best suits the Russian people and culture. Knowledgeable observers such as Mary McCauley in Britain, Yury Afanasyev in Russia, and Peter Reddaway in the United States[7] attribute *perestroika*'s failure to the resistance of "powerful vested interests," primarily the *nomenklatura* bureaucrats and managers. Other observers similarly stress context rather than Gorbachev's leadership, which they praised to the end.[8] I would add at least three other factors: the rivalry between Gorbachev and Yeltsin; the conflict of aspirations within the part-democrat, part-Communist Gorbachev; and the legacy of Communist political and social cleansing described in the previous chapter.

This chapter begins with the achievement of *perestroika*—that is, the freedom it allowed. It reviews the onset and nature of radical "new thinking." Its practical implications for democratization included the legal recognition of civil liberties, while civil rights to due process and personal inviolability lagged behind. Moving into the area of economic and social choices, this chapter depicts an embryonic civil society becoming disillusioned with *perestroika*, owing to growing economic ill-being. I next address the growing separatism of nationalist movements amidst economic discontent and Gorbachev's inadequate responses to growing demands for equality and self-determination by republics and ethnic minorities. The chapter closes with the coup attempt; the breakup of the USSR, which the coup plotters intended to forestall; and a summation of the implications of *perestroika*'s failures and successes, of conflict between friends and foes, and of the costs and benefits of change.

New Thinking

The worst thing about the Soviet system, said the late Nobel Prize-winning poet Joseph Brodsky early into *perestroika*, was "that it curbs the human potential."[9] Gorbachev preferred to blame not the Soviet system as a whole, but the bureaucratic "mechanism braking progress," which he depicted as a distortion of an otherwise viable system. Yet it is hard to imagine that system bereft of its administrative core of censorship and surveillance.

Glasnost' expanded by 1987–88 into a program of democratization as well as free expression. By then, Gorbachev and his advisers concluded, old thinking on law and rights, particularly the dependency principle, which made the meaning of law and rights dependent on their serving the Communist cause (as discussed in Chapter 3), had become glaringly incompatible with the new democratic freedoms. Law students, for example, were taught that constitutional law and rights "cannot always be fixed within the 'narrow legal interpretation,' for the central place in state-legal sanctions belongs to a politico-ideological evaluation of the citizens' conduct."[10] Thinking needed to shift to the supremacy principle of law, under which governors rule beneath the restraints of higher law as well as through the laws themselves.[11]

Gorbachev initiated a momentous shift toward the supremacy principle of law and rights in the "new thinking" he began to allow into constitutional commentary by 1987. As Andrei Sakharov later reminded us, the term "new thinking" was a "half-truth," as it was new only for the party leadership, not the dissidents: They, not the CPSU, first advocated the rule of law.[12] From his foreign exile, the late Boris Shragin anticipated Gorbachev's later affirmations when he wrote that law which protects freedom "turns out to be the basis of social, intellectual, religious, and any other pluralism."[13]

Kommunist, the Communist Party's theoretical journal, early in 1987 broached the idea of a real "law-governed state" (*pravovoe gosudarstvo*), with a new socialist constitutionalism, featuring perhaps a "constitutional court," for judicial review.[14] Up to then, the Central Committee apparatus had helped to purge and regiment the legal profession. Now its publication, *Kommunist*, was chiding the jurists for churning out "stereotypes and prejudices . . . , glossing over reality, avoid[ing] exposing and studying our society's real contradictions," and failing to increase the protection of citizens' rights and to curb illegality.[15]

For the first time, through Yury Kudriavtsev, the regime depicted international human rights norms as "mutually acceptable and universally democratic." He urged (as the dissidents had already done for more than twenty years) that the fulfillment of rights to presumption of innocence, protection against unlawful psychiatric commitment, and freedom of expression live up to standards such as those set in the 1966 International Covenant on Civil and Political Rights.[16] Kudriavtsev told me that such articles augured a party commitment to the rule of law and international human rights without the ideological qualifications of the past. Responding to the call for new thinking, experts V. A. Vereschetin and R. A. Miullerson urged colleagues to stop putting down "bourgeois" international law, which they insisted be considered as one entity and "not divided artificially into capitalist international law, socialist international law, and the international law of developing countries." Soviet citizens, as subjects of international law human rights law, could bring claims of violations against even their own governments.[17]

Soviet doors began to open to human rights nongovernmental organizations (NGOs) like Amnesty International, Human Rights Watch, and the Lawyers Committee for Human Rights. This followed an initially tense encounter between the International Helsinki Federation (IHF) and the Soviet GONGO (government-organized nongovernmental organization), the Human Rights Commission, in January 1988. The GONGO representative, Fyodor Burlatsky, backed down on his efforts to prevent the dissident Lev Timofeyev from speaking at the meeting, when the IHF insisted on dissidents' right to participate as group members of the IHF.[18]

Before my lecture in June 1988 on human rights at the Institute for State and Law of Moscow, Secretary Willy Smirnov of the Soviet International Political Science Association called my talk "premature." But some institute scholars who had followed the old thinking on human rights, including Human Rights Sector head Yelena Lukasheva, welcomed the talk and concluded the crowded meeting with a call for dialogue on human rights—already the goal of our dialogue group, which had been started by Bertram Gross in the United States.[19]

Where practice depended on officials' discretion, it lagged behind thinking. For example, Lev Timofeyev, the controversial speaker at the January 1988 meeting, never received a visa to attend in August 1989 the inaugural human rights dialogue meeting at the University of California at Berkeley to which he had been invited. Still, with the new thinking the ideological cold war was basically over.[20] A former participant in that cold war, Viktor Chkhikvadze, told the public meeting that "what I wrote and what my colleagues wrote in their day were the fruits of a limitless praising of Soviet democracy, of excessive praise for our legislation in the human rights field . . . but something not reflecting realities in our country in any way."[21]

New and old thinking battled in Gorbachev's outlook. For example, by 1986 he was traveling out to Siberia to exhort workers to become masters of their own enterprises, to shake managers out of their lethargy. Yet he kept the stringent limits on liquor sales that he imposed in March 1985. Thus he simultaneously alienated his purported worker allies, focused the blame on symptoms (slackness and drunkenness on the job) rather than on causes of "stagnation," and perpetuated past authoritarian methods of leadership relations with the working people.[22] Needing allies outside the government, Gorbachev turned to the leading human rights champion. On December 16, 1986, he telephoned an invitation to exiled human rights activist Andrei Sakharov and his wife, Dr. Yelena Bonner, in Gorky (Nizhnyi Novgorod) to return to Moscow, no strings attached.[23] Yet Gorbachev alienated supporters of reform in the Communist Party.

When Boris Yeltsin, future president of Russia, criticized the slow pace of reform at a closed Central Committee meeting in October 1987, Gorbachev led the attack on him. He summoned Yeltsin from the hospital sickbed where he was nursing a heart ailment, subjecting him to a storm of denunciations and confirming his removal as candidate (nonvoting) member of the Politburo and First Secretary of the Moscow Party Committee. Yeltsin's demotion into construction administration marked a step forward in the treatment of defeated critics, but raised questions about Gorbachev's commitment to real openness and change, and about his judgment.[24] Yeltsin's expulsion lost Gorbachev a potential ally against conservatives in the party and created in him a political foe who later became a popular president of the Russian Republic. This was the "first of Gorbachev's major political blunders," says Ambassador Jack Matlock. Envy had blinded Gorbachev's judgment. In the old tradition, he preferred to have yes-men around him and viewed charismatic associates as potential competitors rather than valuable allies. That same emotion would lead him not only to continue mismanaging his relations with Yeltsin but to pick weak—and ultimately disloyal—associates in the belief that they could not compete with him.[25]

This conduct proved counterproductive, to put it mildly. After all, Gorbachev faced bitter opposition to openness and economic reform within the *nomenklatura*. The resistance to change went as high as Gorbachev's deputy party leader, Yegor Ligachev. He appears to have at least approved, if not coauthored, a stalinist and anti-Semitic polemic, published on March 13, 1988, during the absence of Gorbachev and his close associate Alexander Yakovlev. Over the signature of Nina Andreeva, a teacher in a Leningrad chemical institute and later staunch nationalist Communist opponent of Russian reform, the polemic attacked *glasnost'* or its alleged corruption of youth, the acceptance of "bourgeois" freedoms, and the defamation of Stalin and the glorious Soviet past. Three suspenseful weeks of silence followed. But the fear of renewed repression abated after Gorbachev persuaded a Politburo meeting to order a rebuttal on April 5 that reaffirmed support for *glasnost'*.[26]

Nobody knew for sure in 1987–88 when the government might clamp down on openness, when a public speaker in Moscow's new Hyde Park Corner, Pushkin Square, might be hustled off and detained by the police, as some were, or what the limits of censorship were. Dissident groups were "still paying various prices in careers and harassment for their independent activities," I wrote in 1988.[27] New freedoms lacked legal underpinnings. Quite possibly, a desire for better relations with the United States and other industrial democracies, and the upbeat Moscow summit in 1988, played their part in preserving and deepening *glasnost'* and influencing Gorbachev to broaden reforms and emphasize his commitment to international human rights. In Moscow, President Reagan emphasized his country's commitment to human rights and freedoms to a meeting of ninety-eight dissidents invited to the ambassador's residence, Spasso House, on the evening of May 30 and, on May 31, to enthusiastic Moscow University students who gave him a standing ovation.

By July 1988, Foreign Minister Eduard Shevardnadze was expounding new thinking in foreign policy to his diplomatic corps.[28] Future foreign minister of Russia Yevgeny Primakov renounced a priority for revolutionary liberation struggle in foreign policy as being counterproductive to peace.[29] Gorbachev's UN speech of December 7, 1988, praised the Universal Declaration of Human Rights and urged the "highest standards" of human rights as "universal values" essential to security in an interdependent world.[30] By then East–West confrontation over human rights had changed to cooperation.

The document of the Vienna meeting of the Conference on Security and Cooperation in Europe (CSCE), signed in January 1989, expanded on the scope of human rights. It included a new right to recognize and actively promote human rights, and noted the mutual accountability of member states for their observance.[31] CSCE agreements added new language by relating human rights specifically to pluralist, multiparty democracy.[32] The Cold War was winding down.[33]

The new thinking seemed aimed both at domestic revitalization and at useful international cooperation and assistance.[34] But whatever the original motivations of the turn to *glasnost'* and new thinking, no other regime, aside from that of a conquered country, has so radically and swiftly shifted ideologically from rejection to acceptance of the supremacy principle of law and rights, and to human rights universalism.

The Party Dethroned

Putting the new thinking into practice ran up against holdovers in outlooks, interests, and goals.[35] No international enforcement existed to push reforms along. The Vienna agreement and later declarations were not self-executing, given the CSCE's weak enforcement mechanisms.[36] Small wonder that the democratic reforms of 1988–89 fell short of the "highest standards" evoked by Gorbachev at the United Nations. On the other hand, they were a quantum leap away from the phony, single-candidate, party-stage-managed elections of the past.

Gorbachev's commitment to democratic reform clashed with his loyalty to one-party socialism, of which he had been a devoted and successful adherent.[37] Born in 1931 in a collective farm peasant family in Stavropol Territory, Gorbachev reached adulthood as a law student at Moscow University, from which he graduated in 1955, two years into the post-Stalin thaw. In 1978 he moved from being party first secretary (boss) of Stavropol Territory to become a Central Committee secretary and, in 1980, a full member in the ruling Politburo.[38] Gorbachev espoused "socialist pluralism"—that is, "pluralism" as freedom for diverse views with no CPSU monopoly on truth, but "socialist" in the sense of the CPSU's political monopoly.[39] The political reforms approved at the 19th Communist Party Conference in June 1988 and enacted into law in November preserved that monopoly; but they signaled the end of single-candidate elections to rubber-stamp parliaments, the Supreme Soviets, and the local soviets (councils).[40]

The constitutional reforms set up a new parliament, the USSR Congress of People's Deputies, which was elected in March 1989 to a five-year term. Gorbachev's team disregarded advice to democratize fully.[41] First, they reserved 750 seats, one-third of the 2,250 total, for deputies elected within officially recognized, old-line "public organizations," including the CPSU (100 deputies). Second, the reforms compromised with representative democracy by having the unwieldy congress elect from itself a 542-seat USSR Supreme Soviet to meet for longer periods between sessions of the congress. Third, Gorbachev lacked a democratic mandate. He entered the congress on the Communist Party's quota. The congress then elected him president (speaker) of the USSR Supreme Soviet.[42]

Despite these limitations and the electoral machinations of some local party organizations, the reforms began to open government and legislative office to candidates not approved by the Communist Party, or even opposing it. Elected deputies included former political prisoners and dissidents such as Sergei Kovalyov and Andrei Sakharov. Slates of CPSU officials went down to defeat in Moscow and Leningrad.

Sakharov told our Berkeley, California, dialogue meeting in August 1989 that the congress and the revelations emerging from debates had given the public the most complete picture ever of their country's sorry state. For the first time in their lives, his wife Yelena Bonner told us, "the people, who for decades could not be involved in politics . . . learned about politics . . . the whole country witnessed hundreds of people—totally independent people, clever, well-educated—who are troubled over the fate of their land."[43] Later, disillusionment and disinterest set in, as public attention shifted to having to cope with shortages of food, sugar, and cigarettes. In another sign of the difficulties of democratization, Gorbachev and Sakharov fell out over Sakharov's demands for full democracy and an end to the CPSU monopoly.[44] Sakharov died on the night of December 14, 1989, after clashing with Gorbachev over the pace of democratization before a hostile congress.

But Sakharov's campaign outlived him. Pressures from human rights advocates, the democratic minority in parliament, and active republic delegations brought Gorbachev around to an accommodation. In February 1990, he assented to a constitutional amendment, enacted in March, to replace the CPSU's legal monopoly under Article 6 of the much amended Brezhnev-era constitution, with endorsement of a multiparty system. A companion amendment created the post of president of the USSR, to be appointed by vote of parliament the first time around, then directly elected. The congress voted Gorbachev president by a narrow majority.[45]

Legalizing Civil Liberties

Before it ran off the rails, the democratization of Soviet public life went far enough to pry long-delayed reform bills on individual rights out of the bureaucracy and bring them to passage. This legislation provided models for the legalization of rights in the Union republics and in those post-Soviet successor states inclined to carry over the new freedoms. A law of July 1989 reversed the repressive direction of recent legislation and narrowed crimes of expression to the advocacy of "the violent overthrow or change of the Soviet state and social system," pornography, war propaganda, incitement to ethnic hatred, and revealing state secrets.[46]

Laws of 1990 included those legalizing freedom of the press and mass media (and abolishing censorship), freedom of conscience, and freedom of association, for the first time in the USSR.[47] The laws required registration in order to have legal rights to property, housing, bank accounts, and mailing privileges.[48] The law on assembly, however, enabled authorities to deny permission to assemble in public and to prosecute demonstrators assembling without permission, which they did in reaction to various nationalist manifestations.[49] The first hostile May Day parade slogans (see below) prompted President Gorbachev to infringe on freedom of expression by decreeing punishment of up to six years' confinement for "public insults or slander of the President."[50]

A liberalized law on procedures for leaving and entering the country, fully effective by January 1993, left in place stumbling blocks such as a five-year ban on emigration for holders of state secrets. But it dropped the requirement of an invitation from a close relative. It also annulled the automatic loss of citizenship for emigrants to Israel.[51]

The reform laws were the product of "struggle and compromise," in the words of Ernest Ametistov, later justice of the Russian Constitutional Court.[52] Together with parliamentary-electoral reform, they formalized the new freedom and embodied the greatest gain for freedom in the uneven process of *perestroika*.

Rights in Jeopardy

President Gorbachev's alliance with the liberals ended just as he was awarded the Nobel Peace Prize in October 1990. He abandoned an agreement to sponsor decisive steps toward a market economy. The president's new allies in government favored a Soviet technocratic, authoritarian, patriotic "third path" toward national salvation through a mainly state socialist market economy and the preservation of the centralized Union.[53] This program resembles the 1995–96 electoral platforms of the Communist Party of the Russian Federation (CPRF). Not surprisingly, those conservatives, later coup plotters, entered the leadership of the CPRF.

Gorbachev ignored the warnings of a possible coup and turned a deaf ear when Foreign Minister Eduard Shevardnadze's warned that "a dictatorship is coming" in his dramatic resignation speech on December 20, 1990.[54] Russian acquaintances of mine concluded that Gorbachev's reneging on a reform plan, and his appointment of the coup plotters to leading posts, gave the plotters reason to believe that he would be with them in their attempted restoration of Communist rule. Also, did not Gorbachev highlight the contradictions of his outlook in Belarus? There, he plumped for "democratic socialism" as the vehicle for "a law-governed state, separation of powers, mixed market economy, social justice and human rights and freedoms," and mass public political participation in policy-making. On the other hand, he also affirmed his Communist faith. The CPSU, he said, "must become the integrating factor of all centrist forces."[55] ". . . I am a communist and faithful to the idea of socialism. I will . . . go on to the next world with this. [T]hat we serve within the framework of the Communist Party is an idea that unites and reflects the interests of all strata of our people."[56]

Yet, by that time in early 1991, the CPSU had lost many liberal members, including Boris Yeltsin, and had become a stronghold of reaction[57] and of the ruinously absorbent industrial military complex, a haven for the coming coup-makers. A strong mafia operated, in the words of Yury Afanasyev, "from the top of the social and political structure to the bottom."[58] By then, too, international "cooperation" on human rights was coming to mean the West's near disregard of the intensified rights violations under Gorbachev in the Union republics.[59]

Moscow responded to Lithuania's March 11, 1990, declaration of independence (which as an annexed state it had formally never lost) with an economic blockade, threats to use force, and the dispatching of troops to enforce conscription.[60] During their seizures of communications centers,

Soviet troops surrounded the television tower in Vilnius and took it on the night of January 12–13, 1991. They killed thirteen unarmed civilians and injured many more. Firing by special security troops of the Ministry of the Interior killed five more people in Riga a week later. The building takeovers and shootings in Vilnius and Riga appeared to have been botched local coup attempts, planned within the CPSU Politburo and Central Committee and carried out under the illegal command of mysterious "Committees of National Salvation" formed under pro-Moscow Communist parties.[61]

The president denied involvement and expressed regrets. He failed to convince critics on the left (pro-reformers) or the right (nationalist reactionaries).[62] The blatant abuse of human rights in the Baltic region continued into the summer.[63] After the violence in Vilnius, Yelena Bonner wrote a letter to the Nobel Prize Committee, asking the retraction of the late Andrei Sakharov's Peace Prize so that his name would not appear alongside Gorbachev's on the same list of Nobel Prize winners. Stung by the Russian publication of her letter in an issue of *Moscow News* that condemned the government's "criminal policy" in the Baltic, Gorbachev tried in vain to get a law passed to safeguard "press objectivity." But popular and frank news programs suddenly went off the air, to be replaced by obedient announcers reading the official line on events.[64]

Procedures for complaint remained weak in cases of the government's violation of individuals' rights.[65] Courts also had no power to conduct a judicial review of laws for constitutionality. In a first step toward judicial review, the government had put through parliament a law setting up a Constitutional Oversight Commission (COC) in 1989. The COC's statute charged it with monitoring the constitutionality of governmental acts (laws and decrees) and acts of public organizations and their conformity with international human rights norms. The COC did not review private complaints. On the positive side, legislative acts or offending parts of them were to lose force immediately (rather than pending possible appeal) when the COC found that "they violate[d] basic human rights and freedoms enumerated in the USSR Constitution and in international acts in which the USSR is a participant."[66] The COC was no match for an executive determined to ignore its findings, as in the case of outlawing required residence permits as a violation of the right to freedom of movement.[67] Nor could it compensate for the weaknesses of the legal profession.

The legal profession did contain some brilliant and dedicated reformers, such as the criminal proceduralist Igor Petrukhin,[68] and attorneys Boris Zolotukhin, Andrei Makarov, and Mark Reznik—though too few. Lawyers lacked a strong autonomous professional bar association, the protections of at least a relative judicial independence,[69] and the legal wherewithal to defend rights to presumption of innocence, due process, humane treatment, and protection from intrusive security agencies and continuing psychiatric abuses. The releases of political prisoners left as many as 157 confined as of October 31, 1991.[70]

Despite these persistent violations of human rights, the USSR had become a much freer country than it had been when Gorbachev took over. President Yeltsin of Russia banned the CPSU and the Communist Party of Russia on November 6, 1991, leaving in operation the local party cells. The USSR president lost to Russian President Yeltsin whatever influence he had over events. Some final acts of the USSR set precedents for post-Soviet legislation, such as the Declaration of Human Rights and Freedoms of September 5, 1991, and the reduction of the use of the death penalty in law and sentencing practice.[71]

The Part-Civil Society

Gorbachev had counted on openness about problems to "help to modernize the regime," Rasma Karklins notes, "but *glasnost'* developed its own momentum and challenges to the regime."[72] Conflict mounted between conservative CPSU and reformist public ideals. Thousands of NGOs, or *neformaly*, had formed and expressed a range of concerns about environmental pollution, charitable needs and religious freedom, nationalist self-assertion, and monarchist and Stalinist nostalgia for a real or imagined past through extreme right and left organizations.[73]

By 1988, after three years of *perestroika*, the reader of monitoring literature and visitor to the Soviet Union could notice the beginning of a new and more open phase in human rights advocacy. Alongside monitoring and the protection of political rights, advocates began to think, as the late Andrei Sakharov always had, in terms of a positive program of education, empowerment, and community building. By 1988, the advocates included, along with the Helsinki groups, the Group to Establish U.S.–Soviet Trust; the Glasnost Press Club; Democratic Perestroika (a nondissident group of scholars); Vybor (Choice), a cultural-historical-philosophical group of Russian Orthodox believers; the Democratic Union for radical political reform; a group of reform-minded teachers calling themselves "Children of the Twenty-First Century"; members of the new "Memorial" society, who were gathering signatures on the streets and in theater lobbies to petition for a memorial to Stalin's victims; and activists of nationalist movements in the Union republics, along with the long-standing groups defending the rights of dissidents, prisoners of psychiatry, refuseniks, Pentacostalists, and so on.

People learned to be "civil" to the extent that they acted autonomously and with restraint, as did Memorial and the pro-Yeltsin crowds in March 1991. Hundreds of thousands of peaceful demonstrators filled Moscow streets on March 28, 1991, to demonstrate against Communist efforts to have Yeltsin unseated as speaker of the Russian Republic parliament, and to demand Gorbachev's resignation. They assembled in defiance of Gorbachev's twenty-day ban on demonstrations in Moscow, and despite his deployment of 50,000 troops. Resolutions of the Moscow City Council and the Russian parliament denouncing the attempt to prevent demonstrations signaled Gorbachev's waning authority even in Russia. President Gorbachev agreed to marches held away from the Kremlin, and to withdrawal of the troops on March 29.[74]

Deputy Vitaly Korotich, editor of the magazine *Ogoniok*, remarked that it was simpler to organize demonstrations than political parties—or effective accountable authority.[75] Pro-democrats like the demonstrators had neither the experience nor the motivation to form large, inclusive democratic political parties or otherwise to unite effectively in defense of democratic reforms and human rights. Moshe Lewin remained optimistic about civil society. He wrote: "Elected bodies, political groups and alliances, an active press—all the necessary institutions of a democratic civil society are in place and are doing their homework. Once the transition is completed, the Gorbachev phenomenon will come to its fruition, and the special role of this individual will have been concluded."[76] Mary McCauley wrote later, and less positively, that political leaders in pre-Bolshevik Russia "were better educated, they were better organized, and there was a stronger tradition of engaging in political struggle for democratic rights and freedoms. . . . The evidence there suggests that Communist Party rule has created a society, weak on elite groups, with a population democratically inclined, opposed to privilege, short on political knowledge and organization, and seeking new group identities."[77] Democrats lacked the skills and the resources, and society the private economic and philanthropic base or the experience, to complete formation of a civil society.

Intellectuals did well what they knew best: they opposed, wrote, and spoke out eloquently for the new free media. But they elevated party politics into principles over compromise and lowered party politics to personalities over unity. Geoffry Hosking noted that, under Gorbachev, the elements of pluralism emerging were "formed on the basis not of material interests, but of culture and ideas, in keeping with the society to which they belong." Elements of the "deeply segmented society" created by Communist totalitarianism carried over to and impaired political cohesiveness and the formation of a democratic political community.[78]

Unlike Russians after 1917, Russians seventy years later had no understanding, experience, or memory of democracy. Philip E. Mosely, a pioneering specialist on Soviet policy, reported in the early 1930s that, although Russia was being ground under the heel of tyranny, "there was no need to explain to educated Russians . . . the meaning of individual freedom, the rights to personal judgment, or the institutions of representative democracy." "Twenty or thirty years later," wrote Thomas Riha, "a visitor to the Soviet Union had to go back to elementary notions of high school civics to explain the nature of free political competition, freedom of association, the role of pressure groups, and all the other institutions and customs the West takes for granted."[79] "In place of totalitarian power," said an exasperated President Gorbachev, "we have a vacuum of power,"[80] The Communists' "social cleansing" had done its work well.

After a euphoria of novel and rousing frankness in the new parliament in 1989, the obvious lack of results, growing hardships, and bitter political confrontations among party factions produced a society more sullen than civil, a society increasingly alienated from pro-democratic Soviet politics where it had, briefly, been hopefully involved,[81] a society morally adrift and economically distressed.[82]

III-Being

The talk of Moscow in mid-1988 was "Sources," a long article written by the economist Igor Seliunin. Seliunin questioned the relative efficiency of state enterprise in both Imperial Russia and the USSR. He reviewed the human and economic costs of the brutal methods of Lenin and Stalin, and concluded that only rapid sweeping reforms (decentralization and increases in private enterprise rights) could overcome stagnation. The article struck at the heart of Soviet Communism's revolutionary legitimacy—Lenin's and the Party's infallibility. A researcher into artificial intelligence said in Moscow in June 1988: "We are going back to the beginning now. Anyone can see the results of the experiment: Finland, independent in 1918, flourishes, and look at us."[83] Whether because of preference or pressures, but apparently both, Gorbachev ignored the advice of Seliunin and a host of pro-market economists. He resorted, at first, to exhortation and compulsion, through campaigns for sobriety and work discipline. He imported high technology, which was wasted in the unreformed Soviet economy.[84] The government's criminal punishment of entrepreneurs as "speculators" compounded economic difficulties, while organized crime flourished.[85]

Bringing the market to a poor, post-totalitarian, multinational country was proving to be a long and difficult process at best.[86] Gorbachev seemed ever less actively positive as an enthusiast for change, and ever more actively negative in the busy defense of his power, according to James David Barber's classifications of "presidential character."[87] As precious years slid by, Gorbachev backed away from his previous support of reform proposals made by a group of economists in October 1990 and by Grigory Yavlinsky in May–June 1991. Frustrated economic reformers wrote of "irreparable losses" and a possible "paralysis of power."[88]

The reformers lost ground to conservatives owing to the inabilities of Gorbachev, Yeltsin, and pro-reform democrats outside or still within the Communist Party to compromise on differences, surmount personal animosities and ambitions, and converge around a new program of democratic reform before the conservatives united to prevent them from doing so. Gorbachev's refusal to heed warnings of an impending coup dashed the hope of any united democratic movement for effective reform and the preservation of the Soviet Union. Accepting his 1990 Nobel Peace Prize on June 5, 1991, President Gorbachev asked for "large-scale support" from the industrialized countries. But the economic and ethnic troubles that had delayed his acceptance of the prize, awarded on October 16 of the previous year, discouraged Western loans and investments.[89] U.S. President Bush did nothing to assure Gorbachev of massive foreign support should he go through with anything resembling "shock therapy."[90]

By 1991, the deterioration of people's economic and social rights was distancing them ever further from the human right to "a standard of living adequate for the health and well-being of himself and of his family, including food, clothing, housing and medical care and necessary social services, and the right to security in the event of unemployment, sickness, disability, widowhood, old age, or other lack of livelihood in circumstances beyond his control."[91] As a result, democracy, its leaders, and *perestroika* were failing their credibility test with a disillusioned public. In a 1990 poll by the All-Union Center for the Study of Public Opinion, when asked, "What do you see as the main result of five years of *perestroika* in the USSR?" 43 percent of the respondents checked off "growing uncertainty about the future"; 37 percent, "crisis of interethnic relations"; 31 percent, "growing chaos and confusion in running the country"; 30 percent, "deepening economic crisis"; but only 19 percent, "an increase in political and economic activity"; 12 percent, "extension of political rights and liberties"; and 10 percent, "the beginning of the country's economic renewal."[92] Coal miners' and factory strikes spread in 1989–90.[93]

The May Day and Revolution Day parades in 1990 featured anti-Gorbachev sloganeering, jeering, and hostile banners in place of the usual mobilized cheers by compliant crowds. Gorbachev, speaking on November 7, 1990, about "the scarcity of goods, long lines, high prices, and the slackening of law and order," only repeated the obvious. The Communist part of the parade carried slogans saying: "No to Private Property," "We Are for Socialism Not Capitalism," and "No Unemployment." The pro-democratic banners carried slogans supporting Yeltsin, a partisan of market reform and Russia's autonomy, and informing the Soviet president, "Gorbachev, you are winning points abroad but you are losing them in your own country."[94]

Separatism

Referring to the Union republics' constitutional right of secession, Stalin had declared that "not a single republic would want to secede from the

USSR."[95] The 1977 USSR Constitution carried over the right of secession in Article 72. It declared that, on the basis of the "equality of all nations and nationalities, and their brotherly cooperation, there has formed a new historical community of people—the Soviet people." For this "new historical community of people" to become a reality, wrote Roman Szporluk, "the 'Soviet dream' also had to become a reality."[96] When it did not, a "parade of declared sovereignties" (autonomy) and of secession movements became the reality.[97]

Some movements, such as that in the largely Armenian Nagorno Karabakh Autonomous Region (NKAO), part of Azerbaijan, sought independence from their own Union republics. Gorbachev ignored the advice of Andrei Sakharov and other human rights advocates that the government intervene directly to avert bloodshed over the NKAO. The conflict had its Soviet origins in Stalin's decision in 1921 to transfer Karabakh and intervening land to Azerbaijan from Armenia, already reduced by concessions to Turkey that included the sacred Mount Ararat. Merciless fighting began in the NKAO in early 1988, after its Supreme Soviet voted to secede from Azerbaijan. There followed massive outflows of refugees; an anti-Armenian pogrom in the town of Sumgait, Azerbaijan; and gross violations of Armenians' rights in Karabakh and the belt of land separating it from Armenia, apparently with help from the Soviet Fourth Army troops. The Soviet government and forces failed to intervene to head off the Anti-Armenian pogroms in Sumgait (February 1988) and Baku (January 1990), to prevent brutal retaliation by Armenian irregulars, or to lift the choking blockade on road and rail traffic into Armenia.[98]

Perestroika's freedoms permitted the expression of minority groups' discontent with their treatment by a dominant group in their republic and of their resentment of Moscow's imposition of ethnic culture "national in form and socialist in content."[99] Researcher on nationalities Algiras Prazauskas concluded: "The forced internationalization . . . excesses in language policy, violation of the principles of social justice and equal rights for all nations—all this aggravated markedly national relations, hampered a natural process of rapprochement of nations and paved the way for the recurrent outbursts of nationalism."[100] President Mircea Snegur of Moldova noted the socially and politically destructive legacy of "territorial dismemberment, ethnic assimilation, organized migration seeking to change the composition of the population of this land . . . aberrant economic experiments . . . , ecological disaster . . . , and a social infrastructure incapable of meeting elementary human needs."[101]

By destroying civil society, moreover, the Communists had diminished the chances for a timely, open, and democratic settlement of grievances. As old and new grievances fueled nationalist demonstrations during *perestroika*, the government used force against nationalist demonstrators—for example, in Alma Ata, Kazakhstan, in December 1986;[102] in the "mini-

Tiananmen" in Tbilisi, Georgia, in April 1989, where troops' use of gas and sharpened shovels killed nineteen peaceful demonstrators; and in Baku in January 1990. Such shows of force were sufficiently excessive to inflame passions but not enough to crush growing separatism.[103] All but one Union republic, Kirgizia, followed the lead of Estonia, which declared sovereignty in 1988. Republics carried on "wars of laws" by vetoing central government legislation. They began to display pre-Soviet state flags and place-names. The political commentator Otto Latsis concluded that, "against the background of increased democratization," Communist reformers' "attempts to use the imperial language of force failed."[104]

Gorbachev delayed treaty concessions to greater republic autonomy until the spring of 1991. By then the Union was rapidly decentralizing from below, as republics asserted their growing autonomy. He began negotiating Baltic independence and the autonomy of other republics only in April. On April 23, at the government dacha (country home) at Novo-Ogaryovo, he concluded the "nine plus one" agreement with leaders of Russia, Ukraine, and seven other Union republics (except for the Baltic states Georgia, Armenia, and Moldova) to draw up a treaty for a new decentralized "union of sovereign states."[105] But Gorbachev's belated treaty concessions were overtaken by rising local nationalism, combined in places with anti-Communism, and everywhere with the impact of economic chaos and decline.[106]

Breakup

Only a "people" in the legal sense—that is, the inhabitants of an overseas colony or an oppressed population of any country—has the right of self-determination as either autonomy or secession from an internationally recognized state. Only the Baltic republics within the USSR had such a right, at least in the view of those governments that recognized their legal independence from the USSR.[107] Still, legal rights aside, the dissolution of the Union calls to mind Douglas Sanders's proposition: "Cultural minorities are a fact of life. Political stability requires that minority rights be acknowledged and accommodated."[108] Moscow's responses to republic and local grievances and claims to a share of power came too little and too late. Any hopes that the new Union treaty slated for signature on August 20, 1991, might have preserved the Union faded with the August coup attempt.

Politburo member Yegor Ligachev had warned that a multiparty system would be "the ultimate betrayal of Communism" and "would mean the breakup of the Soviet federation."[109] Two years later, like-minded leaders launched a coup attempt to restore the Party's monopoly and save the Union. The coup plotters included Gorbachev's leading government appointees: Prime Minister Valentin Pavlov, Vice President Gennady Yanaev (whose nomination Gorbachev had pushed through a reluctant Congress of People's Deputies), KGB head Vladimir Kryuchkov, Interior Minister Viktor Pugo, Minister of Defense Dmitry Yazov, as well as leading industrial and agricultural administrators.

On August 19, the plotters made their bid for power in the name of preserving the Union. On the pretext that the president, vacationing in the Crimea, was ill and unable to carry out his duties, they claimed authority as the State Committee on the State of Emergency. When Gorbachev did not join the plotters, as they seem to have expected he would, they kept him isolated in his Yalta holiday villa by the sea. Gorbachev's rival, Boris Yeltsin, bolstered by his election as president of Russia in the first round of elections on June 12, had been a leader in the contest with Moscow over the division of powers and the controls over resources. Yeltsin emerged as a hero in the defeat of the coup, and the lead player in Gorbachev's political eclipse and fall.

Thousands of Muskovites gathered to stand in the rain, at risk of worse than a drenching, to defend the center of defiance to the coup, the Russian Republic White House (government building), where Boris Yeltsin and coup opponents took shelter between August 19 and the end of the coup attempt on August 21, 1991. General Alexander Lebed, sent to seize the White House, turned his tanks around in support of it. Three young men, a Russian, a Ukrainian, and a Jew, died in encounters with armored vehicles a few blocks away. They were later accorded the funerals of martyred heroes in Vagankovsky Cemetery. Support also came from Anatoly Sobchak and a portion of the public in St. Petersburg and other cities. Air Force Commander Yevgeny Shaposhnikov and Airborne Troops Commander, later Minister of Defense, Pavel Grachev refused to obey the plotters of the coup. When General Lebed, a foe of Grachev and later ally and Security Council Secretary of Yeltsin, led his troops up to the White House but no farther, some troops even went inside to join the defenders. The Alpha and Beta special strike teams of the KGB also disobeyed orders to storm the erstwhile symbol of democracy.[110]

Central government had, in Bonner's words, "no legitimate authority" after the collapse of the coup.[111] Its purpose had been to save the Union by preventing the signing of a new Union treaty on August 20 to replace the original treaty engineered on December 30, 1922.[112] The failed coup also brought on Yeltsin's banning in Russia of the CPSU and the Communist Party of Russia rather than increased power for it; and the breakup of the Soviet Union rather than its intended salvation.[113]

Martha Brill Olcott aptly summarizes: "Gorbachev consistently stumbled over nationality relations by offering the republics too little too late."[114] Former Foreign Minister and Politburo member Eduard Shevardnadze looked back at lost opportunities and surmised that "if we had proposed the treaty three or four years ago, I am certain that the people would have voted for it without hesitation. We were tardy, timid."[115]

The coup left Gorbachev with little choice but to reach out to Yeltsin and the other republic leaders for whatever cooperation they could negotiate with the center. By then the "parade of sovereignties" became a parade toward full independence. After the coup, the Union republics followed the lead of Lithuania's earlier declaration of independence (March 11, 1990). The new USSR State Council, or upper chamber, recognized the Baltic republics' independence on September 6.

Two mortal blows to the Union followed. First, the Ukrainian public voted overwhelmingly for independence in a referendum of December 1, 1991 (see Chapter 5).[116] Second, in the wake of the Ukrainian referendum, Presidents Yeltsin of Russia, Leonid Kravchuk of Ukraine, and Stanislav Shushkevich of the host republic, Belarus, met in a hunting lodge in the Belovezhskaya Pushcha (Bison Forest) and, without either constitutional authority or a popular mandate, except in Ukraine, proclaimed on December 8 the end of the Soviet Union as a state and the formation of a new loose Commonwealth of Independent States (CIS). The CIS lacked any central intergovernmental institutions.

Leaders of the other eight newly independent states, excepting Georgia, joined the Commonwealth at Alma Ata, Kazakhstan, on December 21. President Gorbachev announced his resignation on December 25, 1991. When Gorbachev returned to his offices the next day, he found that Yeltsin and other Russians (most of them once good Soviet Communists) had taken them over. By then the white, blue, and red Russian tricolor had replaced the banner of the USSR with its hammer and sickle atop the Kremlin and other public places, if not in the hearts of all Russians.

The CIS provided nothing to replace the lost Soviet identity. Its founding statements pledged military cooperation under a united command, respect for each other's territorial integrity, and a commitment to uphold international standards of human rights on the model of the September 5 declaration of the USSR Congress of People's Deputies.[117] But the lack of any CIS enforcement mechanism left regional monitoring up to the new human rights agencies of the CSCE. They would be hard-pressed to realize the lofty commitment to human rights and democracy formulated in the meetings held at Vienna, Copenhagen, Moscow, and Paris.

Conclusions

Perestroika failed to resolve the long-standing Soviet conflict between "friends and foes of change."[118] Opposition to reform lodged in the entrenched bureaucracy, the *nomenklatura*. Gorbachev's temporizing on reform and alliance with conservative appointees, who then plotted the failed August coup, reflected his conflicts of values and interests as leader. On one side shone his commitment to a new freedom, impressively voiced to the UN in 1988. On the other side loomed a commitment to socialism, voiced as late as 1991, "within the framework of the Communist Party," which "unites and reflects the interests of all strata of our people." Gorbachev felt uneasy with pluralism, whether of parties, interests, economic ownership, ethnic values, or regional authority.

Also playing their part in undermining reform were the legacies of Communist social cleansing: the lack of democratic experience, economic autonomy, and civil society, both generally and in regard to the airing and resolution of issues of ethnic tensions and minority rights. Finally, the USSR faced the "cruel dilemmas of development," known around the world, which inevitably accompany efforts to balance growth with the protection of individual economic and social rights.

As in tsarist Russia, the conflicts between past and future framed a difficult ordeal for freedom in the Soviet Union. They contributed to the failure, once again, as Guchkov had put it in 1913, "to effect a peaceful, painless transition from the old, condemned system, to a new order." Gorbachev incorporated the new thinking on human rights and freedoms, originally voiced by some democratic Soviet dissidents some two decades earlier, into the official "new thinking." If this fell apart in practice, it might well have been because political freedoms ran ahead of the essential commitments to the rule of law, economic reform, and inclusiveness in center-regional relations and minority rights.

But, unlike the case in late 1917, the collapse of the regime in 1991 left a legacy of democratic freedoms that at least partially survived the Soviet collapse. David Remnick gives Gorbachev his due: "Spurred by a shuddering economy to open Soviet society, he freed political prisoners and granted considerable liberty to religion, the press, and dissident political groups. Censorship eased; intellectual life revived. Almost single-handed, he ended the Cold War."[119] Freedom was passed on to the fifteen post-Soviet states to preserve or destroy, depending on how they handled the enduring conflicts between reform and reaction, growth and equity, and inclusiveness and inequality.

Chapter 5
Free at Last? Democracy in the Newly Independent States

> Physicists know that you can move from one order of things to another
> only by passing through a state of chaos.
> —President Askar Akayev of Kyrgyzstan.[1]

Democracy in Post-Communist States

The post-Communist countries of Eastern Europe, to the west of the former Soviet Union, are successor states to the Austro-Hungarian, German, and Ottoman empires. The fifteen post-Soviet states cover an area that belonged almost entirely to the Russian Empire. By the end of 1991, those former republics of the USSR were free, like it or not. Majorities in the three Baltic states liked it; they regained the full independence they had enjoyed from 1918 until the Soviet takeover, and a chance to make democracy work this time around. Majorities in the newly independent states of Ukraine, Moldova, Armenia, Georgia, and Azerbaijan also liked it. The other seven newly independent countries—Russia, Belarus, and five in Central Asia—were also free at last. Some newly independent states hung on to and strengthened a still rudimentary democracy. Others slipped into authoritarianism and, in its extreme form, dictatorship.

The results of independence do not confirm the predictions of cultural relativists who see democracy as mainly a Western form of government. Nor do they confirm the expectations of those universalists who have anticipated the triumph of liberal democracy and human rights around the world. Rather, the story turns out to be one of diversity, one that reflects the outcomes of a struggle among powerful former Communists, democratic reformers and human rights advocates, nostalgic and disadvantaged pro-Communists, and nationalists. These groups overlap considerably in the political arena of mixed motivations.

During the 1990s the number of liberal democracies in "free" countries with relatively full ranges of all basic human rights had—according to the human rights NGO Freedom House—reached seventy-nine by 1997, as compared with fifty-seven a decade earlier. "Partly free democracies" (so rated by Freedom House) numbered another thirty-nine in fifty-nine partly free countries. About 60 percent of the world's countries and nearly 55 percent of its population in 1997 lived under governments and legislatures chosen in generally free and fair elections. Most of the even partly free democracies, reported Freedom House, "have a substantial degree of freedom, as well as some measure of respect for basic human rights." Above the world average, about 70 percent of inhabitants live in "partly free" and "free,"—that is, "liberal"—democracies among post-Communist states of Eastern and post-Soviet Europe.[2]

About half of the post-Communist states of Eastern Europe enjoy a broad enough range of human rights to merit a "free" rating, though they are prone to discrimination against certain minorities; four or five are "partly free"; two "not free."[3] Among the post-Soviet states, only the three Baltic states are free, or liberal, democracies—but "ethnic" democracies. None of the twelve post-Soviet newly independent states can be rated as free democracies by any stretch of the concept. Five of them, fewer than half, are "partly free" democracies, or approaching that status. Altogether, though, they contain over 70 percent, and with the Baltic states, three-quarters, of the total post-Soviet population.[4] The survival of freedom after *perestroika* gives some grounds of hope for its future. But the incompleteness of freedom in post-Soviet democracies and nondemocracy in the other post-Soviet states point to the dangers lying ahead.

This chapter considers the shifting patterns of democracy and rights in the post-Soviet states since independence and reviews freedom and human rights in the partly free democracies of Ukraine and Moldova and the near-democracies in transition of Georgia and Kyrgyzstan.

Human Rights and Democracy

Timothy Colton listed six "protodemocratic" states when independence came in 1991. These states' Soviet-era parliamentary elections of 1990 were "passably fair, and anti-Communist groups, usually under the umbrella of a 'popular front,' had a chance of winning." They included Estonia, Latvia, Lithuania, Russia, Ukraine, and Armenia. All except Armenia remained free or "partly free" democracies. Colton listed nine other states as "pre-democracies": Azerbaijan and Georgia in the Caucasus region and the five Central Asian countries plus Belarus and Moldova to the west.[5] One should change the "pre" to "non" for most of these, except for the new democracy, Moldova, and the near-democracies of Georgia and Kyrgyzstan.

On the civil rights front, reforms in law enforcement, security, and justice lag behind reforms in civil liberties.[6] The lapses in civil rights make a mockery of constitutional "guarantees" to rights of due process, personal inviolability, even life itself. The lack of the rule of law in day-to-day administration in the post-Soviet states (and in Eastern Europe as well) prevents the accountability of officials and other violators of civil rights. It facilitates the persecution of those who oppose the government in power. It allows a continuation of brutal and inhumane treatment by police and jailers, denial of vital medical treatment to prisoners and of their access to legal counsel, a slow pace of change in the jury system coupled with a scarcity of impartial tribunals, and the prosecutors' vast powers. People face an increased danger of victimization by street and organized crime, abetted by corrupt police and local authorities. In complicity with organized crime, "underpaid policemen and rogue armies all inflicted damage on the delicate democratic structures."[7] The residence permit system also continues to deny freedom of movement and creates new opportunities for abuses by officials and corruption that affects more than half the post-Soviet population.[8]

As Ariel Cohen has written, "The development of the rule of law is a key element of democratic reform."[9] Where the rule of law falters, economic reform is undermined by corrupt practices and the lack of sanctity of contracts and property. This in turn imperils democratization. Former Communists of the old *nomenklatura*—bureaucratic power elite—prosper by participating in privatization at such bargain rates that it can more accurately be called piratization, or, as the Russians say, not *privatizatsiya* but *priekhvatizatsiya*—not privatization but the big grab. A "corrupt business class" appears "which is intimately entwined with a corrupt and criminally connected political class."[10]

Outside the privileged circles of power and wealth, the decline in economic and social rights for most people continued into independence, to the detriment of citizen involvement in politics.[11] The most deprived have been the most vulnerable—the old, the pensioners, children, salaried employees who go unpaid (and soldiers who have literally starved in Russia), while the corrupt power elites siphon off untold wealth.[12] The old trade unions take care of their own as best they can, but nothing more. They lag behind the much smaller but more militant independent unions, such as the coal miners', in exercising their formal rights to strike (used ever more often) and to bargain collectively.

Both democracy and the attainment of human rights under rule of law are the tasks of difficult decades, not a few years. They must be the work mainly of the people of post-Communist countries. But outside help through investments, credit, and broad-based dialogue about common problems and dilemmas of economic growth with equity remain crucial in the struggle for human rights and democracy.

Women have borne the brunt of economic and social disruption in the transition since *perestroika*. They face discrimination in employment, advancement, and access to appointed and elected political posts, sexual exploitation, and almost unchecked domestic violence. In response, women here and there are forming their own advocacy groups and self-help centers.[13] Discrimination and harassment against homosexuals also remain, even where homophobic laws have been repealed.

Jews, formerly the most culturally repressed minority, have made the greatest gains in cultural freedom. *Perestroika* brought new freedoms for Hebrew instruction, cultural and communal life generally, and religious worship and instruction. Where there is a preeminent church associated with the majority ethnic group, as in Armenia or Russia, this may sway the government away from neutrality and toward the dominant church, at the expense of the equal rights of other faiths to registration, support, or the return of property confiscated by the Communists. Various resident faiths may encourage the government to limit proselytizing by foreign-based groups, which is banned in six post-Soviet states, and to organize religious instruction in state-supported schools.[14]

Governments or citizens of most free democracies practice some discrimination against certain minority groups. Shortcomings in the rule of law expose Jews to possible anti-Semitism and other minorities to possible discrimination in violation of their constitutional and human rights.[15] Violent interethnic conflict has taken a toll in human rights, democratic participation, and stability. The lingering victimization of deported and expelled nationalities affects, for example, the Tatars, who encounter hostility and worse as they return to Crimea.

Any assessment of shared human rights problems should include the uprooting in the post-Soviet states of some nine million refugees, displaced persons, and other involuntary migrants.[16] They have fled present or anticipated persecution and discrimination, civil strife, ethnic cleansing, environmental disasters, and misgovernment in the Caucasus region, Central Asia, Moldova, and Russia. Arthur C. Helton, director of Forced Migration Projects at the Open Society Institute, spoke at a CIS (Commonwealth of Independent States) Conference on Forced Migration in Geneva. The conference brought together officials from the CIS and European countries, the UN High Commissioner for Refugees, the International Organization for Migration, the OSCE, and representatives of eighty NGOs. Helton warned that a lack of international commitment to effective remedies will leave people "uprooted, unprotected, and unassisted."[17] One might add that the uprooted are unrepresented, to the extent that their status where fate has tossed them excludes them from political participation and advocacy.

Partly Free Democracies: Ukraine and Moldova

Ukraine

Ukraine is the second largest of the post-Soviet states. It covers an area of 240,000 square miles, almost as much as Texas. Ukraine's borders have shifted often since it united with Moscow in 1654, under which it suffered cultural Russification. Forcefully reunited after separation in 1918 and the subsequent civil war, Ukraine was enlarged to the west by Stalin's annexation of Transcarpathian Ukraine from Hungary in 1945. Stalin had annexed the rest of western Ukraine, including L'viv (Lvov), at the expense of eastern Poland under the Nazi–Soviet Pact of August 23, 1939. Western Ukraine is heavily ethnic Ukrainian and Ukrainian ethnonationalist in comparison with mainly Russian-speaking, ethnically mixed eastern Ukraine.[18]

Under a healing leadership, Ukraine has set an example of ethnic peace and democratization for the post-Soviet states. The Chernobyl Nuclear Power Station meltdown in eastern Ukraine on April 26, 1986, and Moscow's subsequent indifference tended to unify the country. "Ecological disasters," said mother activists, "did not recognize ethnic boundaries."[19] Chernobyl prompted ecological movements and political associations in eastern Ukraine to join with pro-independence movements in the more separatist western Ukraine. Rukh, the nationalist Ukrainian Popular Movement for Perestroika, has taken care to be inclusive in membership and staffing and to avert anti-Semitism and other forms of extremism.[20] The aim has been, in the words of Ukrainian poet and philologist Oksana Zabuzhko, to resume Ukrainian "identity in a very broad sense."[21] On July 16, 1990, the Supreme Rada (Soviet) voted 355 to 4 for a Declaration of State Sovereignty. The declaration pledged Ukraine to becoming a "nuclear-free zone," which it achieved in 1996.[22] The declaration also obligated Ukraine "to respect the national rights of all peoples."[23]

By 1991 Leonid Kravchuk, speaker of the Supreme Soviet since July 23, 1990, and former ideological secretary of the CPSU, had changed from "a colorless apparatchik to an ardent pro-independence nationalist."[24] Under his leadership, the Supreme Rada declared full independence on August 24, 1991, a few days after the attempted Moscow coup. Kravchuk won election as president of Ukraine with 62 percent of the vote on December 1, 1991, the day on which a referendum approved Ukrainian independence. Pro-independence votes occurred in heavily Russian areas: 77 percent in Donetsk, and 54 percent even in Crimea, despite its close Russian ties and 70 percent Russian majority.[25]

The country's 1991 law on national minorities is said to have "played an instrumental role in preventing ethnic strife by allowing individual citizens to use their respective national languages in conducting personal business and by allowing minority groups to establish their own schools."[26] To be sure, in Ukraine inclusiveness carries far fewer risks to titular ethnic culture and identity—with a 74 percent Ukrainian majority in the population of 52 million and the next largest group, the Russians, at 22 percent[27]— than it does in Estonia and Latvia, which have slim ethnic majorities.

While President Kravchuk dithered on market-oriented reforms, privatization, and the introduction of fiscal discipline, the economy sank far below even the disastrous Russian decline. Ukraine had an unhealthy dependence on Russia for most of its fossil fuels, which no longer flowed in at a fraction of the world price. The country spent several times more on the lingering costs of the lethal meltdown at its Chernobyl NPS than it did on regular health care, culture, and education. It was loathe to shut down remaining Chernobyl reactors because of the fuel shortage.[28]

Ukrainians elected a new 450-seat Rada (parliament) in March–April 1994, with a high voter turnout of 74 percent. One must agree with Anders Aslund that "Ukrainian society displayed an extraordinary peacefulness amid its squalor." The parliamentary election, held with Kravchuk's reluctant agreement, "was the first victory for Ukrainian democracy."[29] In elections of June–July 1994, former prime minister Leonid Kuchma beat Leonid Kravchuk and four other presidential candidates. He won the four-year term in a runoff against Kravchuk, with 52 percent of the vote versus 45 percent for Kravchuk.

President Kuchma quickly eliminated the censorship that Kravchuk had imposed on state and private media. However, the potential for pressures on the media remained through the government's newsprint monopoly and state-owned television and radio stations. Freedom of assembly has held despite the Soviet-era law, common to the NIS, which requires permission to hold public meetings and demonstrations.[30] Freedom of association is nonetheless qualified by provisions, as in other post-Soviet states, that registration is required for a party or an association to have a bank account, acquire property, or enter into contracts. Political parties enjoy less than full freedom. They may not receive funds from the state or from abroad or maintain foreign bank accounts. Under Ukrainian law, also, registered groups are supposed to inform the government of their activities and meetings, open meetings to all persons, present registration documents to any government official on request, and prove that activities comply with the group's registered purpose. No registered organization may duplicate a government function or service. Thus, the Ministry of Justice forbade human rights lawyers to form an association to represent prisoners because, it said, the government already provides lawyers for the accused.[31]

Ukraine joined the Council of Europe in November 1995—not with a flawless record, however. The Human Rights Committee associated with the International Covenant on Civil and Political Rights (ICCPR) has strongly recommended attention to such lapses in civil rights as discrimination against women, police torture and ill-treatment of detainees, inhumane conditions in prisons, and the lack of judicial impartiality.[32]

Freedom of religion in Ukraine has been marred by rivalry among three churches over the control of church buildings and other property. The Russian Orthodox (renamed the Ukrainian Orthodox) Church goes back to Vladimir's conversion of Kievan Rus' in A.D. 988. The Uniate (Eastern rite Catholic) Church looks back on four centuries of union with Rome. The (Ukrainian) Autocephalous Orthodox Church originated in Lenin's encouragement of indigenous churches in contrast to the Russian Church. Stalin preferred the Russian Church, which applauded his dissolution of the Uniate and Autocephalous Churches in 1946.[33] Religious freedom exists for established Jewish, Moslem, and Protestant groups. But anti-proselytizing law and policy limit the religious activities of foreign groups.[34] The Jewish minority, the second largest after the Russians, received the satisfaction of President Kravchuk's commemoration of the Holocaust and his apology for the Ukrainians' part in it at the massacre site of Babyi Yar in 1991. The government encourages the revival of Jewish communal, cultural, and religious life.

Nationalism in western Ukraine perpetuates lingering issues of minority rights. Thus, Russian speakers in L'viv have complained that schools do not offer enough instruction in Russian. They object to the Ukrainian language examination for admission to colleges and universities. Jewish and Russian minorities in parts of western Ukraine also complain, with cause, that ultranationalists foster ethnic hatred. The city of L'viv granted registration to the anti-Semitic and ultranationalist Organization of National Unity (ONU) after Kiev had refused to register it. L'viv also refused the Jewish community permission to build a memorial on the site of the only former German concentration camp where a memorial has yet to be erected.

Crimea has been a more serious ethnic trouble spot. Until the breakup of the USSR, nobody took seriously the possible consequences of Khrushchev's "gift" of the Crimean peninsula to Ukraine in 1954 to mark the tricentennial of Ukraine's union with Russia. After independence, however, a Russian-speaking movement demanded Crimea's autonomy or reunification with Russia. Ukrainians and Tatars have felt the sting of discrimination in Crimea. The rebellious Crimean government cut off its subsidy of the only Ukrainian-language paper in Simferopol. With the complicity of local authorities, some Russian settlers have obstructed the resettlement of the Crimean Tatars returning from the deportation of 1944. The Kiev authorities ran out of money to assist the Tatars' resettlement after 250,000 had returned.[35] The Tatars have formed their own representative assembly, the Medzhlis, under their determined leader Mustafa Dzhemil.[36]

Running out of patience with Crimean separatism, President Kuchma in 1995 convinced the Rada to annul Crimea's constitution and presidency as violations of Ukrainian law. Two weeks later, Kuchma introduced direct rule from Kiev over the Crimean administration and assembly. Despite this, four Tatars died in a violent confrontation in June 1995.[37] Furthermore, the alliance between the underworld and the political world in Crimea resulted in the murder, with impunity, of six people, half the leadership of the Crimean Christian Liberal Party, because the party's platform favored economic reform. The remaining party leadership fled Ukraine and the party disbanded.[38]

Women in Ukraine organized inclusively to support independence and environmental protection. They realized that ecological disasters, which went back years before Chernobyl, threatened them and their families and did not stop at ethnic boundaries. Well represented in local and provincial government, women make up less than 3 percent of Rada deputies. Prompted by women's NGOs, parliamentary hearings concluded: "Women are the most vulnerable . . . to the wave of exploitation, criminality and violence. Women suffer discrimination in the workplace. They constitute more than 70 percent of the unemployed. The mean income level of women is one-third less than the equivalent among males."[39]

After two years of wangling over a new constitution to replace the amended 1978 Soviet-era document, the president on June 26, 1996, called a referendum to approve a draft constitution that would have given him dominant power of appointment and divided parliament into two chambers—the better to conquer it. The Rada promptly passed a draft of its own the next day which provided for a balance of power among the three branches of government. Ministerial appointments are made in consultation with the Rada. The judicial branch is formally independent. The constitution retains Ukrainian as the state language, but it recognizes languages of minorities for official use in regions where they are concentrated. Rejecting Rukh's proposal to turn Crimea into an ordinary province, it retains an "Autonomous Republic of Crimea" with its own parliament and constitution.[40]

After his election, President Kuchma brought inflation and deficit spending under control, stepped up privatization, and qualified for growing credit and project aid from the IMF and the World Bank. He managed to push through a conservative parliament a stringent budget, a constitutional law that enhanced his executive authority to forge ahead with reform, and ratification of the Nuclear Non-Proliferation Treaty.[41]

Stubborn resistance to tax and property reforms still persist. Corruption thrives at all levels, even to the bribes needed to start a small business. A thriving, tax-evading black market accounts for about half of the economy. Discouraged foreign investors tend to stay away. Ukraine has one-hundredth the foreign investment per capita that Hungary has. It must also overcome the survival of defense-industry dinosaurs, the lethal legacy of Chernobyl, the insecurity of private property rights, rampant organized crime—in short, the lack of the rule of law with its essential guarantees of political, economic, and social rights.[42] On the brighter side, in two years (1994–96), inflation fell from more than 10,000 percent to a few percent annual rate, and the average monthly wage increased from U.S. $11 to U.S. $80.

A study conducted for Freedom House summed up Ukraine's progress and problems: "Ukraine has made steady progress toward political and national stability. The Crimea crisis has been temporarily defused. It has managed to avoid ethnic strife and extremist violence. There is a vibrant independent media, established trade union and other elements of a burgeoning civil society. But foot-dragging on reforms could undermine foreign assistance and prompt Russia to use economic means to provoke crisis and unrest."[43] Conversely, the modesty of foreign assistance now furnished will slow reform. To push on with reform, Ukraine needs not more high-paid foreign experts but steps to lower barriers to its exports of metals, agricultural products, chemicals, and clothes to Europe, the United States, and other countries.[44]

Moldova

Moldova has won plaudits from Freedom House as "a model of post-Communist reform."[45] A country of some 4.4 million people, Moldova lies sandwiched between Ukraine and Romania. Ethnic Romanian Moldovans make up 65 percent of the population, Ukrainians 14 percent, and Russians 13 percent.[46] Its parliament unanimously declared independence on August 27, 1991, less than a week after the coup attempt in Moscow. At the same time, as in most post-Soviet states, the Moldovan parliament undertook international human rights commitments by declaring its readiness to adhere to the Helsinki Final Act of 1975 and the Paris Charter for a New Europe, to join the UN, and to guarantee the human rights of all citizens.[47] Moldova evolved into a democracy, as betokened by peaceful and generally free and fair elections.

Parliament elected Mircea Snegur president in 1990. Snegur, once a Soviet official, quit the Communist Party in 1989. In his moderate nationalism and political pragmatism he resembled Ukraine's President Kuchma. Snegur stood for and won direct election overwhelmingly in 1991. The new Moldovan Constitution of August 27, 1994, provides for a multiparty system and a strong president as chief executive. The judicial reforms of 1995 set up a Constitutional Court.

Moldova has asserted an identity separate from that of Romania, to which much of Moldova once belonged. It managed a peaceful electoral change of parliament in what OSCE observers deemed the essentially free and fair elections of February 1994. The Moldovan government has made peace with the 4 percent of Turkic, mainly Russian-speaking, Christian Gagauz by granting extensive autonomy to their southern homeland. The government has preserved political freedoms where it holds authority, despite the ravages of civil war with the breakaway, predominantly Slavic,

Transdniester region to the northeast in 1992. Stalin tacked that region onto Moldova in 1945.[48]

The media present diverse viewpoints. Bans on anti-independence and anti-democratic expression and parties seem to be directed against the proponents of reunification with Romania, who dispute independent Moldova's right to exist.[49]

The religious freedom law of 1992 includes the right of conscientious objection and freedom of religious profession, worship, and the formation of associations and foundations. The law requires government permission to hire foreigners. Proselytizing, though banned, still continues. Protestants, followers of Krishna, Baha'i, and other sects worship freely. Only a branch of the Orthodox Church recognizing the authority of the Romanian Orthodox Church was denied registration and reports local harassment.

The active Jewish community has cooperative relations with the government and local authorities. Anti-Semitism breaks out unsystematically as, for example, in the toppling of Jewish gravestones in Chisinau or the beating of Jews in Bender, Transdniestria. In a gesture to minorities, many of whom do not speak the state language, Moldovan (Romanian), parliament postponed from 1994 to 1997 the operation of a law requiring competence in Moldovan as well as Russian. Although Russian speakers tend to lack competence in Moldovan, most Moldovans can speak Russian. The new constitution guarantees to parents the right to choose their children's language of upbringing. The parliament includes deputies from the Russian, Ukrainian, Bulgarian, and Gagauz minorities. It debates either in Moldovan or Russian, with translations provided.

Foreign observers from the Conference on Security and Cooperation in Europe (CSCE) and foreign NGOs have reported favorably on human rights in Moldova, as did a delegation of the old Russian Supreme Soviet.[50] Moldova has an outstanding record of cooperation with such human rights NGOs as Helsinki Watch groups and the Helsinki Citizens Assembly. OSCE's Office of Democratic Institutions and Human Rights praised Moldova's "zero option" law of June 1991, which gave the right of citizenship to all residents in Moldova. But this cut no ice with the separatist movement in Transdniestria.

Slavs in Transdniestria comprise about 54 percent of its roughly 600,000 inhabitants; 28 percent are Ukrainians, 25.4 percent Russians, 40 percent Moldovans.[51] Non-Moldovan founders of the Dniester Moldovan Republic (DMR) on September 2, 1990, feared possible union with Romania. They objected to the 1989 language law making Moldovan the state language and changing from Cyrillic to the Latin alphabet. The separatists vowed to remain part of the Soviet Union;[52] they supported the Moscow coup attempt of August 1991. "It was the Moldovans, not Russian residents, who rallied to Yeltsin, 'Democratic Russia,' and the Russian flag," Deputy Vladimir

Solinar' from Chishinau told me in September 1991, soon after the coup attempt. "None of these is popular with Moldova's Russian residents."[53]

The Union's demise fed an armed rebellion demanding a separate Transdniestrian republic. During the hostilities in 1992, tens of thousands of Moldovan refugees fled the rebellious left bank and the right-bank town of Tighnina.[54] Moldova has averted serious conflict with Russia, despite popular sympathy for the separatists, the participation of Russian Cossacks on the separatists' side, and assistance extended to them by the Russian 14th Army under General Alexander I. Lebed.[55]

Russia's President Boris Yeltsin joined the mediation of a cease-fire agreement in July and August 1992. Negotiations for a cease-fire brought together ministers of Moldova, Romania, Russia, and Ukraine. The negotiations marked the first peacekeeping mission of the CSCE.[56] The agreements provided for a Russian-Moldovan-DMR peacekeeping force. After two years of Moldovan cooperation with the OSCE (formerly CSCE), the separatist Transdniestrian rulers finally agreed to allow OSCE representatives to participate in the mediating commission formed under the 1992 cease-fire. The mediators ran up against the clash between Transdniestrian demands for independence in a loose confederation and the Moldovan offer of autonomy.[57]

After Mircea Snegur broke with his Agrarian Party and turned to support reunification with Romania, another former Communist leader, Petru Lucinschi, who opposed reunification with Romania, defeated Snegur in the December 1996 elections and took office January 16, 1997. Lucinschi favored improving relations with Russia and continued talks with the DMR and its pro-independence president, Igor Smirnov, also reelected in December. Human rights in the DMR sank to the oppressive levels of a dictatorship.[58]

Moldova, a fertile, primarily agricultural republic, began to develop a mixed economy by the later 1990s. Privatization lagged in agriculture, its main sector. But from the standpoint of marketeers, gains have been impressive. The gross domestic product had dropped by nearly a third in 1992. It registered its first small gain in 1995, not counting the extensive shadow economy operating beyond the reach of the tax collector and official statistics. Annual inflation rates dropped from nearly 2,200 percent in 1992 to about 10 percent in 1995. The budget deficit, a feeder of inflation and high interest rates, dropped from 23.4 to 3.5 percent of the GDP between 1992 and 1995.[59] Economic hardships and the tensions with and inside Transdniestria continued to intensify freedom's ordeal in one of the two "most free" newly independent states.[60]

Near Democracies: Georgia and Kyrgyzstan

Georgia

Georgia's turbulence and brutal treatment of prisoners leaves it short of "partly free democracy" status.[61] Yet, under President Eduard Shevardnadze, the country enjoys a tense but freer peace after several years of bitter internal war. Georgia declared independence in April 1991. Its population of 5.6 million is almost 70 percent Georgian. Its minorities include 9 percent Armenians, 7 percent Russians, and 5 percent Azerbaijanis.[62] Zviad Gamsakhurdia's tyrannical presidency ended with his violent ouster in January 1992. This opened the way to a cease-fire, monitored by the CIS and CSCE, in the war against its South Ossetia region. Gamsakhurdia had met its demands for autonomy with force.

Georgia took another step away from dictatorship after holding generally free and fair multiparty parliamentary elections in October 1992. The new parliament appointed Eduard Shevardnadze, former Soviet foreign minister, supporter of *perestroika*, and once Georgia's Communist First Secretary, as chairman, head of state, and head of the executive branch.[63] Parliament adopted a new constitution on August 24, 1995. Fair elections of November 5 produced a new single-chamber parliament and elected Eduard Shevardnadze president of Georgia with 74.3 percent of the vote. Shevardnadze's Centrist Union Party won a clear majority, with 150 of 225 seats in parliament. Fighting with followers of Gamsakhurdia had ended by 1993. He was reported to have died in exile in December.[64] Fighting continued in separatist Abkhazia.

Abkhazians had dropped to 18 percent of the Abkhaz Autonomous Republic, strategically located on the shores of the Black Sea. By the time of a UN-brokered cease-fire in December 1993, the Abkhaz rebels had defeated the Georgians with help from Russian forces and Moslem brethren from the North Caucasus region of Russia. The carnage took a high civilian toll and produced an outpouring from Abkhazia of an estimated 250,000 surviving refugees, mainly ethnic Georgians. Representatives from Georgia, Abkhazia, Russia, and the UN signed a cease-fire agreement on May 14, 1994.

The price for Russian assistance, and the protection of Georgia's railroad communications from various foes, was Georgia's entry into the CIS and its agreement to the presence of 19,000 Russian troops in five bases. Russian troops have served as peacekeepers for the CIS in South Ossetia since June 1992. They patrolled the border with Abkhazia under the cease-fire agreement of May 14, 1994. The 1994 agreement's provisions on refugee resettlement remained largely unfulfilled, despite the presence of a UN observer group and the CIS peacekeeping force of Russian troops. Abkhazy continued to commit ghastly atrocities of rapine, torture, and murder against Georgian families remaining in Abkhazia.[65]

Criminal justice remains defective. Prisons are overcrowded; inmates are starved, tortured, and beaten. The right to counsel is violated. Forty suspects died in pretrial detention in 1995. They were denied access to adequate counsel of their choice. Rather than ignore the police abuses, the government arrested more than 350 police officers, and it has created the Office of Human Rights Defender to respond to claims of violations.

After the attempted car-bomb assassination of President Shevardnadze on August 29, 1995, accusations of complicity reached high into the State Security Service, parliament, and the leadership of the Mkhedrioni (Horsemen) paramilitary force, which had been Shevardnadze's ally in the 1992–93 war against followers of Gamsakhurdia. The president had it disbanded on October 1, 1995.

Electronic eavesdropping intrudes on privacy in Georgia, as in other NIS. Before his assassination, and the serious wounding of his wife, a deputy, on December 3, 1994, Gia Chanturia, head of the National Democratic Party, had complained that his office was bugged. During Shevardnadze's presidency, security agencies' invasions of privacy have diminished.

Media freedoms increased after the fighting ended, contrary to trends in neighboring Armenia. There was notably fairer access to television broadcasts in Georgia than in Armenia during the 1995 electoral campaigns. The government allowed more certain freedom of assembly despite lingering political tensions between supporters of Shevardnadze and those of the late Zviad Gamsakhurdia. It maintained freedom of residence, without a permit system.

A minority rights law of March 10, 1995, and the new constitution bolstered the legal framework of once chaotic Georgia. Mskhetian Turks, a group deported by Stalin to Uzbekistan in 1944, began to return despite threatening local opposition. The Jewish community shares in Georgia's religious and cultural freedom. It was much diminished by emigration to Israel in the early 1970s and later flights to escape robbery and kidnapping for ransom by predatory gangs during Georgia's civil conflict in the early 1990s.[66]

The government has cooperated with international NGOs. Some exceptions exist with respect to access to political prisoners who are possible victims of abuse. Domestic human rights monitoring appears to be polarized: The State Committee on Human Rights and NGOs find each other to be biased. The projected human rights ombudsman may make a needed contribution to domestic human rights monitoring. Women's human rights have become the subject of concern for a growing number of new women's NGOs, such as Georgian Women's Choice and the Party for Defense of Women's Rights.

Georgia's economy, like that of Armenia, fell into ruins and an energy crisis. Georgia has depended on humanitarian grain shipments to stave off hunger and on foreign aid to avert financial collapse. Freedom House published an upbeat report about an austerity campaign "that stamped out hyperinflation in less than a year. Prices were freed, state spending was frozen, and large scale privatization was launched. Moreover, oil reserves were discovered in eastern and western regions by a British investor and after much wrangling, Russia agreed to a pipeline carrying Azeri oil through Georgia."[67] That agreement bears watching. Economic recovery has begun but will take time to improve the lot of refugees, pensioners, orphans, growing numbers of street waifs, and, as in other newly independent states, the handicapped.

All signs point to the correctness of the report for Freedom House that found, "despite episodes of political violence, persistent corruption, Russian meddling, human rights abuses and Abkhazia, democratic elections, a new constitution and economic reform have set Georgia on the road to strengthening democracy."[68]

Kyrgyzstan

Kyrgyzstan is a small, poor, mountainous country of about 4.6 million people squeezed up against China in northeast Central Asia. The country moved toward democracy after independence. Earlier, violence had erupted in Osh, Fergana Valley, on June 4, 1990, between Uzbek farmers and Kyrgyz seeking their land.[69] In the wake of that bloodshed, Soviet President Mikhail Gorbachev had Askar Akayev, then a Supreme Soviet deputy, flown back to Bishkek and elected president, unopposed, in November.[70] President Akayev, a physicist, had been head of the Kyrgyz Communist Party's Science Department.

Determined to calm his country with a firm hand, President Akayev managed to avert repetitions of the clash in Osh. In the name of order, he established an authoritarian regime[71] that lacked accountability due to the absence of alternatives to Akayev, the rudimentary party system, and the muzzling of the critical press.[72] Akayev had his presidency reaffirmed in the dubious, Soviet-style referendum of January 1994, when he ran again unopposed. The president circumvented the constitution when he decreed, on September 20, 1994, the holding of elections to a new 105-member bicameral parliament on February 15, 1995. The decree seemed to be aimed at heading off corruption inquiries through parliament that might embarrass his government. Observers reported widespread violations such as ballot stuffing in the February elections; but no one party or group weighted the results enough to subvert the elections. "All of us Kyrgyzstanis are still beginners in democracy, and perhaps we understand it only in our heads, not in our hearts," President Akayev said after the elections. He expressed hope that the next elections would be "truly democratic."[73]

Parliament rejected a petition for a referendum on the president, on the grounds that referenda to extend a president's term were unconstitutional —a consideration that did not deter the other Central Asian countries. The relatively free, multicandidate presidential election of December 24, 1995, retained Askar Akayev in office for a term running through the year 2000. In February 1996, Akayev held a referendum that illegally amended the constitution to give him full discretion in ministerial appointments. Akayev resorted to criminal prosecutions of opposition leaders.[74]

There is notable corruption in government. Pressure on the media has abated but continues. The prosecution and beating of journalists who displease the government has remained a matter of concern for the United States and human rights organizations.[75] As in other newly independent states, the presidency overshadows the legislature and Constitutional Court. "Nevertheless," concludes the State Department, "a strong desire for consensus gives many different interests a role in decision-making."[76] Compared with other Central Asian countries and the authoritarian newly independent states, Kyrgyzstan enjoys greater freedom of expression, association, and assembly, unmarred by disappearances and killings of oppositionists.

Imposing no limits on proselytizing, and banning the teaching of religion or atheism in public schools, Kyrgyzstan leads the newly independent states in its degree of religious freedom and separation of church and state.

Kyrgyzstan's population has a Kyrgyz majority of 57 percent, and minorities of Russians (18.8 percent), Uzbeks (13.5 percent), and Ukrainians, Tajiks, Kazakhs, Koreans, and others. Kyrgyz lawyer (then deputy) Timurbek Kananbaev said that, positive as Kyrgyz feel about keeping up economic and political relations with Russia, they relish their independence, which was declared on August 31, 1991. They still remember the Russian takeover in the 1860s, later Russian massacres of rebels in 1919, and ethnic Russian control behind the scenes under Soviet Communist rule.[77]

Women in Kyrgyzstan fare relatively well in employment, although recent job losses and the hardships of pensioners affect them disproportionately.[78] The government appears committed to leave behind as soon as possible its legacy of a state-run economy isolated from the non-Soviet world. It has cooperated with foreign human rights NGOs and allowed local ones to monitor and advocate for human rights.

Now Kyrgyz are compensating for their past subjugation. Minorities claim governmental discrimination in favor of Kyrgyz in jobs, education, and politics.[79] On the other hand, parliament made an inclusive move with a majority proposal, approved by the Constitutional Court and sent to the president for approval, to make Russian an official language, alongside the state language of Kyrgyz, as a means for speeding up economic reform and expanding communication with other CIS countries.[80]

Advancing beyond earlier assessments,[81] Kyrgyzstan inched toward democracy in the mid-1990s. Perhaps the country will live up to its obligations as a member of the UN, the OSCE, and as a party to the ICCPR. It acceded to the Covenant in January 1995.[82] The country's exports of cotton, wool, tobacco, meat, gold, mercury, uranium, and hydroelectricity go only part way toward meeting its needs. What the country lacks in natural resources it appears to be trying to compensate for by offering a more democratic choice and attracting foreign investment and credits.

Conclusions

Three-quarters of the post-Soviet population live in countries that may, however imperfect, be called democracies. The subjects of this chapter have been the partly free democracies of Moldova and Ukraine and the near democracies of Georgia and Kyrgyzstan. The inclusiveness of governmental choices in Ukraine and Moldova and their cooperation with local and international human rights organizations have given them a chance, despite all difficulties, to evolve into stable democratic political communities under eventual rule of law. In order for freedom to strengthen and democracy to consolidate in those countries and the near democracies, an active public and their representatives must do more to curb civil rights abuses, to expand the rule of law, and to make administrators, security ministries, law enforcement, and organized crime accountable for their actions. The *nomenklatura* power elite must become accountable to the society it has so long robbed and to which it can no longer offer the shabby security on which the Communist regime based its legitimacy. Progress toward deeper democratic freedoms will depend also on achieving less corrupt, more effective, and equitable economic reform.

Freedom's ordeal has an international dimension. The newly independent countries live in ever-decreasing isolation. Enhanced global intercommunications via fax and e-mail assist networking and swell the flow of information, increasing the public's awareness of democratization around the world.[83] Taking advantage of the new electronic and political openness are agencies of the United Nations and regional organizations such as the Council of Europe and OSCE, as well as philanthropic foundations, human rights NGOs, the international women's movement, and various public and private sources of investment and credit. The international dialogue should incorporate issues of democratic rights and freedoms in their broadest sense.

Chapter 6
Varieties of Authoritarianism

There can be no doubt that the moment when political rights are granted to a people who have till then been deprived of them is a time of crisis, a crisis that is necessary but always dangerous.
—Alexis de Tocqueville[1]

In the spring of 1991 I wrote that "sooner or later," changes occurring in the USSR would bring "the emergence of democracy in most former or present parts of whatever replaces the . . . present USSR." I quoted the historian Leonid Batkin telling David Remnick that "No dictator possesses a narcotic strong enough to put us to sleep again."[2] The prognosis was only partly correct. The people in nondemocratic post-Soviet states who had advocated on the issues of the environment, minority rights, and independence found themselves silenced, or neutralized, after independence.

Universalist assumptions about democratic freedoms and rights find support from diverse cultures in post-Communist democratizing countries. Across the old Soviet border in Asia, the Republic of Mongolia, a former Soviet satellite and once Moscow's medieval model of despotism, is a democracy, and is rated freer than all the newly independent states—much freer than its post-Soviet Asian neighbors.[3] Patterns of freedom's demise in post-Soviet states backhandedly support universalist assumptions as well. Nondemocratic, partly free, and unfree countries reach across cultural lines from Belarus, through the Caucasus, and into Central Asia. Admittedly, the nondemocracies cluster mainly outside Europe, in Asia Minor (the Transcaucasus) and Central Asia. But it is still early. The essential developmental choices are just being made.

The nondemocracies appear here as "pseudodemocracies" and dictatorships. They lack even the imperfect and partial accountability of the new democracies. Pseudodemocracies are authoritarian states behind unfree electoral facades. In Larry Diamond's definition, pseudodemocracies "have legal opposition parties and perhaps many other features of electoral democracy, but fail to meet one of its crucial requirements: a sufficiently fair arena of contestation to allow the ruling party to be turned out of power."[4] The pseudodemocracies include Armenia, Azerbaijan, Belarus, and Kazakhstan. The least free countries of all are the dictatorships of war-torn Tajikistan, Turkmenistan, and Uzbekistan.

Pseudodemocracies

Belarus

Belarus is a pseudodemocracy veering toward dictatorship. It was long a western buffer for Russia. Its population, now a little over ten million, has suffered repeated invasions, dictatorships, and 70 percent of the lethal radioactive fallout from the Chernobyl reactor meltdown of April 26, 1986. The fallout caused countless physical and psychological casualties and left 25 percent of the country uninhabitable. Two million people in seriously affected areas live under constant stress, are prone to greater risk of diseases, and receive inadequate foreign assistance.[5]

Belarus declared indepedence on August 25, 1991, after the failed coup in Moscow. A "zero option" law granted citizenship to all residents as of October 19, 1991, following the general pattern in the newly independent states. Belarus's first head of state, Stanislav Shushkevich, chairman of the Supreme Soviet, was elected president in 1990 under relaxed, partly competitive conditions. On July 10, 1994, Aleksandr Lukashenka won election over Prime Minister Vycheslav Kebich, as the first democratically elected president of Belarus, after campaigning on a platform of anticorruption. The post-Soviet constitution of 1994 creates a powerful presidency and a new Constitutional Court.

The president soon put himself above the law. His rule prompted the novelist Vasil Bykov to view the first four years of his country's independence as "a moment when individual freedom and state freedom emerged on the horizon, waved to us, and then disappeared again."[6] The two rounds of parliamentary elections in May and December 1995 finally produced a quorum of 197 deputies in the 260-seat parliament, despite government attempts to discourage voter turnout to below the 50 percent required for valid elections.[7] Elections proved to be "less than free and fair," according to international observers. They noted restrictions on campaigning and political party activities and limited voter information. "Political parties," monitors reported, "were not permitted to campaign for candidates, and presidential decrees restricted political gatherings and candidates' use of the mass media. A vicious 'smear' campaign broadcast on state-run television in the final days . . . ensured that not a single candidate from the opposition Belarusian Popular Front was elected."[8]

Lukashenka flouted the constitution by refusing to work with the "illegitimate" old parliament. He instructed executive agencies in December 1995 that they must obey his decrees, which had been struck down by the Constitutional Court as unconstitutional. The government censors the broadcast media; it uses libel laws and its monopoly control of printing and distribution facilities to silence press criticism of its officials and hush up exposés of corruption in the self-proclaimed anticorruption Lukashenka government. Judge Lyubov' Zholnerchik sued the newspaper *Svaboda* (Freedom), a frequent target of government libel suits, for one billion rubles, claiming defamation of her character after the paper questioned the objectivity of her decision in a case against opposition MP Sergei Antonchik. He had been detained and held incommunicado for three days for his support of a peaceful Minsk metro workers' strike.[9] His three companions, also trade-union leaders, served ten to fifteen days' administrative arrest for "organizing an unauthorized meeting."[10] On government orders, the state printing house annulled contracts to print four leading independent newspapers, including *Svaboda*, forcing them to look abroad for printers.

The slow start of reforms and economic decline in Belarus cloud Lukashenka's regime. The president's administration has given neither more bread nor more freedom. Rather than make needed economic reforms, Lukashenka turned to rapprochement with Russia to solve the country's problems, a policy approved in the referendum of May 14, 1995. The government has dealt with the protests from the Belarus Popular front by banning its demonstrations, beating demonstrators, arresting and trying leaders.[11] Popular Front members were also infuriated by the return to a Soviet-type red flag and national emblem. Two oppositionists, Zenon Poznyak and Sergei Naumchik, sought asylum in the United States on the grounds that their lives and freedom were in danger in Belarus.[12]

An agreement with Russia on progress toward a "union" of separate states came in the treaty of April 2, 1996. That Russia would proceed far toward unity with its impoverished neighbor appeared uncertain.[13] But the agreement stirred unease in Russia's "near abroad," coming on the heels of a Russian Duma resolution in March 1996, pushed through by the Communists, which declared the dissolution of the Soviet Union illegal and called for its reunification.[14]

The constitutionally proclaimed freedom of religion did not come to pass for the growing Protestant and Catholic churches. Lukashenka imposed controls on those churchs' clergy, banned foreign proselytizing, and favored the Orthodox Church, calling its development a "moral necessity." The return of property to churches and restitution to Jews continued to face difficulties into the later 1990s.[15]

Among other lingering restrictions, the *propiska* residence-permit system infringes on the freedom of movement. Selective denial of travel visas raises other barriers, as in the case of Free Trade Union President Gennady

Bykov, whom the government denied a visa to attend a union conference abroad after it had detained him for his connection with the Minsk metro workers' strike. The shooting down on September 12, 1995, of a racing balloon, with its American crew, which had strayed across from Poland added to the impression of governmental callousness, suspicion, and isolationism. Some foreign satisfaction was derived from Belarus's cooperation with an international investigating commission after the fact. The government has been willing to admit foreign human rights monitors and to begin talking with local NGOs.

"If Ukraine has stagnated," George Zarycky writes, "Belarus is in full retreat. Nonparty President Lukashenka has acted more like a Bolshevik than a Belarusian patriot."[16] Belarus remains a pseudodemocracy unless and until the government permits free and fair elections and lives up to its obligations to respect political human rights. Belarus's economic slide under Lukashenka's conservative leadership may be the biggest reason for shaking off his autocratic rule.

Armenia

Armenia has clung to its identity and cohesion as an ethnic nation through millennia of domination by Macedonia, Rome, and Persia, from which Russia acquired it in 1828. The country fell under Soviet rule after the massacre and flight of Armenians in Turkey caused the deaths of at least a million and half Armenian men, women, and children. A brief de facto and unsuccessful independence under a government headed by the Dashnak Party in 1918–20 was followed by recovery under Soviet rule. The Soviet government reduced what was left of Armenia in 1921 by returning to Turkey a region formerly ruled by the Ottoman Empire including Mount Ararat, and by moving Armenia's border with Azerbaijan westward, thus isolating the mainly Armenian Nagorno-Karabakh Autonomous Oblast (NKAO) within Azerbaijan and leaving the mainly Azeri enclave of Nakhichevan within Armenia. This planted the seeds of war, which broke out in the NKAO in 1988. In the latest historic crisis of self-determination, the Armenians have fought a bitter war with their neighbor, suffered blockade, and slipped away from democracy.

Armenia reached the peak of national unity when it declared independence from the Soviet Union in December 1991. This followed an overwhelming and fair "yes" vote in a referendum on independence on September 21, 1991, during which I served as an election observer. Armenia joined the Commonwealth of Independent States in December 1991, and the United Nations in March 1992.

The tide of battle over the future of the NKAO has turned in favor of the Armenians since my visit in 1991. The determined economic reform and privatization measures yielded their first positive growth figures by

1994 and control of inflation by 1995. But democracy, in contrast, suffered a series of defeats. After independence, Armenia regressed to a pseudo-democracy that features dubious elections and the persecution of leading opposition parties and media under its authoritarian president, the former human rights champion Levon Ter-Petrossian.

In the relatively free multiparty elections of May 1990, the Armenian National Movement (ANM) had beaten the Communists but fell short of a majority in the politically fragmented, 249-member parliament. A 1990 law on the presidency and a 1991 law on parliament provided the legitimacy for those branches in the absence of a new constitution. ANM's leader, Levon Ter-Petrossian, won the fair presidential election by a large majority on October 16, 1991.[17] Parliament adopted a resolution declaring the International Covenant on Civil and Political Rights (ICCPR) to be the law of the land as well as ratifying its optional protocol, which permits individual complaints to the Human Rights Committee. However, the accession to the ICCPR did not avert the government's growing violation of democratic rights and freedoms.[18]

Once an oppositionist himself, President Ter-Petrossian had achieved prominence in the Karabakh Committee, which supported coethnic rebels in the NKAO in the face of Soviet favoritism toward Azerbaijan's forces. But the president argued against the opposition demand to recognize the NKAO's independence, because that would bring on a formal state of war between Armenia and Azerbaijan. After two years of deteriorating relations with the opposition, the president on December 24, 1994, went on television to announce a decree suspending Armenia's oldest and most popular opposition party, the Armenian Revolutionary Federation (ARF), or Dashnak Party, for allegedly harboring terrorism. The Supreme Court approved the ban.

The opposition had insisted that the new constitution be approved by a constitutional convention instead of the 1995 referendum, and that it provide for a parliamentary system rather than the final draft's strong presidential rule. They lost on both counts.[19] Armenia held parliamentary elections and a constitutional referendum on July 5, 1995.

The elections were ostensibly competitive and multiparty. They featured diverse viewpoints and frequent public rallies critical of the government. Yet the government turned the elections into a pseudodemocratic charade, limiting rights of association and expression, denying registration to 500 opposition candidates, refusing to register the Dashnak and eight other parties,[20] manipulating the media, rigging votes, and suspending the opposition Dashnak Party. The president decreed the closing of twelve newspapers and news agencies supposedly linked to the ARF. Interior Ministry troops then sealed off the ARF offices and the suspended newspapers and news agencies. Not stopping at the closure, police took away archives, computers, and other equipment. The government's interference handed its

ANM party a decisive, if unfair and fraudulent, electoral victory. It turned the constitutional referendum into a rigged affirmation of the president's vast executive and appointative powers. A European Union resolution condemned the suspension of the ARF as an "attack on the basic principles of democracy."[21] After the elections, police packed Vahan Hovanesian, an ARF leader, off to jail on a raft of charges including high treason and terrorism.[22]

The government has used registration and accreditation procedures, control over high-priced newsprint, and its own chain of kiosks to hamper opposition newspapers, causing several to close down. In 1994 the almost entirely state-owned and tightly controlled broadcasting industry canceled a contract to carry broadcasts of Radio Liberty. The government was unable to explain or prevent attacks on journalists and the offices of government and opposition media. In the absence of military censorship, however, papers continue to publish articles critical of the government.

The government also flouted due process rights of political actors, including seventeen members of the "Dro" group, associated with the Dashnak Party, on charges of economic crimes, drug trafficking, murder, and the recruitment and training of new members. The authorities have restricted access to counsel, tortured suspects to extract confessions, and tried defendants before courts favoring the prosecution. Apparently government-connected assailants beat up three Dro attorneys and several opposition journalists. At least two detainees died in police custody. The Dro defendant, Artavast Manukian, died of pneumonia on May 17, 1995, after being denied adequate medical treatment for a stomach tumor. Eight Azerbaijani POWs died in a military prison in 1994, forensic evidence suggests, by execution-type shootings.[23]

Freedom of religion is limited under a 1991 law that bans proselytizing and restricts registration to those religious organizations whose doctrine rests on "historically recognized holy scriptures" and is "free from materialism and [is] of a purely spiritual nature."[24] Denial of registration also means denial of the right to issue its own publications, rent a hall or meeting place, run its own radio station and television program, or sponsor the visas of foreign visitors.

The country is nominally 80 percent Armenian Christian. A presidential decree of December 22, 1993, bolstered the special position of the Armenian Apostolic Church by requiring the Council on Religious Affairs to investigate representatives of registered religious organizations and to ban missionaries exceeding the permitted bounds of their activities. Devotees of Hare Krishna allegedly were beaten in police custody in Yerevan on August 31, 1994, soon after a group assaulted sect members in their temple. The government held up delivery of thirty tons of religious literature to the Krishna group on grounds of the ban on proselytizing. Brutal beatings, the ransacking of offices, and arrests by government-connected armed groups victimized Jehovah's Witnesses, Pentacostalists, and Hare Krishnas with impunity in 1995, after months of press criticism directed against the groups.[25]

After the flight of some 200,000 Azerbaijani refugees during the early days of the war in the NKAO, the population of 3.6 million remained about 93 percent Armenian.[26] Small minorities of Kurds, Russians, Jews, Georgians, Greeks, Assyrians, and others suffer no discrimination. Under the 1992 law on language, they are guaranteed the right to publish and study in their own languages.

Another law of 1992 which protected women against discrimination has been negated by the high rate of unemployment. Women encounter discrimination in career choices and politics. None served in the cabinet during the first years of independence. Rape is rarely reported or punished; spousal abuse is virtually never reported.[27]

Press-gangs carried out forcible conscription of men in the undeclared NKAO war with Azerbaijan. The war featured brutal ethnic cleansing first by the Azerbaijanis and then by the Armenians. The war took thousands of lives and produced more than a million refugees and displaced persons. An informal cease-fire in May 1994 was confirmed in July.

The Azerbaijan and Turkish blockades and the disruption of transport from Georgia forced most people below the poverty levels necessary to sustain health and well-being. Fuel shortages necessitated the reopening of the Metzamor Nuclear Power Station, one of the world's most dangerous, which had been closed in 1989. As a result of hardships and the uprooting of Armenians from Azerbaijan, Armenian emigration reached alarming levels—as many as 700,000 persons in 1992–95, or nearly one-fifth of Armenia's population.[28] Armenia pushed ahead with reforms, even as it stepped back from democracy, aided by budget tightening, a wealthy diaspora, and minimal inflation and foreign debt. The fall of production has been reversed.[29] Meanwhile, foreign and domestic human rights monitors continue their work.

Azerbaijan

Azerbaijan, a predominantly Moslem country of 7.6 million inhabitants abutting the oil-rich Caspian Sea, declared independence on August 30, 1991. One of Colton's "predemocracies" (see Chapter 5), it has lapsed into authoritarianism under pressures of war and foreign intervention. Armenia's pseudodemocracy still merits a "partly free" rating, but Azerbaijan is a "not free" pseudodemocracy.

Supporters of a Moscow favorite, Ayaz Mutalibov, dominated the Supreme Soviet after fraud tilted the voting results in the first "democratic" election of 1990. The Supreme Soviet elected Mutalibov president in October 1991, but this did not prevent a nationalist rival, Abulfaz Elchibey, leader of the "pro-independence, anti-Communist and anti-Russian" Azerbaijan Popular Front (APF), from winning the democratic presidential elections of June 7, 1992.[30] That year, the APF government dissolved the Supreme Soviet and transferred its legislative powers to the National Council, a permanent legislature formed in October 1991, with half of its fifty members to be picked by the president and half by the opposition.[31]

The internal war over Nagorno-Karabakh overshadowed all choices. In 1993 Armenian offensives swept to the west, south, and east of the tiny NKAO, a region comprising 5 percent of Azerbaijan, and took over 20 percent of the country as far south as the border with Iran. Monitors reported that "Both sides engaged in frequent human rights abuses and violations of humanitarian law, including the killing of civilians, hostage-taking, and ransoming the remains of the dead." The Armenians took hostages and practiced ethnic cleansing of Azeri villages, as once the Azerbaijanis had done in Armenian villages in the NKAO.[32] Burning and looting as they advanced, the Armenians forced 500,000 new and already displaced persons to flee. The total refugee population rose for a while to over a million out of the population of 7.5 million. Refugees included 48,000 Meskhetian Turks who had fled pogroms in Uzbekistan in 1990 and over 200,000 Azerbaijanis and Kurds expelled from Armenia.[33] Fighting continued until the internationally mediated cease-fire of May 1994.

The regression toward authoritarian rule continued when a military coup overthrew Elchibey and replaced him with Haidar Aliyev, former member of the CPSU Politburo and the Communist Party first secretary of Azerbaijan. After the National Council elected Aliyev speaker and president, he was confirmed for these positions by a questionable election, boycotted by the opposition, on October 3, 1993. Aliyev resorted to censorship, arrests, mistreatment of detainees, and harassment of APF, Musavat, and Azerbaijani Independence Party oppositionists. An attempted military coup brought political assassinations and more insecurity on September 30, 1994.[34] But opposition parties and a diverse press carried on, while Aliyev warded off two more coup attempts in 1995 that were widely believed to have been masterminded by Moscow in its pursuit of the "great game" over Caspian oil fields, and that could well have been planned from Moscow after Baku signed a deal with a consortium of Western petroleum companies.[35]

In the name of stability, President Aliyev set about excluding opposition parties and leaders from participation in the elections of November 12, 1995, to a 125-seat parliament. Under international pressure, the Ministry of Justice registered opposition parties including the APF and the Social Democratic Party, though not the Iranian controlled and funded Islamic Party. The government harassed and intimidated would-be registrants. On the pretext that 5,000 signatures were falsified, the government banned the venerable and large Musavat Party from registration.

The government's fraudulent report of 80 percent voter participation in November doubled the monitors' estimates of 40 percent. The restraints on opposition parties and candidates and the widespread voter fraud prompted a joint mission of the OSCE and the UN to conclude that the elections "did not correspond to internationally accepted standards."[36] After the final round of voting in February 1996 in 15 of 125 electoral districts, opposition parties held 9 out of 125 seats.[37] A new constitution, allegedly supported by 91 percent of the vote, increased the president's already wide powers.[38]

In violation of civil rights, the government mounted a campaign of arrests, criminal investigations, trials, convictions—even murder—against opposition leaders from the Musavat, Social Democratic, and Popular Front Parties. Its operatives raided and ransacked homes and took away oppositionists and human rights advocates, sometimes without arrest warrants. Jails held 70 to 100 political prisoners by 1996, compared with about 25 at the end of 1994. The government limits opposition activities, especially outside Baku, and censors opposition newspapers. Former foreign minister Tofiq Gasymov was arrested in September 1995, allegedly for masterminding the March 1995 coup attempt, apparently to prevent his participation in the November elections. The government released him from solitary confinement the following February. The frail and not always lucid Gasymov says he was given injections while in prison. The government postponed his trial indefinitely after a visiting mission of the U.S. Commission for Security and Cooperation in Europe interceded on his behalf.[39] Along with the familiar police brutality in post-Soviet states, the authorities reportedly harassed, assaulted, and detained wives and children of political fugitives in order to secure their capture.[40]

Unlike the case in freer though still not democratic Armenia, the Azerbaijani government systematically censored the press. In March 1995 it jailed five journalists who cartooned or wrote critically about the president. After their conviction in a Baku court and sentencing to two to five years' imprisonment, President Aliyev pardoned all five in November.[41] The OSCE/UN Joint Electoral Observation Mission found that "Political censorship of party and independent newspapers . . . restricted the freedom of speech of political parties."[42] In the words of the State Department, "The Government tolerates the existence of some opposition parties. It has demonstrated, however, a disregard for the right to freedom of speech, press, assembly, association, and privacy when it has deemed it in its interest to do so."[43] The Armenians of the so-called Nagorno-Karabakh Republic carried out a policy of ethnic cleansing of hundreds of thousands of Azerbaijanis from seized territories, causing great hardship. Negotiations stalled in 1996 on proposals that Armenia agree to autonomy rather than independence for Nagorno-Karabakh, in exchange for Azerbaijan's agreement to Moscow's demands for military bases, joint border patrols, and joint air defenses.[44] Presumably there would be a sweetener for Armenia, including the lifting of the land blockade.

Azerbaijan respects the religious freedom of Christians and Jews to worship and carry on educational activities, but the largely abandoned Armenian churches have been vandalized and shut down. The 10,000 to 20,000 Armenians left in the country face discrimination and live in considerable fear. Kurds and immigrant refugee Mskhetian Turks occasionally report discrimination.

Unlike the dictatorships of Central Asia, Azerbaijan did not bar foreign NGOs, but it broke up a meeting in 1994 between political oppositionists and a delegation from Human Rights Watch/Helsinki. It allowed monitoring of the condition of military prisoners and persons internally displaced by the war over Nagorno-Karabakh but hampered the monitoring of political cases. The police picked up or interfered with groups circulating petitions or otherwise advocating for the rights of political detainees and prisoners.

Women in Azerbaijan legally have equal rights in public and economic life. In contrast to Armenia and Georgia, several women hold prominent places in the Aliyev government and in what is left of the opposition in the APF. In a departure from past passivity, women have formed over a dozen advocacy groups, including the Association for the Rights of Azerbaijani Women. Most women remain traditional homemakers. Monitors widely noted a continuation of the practice of men's voting on behalf of female members of the family. Beatings and rapes of women go underreported. Women have suffered not only due to economic difficulties, but also as a result of the practices of hostage taking and sexual slavery. The exchange price for a young officer, aid workers reported, was five female hostages, forty-five gallons of gasoline, and a million rubles (at 1993 levels). Bride abduction continues in some parts of the country.[45]

Given the U.S. Congress's limitation on economic and humanitarian aid to Azerbaijan because of its blockade of Armenia, the unlikely remaining leverage in human rights issues might come from the shares of U.S. companies in multibillion-dollar international–Azerbaijani oil consortiums. The U.S. embassy played a leading part, along with European embassies, in pressuring the government to register the Popular Front Party, though it was clearly unable to head off the government's authoritarian control over the election's outcome. Despite riches of oil, natural gas, and cotton agriculture, and a growing private sector outside of the law, the economy has continued to suffer from the results of the war over Nagorno-Karabakh, the burden of internally displaced persons and refugees, the Armenians' occupation of vast reaches of productive farmland, delays in reform, the breakup of the Soviet Union, and border closings with Russia and Iran.

Nondemocracy in Central Asia

The five states of Central Asia—Kazakhstan, Kyrgyzstan, Uzbekistan, Tajikistan, and Turkmenistan—were originally autonomous khanates and emirates; they were designated by Stalin as republics after they were subsumed beneath Soviet power during a civil war fought in the 1920s. Central Asia is diverse in political choices and in resources and income levels. The most tranquil and democratic country, Kyrgyzstan, is also one of the two poorest, along with Tajikistan, the least tranquil and among the least democratic.[46]

Central Asia suffered greater violations of Muslim rights and destruction of formal Islamic learning and religion under Communism than it did under the relatively tolerant tsarist governments.[47] But the Communist local leaders became steadfast adherents to the Union. In the late Soviet era, catastrophic unemployment levels accompanied regional underdevelopment, high birthrates, lack of family-planning programs, and low out-migration. Soviet development policies heedlessly inflicted environmental and health catastrophes, whether from careless use of herbicides on cotton crops, unsafe testing of nuclear weapons, or the shrinking of the once magnificent Aral Sea through excess water use, which generally devastated its environs in northern Uzbekistan and southern Kazakhstan.[48]

The fragmentation of the Soviet economy and the considerable chaos of economic reform have made economic matters worse for most people. Local leaders have justified their dictatorships as bulwarks against the threat of ethnic conflict and Islamic fundamentalism.[49] Islamic fundamentalist movements aim at strictly interpreted Islamic theocracy. The fundamentalist movements based in Iran, Afghanistan, and Saudi Arabia compete among themselves in Central Asia. They must, in turn, compete with many other cross-currents of involvement from the east, west, and north of the area. Outside observers such as Graham Fuller and Martha Brill Olcott downplay the present influence of fundamentalism in Central Asia. But they see no guarantees against a future tide of fundamentalism, should future governments fail to come up with solutions to interethnic tensions, economic hardships, repressiveness, and lack of regional integration.[50]

Islamic scholars also have warned against rushing to label nationalist, pro-reform, and environmentalist movements, most now repressed, as "fundamentalist."[51] Fundamentalist movements appear to thrive on a Muslim area's poverty, the sense of victimization by foreigners and their local accomplices, and their governments' denial of freedom to nonfundamentalist Islamic and secular opposition movements and media.[52] Fundamentalism's emergence is more likely where Islam has been most developed—that is, in Tajikistan, Uzbekistan, and Azerbaijan across the Caspian Sea. Russia, not Islam, has remained the leading outside influence into the later 1990s. Turkey, the United States, Western Europe, Japan, and other industrial powers of the Asia-Pacific rim are discovering growing interests and opportunities in the region. The governments are beginning to welcome foreign investors and, except in Turkmenistan, to tolerate human rights monitors.[53]

Kazakhstan

Kazakhstan declared its independence in December 1991, becoming the last republic to do so. Its president, Nursultan Nazarbayev, continued his hold on power when his presidency was confirmed in an election that same month. Under Nazarbayev's leadership, the country averted violence between Russians and Kazakhs, but its government became less accountable and more authoritarian. International observers declared unfree and unfair the flagrantly fraudulent March 7, 1994, elections to the Supreme Soviet and local councils.

After the parliament voted no confidence in the cabinet's economic and social policies on June 1, the president took advantage of a constitutional court ruling that held the 1994 elections unconstitutional; he dissolved parliament and ruled by presidential decree. On December 9, 1995, the suspension ended with elections to a new bicameral legislature,[54] under the eyes of international and domestic observers. The observers reported local violations and possible exaggeration of voter turnout, but a fairer election than that of March 1994.

The president had his term extended by four years to the year 2000 by a procedurally flawed, unconstitutional referendum on April 29, 1995. As a further boost to presidential power, a referendum majority reported at 89 percent approved a new constitution on August 31, 1995. The constitution increased the president's power by giving him authority to dissolve parliament for denying approval of his nominee for prime minister, and by making him virtually irremovable by impeachment, while undercutting the Constitutional Court's authority to challenge the president's elevation to virtual dictator.[55]

With the constitutional referendum looming in August, members of the pressure group Anti-Dictatorship Bloc went on a hunger strike to urge a boycott of the referendum. They were arrested on the charge of holding an unauthorized protest: Arbitrary conditions set by local authorities include their pre-approval of the slogans on banners.[56] An organizer of the hunger strike, Vladimir Chernyshev, deputy of the dissolved parliament, was beaten at the entrance to his apartment, apparently in an effort to persuade him to end the strike.

"There is a certain freedom of association" in Kazakhstan, according to Yevgeny Zhovtis, executive director of the independent US–Kazakhstan Human Rights Bureau, but not of participation in the policy process.

"Kazakhstan is absolutely authoritarian when it comes to the ability of people to influence their country's policies. This ability has been liquidated."[57]

A fire in the warehouse of *Karavan*, the most independent newspaper in Kazakhstan, destroyed a million dollars worth of newsprint after its critical coverage of the parliamentary dissolution. The paper's investigation found evidence of arson. After it reopened, the paper reduced its political coverage, but this did not silence all press criticism of policy and legislation, nor did it deter opposition group publications.

President Nazarbayev explains that his strong powers are necessary for preserving peace and stability in the face of obstructionism by conservatives and Kazakh ethnic nationalists in parliament. The government has refused to register parties and associations identified with Russian and other ethnic and religious groups. The nationalist and pan-Turkic Alash Party and the Social Democratic Party refused to apply for registration because they sensed a return to Soviet-era surveillance in the requirement that organizations submit lists of members with dates and places of birth, addresses, and places of employment.[58]

Although it is the size of the Indian subcontinent, Kazakhstan contains only 17 million people, including ethnic Kazakhs (about 42 percent), Russians (36 percent), Ukrainians (5.2 percent), and lesser percentages of Germans (4.7), Uzbeks (2.1), Tatars (2), and others (7.1).[59] Non-Kazakhs' sense of discrimination by Kazakhs and issues of language law breed tensions between the mainly Russian-speaking north and the mainly Kazakh south. In 1995 the government sentenced Boris Suprynuk, a Russian citizen, to two years for insulting the prosecutor in his previous trial for inciting inter-ethnic hostility.[60] According to the State Department, discrimination continues against Russians and other non-Kazakhs in government jobs, education, housing, and other areas of contention. Kazakh supporters of such policies believe affirmative action is justified in the wake of two hundred years of Russian domination.[61]

In November 1994, the Ministry of Justice suspended the activities of the Semirechiye Cossack Society, charging it with paramilitary activities and the promotion of ethnic intolerance. It arrested two organizers of an unauthorized demonstration in Almaty (Alma Ata).[62] In January 1995 a local court sentenced Nikolai Gunkin, the leader of the Semirechiye Cossacks in south Kazakhstan, to six months in jail on the charge of holding an unauthorized demonstration; upon his return from flight to Russia, he was given an additional three months in a labor camp.[63] Gunkin's lawyer, Ivan Kravtsov, withdrew from the case after an episode of intimidation, "including a physical assault on his wife, Iraida Kravtsova, by unidentified people who broke into the family's apartment."[64]

There is freedom of religious worship and proselytizing in Kazakhstan. The potential for interference lies in constitutional requirements that the appointment of heads of religious organizations by foreign centers and the activities of foreign religious organizations take place "in coordination with the government." Legal freedom to proselytize is occasionally negated through interference by local officials. The government returned the main Orthodox church in Almaty to the Russian Orthodox Church in April 1995. The issue of religion so far has avoided adding to intergroup discord. In fact, the Islamic mufti and Russian Orthodox archbishop have appeared together in public in order to promote religious and ethnic harmony.

The hardships subsequent to the Union's and economic reform hamper the opening of Kazakh society. But Kazakhstan is rich in oil and minerals. The economy's contribution to political development will depend in part on how Russia and other foreign partners participate in the oil and other industries (see below, "Regional Cross-Currents"). Economic development will also depend on domestic and foreign efforts to modernize — for example, by reforming the laws of commerce and taxation, and by reorganizing inefficient agricultural and industrial survivals from the Communist era.

Kazakhstan permits human rights monitoring. NGOs may report on behavior of police and other official corruption and abuses of power by security agencies. Reducing these obstacles to democracy and a free-market economy depends mainly on choices made within Kazakhstan; for now the country remains authoritarian due to presidential rule by decree, the presidential referendum, and infringements on other political freedoms. The government preserves a modicum of media freedom; it desists from killing and kidnapping oppositionists and critics. By the late 1990s Kazakhstan remained a partly free but authoritarian country.

Dictatorships: Tajikistan, Turkmenistan, Uzbekistan

When the Union fell apart, Tajikistan, Turkmenistan, and Uzbekistan emerged as dictatorships under their previous leaders. They formed the least free and accountable post-Soviet governments. They have made Freedom House's list of the "20 worst-rated countries." Their human rights commitments as members of OSCE and the United Nations remain unfulfilled.[65] Uzbekistan's government began to open up to dialogue with international human rights organizations in the mid-1990s.

Tajikistan

Tajikistan's war-torn, mainly Farsi (Persian)-speaking society is tied linguistically to Iran rather than to Turkey. Its government of former Communists, under parliamentary chair and head of state Emomali Rakhmanov, depicts itself as a bulwark against Muslim fundamentalist foes.

The Soviets took over present-day Tajikistan, once part of the Emirate of Bokhara, in a civil war that lasted until 1928. Moscow then turned the subjugated area into an autonomous Tajik region. The government tried to cut linguistic ties with Iran and Afghanistan by replacing Arabic script with Latin, then Cyrillic. In creating the Tajik Soviet Socialist Republic, Stalin deliberately cut off the Farsi cultural centers of Samarkand and Bokhara by including them in Uzbekistan while incorporating part of the Uzbek-settled Fergana Valley into Tajikistan. This demographic manipulation produced a new country that is now about 60 percent Tajik, 26 percent Uzbek, and less than 2 percent Russian.[66]

Stalin ruled through a coalition of Khojandi clans to the north and dominant Kulyabis to the south. He brought down mountain people, Gharmis and Pamiris, to work the cotton fields. "By this discriminatory distribution of power," with traditional clan rule under the guise of the hammer and sickle, Anthony Richter writes, "Moscow helped create hostile regional ethnic groups where no particular ethnic consciousness had existed before."[67]

Tajikistan was the first Central Asian republic to introduce a multiparty system. But it did not last long. In the 1991 elections Rakhmon Nabiyev, the candidate of the Kulyabi coalition, emerged the apparent majority winner over the opposition coalition of Gharmi and Pamiri Islamists, nationalists, and democratic reformers headed by the Islamic Revival Party (IRP). The Russian, Tajik, and Uzbek governments labeled the IRP "radical." After three months of demonstrations and violence in Dushanbe, Nabiyev yielded in May 1992 to demands for a coalition Government of National Reconciliation. Communal violence in June between Islamists and supporters of Nabiyev and the Kulyabis based in Khojand to the north pitted rich, governing clans led by Emomali Rakhmanov against poor, governed ones. The country plunged into civil war.[68]

With the help of Russian and Uzbek troops sent in to quell the fighting, the Rakhmanov faction overturned Nabiyev's coalition government in December 1992. It then wreaked a bloody revenge on the opposition. Survivors ended up in exile or prison.[69] By the time of the cease-fire in January 1993, the war's toll included as many as 50,000 killed and over 800,000 displaced persons in a country of only 5.6 million. Close to 100,000 of the refugees survived a perilous flight to refugee camps in Afghanistan along with defeated leaders and fighters.[70]

Rakhmanov was elected president in the questionable ballot of November 6, 1994, and a new parliament, the Majlisi Oli, was elected in the ballot of February 1995. The elections of 1994 and 1995 proceeded, according to monitors, "in a climate marked by intimidation and fraud." A simultaneous referendum in 1994 approved a new constitution.[71]

The constitution's bill of rights fades before the will of local warlords, strict censorship, the banning of most opposition organizations and meetings, lingering regional animosities, feuding among pro-government militia groups, and the beating, raping, and killing of civilians and looting of their homes after renewed fighting in July–September 1994. Both sides have executed prisoners of war. Antigovernment forces reportedly have killed Russian army officers, medical personnel, and enlisted men, and attacked buses carrying Russian military dependents.[72] After the first 1993 cease-fire, Gharmis and Pamiris returned to homes and schools occupied or looted by Kulyabis, Uzbeks, and other government supporters. Despite some government efforts to prevent it, Kulyabi mistreatment of Gharmis and Pamiris continued.

Under a CIS–Tajik treaty of 1993, 24,000 Russian troops—7,000 soldiers and 17,000 border troops—have guarded the unquiet Tajik-Afghan border and taken casualties as protectors against "Islamic insurgency." The UN and its United Nations Mission of Observers to Tajikistan (UNMOT) sponsored another cease-fire with the opposition, the Coordinating Center of Tajik Democratic Forces of Islamic, nationalist, and democratic groups, effective October 20, 1994. The UN High Commission for Refugees, the Red Cross, and Médecins Sans Frontières, rendered humanitarian aid.[73] President Rakhmanov and the opposition leader, Mullah Abdullah Nuri, met, but mutual distrust remained. Fueling the mistrust were opposition raids across the border from Afghanistan; Dushanbe's lack of firm control over militia forces; government human rights violations in its courts, prisons, and unquiet regions; and opposition activity and government military buildups in the mountainous Gharm and Gorno-Badakhshan areas.

The country cannot provide enough food or heat due to its waning exports of tin and cotton and its nearly idle factories. Wages and pensions go widely unpaid. The UN Development Program tries to make a difference in the economically desperate situation by promoting community development and new income-producing roles for women.[74] Women in the cities have relatively equal career opportunities. Another positive factor for human rights are the survivals of *perestroika*: a closely watched religious revival and the presence of international humanitarian and human rights organizations.

Local human rights NGOs avoided issues of government violations. International NGO monitoring and mediation continued, however, with cooperation on the part of the Dushanbe government. Human Rights Watch/Helsinki, the International Committee of the Red Cross, and the International Organization for Migration worked out of offices in Dushanbe. Human Rights Watch faults the OSCE mission for being "reluctant to address individual cases of human rights violations." It also notes Russia's economic and political interests in Tajikistan and its role as government supporter rather than peacekeeper. Here, as in the other war-torn newly independent states, Russia's intervention both fans war and enforces the uneasy peace.

Turkmenistan

Turkmenistan became independent after a 94 percent "yes" vote on the referendum of October 27, 1991. The president of the gas-rich country, Saparmurad Niyazov, had been first secretary of the Turkmen Communist Party since 1985. He was elected president on June 21, 1992, by Soviet-era proportions: 99.5 percent of the 99.9 percent of eligible voters participating. After independence he destroyed the Gorbachev-era glimmer of democracy and freedom and replaced it with one-party rule through the Democratic Party, as the Communist Party was renamed. President Niyazov had his term extended from 1997 until 2004 in a 1994 referendum with an officially reported "yes" vote of 99.9 percent.[75] In 1994 the parliament, the Mejlis, was elected with only the Democratic Party of Turkmenistan allowed to participate—reported participation: 99.8 percent of eligible voters.[76]

Human Rights Watch terms Turkmenistan "one of the most repressive governments in the world," complete with rigid censorship, police brutality and torture, and the suppression of independent political activity.[77] Oppositionists and dissidents are jailed, beaten, falsely charged as murderous traitors and drug addicts, and given severe prison sentences of up to fifteen years. Even the Soviet-era Women's Council of Turkmenistan has been disbanded. Fear of retaliation silences local human rights advocacy. The government's noncooperation hampers international monitoring efforts. Restrictions have let up only in the sphere of religious freedom and emigration.

Turkmenistan has the world's fourth largest reserves of natural gas. The president has justified his tight control over the country of 3.9 million as essential for the stability necessary for foreign investment in gas extraction and other sectors and for peace among ethnic groups. Such control certainly serves to protect the corruption that extends to the top levels. Besides the 72 percent Turkmen majority, the population comprises a declining minority segment—at last count—of Russians (about 9 percent), Uzbeks (9 percent), and numbers of Kazakhs, Ukrainians, Armenians, Azerbaijanis, Jews, and other ethnic groups. As in Kyrgyzstan and generally in Central Asia, Russians and other nonindigenous groups complain of discrimination because of one official, titular language and preference for the titular group—in this case, Turkmens—in hiring and promotion.[78]

Opposition lingers underground. On July 12, 1995, a group of several hundred residents marched peacefully in the capital, Ashghabad, handing out leaflets that called for new elections. After an hour, the police closed in and beat the demonstrators. They arrested some two hundred and kept fifteen in prolonged custody, incommunicado. One detainee from the demonstration, Sukhanberdy Ishonov, hanged himself after his release. He had been brutally beaten to extract a forced confession, which the government broadcast on television. The authorities interrogated and deported an *Izve-*

stiia correspondent for reporting on the protest march. His interrogator stated, "We never had and never will have protest marches."[79]

Uzbekistan

Uzbekistan declared its independence in August 1991. It is the most populous of the newly independent Central Asian states. Its approximately 23 million inhabitants include Uzbeks (71 percent), Russians (8 percent), Tajiks (5 percent), Tatars (4 percent), Kazakhs (3 percent)—altogether 115 ethnic groups. Unlike Tajikistan, Uzbekistan has been spared internal war.

The Communist Party, renamed the National Democratic Party of Uzbekistan, continued to be the ruling party. Its former boss, Communist First Secretary Islam Karimov, continued running the country as president, having been elected without significant competition in December 1991. After independence, Human Rights Watch/Helsinki monitors recall, "the exercise of fundamental freedoms . . . flourished on a broad scale . . . , public rallies filled the streets, opposition political parties and movements sprang up and functioned actively, and an independent human rights movement began to take root."

Beginning in 1992, soon after independence, the fruits of *perestroika* withered. In all but freedom of movement and of religion (save the persecuted independent Islamic groups), the government resumed Soviet-era repression, minus the Communist ideology. It resorted to censorship, "discriminatory dismissals from work, and intimidation through surveillance of homes and telephones," deregistering the National Association "Russian Culture," human rights groups, and opposition associations, and banning public rallies.[80] The parliamentary elections of December 25, 1994, the first multiparty elections since independence, were competitive in form but intimidating and unfree in substance. Karimov's government crushed main opposition parties such as the Birlik (Unity) Popular Movement and Erk (Strength of Will) Democratic Party. Police and security agents arrested and beat their leaders and activists and other critics. The courts sentenced them to terms of up to at least twelve years, on various political and trumped-up charges such as insulting the president, conspiracy to seize power, illegal business activities, drug dealing, and smuggling.

In one bizarre case, Nadira Khidoiatova, the niece of Uzbekistan's former ambassador to the United States (who was granted political asylum in 1993), was reported arrested around July 11, 1995. A coworker arrested along with her, Asia Turaniyazova, also in her twenties, was a recipient of a Rockefeller Grant and is working on ecological issues in her native Karakalpakistan (an area devastated by the shrinking of the Aral Sea). The women were charged with exporting animal skins illegally. Both were forced to undergo abortions, perhaps to try to force confessions from them or perhaps because pregnant women are, by law, to be released pending trial—by terminating their pregnancies, the authorities avoided this necessity. The women gained their release on bail on October 5, 1995, following a campaign launched by Human Rights Watch.[81] Before the month's end, the government had reportedly forced the retirement of the head of the National Security Service (former KGB) responsible for the mistreatment of the two women[82] and dismissed the security official in charge of the case.[83]

A wave of crackdowns began in late 1994 against independent Muslim communities. Muslim religion and religious teaching has flourished since the lifting of Soviet-era bans, with the government's active support. But the government looks with suspicion on Muslim organizations unaffiliated with the state. It sees them as subversive and as conduits of militant influences from abroad. Human Rights Watch/Helsinki gathered reports that individuals, usually men, "reportedly are detained for as little as wearing a beard, failing to praise or praise sufficiently the government in their prayers," although the teachings of Islam enjoins saving one's praises only for God, "showing solidarity with practitioners of conservative Islam; or being independent financially from the [government's] Spiritual Directorate."

Apart from the abuse and imprisonment of "independent" Muslims and the closing of their mosques, the government appears to have been involved in the disappearance of three "independent clerics." The head of the Islamic Renaissance Party, Abdullah Utaev, disappeared in 1992. Imam Sheikh Abdulavi Qori Mirzoev disappeared at Tashkent airport on August 29, 1995, on his way to address an international Islamic conference in Moscow; also disappeared was his companion, Ramazanbek Matkarimov, a train conductor and unpaid assistant, who was married and the father of four children. The government disclaimed all knowledge of their disappearance, to the general disbelief of fellow Muslims and of human rights organizations.[84] The government says that it must stay in control to head off fundamentalism and civil strife such as beset Afghanistan and Tajikistan. To reinforce that control, an orchestrated referendum on March 26, 1995, extended President Karimov's first term by three years to the year 2000.

By 1995 the kidnapping of human rights advocates returning from neighboring countries ceased. Seven political prisoners regained their freedom through early release in late 1994 and 1995. Despite the absence of freedom of expression, academic institutions began to receive increasing leeway to pursue reforms and to use Western textbooks. Religious freedom prevails for non-Muslims, though with bans on proselytizing. Jewish cultural life and worship are reviving.

In 1994 the government began to cooperate with foreign human rights NGOs. The government in 1995 welcomed an OSCE regional liaison office. It lifted a three-year ban on Human Rights Watch/Helsinki and enabled it to open an office in Tashkent in November.[85] The European Commission of the European Union began negotiations over an agreement on cooperation. These openings and the new governmental Human Rights Commission and the Parliamentary Commission on Human Rights may be either little more than window dressing or the beginning of a cautious reduction of dictatorial repression.

Economic development promises to make the biggest inroads vis-à-vis the patriarchal denial of women's equality, as on repressiveness in general. The growth potential is there. As market reform proceeds, this heavily agricultural country, the world's fourth largest producer of cotton, can draw on substantial resources of gold, strategic minerals, gas, and oil, given the requisite foreign investments and legal framework. On March 2, 1995, the president decreed a program to increase the role of women in society and administration. It set up a National Women's Committee, whose head became a deputy prime minister charged with monitoring women's rights and welfare, and a network of provincial and local heads of women's affairs. Culture rather than government policy keeps nonprofessional women busy bearing many children and working in the cotton fields. Wife beatings continue to be considered a family affair. A female journalist reported in the early 1990s that about 50 percent of women's suicides through self-immolation in Central Asia appear to be a means of escaping from chronic beatings.[86]

The government's return to a human rights dialogue may be linked to its efforts to form closer ties with the West and thus to gain access to foreign investment and development assistance. Says Human Rights Watch/Helsinki, "Self-interest may lead to the beginning of genuine reform, if the international community insists on it"—which it should.[87]

Regional Cross-Currents

Russia is the most powerful regional player in the more-than-century-old "Great Game," the competition among outside powers to control the politics and economic—especially oil and gas—resources of the Caspian basin and Central Asia. Russia's influence on the economic and political fates of its southern neighbors should present no surprise to anyone familiar with the history of the U.S. Monroe Doctrine and U.S. hegemony in Latin America, or with the history of other one-time continental great powers, such as Napoleonic France. Actually, Russia has not propounded its own "Monroe Doctrine" of "European powers keep out." But its economic and strategic interest in the Caucasus leads Russia to engage in "destabilizing intrigues" there.[88] Going into the late 1990s, Russia had some 23,000 troops in Armenia and Georgia, plus about 8,000 peacekeepers in the two republics.[89] Russian and Armenian troops jointly patrol the border with Turkey and Iran. Russia is involved in OSCE mediation to end local wars. Russia maintains military bases, peacekeeping forces, or both in nine former Union republics.[90]

Diplomats from Western countries and Azerbaijan have connected the impasse in negotiations over the NKAO with Russian attempts to gain more influence over Azerbaijan's oil policy and with Russia's desire to have their peacekeepers stationed there. As a riparian, shoreline power on the so-called Caspian "Sea" (more accurately classed as a lake), Russia is pressing what appears to be a legal claim to a voice and a share in the revenues and decisions, regarding the exploitation of Caspian oil resources. U.S. and other foreign investors have confronted the additional disincentives of unresolved internal conflicts, corrupt practices of local governments, and inconclusive environmental and economic issues regarding where to lay pipelines and how much of the oil produced should flow west in pipelines across Russia rather than across Georgia, or to Iran. Pending agreement on these issues among littoral states, Russia poses a threat to the integrity and possible democratization of political processes in Kazakhstan and Azerbaijan.

Russia has close security and economic ties with Central Asia. It has acted to limit the bypassing of its own pipelines by Kazakh and Uzbek petroleum exports.[91] It has no particular interest in regional democratization and human rights, except perhaps for the human rights of Russians. A discontented Russian minority in Kazakhstan provides a form of leverage there, as does control of oil flow from Kazakhstan through Russian pipelines.[92] The destabilizing effect of Russian intervention showed up in Tajikistan. Russia backed former Communist hardliners there against the coalition of Islamists, democrats, and nationalists, which they overthrew in December 1992. The price for Russia's military support was reported to be a 50 percent share in the Nurek hydroelectric plant and extensive industrial properties. Turkmenistan's 700 million tons of oil reserves and 8,000 billion cubic meters of natural gas attract attention from East and West—and North. Turkmenistan balances influences from Iran and Russia, and cultivates trade with Turkey and Pakistan. But Russian troops patrol Turkmenistan's border with Iran.[93]

The specter of a possibly hungrier Russian irredentism has prompted its "near abroad" (except Belarus) to form regional bodies and to strengthen ties with Europe, the World Bank, IMF, WTO, OSCE, and possibly the North Atlantic Treaty Organization (NATO) for common defense and joint actions. The six Muslim republics have joined the Economic Cooperation Organization reactivated by Iran, Turkey, and Pakistan. Kazakhstan, Kyrgyzstan, and Uzbekistan have signed on to an economic union. The countries of the "near abroad" have expanded their system of unilateral treaties with East Asian countries.[94]

Part of the road to peace and stability lies through inclusive nation building of a shared multiethnic identity among citizens of each Central

Asian country (as among citizens of the other post-Soviet states); part of that road leads also through increased regional cooperation to compensate for the shattering of economic ties among republics in the former Soviet Union.[95] Asian human rights workers reject the idea that Central Asians are culturally unsuited for democracy. Natalia Ablova, director of the Kyrgyz-American Bureau on Human Rights and the Rule of Law says that educated Kyrgyz "are oriented toward Europe [and its] stability, tolerance, and a certain independence from the state."[96] S. V. R. Nasr concludes, from the experience of numerous secular and Islamic states, that democracy does not make the Muslim countries more vulnerable to fundamentalism. It may well be "the best means for contending with revivalism. . . . Rather than radicalizing revivalism, participation in the political process will push it in directions that will constrict its political growth."[97]

Conclusions

The more democratic these countries become, the harder it will be to meddle covertly in their politics or to cut a corrupt deal behind the public's back. George Zarycky of Freedom House concludes that the cohesion and independence of Russia's new neighbors will depend on their achieving "a sense of statehood buttressed by meaningful economic reform, a strong civil society and the development of democratic institutions . . . the elimination of corruption, . . . and rule of law."[98]

The outcomes of any new activism will reflect choices of which social, ethnic, and religious groups to include and which to exclude from the community. Armenians, Azerbaijanis, Georgians, Ingush, Ossetians, Abkhazy, Slavs of Transdniestria, Tajiks of rival clans and persuasions, Russians, and Chechens have chosen to fight over who belongs in and out, and where they belong. Most of them live through uneasy truces and peacemaking. So far, the dictatorships have outdone Kazakhstan and the pseudodemocracies in their silencing of opposition. Still, nine out of ten inhabitants of the newly independent states live in greater freedom than they did under Communism.

New struggles and times of trial for freedom, as envisaged by Tocqueville, are to be expected in the nondemocratic states. Even the least free countries have opened up more than ever before to contacts and cooperation with potential investors, foreign donors, and, in the case of Uzbekistan and Tajikistan, to regional human rights and humanitarian organizations. Foreign investment and aid will always be a double-edged sword for human rights. But it could well be in the investors' and the donors' self-interest to foster equitable development and democratization.

Chapter 7
Democracy for Whom? The Baltic States

> We shall not back down, so that we no longer feel as if [we were] in
> Orwell's *Animal Farm*, where all are equal but some more equal than
> others.
>
> —Teacher Maare Grossman from Rakvere, delegate
> to the 19th Communist Party Conference[1]

Democracy for Whom?

When Maare Grossman made this statement to the Estonian Popular Front
Rally in Tallinn on June 17, 1988, neither my Estonian companions nor I
seriously expected that in a little over three years Estonia and its Baltic
neighbors would have carried their demand for equality to the point of
full independence. But in March 1990 Lithuania became the first Soviet
republic to declare independence unilaterally. As Moscow's grip loosened,
Estonia, Latvia, and Lithuania regained full independence in September
1991. By then, it was not the Soviet immigrants but the recently subject indigenous populations who were more equal in Estonia and Latvia.

Issues of ethnic group rights and sovereignty in the Baltic republics
have attracted international attention out of all proportion to their small
total population of eight million. There is sympathy in the West for the
Baltic countries' struggle for independence, and there is admiration for
their determined moves toward economic recovery despite great difficulties and wide hardship. On the other hand, both human rights advocates
and nationalists in the Russian Federation have expressed concern for the
rights of Russian coethnics in the Baltic states. Those states also occupy a
strategically sensitive location along the old Cold War East–West dividing
line on the rimland of Scandinavia. Finally, for many, the Baltic states are
somehow seen as a lost part of the West regained.

The Baltic countries remind us of the limitations even of human rights
as standards and prerequisites for democracy; they cannot simply be me-
chanically activated during a democratic transition.[2] Perhaps such rights,

especially the rights to citizenship, do not go far enough to prevail against states' sovereign rights. Perhaps the international organizations, in applying them to Estonia and Latvia, applied them too flexibly. Certainly, human rights, like rights in general, carry the seeds of disagreement regarding as to their implications.

The freedom and autonomy asserted during *perestroika* opened the political arena to growing conflicts between the indigenous nationalists' claims to the human rights of self-determination and national survival and claims of Soviet-era immigrant populations to nondiscrimination and citizenship. The question became: Democracy, and equality, for whom? The answer turned out differently in Lithuania than in the other two republics.

The subjects of this account are all "free" democracies. Lithuania is a "liberal" version: It includes equal rights of citizenship for immigrant minorities among its other equal and extensive human rights. Estonia and Latvia are, rather, "ethnic" democracies. They differ from liberal democracies in that they have chosen full inclusiveness of all rights mainly for the dominant ethnic group. They regard "the non-dominant groups as having relatively less claim to the state and also as not being fully loyal."[3] Ethnic democracy does not exclude universal guarantees of civil rights and recognition of certain group rights, such asrights to an autonomous cultural life reflective of one's ethnic identity. The results of policy in the ethnic democracies of Estonia and Latvia leave human rights standards difficult to apply and the future of democratic community clouded, though surprisingly less threatened by violence than is the case even in some post-Soviet states that accorded automatic citizenship, "zero option," to permanent residents.

This chapter examines the impact of the Soviet occupation, the regaining of independence, and the acquisition of citizenship and minority rights in Lithuania; the contrasting outcomes for citizenship and minority rights in Estonia and Latvia; conflicting claims as to rights; international findings; and the implications that lie beyond human rights law for democratic community in the Baltic states.

The Soviet Occupation

Baltic majorities' claims of threats to their identity and existence as peoples reflect the experience of imperial colonization. Estonia, Latvia, and Lithuania became part of the Russian Empire upon their seizure from Sweden by Peter the Great in the early eighteenth century. They enjoyed independence between 1918 (recognized by Soviet Russia in 1920) and their annexation and occupation by the USSR in 1940. They were reoccupied at the end of World War II. Nearly fifty years later, the Soviet Union recognized the Baltic states' independence on September 6, 1991, some three months before its own collapse.

The brutal deportations and purges under Stalin's Soviet rule brought the Balts severe economic deprivation compared with their free neighbor Finland, with which they had lived on a par before World War II. Soviet occupation also brought an influx of Russian-speaking industrial workers, military, security and political personnel, and professionals—an inflow that came close to making minorities out of Estonians and Latvians.[4] It reduced the proportion of ethnic Estonians and Latvians in their homelands from about eight out of ten inhabitants before the Soviet occupation to 61.5 percent of Estonia's population of about 1.5 million, and 52 percent of Latvia's population of 2.5 million, in 1989.[5] Russians are the largest minority group in Estonia and Latvia. Their share of the population in Estonia rose from 8 percent before the Soviet occupation to about 30.3 percent in 1989. The rest of the population includes Ukrainians, Belarusians, Finns, Jews, and a smattering of other nationalities. Estonia's Russian-speakers are concentrated in the capital, Tallinn, where they comprise half the city's population and unemployment is lowest, and in the northeastern industrial rust belt, where unemployment is relatively high.[6] Latvians are the minority in all seven of the largest cities of their country. They make up only one-third of Riga's inhabitants.[7] During the fifty years of occupation, Latvia's proportion of Russians increased from 9 percent to about a third of the population; the rest consists of Belarusians, Ukrainians, Poles, Lithuanians, Jews, and a smattering of others.[8]

Soviet immigrants served as conveyers of Moscow's rule. They formed a privileged enclave, using their own language.[9] Their schools did not even teach the local languages. The newcomers concentrated in the industrial sector implanted by Moscow. They enjoyed favored access to new housing constructed for workers.[10] Russian-speakers flocked into the professions of medicine and policing. Estonians and Latvians complained that police and physicians often could address the indigenous populace only in Russian.[11] On the other hand, the separation of Russian-speakers from the rest of society has been far from complete. For example, substantial minorities within the Russian-speaking population supported Estonian and Latvian independence. Also, an estimated 100,000 ethnic Russians out of 475,000 in Estonia automatically retained Estonian citizenship along with other pre-occupation citizens and their descendants.[12]

Regaining Independence

As independence became a reality, radical nationalists took over in Estonia and Latvia. Political platforms changed from inclusive to exclusive on the issue of citizenship for Soviet-era immigrants. A demonstration on June 14, 1987, in Riga, Latvia, defied the police to mark the anniversary of the 1941 deportations. It sparked a series of patriotic demonstrations in Latvia and then in its Baltic neighbors. During 1988 environmentalist movements grew into popular fronts for national sovereignty. On June 16, 1988,

Gorbachev responded to the groundswell of discontent in Estonia and replaced its Communist Party first secretary, Karl Vaino, with Vaino Valjas, the former ambassador to Nicaragua. "Valjas, a fluent speaker of Estonian at last!" Estonian friends exulted. By moderate national standards of the time, Valjas was "our Communist." Upon its founding in April, five of the seven members of the executive committee of the Popular Front were Party members. The front grew out of the new environmental movement and the liberal (proautonomy, proreform) wing of the Communist establishment.[13]

On June 17, 1988, a mass rally organized by the Popular Front brought together 150,000 people—one of every ten in Estonia—ostensibly for a send-off for the delegates to the 19th Conference of the Soviet Communist Party. The cheering, singing throng filled Tallinn's huge Festival Field. Police stayed away, and competent activists of the Popular Front reminded one of the marshals at nonviolent peace marches in the United States. No delegates to a Communist Party meeting had ever before received this sort of local nationalist send-off. The crowd waved the white, blue, and black flags of the prewar republic. Because the flags were still illegal, they passed from hand to hand. Banners spelled out the issues: "We'll Eat Our Food and Sell the Rest," "Stop Immigration," "We Want a Clean Environment," "We Demand a Sovereign, Self-Managing Estonia." Other banners demanded historical truth, the designation of Estonian as a state language, and so forth.

Five of the thirty-two Communist delegates spoke at the rally. They voiced support for the unprecedented Estonian Communist Party platform and its demands for autonomy. These demands had support in Estonia's national-Communist Party leadership, and then in the Supreme Soviet, where Estonian nationalists outnumbered the Russian-speaking pro-Unionists.[14] By November 1988, the Estonian Supreme Soviet expressed its dissatisfaction with Soviet parliamentary reforms of that same month by asserting a right of veto over federal legislation.[15]

By 1989, people were rallying for full independence. During the "Baltic Way" demonstration of August 23, 1989, the fiftieth anniversary of the Nazi–Soviet Pact, four out of every ten native Balts, two million of them, joined hands in a human chain linking the capital cities of Vilnius, Riga, and Tallinn in a nonviolent demand for independence. Amid growing tensions between Tallinn and Moscow, the Russian-speaking opposition to Estonian self-determination formed Intermovement and the Union of Work Collectives as anti-autonomy groups with a conservative, pro-Communist ideology.[16] They echoed international criticism of the government when, in August 1989, it set residence minimums for voting and candidacy in local elections. The government backed down but kept five-year residence requirements for candidates—a mild limitation compared to what was to come.[17]

Lithuania became the first Baltic republic to proclaim restored independence. Its unilateral action in the Supreme Soviet resolution of March 11, 1990, goaded the center into a blockade lasting several months, followed by the Soviet forces' violence in January and July 1991. When other republics later followed Lithuania's lead, the single system of Soviet government and law disappeared in the USSR, along with "the Soviet people."[18] Estonia declared its restored independence on August 20, 1991, during the Moscow coup attempt; Latvia declared its independence on August 21. The USSR recognized the independence of the Baltic states on September 6, 1991. All three then entered the United Nations and the Conference on Security and Cooperation in Europe (CSCE), now the OSCE. On May 14, 1993, Lithuania gained membership in the Council of Europe (COE) along with Estonia.[19] Latvia's delay in legislating naturalization rights and procedures held up its admission to the COE until February 1995.

A Troubled Consolidation

Estonia, Latvia, and Lithuania shared the European experience of democracy's drift into authoritarian presidential rule during the 1930s.[20] Upon regaining independence, they held on to democracy. Freedom's decisive ordeal of democratic consolidation began. Democratic consolidation is the period of completing the transition to guaranteed democratic rights and accountability of free democracies, and to democracy's legitimacy in the people's eyes.[21]

The internationally monitored fair and free elections of September 1992 in Estonia were the first post-Soviet legislative elections in the former Soviet Union. Estonians approved a new constitution; elected a renewed parliament, the 101-seat Riigikogu (State Assembly). Parliament elected a new president, Lennart Meri, to replace Arnold Ruutel, a Communist nationalist who had helped steer Estonia toward independence; and a new prime minister.[22] Elections came at a time of great economic hardship associated with the disruption of former patterns of trade, fuel supply, and so on. They produced a majority coalition committed to speeding up the pace of reform toward a capitalist, market economy. Elections of March 1995 produced the second post-independence parliament. It approved a coalition government under Prime Minister Tiit Vahi, which later reformed in the wake of the October 1995 wiretap scandal (see below). Parliament reelected Lennart Meri president in 1996.[23]

The Latvian elections of June 5–6, 1993, replaced the old Supreme Soviet of 1990 with a freely and fairly elected restored 100-seat Saeima, which approves the prime minister and his cabinet, and elects the president as head of state. A broad spectrum of parties competed for the votes of the 72 percent of eligible citizens who voted in the Saeima elections of September and October 1995. That Saeima reelected Guntis Ulmanis as president on June 18, 1996. The May 1995 electoral law restricted participation by barring the candidacy of persons who continued to be active in the Communist Party and other pro-Soviet organizations after January 13, 1991, when Soviet troops began a failed attempt to topple the government in Lithuania and Latvia.

In Lithuania, the head of state was Supreme Council Chairman Vytautas Landsbergis, leader of the Sajudis popular front and champion of Lithuania's independence. In a democratic turnover on May 25, 1992, this eminent figure lost the referendum on his proposal for a strong presidency. CSCE observers adjudged as free and fair the parliamentary elections of October 25 and November 15, 1992. The voters approved a new constitution and a restored parliament, the 141-seat Seimas. They favored the Lithuanian Democratic Labor Party (LDLP), successor to the Communist Party of Lithuania. The LDLP leader, Algirdas Brazauskas, had led a Communist split from the CPSU in 1989, when he served as first secretary of the Lithuanian Communist Party. Brazauskas was appointed acting president by the Seimas, replacing Vytautas Landsbergis. Brazauskas then won the presidential election of February 14, 1993. Landsbergis replaced Brauzaskas after crime, corruption, and declining living standards brought a crushing defeat to Brauzaskas and the LDLP. The president appoints the prime minister and cabinet with the approval of the Seimas. Right-of-center parties captured a majority of local government councils from the LDLP in the elections of March 1995.[24]

Estonia, Latvia, and Lithuania adhere to basic international human rights covenants, including the European Convention on Human Rights and Basic Freedoms of the COE. They inscribe individual equality and rights in their constitutional documents and have welcomed international human rights monitors, including resident OSCE missions in Estonia and Latvia.[25]

The foreign refugees' rights to asylum concerns mainly refugees from countries outside the former Soviet Union. Suffice it to say that none of the Baltic republics accords them refugee status or recognizes rights of asylum. On the other hand, vis-à-vis internal politics, the constitutions, laws, and in large part the practice of the Baltic republics guarantee extensive democratic freedoms of the media and expression generally, of association and assembly, of academic freedom, and freedom of movement within the countries and abroad. In March 1995 Estonia deported Russian citizen and resident of Estonia Pyotr Rozhov, the representative of Vladimir Zhirinovsky's Liberal Democratic Party of Russia, for alleged activities against the Estonian state since 1989. Reporters working in the state-owned sector of Lithuania's television and radio broadcasting have reported pressures not to criticize government policies over the air.

The Baltic republics support cultural centers for various minorities and ban discrimination against them. The governments grant religious freedom, but within varying limits. Lithuania grants property rights in buildings to religious communities, centers, and associations. It subsidizes nine "traditional" religious communities and does not ban proselytizing. Leaders of one of the "traditional" communities, the small Jewish community, has asked the government to prevent further vandalism and theft at Jewish cemeteries in Kaunas, Vilnius, and Klaipeda.[26]

Latvia allows only religious organizations that are already in the country to invite foreign missionaries. Mormon missionaries and other "nontraditional" religious groups have difficulty getting visas and residence permits. In May 1995 the "Rubiks sabotage group" bombed Riga's one synagogue and threatened to bomb the Monument of Freedom and Moscow–Riga trains unless the government freed the long-detained former Communist first secretary Alfreds Rubiks, held on charges of conspiracy against the Latvian state since 1991. Rubiks was convicted after a twenty-five-month trial and an excessive sojourn in detention; he was sentenced to eight years in prison.[27] Other disturbing manifestations of extremist behavior and groups had occurred the year before.[28]

The Baltic constitutions proclaim extensive rights of due process and judicial impartiality as preconditions for governmental accountability and citizen protection. Legal reforms of the Soviet-era systems are preconditions for fully realizing the civil rights already proclaimed. The reforms proceed at an uneven pace. The targets of reform have been holdovers from Communism and threats to human rights,[29] including inroads on full democratic accountability under rule of law, an overly powerful prosecutor's office, police brutality and inhumane prison conditions, pervasive organized crime and corruption, and, in Latvia especially, the persistent habit of brutally hazing military recruits. Estonia and Lithuania have constitutional courts and relatively independent judges. In Latvia, courts tend to remain corrupt and too weak to enforce their decisions. Still, justice seems to have been served in notable political cases tried by Latvian courts —the Rubiks case just mentioned and the Noviks case, wherein the Riga district court convicted Alfons Noviks, former head of the Latvian secret police, of "genocide" and imposed a life sentence for his part in mass killings, deportations, and torture between 1940 and 1953.

Estonia has progressed further than Latvia and Lithuania in tangible efforts to reform inhumane prison conditions and conduct of prison staff. The Estonian government has begun to discipline abusive prison guards and provide more space in pretrial detention centers. It has opened new training and recreation centers in the Harku women's prison and embarked on a general plan to upgrade prisons. Incidents of prisoners killing prisoners dropped from thirty-two in 1992 to one in 1995. Representatives of the COE visited prisons on government invitation and made recommendations for bringing them up to COE standards. The pace of reform depends on finding resources and training better prison staff.[30]

One example of advanced accountability on personal security issues that compares favorably with the situation in Russia, where politicians assume their phones may be tapped, occurred in Estonia. In October 1995, parliament appointed a special committee to investigate charges that Interim Minister Edgar Savisaar had illegally recorded his conversations with other ministers, without the requisite court permission to wiretap. During the course of the investigation, Minister Savisaar and the entire cabinet resigned, and a reconstituted governing coalition assumed office.

The threats to human rights by organized crime in Lithuania include blackmail attempts against the already unsafe Ignalina nuclear power plant, the leading source of electric power and the only operating nuclear power plant in the country and the Baltic region. The criminals have trafficked illicitly in nuclear materials from the plant.[31] They have committed arson and murder to silence investigative reporters.[32] In October 1994 the Supreme Court convicted four persons with criminal records for the 1993 murder of the copublisher and editor of a popular daily paper that had published a great deal about organized crime. One of the criminals was executed in July 1995.[33]

For a year Lithuania's Preventive Detention Law of 1993 allowed police to detain persons suspected of being violent criminals for up to two months, subject to permission of the procurator general in each case. Later extensions of the law added safeguards, such as the habeas corpus requirement to bring the detainee before a court for its approval of the detention's legality within forty-eight hours of arrest and the detainee's right to meet with an attorney during detention. A few well-publicized convictions out of over five hundred cases leaves the impression that the police have abused the possibilities of long detention.[34]

The Lithuanian government has on occasion been less than enthusiastic and supportive of investigative reporting about organized crime. A bomb destroyed a new building intended to house the largest daily, *Lietuvos Rytas*. The paper had been publishing a series on organized crime families. The government had uncovered no leads in the bombing by year's end and troubled some observers by sending tax collectors to the bomb scene. Press reports stated that, in a meeting two days later with the editors of *Lietuvos Rytas*, President Brazauskas chided them for allegedly publishing unsupported charges against organized crime figures. Meanwhile, in parliament, opposition members denounced the government's criticism of the press's investigations into official corruption.[35] The press obviously has a hard road ahead as it attempts to achieve governmental accountability for corruption and the criminals' responsibility for racketeering.

Estonia's rapid currency, property, and fiscal reforms produced enough of a market economy to merit associate membership in the European Union in June 1995. The export trade in food, textiles, and timber products has shifted mainly from east to west. Troublesome rates of unemployment continue in the countryside and in the northeast, among the predominantly industrial and ethnic Russian workforce. The issues of citizenship rights and economic conversion of obsolete enterprises in the northeast exacerbate discontent there. Economic reforms, such as inflation curbs, privatization, the reorientation of trade from east to west, and the growth of the economy in Estonia have outstripped the pace of similar processes in Latvia and Lithuania, and in other post-Soviet states. Still, by 1996 in Lithuania, more than 40 percent of state property was privatized, including most housing and small business.

In the Baltic states, reforms exact costs in economic and social rights. They have meant increased hardships for farmers, for Russian-speakers in obsolete state-owned industries, for the unemployed and persons on fixed incomes. Social services and health care totter on an inadequate base.[36] The now free Baltic trade unions are beginning to exercise their right to collective bargaining.[37] They tend to ignore rising job discrimination against women, a by-product of unemployment, conditions of widespread economic hardship, and the absence in the past of effective women's rights advocacy. Women's and children's protection against domestic abuse and violence generally remains inadequate throughout the area. But active women's rights organizations have begun to emerge. In Latvia, for example, women's advocacy groups try to find women jobs, lobby for better social benefits, help victims of domestic abuse, and attempt to stop the hazing of draftees. Unlike the case in Poland, none of the Baltic states, including Catholic Lithuania, has restricted the right to abortion, a principal means of family planning.

The disabled suffer no legal discrimination, but, as elsewhere, general shortages of funds usually inhibit the provision of special access laws. Riga, Latvia, has adapted intersections for wheelchairs. Estonia has made special new provisions for children's welfare: It has programs for refurbishing schools, free medical care, and subsidizing school meals. A few children's advocacy groups in Estonia are lobbying for new child protection laws. One of their targets is likely to be the present failure to carry out programs for juvenile rehabilitation and correction law, leaving juveniles housed with adult convicts.[38] International human rights law is silent on consenting homosexuality; the Baltic states have decriminalized it.[39]

George Zarycky attributes the poverty among pensioners, country folk, and other vulnerable people, not to market building alone, but also to the way the market grows under bureaucracies that make sure to benefit from the process:

Since breaking with the Soviet Union after fifty years of often brutal occupation, the three small Baltic states have made striking progress toward establishing market economies, multiparty democracies, a vibrant independent press and a healthy civil society [if one ignores the immigrants]. Yet in 1955, all three faced growing public unease amid persistent unemployment, banking crises, high inflation and the perception that the old Communist nomenklatura was exploiting the privatization process.[40]

Minority and Citizenship Rights in Lithuania

After the failure of the 1991 coup attempt, Baltic governments banned organizations they found to be subversive and those with reputed ties to Moscow. Briefly also, the Estonian government dissolved three Russian-speaking local government councils, but quickly held new elections in which the same Russian-speaking, allegedly pro-Moscow, leaders were returned to office.[41] In Lithuania, the confrontation with alleged subversives, especially among the Polish autonomy-seeking minority, grew more serious. The central government took over predominantly ethnic Polish local councils in areas acquired through Stalin's territorial shifts. The takeover left suspicions on both sides and a sense of betrayal,[42] according to pro-independence, ethnic Polish deputies.[43] Deputy Romualdas Ozalas, a former leading Communist, then head of the Commission on Affairs of East Lithuania, the area of Polish concentration, stated that the suspension of the local councils contained procedural irregularities, but attributed them to the urgent priority of "first restoring the state, as it was, under the law" and averting threats to that state.[44]

The priority of national restoration has been widely accepted among Lithuanians. They were embittered by the occupation, and by the bloodshed of January and July 1991. Just after full independence, in October 1991, a cosmopolitan expert on comparative literature pointed to the statue of Pushkin in central Vilnius and said: "Pushkin should be moved to the outskirts, leaving only Lithuanian cultal figures in the center. It represents the Russian cultural oppression of Lithuania." Later, she asked angrily why her companions from Estonia and the United States showed so much concern for the Poles (and the suspension of their local government), when it is "we Lithuanians who have suffered so much." The identity of ethnic Lithuanian nationalists is the identity of martyrs abandoned by the West to suffer at the hands of the Soviet oppressor.[45]

Ethnic Lithuanians approached independence with a strong majority of 80.6 percent, compared with 9.7 percent for Russians and 7.1 percent for Poles,[46] in addition to Belarusians, Ukrainians, and Jews. Hence the Lithuanians have had less reason to fear national extinction than have the smaller indigenous majority populations of Estonia and Latvia. For all their bitterness about the Soviet past, the Lithuanians have admitted the immigrant legacy of that past into their democratic community.

Before the bitter confrontation with Moscow in 1990–91, the Lithuanian Supreme Council passed an interim citizenship law on November 3, 1989. The law recognized continuity of citizenship for survivors from the pre-

Soviet era and their descendants. It gave the option of citizenship to all permanent residents of Lithuania who would register their assent to citizenship within a two-year period. Most immigrants took advantage of the interim law: fewer than 2 percent remained noncitizens. Thus enfranchised, ethnic Russians, the largest non-Lithuanian minority, participated actively in elections. In 1992–93 they voted mostly for ex-Communist Brazauskas and the LDLP.[47] The follow-up Lithuanian Citizenship Law of December 10, 1991, recognized the citizenship of those who were citizens up to the Soviet occupation, their descendants, and citizens naturalized under the 1989 law.[48] For others, the law stipulates naturalization, with requirements including knowledge of Lithuanian and residence of ten years.[49]

Poles, particularly, have expressed concern that the language law, resembling the laws of Estonia and Latvia, discriminates against them by requiring a working proficiency in Lithuanian. As in its Baltic neighbors, the Lithuanian government has granted liberal extensions of the law's deadlines as non-native speakers of Lithuanian continue to take tests of language proficiency. No one was known to have been dismissed for lack of proficiency by the end of 1995.

Immigrants' Rights in Estonia

The repressions and mass immigration during Soviet occupation prompted the governments of the Baltic states, as they gained autonomy, to reject the Sovietization and Russification of their countries and languages; they asserted their right of national self-determination and the principle of legal continuity from the pre-Soviet period in statehood and laws, including citizenship laws. They also undertook to respect minority groups' cultural rights.

Estonia and Latvia became the only post-Soviet republics not to offer immigrant residents citizenship without waiting under some form of "zero option."[50] The moderate nationalist Estonian Popular Front had included Russian-speakers as well as Estonians in the struggle for independence, but failed before it disbanded in its attempt to get naturalization requirements waived for Soviet-era immigrant residents. Excluding Soviet immigrants from citizenship appeared also to serve a purpose other than of that group self-preservation by effectively limiting the opposition to their governing coalitions.[51] Whatever the legislators' motives, the once-privileged immigrants felt the sudden shock of statelessness.[52] Stripped of Soviet identity, citizenship, and protection, they became stateless speakers of a foreign tongue. Some radical nationalist leaders even openly but vainly sought the immigrants' expulsion as illegal occupiers.[53]

Naturalization requirements stiffened with time. The 1992 law, echoed later in Latvia, carried over the pre-Soviet citizenship law of 1938. It recognized as citizens only persons who had been citizens before the Soviet occupation, and their maternal or paternal descendants. The law made exceptions for meritorious service (a few hundred so far) and for stateless residents who were never Soviet citizens. An amendment of February 18, 1993, also exempted applicants who had registered for citizenship by February 24, 1990, with the unofficial Congress of Estonia (elected and filled by pre-occupation citizens and their descendants). The law required a two-years' residence before applying, plus an additional one-year waiting period, a language test for proficiency in Estonian, an oath of loyalty to the Estonian state and its constitutional system, and an adequate, permanent, and lawful income.[54] The new citizenship law of January 1995 raised the residence requirement from two to five years, for a six-year wait in all. This longer residency affected few Soviet-era residents.[55] The law requires that applicants be tested for proficiency in oral and written Estonian; they had to pass another test, in Estonian, of their knowledge of the constitutional framework of governmental institutions, basic rights, freedoms, and duties of all persons, and naturalization procedures under the law.[56] The law also disqualifies from citizenship certain categories of applicants with past criminal convictions, anti-Estonian activity, or career foreign military service.[57]

By mid-December 1995, about 65,000 applicants had received Estonian citizenship. With applications coming in at about 2,000 a month, almost 83,000 more cases were pending. The citizenship and occupational language requirements force a diminishing majority of the immigrant population to confront the consequences of their past indifference to Estonian language and culture.[58] About 40 percent of the Soviet-era immigrants and their descendants had been born in Estonia.[59] With time, the language requirement would either present fewer difficulties or be waived because the applicants had studied in Estonian schools or passed the qualifying language examination for various jobs in the public sector.

Anyone dealing with the general public must, by law, speak passable Estonian. Russians and other noncitizens allege discrimination in hiring due to occupational language requirements. They also complain about the lack of free instruction in Estonian. As of the mid-1990s, no one had been dismissed for lack for proficiency in Estonian. The 1993 law on the civil service required that government employees be proficient in Estonian by the end of 1995. As that deadline approached, parliament extended the requirement to February 1, 1997. No noncitzens could be hired into the civil service after January 1, 1996.

Local non-Estonian inhabitants may receive official information in their language where they form a majority, and their local government may conduct business in that language. Yet, for reasons that remain unexplained, the central government broke its own law and denied to the city councils of the heavily Russian cities of Sillamae and Narva in the mainly Russian northeast the right to use Russian for their interdepartmental business and official documents.[60]

Delays and carelessness by the registering authorities in issuing residence and work permits under the Law on Aliens of July 1993 compound anxiety over status and possible expulsion from Estonia on the part of civilian aliens and some 15,000 resident Russian military pensioners.[61] Soviet travel passports for about 300,000 stateless persons expired on July 12, 1995. In order to travel abroad, they could apply for aliens' travel passports, valid for five years, or receive temporary travel documents. The rules of 1993–94 left aliens in suspense about their future in Estonia, owing to government indecision about how many times they may renew the passports or how long they may live in Estonia as persons without citizenship.[62]

Noncitizens are guaranteed basic rights under the Estonian constitution, including the right to unemployment benefits and social services.[63] They also have equal rights to participate in privatization of housing and commercial and agricultural property, with potential exceptions for the ownership of certain categories of property such as the law specifies. Noncitizens may own land with permission of the government and, in practice, the land under real property which they own.[64] Ethnic minorities possess extensive legal rights to preserve "ethnic identity, cultural traditions, native language, and religious beliefs." The government provides subsidies to minority-group cultural organizations run by citizens. Noncitizens may join such groups.[65] As part of its post-independence settlement with Russia, Estonia agreed that about 18,000 military veterans demobilized before Estonia regained full independence in 1991 and who were born before July 1, 1930, may stay, and may receive a pension two or three times higher than the average.[66]

Noncitizens in Estonia have not been permitted to vote in elections to parliament, hold elected office, or form political parties.[67] No Russian-speakers (the bulk of immigrants) were elected to parliament or were left in the cabinet after the parliamentary elections of September 1992. This changed in the 1995 elections. A Russian party, Our Home Is Estonia, sent seven Russian-speakers to parliament, elected by voters among the 100,000 enfranchised Russian-speakers, in the second peaceful and democratic change of parliament and government.[68]

As another exception to political exclusion, the government moved to make local elections meaningful in the mainly Russian-settled northeast and the heavily Russian capital, Tallinn. It bestowed citizenship without naturalization requirements on about a hundred Russian-speaking local politicians under the provision of the citizenship law that exempted from naturalization requirements persons who had rendered "exceptionally valuable service" to Estonia. The mayor of Narva in the northeast disclosed that the entire leadership of the city had received citizenship in that way;[69] so, too, did non-Estonian celebrities in science, culture, business, and so on, amid accusations from others in the Russian-speaking community that these new citizens had sold out.[70] Among the gains in office in local elections of October 17, 1993, twenty-five Russians (or nearly half its membership) were elected deputies to the Tallinn City Council.[71] It was not clear that the local vote compensated immigrants for the uncertainty of their future in Estonia.[72] But most immigrants seem to want to stay in Estonia and Latvia rather than apply for citizenship in Russia or other countries of origin.[73]

Immigrants' Rights in Latvia

Latvia regained independence with the smallest majority of the titular nationality among the Baltic states.[74] The Supreme Soviet elected in 1990 responded by legislating the most exclusive naturalization process and laws on alien rights in the Baltic region and the former Soviet Union.

After the country regained full independence in 1991, parliament passed interim citizenship rules on October 15. The resolution expressed the intent to "liquidate the consequences of the Soviet Union's occupation and annexation of Latvia" and to renew the legal rights of citizens of the Republic of Latvia by reinstating the citizenship law of 1919. Following the principle of continuity from pre-Soviet Latvia, parliament gave automatic extension of Latvian citizenship upon registration to persons who were citizens or who qualified for citizenship (as permanent residents) on June 17, 1940, the date of the Soviet invasion, to and their direct descendants who registered before July 1, 1992.[75] This excluded from citizenship more than 700,000 Soviet-era immigrants.

In June 1994 a nationalist majority in the Saeima, elected by enfranchised nonimmigrants in 1993, sent to the president a law with low annual quotas of applicants. This would have meant permanent noncitizenship for the almost 30 percent of the population who are noncitizens.[76] Under pressure from the COE on human rights grounds, President Guntis Ulmanis refused to sign the bill with quotas,[77] so parliament passed one without quotas. The COE delayed Latvia's admission until February 10, 1995, after an assessment of the new naturalization law.[78] The law of July 22, 1994, retained virtual quotas by including a schedule of waiting periods for application. The applicants able to pass the language test must then wait their turn. The waiting time is in effect proportionally to the probability of assimilation and detachment from a foreign identity and loyalty. The top priority goes to spouses of Latvian citizens, citizens of other Baltic states, and persons born in Latvia. The longest wait, until January 1, 2003, is for persons who entered Latvia after they reached the age of thirty.[79] Applicants have resided for ten years in Latvia, pass a stringent language test and a test on the constitution and Latvian history, and take an oath of loyalty. Among those disqualified are former Soviet KGB and military officers.

The language test taken requires not only conversational Latvian, as in the 1991 draft, but a considerable written knowledge as well. Only 37 percent of noncitizens in one poll thought they knew enough Latvian to pass the test. There is widespread anxiety over the language requirement and the possibility that the language exam may be administered unfairly. A 1995 amendment liberalized the law for some persons by allowing automatic citizenship for all ethnic Latvians returning to their homeland and for persons who have completed a secondary education in Latvian language schools.[80]

Naturalization is not a right, one should note, but something one "can" receive at the discretion of the government—subject to court appeal and the oversight of a parliamentary supervisory committee.[81] The UN Human Rights Committee, the body that receives complaints and reports on compliance with the International Covenant on Civil and Political Rights (ICCPR), has expressed concern that "a significant segment of the population will not enjoy Latvian citizenship due to the stringent criteria established by law . . . and pursuant to a timetable calculated to delay the naturalization process for years."[82]

Latvia returned to its 1922 constitution, which is supplemented with a constitutional law of 1991 that proclaims basic rights and freedoms.[83] Noncitizens have equal basic rights of due process, inviolability of person, and expression. Some fear of statelessness vanished under a law of 1995 that set up a permanent residency status for ex-Soviet stateless persons and facilitates their travel abroad on noncitizen passports.[84] But noncitizens remain outside the democratic community of equals in several ways. For example, they may not vote in Latvia's local or national elections[85] or form political parties.[86]

Latvia's new law on radio and television, passed in August 1995, limits the time for broadcasts in Russian and from Russia.[87] The Riga city council has regularly denied noncitizen groups permission to assemble and demonstrate to protest against discrimination. Russian-language newspapers and members of organizations denied the right of assembly have accused the police of using excessive force to break up demonstrations that proceeded anyway. The courts dismissed charges against demonstrators for allegedly blocking entrances to the city council building. The government has registered about thirty-five political parties. It denies registration to communist and Nazi groups and to other organizations whose activities, it holds, would contravene the constitution. The government denied registration to the League of Stateless Persons on the grounds that noncitizens are prohibited from forming "political" organizations.[88] The noncitizen population enjoys a lesser right to privacy. The protection (such as it is) of the judicial warrant required to invade citizens' privacy of telephones, mail, and so forth, does not apply to the considerable noncitizen population. Russian-speaking journalists have been beaten and threatened by extreme nationalists.[89]

A 1995 law on the status of stateless former Soviet citizens affirms their basic human rights. Permanent residents have the right of freedom of movement within Latvia and to travel abroad and return, as well as to invite close relatives to join them so families can be reunited. The law secures the right of permanent registration for persons lacking permanent housing (a problem in the past for residents of dormitories furnished by the military or Soviet enterprises).[90]

Noncitizens in fact hold unequal rights in several spheres other than the franchise denied to them. They may not hold state administrative, elected, and judicial offices or serve as fire fighters, crew members on Latvian ships and commercial airliners, jurors, litigating attorneys, notaries, or private detectives. Unlike the case in Estonia, noncitizens may not own land except as shareholders in companies holding land; nor may they automatically inherit land use, although they may lease land and own buildings on it. Noncitizens' pensions are 10 percent below those received by retired citizens. They received 10 percent fewer privatization vouchers. Noncitizens may not own firearms, hire armed guards (a potential problem for business people, bankers, and others, owing to organized crime), or work as private detectives.[91] Non-Latvian speakers must have an adequate knowledge of Latvian for any employment in "institutions, enterprises, and institutes," and sufficient proficiency to deal with the public as needed. This requirement has not been strictly enforced.[92]

Human Rights at Issue

The exclusion from citizenship meant statelessness for about 30 percent of the population of Estonia and Latvia.[93] The governments of Estonia and Latvia and supporters of current citizenship and language policies have maintained that naturalization requirements reflect not ethnic bias but, rather, unresolved issues of trust, loyalty, and the survival of the Estonian and Latvian languages, ethnicity, and statehood. Estonia insists that the citizenship requirements are liberal by international standards.[94] To charges of ethnic discrimination, the Latvian government has responded that 30 percent of ethnic Russians in Latvia are citizens[95] and that about a quarter of all citizens (and 46 percent of the total population) are ethnically non-Latvians.[96]

Most ethnic Latvian movements and parties see no contradiction between democracy and Latvian nationalism. Where they did differ among themselves, it becomes apparent, is over the balance in law between protection of Latvian identity and protection of minority rights. Radical nationalists, such as Visvaldis Latsis, of the Movement for the National Independence of Latvia, and Chairman Maris Grinblats and Secretary Anita

Brence, of the Latvian Committee, favored total exclusion of Soviet immigrants from citizenship. They had no intention of sharing their democratic freedom with the Russian "colonizers" who earlier had lorded it over them. Their survival is also a human right, Grinblats argued, in the face of demographic depletion under Soviet rule, when repression and immigration lowered the proportion of ethnic Latvians from 75.5 percent in 1935, to about 50 percent in 1991. (Since then the ethnic Latvian proportion has slowly inched up to 54 percent).[97]

The Estonian and Latvian denial of ethnic bias is technically correct, as their laws center formally not on ethnicity but on legal continuity from pre-occupation days. But legal technicalities and statistics on citizenship do not resolve the issue of the aliens' identity and future in the Baltic region. For immigrants or children of immigrants, with few exceptions,[98] naturalized citizenship is an unclear possibility, not a right of residence or birth. At the same time, persons born outside Latvia who never before set foot in the country may be citizens by virtue of descent from a Latvian citizen[99] or, simply, Latvian ethnicity.

Active supporters of independence among Russian-speakers feel betrayed.[100] A leader of the new League of Stateless Persons in Latvia, Boris Tsilevich, sees the Latvian government as acting not as "arbiter among various linguistic groups, but as defender of the interests of one of them." The "ideology of ethnic statehood" ignores past noncitizen votes for the Popular Front and "prevails over rational considerations."[101] Tsilevich speaks for most Soviet-era immigrants, who prefer citizenship in Latvia, their land of adoption or birth.[102]

Russia turned from supporter to critic of Estonia and Latvia after Russian independence. The Russian parliament, government, and human rights advocates have complained to Estonia, Latvia, and the United Nations that the citizenship and language laws of Estonia and Latvia violate the human rights of the Russian-speaking minorities by discriminating against them, by denying them their dignity, and, President Yeltsin charged, by engaging in "ethnic cleansing."[103]

Findings of Human Rights Organizations

No such crime was described in foreign human rights reports on Estonia and Latvia. The human right to a nationality (citizenship)[104] is a half-right. Implementing the right to citizenship is left to individual states of the world as one of the prerogatives of sovereignty.[105] Human rights delegations from such international governmental agencies as the United Nations, the CSCE (now OSCE) and its High Commissioner on National Minorities, the COE, the Finnish Helsinki Committee, and the Human Rights Committee, which monitors compliance with the ICCPR, found that the citizenship laws of Estonia and Latvia conform to international standards. However, various monitors did express concern about such provisions as the banning of certain social and political undesirables from citizenship, the stringency of the language examination, and the need to apply it impartially and to improve the teaching of Estonian and Latvian. Progress toward a multi-cultural political community has begun in Estonia, where, as one liberal Russian correspondent reported, "the basic principle of national identification . . . is not blood but language." The Council of Europe was sufficiently satisfied with conditions in Estonia that it suspended human rights monitoring there, conditioned on improvement in Estonian language instruction. Three-fourths of young Russians between the ages of eighteen and twenty-nine consider Estonia "their country," compared with 27 percent of the Russians aged sixty and older. By 1997 the Moscow city government conditioned new subsidies for gifted Russian-speaking children on the basis of their learning Estonian.[106]

The NGO Human Rights Watch/Helsinki did find that the language and citizenship requirements as presently administered and interpreted in Estonia and Latvia contravene the prohibition against discrimination on ethnic grounds in the civil and political rights, including citizenship requirements, of minorities who were once also citizens and had reasonable expectations of remaining so. At the same time, Helsinki Watch uncovered in Estonia "no systematic serious abuses of equality of social human rights in the area of citizenship." It concluded: "Non-citizens in Estonia are guaranteed basic rights under the Estonian Constitution, including the right to unemployment benefits and social services."[107]

Children born in Latvia and Estonia of noncitizen expatriates inherit their parents' statelessness. Yet under the international law of human rights, "every child has the right to acquire a nationality," a CSCE mission argued. Children born in Estonia (and presumably also Latvia) since ratification of the International Covenant on Civil and Political Rights should acquire citizenship at birth.[108] This exception for children the monitors identified as a question of morality and goodwill rather than a legal human rights obligation, though Latvia is violating its legal commitment to grant citizenship to such stateless children under the 1954 Convention on the Reduction of Statelessness, to which it is a party.[109] Every third child or so born in Latvia and Estonia is an immigrant, and thus stateless. The governments of those countries should ask themselves, by opening themselves up to native-born stateless children, and living up to their human rights obligations, can they not also build a more inclusive and stable democratic community?

Conclusions

Democratization in the Baltic republics is further along than in any other post-Soviet states. The human rights associated with democracy are especially advanced in Lithuania and, in areas other than citizenship, in Estonia. The large stateless immigrant minorities in Estonia and Latvia are excluded from full participation and representation. But most immigrants still wish to make those countries their home, unlike their Russian-speaking compatriots who are streaming out of Central Asia and the Caucasus.

Standards of human rights provide one of several keys to nation-building toward a democratic community in Estonia, Latvia, and Lithuania. Beyond the questions and standards of human rights remain the political and psychological costs of exclusionary policies. Internally, this means the anxious uncertainty of immigrants about whether they will even be allowed to remain at all, as most of them would like.[110] Externally, this means unsettling pressures and hyperbole about "ethnic cleansing" from the direction of Russia.[111]

Another key to democratic community lies in the realms of politics and equity. Here, mediation by human rights organizations has sustained the process of conflict resolution. The challenge remains to find a reasonable middle ground between: (1) Estonian and Latvian nationalist claims to self-determination and their desire to put the occupation and its legacy behind them and preserve their nationhood and power; (2) the fulfillment of immigrants' claims to full equality of rights, including the right to citizenship. Perhaps the passing of time and renewal of generations will accelerate the needed democratic inclusion of immigrants and their children.

The international missions have noted the tensions over unresolved issues posed by the language and citizenship laws, the insecurity those laws engender, and their potential for creating social conflict.[112] One can only agree with the UN mission that, on the part of Russian, Belarusian, and Ukrainian communities, there is "considerable anxiety about the future and, on the part of some members of the Estonian community, the desire to turn back the clock to the pre-1940 years, notwithstanding the fact that in the intervening period two generations of residents of non-Ethnic Estonian origin have grown accustomed to living in Estonia and perceive Estonia as their homeland."[113]

International and NGO observers have urged government leaders and leaders of immigrant groups to keep their constituencies better informed on issues of minority rights, and to continue their efforts aimed at increasing intercommunal cooperation.[114] On February 15, 1993, in the face of repeated charges by the Russian Federation that Estonia is violating the human rights of Russian-speakers, Estonia agreed with the CSCE to set up a human rights mission in Estonia. Monitoring and evaluation have expanded into an ongoing process of mediation, conflict resolution, and observation through offices in Tallinn and the northeastern cities of Narva and Khotla-Jarve, in conjunction with an independent local round table set up in the East Virumaa county of the northeast.

The Danish government has provided seed money for a nongovernmental legal information center in the Estonian capital of Tallinn. The center gives free legal help to both citizens and noncitizens seeking advice on issues related to their human rights.[115] Foreign aid directed to efficient funding of inadequate instruction in the indigenous languages of the three Baltic states is aid well spent.[116] The president of Estonia established a Human Rights Institute in 1992 as an additional monitor. In 1993 his government organized a national "Round Table" as a meeting place for people from the citizens' Union of Estonian Nationalities, deputies from various political parties, and the Russian-speakers' Representative Assembly.[117]

Latvia has been working on a national program for the promotion of human rights that was recommended by a high-level team put together by the UN Development Program, the COE, and the OSCE. Even when the government finds the funds to fully staff its new Human Rights Office, its monitoring and responses to claims will be dealing only with the symptoms, not with the underlying distrust. This is exemplified in the sentiments expressed by the Latvian activist who in October 1991 insisted that, "for what the Russians did to us, we can never trust them," and by a former member of the Russian Popular Front for Independence who recalls that "we supported them and they betrayed us."

Overcoming the reluctance among nationalist politicians and their constituents in Estonia and Latvia to facilitate naturalization of the immigrants would also play a part in creating the inclusive democratic community. The governments of Estonia and Latvia, but especially the more restrictive Latvia, should keep in mind that restraints on minority rights of association and participation hamper conflict resolution, and in fact may actually intensify conflict.[118] President Guntis Ulmanis of Latvia said that either Latvia must provide "Russians, Ukrainians, Belarusians and Jews with an opportunity to integrate here" or Latvia will commit the "gross mistake" of an exclusionary attitude that "would give an impetus to the development of a two-community state . . . which is inconceivable."[119] But it is possible.

Another important key to a stable and inclusive democratic community, along with human rights fulfillment and external and internal mediation, will be a movement from freedom at the cost of many persons' economic and social rights to freedom that at last proves compatible with, and essential to, the realization of those rights. Inequity of economic development threatens the peace, violates human rights, and may still undo democratic consolidation. In sum, the experience of freedom in the Baltic states once again demonstrates the importance and interdependence of choices concerning regime, inclusiveness, and development.

Chapter 8
Russia's Third Try

> We see just as before . . . how strong the arbitrary rule of the authorities still is, both in the center and locally.
>
> —Boris Yeltsin[1]

Russia's first attempt at democracy ended with the dissolution of the Duma (Parliament) and the collapse of tsarism in March 1917. Its successor, the Provisional Government, tried and failed to found a democratic republic in 1917 under unfavorable wartime conditions. Russia's third try began during *perestroika*, when it was still the Russian Soviet Federated Socialist Republic (RSFSR). After independence, the Russian Federation lived through deadlock, a violent resolution of that deadlock along with major institutional changes, and local civil wars. Lack of governmental accountability, pervasive lawlessness, and grave human rights violations left Russia slipping into authoritarian rule.

Through its trials of freedom, human rights defender Sergei Kovalyov reflected in his letter of resignation from chairmanship of the Human Rights Commission, "Russia was struggling against itself, like a man subject to a terrible vice." In the struggle, democracy lost ground. "You pledged to build a state of the people and for the people," Kovalyov wrote to President Yeltsin, "but have constructed a bureaucratic pyramid on top of the people and against them."[2] A popular journal of opinion, *The New Times*, editorialized about "the nostalgia for order," for the "strong hand."[3]

Less pessimistic Russian advocates of human rights and rule of law such as Ludmilla Alexeyeva, the champion of a new civil society and former chronicler of dissent, have expressed the belief that nothing is foreordained, and that it is up to Russians to build a new open, democratic society instead of bemoaning the survivals of the old one.[4] Outstanding U.S. experts on Russia no less than Russians, are divided in their assessments of democracy's progress and prospects. Contrast, for example, Stephen Cohen's pessimism with the caution and wait and see attitudes of Jack Matlock and Michael McFaul. McFaul sees Russia in a period of "transition without consolidation." The reality of elite rule coexists with the potential for democratic renewal in Russia's relatively free elections.[5]

This chapter examines the deadlock of democracy in 1992–93; the resulting new authoritarianism of 1993–95; its outcome, the disastrous war in Chechnya; the political context of embattled freedoms and threats to those freedoms from outside the law; the interweaving of religion, identity, and freedom; and, as the war ground on, the crucial choices made by the people and their leaders; and the signs of accountability and the restoration of partial democracy that appeared with the elections of 1995 and 1996.

The Deadlock of Democracy

Independent Russia at first appeared to be leading the way toward constitutional democracy among the newly independent states. By 1991 Yeltsin's democratic credentials as elected deputy and then president of Russia seemed confirmed by his leadership of the resistance to the failed August 1991 coup. Russia already had in place some immediate essentials for new democracy: representative government, political freedoms under law, and growing legitimacy with the public.[6]

After a year of independence, however, democracy came under threat. Once independence had removed a common Soviet adversary, a deadlock developed between the president and parliament—the Congress of People's Deputies and its smaller sitting chamber, the Supreme Soviet. The president then resorted to innumerable, often disregarded, decrees. Officials and regions either ignored or bent the decrees or made up their own.[7] Parliament opposed the president's shock-treatment reforms and refused, in December 1992, to extend his special decree powers for another year. It forced the replacement of the pro-reform prime minister, Yegor Gaidar, with the then conservative administrator from the gas and oil sector, Viktor Chernomyrdin. Federal relations featured a struggle between Moscow and the regional authorities over the division of resources and power.[8]

Russia was still making do with the patched-up Soviet-era Russian Republic Constitution of 1978, amended hundreds of times during and since *perestroika*. Its contradictory wording counterposed a strong president armed with veto powers, on the U.S. model, with a parliament that retained supreme power.[9] But the new Constitutional Court proved unable to adjudicate the battle of the branches. It sided with parliament by early 1993.[10] In March 1993, the frustrated president announced his intention to assume emergency powers to save the country. He narrowly survived an impeachment attempt and rallied to negotiate an agreement with parliament for an April 25 referendum.

To the surprise of many, including parliament no doubt, the president won a vote of confidence for his leadership and reform program. Victory in the April referendum was really a victory by default, if public opinion is any indicator.[11] The voter turnout in the April referendum failed to provide the required majority of 50 percent of all eligible voters for an early parliamentary election. Hence the majority vote had no legal force.[12]

Yeltsin's success in the referendum prompted him to convene a constitutional convention, an assemblage more subject to Yeltsin's influence and more likely to draft a strong-president document than was the Constitutional Commission of the parliament. But the draft favored by the president encountered opposition on issues of regions' powers in the federal system and on the balance of power between president and parliament.[13]

As the democratic deadlock continued, Parliament passed a huge deficit budget to fund credits to the ailing state industrial sector with the aim of preventing unemployment. A botched currency reform and ruble recall sprung on the public by the administration in July 1993 wiped out what remained of most people's hard-earned and inflation-ridden savings. Something had to give—but nothing did until, in the name of constitutional order, both sides turned to extraconstitutional solutions in September–October 1993.[14]

The Presidential Coup

After the August 1991 coup, President Yeltsin had shunned advice from several quarters—lest he appear a dictator—to dissolve the tainted, mainly pro-coup parliament and to call for new elections.[15] Two years later, at a less opportune time in light of his declining popularity, the president issued a decree on September 21, 1993, which ordered the disbanding of parliament and set elections for a new parliament under a new constitution yet to be voted on.[16]

The president cited the mandate of the people in the April referendum to justify his move. The resisters in parliament bunked inside the White House (parliamentary building). Their alliance included Communists, nationalists, and extremist paramilitary bands. The rebels elected a new "president," Yeltsin's erstwhile ally and former vice president, Aleksandr Rutskoi. Both sides claimed to be acting in defense of the constitution and rule of law.[17] On October 3, mobs broke through police cordons around the White House to join with its occupants. Then, urged on by Rutskoi and Khazbulatov, they stormed the Moscow mayor's office and made a failed and bloodily repulsed attack on the Ostankino TV station. By the next day, the president had persuaded General Pavel Grachev to send troops to shell, storm, and recapture the White House. For that deed, Yeltsin made Grachev minister of defense.

Former President Mikhail Gorbachev and other critics depicted President Yeltsin's attack on the White House as the authoritarian destruction of the democracy that Yeltsin had once saved.[18] Supporters of the move at the time included Sergei Kovalyov and the older part of the human rights movement. They believed then that President Yeltsin had little choice but to launch the attack: He was faced with armed rebellion conducted by extremists and the prospect of a civil war and the breakup of Russia.[19]

The president imposed a brief censorship control over the media in October, though not long enough to affect the elections. The elections to the 450-seat State Duma excluded the banned hard-line opposition groups associated with the armed assaults of October 3. A wide spectrum of contestants remained. The pro-Yeltsin Democratic Choice Party of Yego Gaidar, Sergei Kovalyov, and other democratic loyalists at the time competed with twelve other parties: democratic moderates and market reformers, pro-Communists, moderate-to-extreme nationalists. The administration and its Democratic Choice allies suffered a shocking defeat. Vladimir Zhirinovsky's populist demagoguery and the disunity and overconfidence of the pro-reform "democrats," as well as public disenchantment with democratic politics, put his Liberal Democratic Party at the top of the party lists for 225 seats, with 23 percent of the vote, in the State Duma voting returns; Russia's Democratic Choice garnered only 15 percent.[20] The upper chamber, the Federation Council, consisted of the heads of the legislative and executive organs of the sixty-eight regions and twenty-one autonomous republics.[21]

Ostensibly to further the constitutional protection of individual rights, the president appointed tireless human rights defender and former political prisoner Deputy Sergei Kovalyov to head the executive branch's Human Rights Commission. Under Kovalyov's direction, and while it functioned as a real monitor, the commission produced two reports in 1994 and 1996 that were critical of human rights in Russia. The president's office would have kept the 1994 report from public view had it not been for protests that secured its official publication.[22]

The 1994 report of the Human Rights Commission detailed serious human rights violations committed by government forces and police during the state of emergency in Moscow of October 3–18, 1993. The government had extensively violated obligations under international law, the constitution, and the Russian Federation Law on the State of Emergency, which had obligated the state to respect its citizens' civil rights. Shooting by troops and police accounted for all but six of seventy-two journalist casualties, and all seven deaths of journalists. Police and troops fired without cause on citizens not participating in the disorders, wounding forty-one and killing six. Police conducted mass roundups of 90,000 persons for alleged curfew and administrative violations. The police detained them under inhumane conditions in jails and sports stadiums; some were made to run police gauntlets, other detainees were beaten and tortured to extract information. The government shut down thirteen opposition newspapers associated with the parliamentary rebellion and fired their editors-in-chief.[23]

The New Authoritarianism (1993–95)

On December 12, 1993, the country voted in the referendum for the first new constitution since the much-amended 1978 document inherited from Brezhnev.[24] The constitution squeaked through the referendum amid indications that voting figures had been padded to reach the required participation of half the registered voters.[25]

The 1993 constitution carries over *perestroika*'s "new thinking" in the formulation of Article 2: "The individual and his rights and freedoms are the highest value. The recognition, observance and defense of the human rights and freedoms of the individual and the citizen are the obligation of the state."[26] The constitution retained the principle that Russia's international human rights obligations were the acting law of the land, along with the constitution itself. The human rights treaties had superior force in the event of conflict with the constitution.[27] The new constitution breaks with Soviet Communist precedent by recognizing ideological pluralism, barring "the imposition of any state or obligatory ideology"; the equality of all associations before the law, excluding subversive ones[28]; and the separation of powers into "independent legislative, executive, and judicial branches."[29] The constitution obligates the president to be "guarantor of the rights and freedoms of the human being and citizen."[30] But the president's vast powers of decree and appointment under the constitution, and its weak checks on executive power, open the way to bypassing the constitution itself.[31] Contributing to the lack of accountability, initially, was the political apathy engulfing a skeptical and economically preoccupied public.[32]

A central feature of Russia's limited democracy is the relative lack of executive accountability between elections. The 1993 constitution eliminates parliament's right to repeal presidential decrees and directives. It gives the president authority to dissolve the Duma and call for new elections within three months after two votes of no-confidence in his government by absolute majority of the Duma members, or after three rejections of his candidate for prime minister.[33] If the Duma rejects the president's request for a vote of confidence in his government, he may accept the government's resignation or dissolve the Duma and call for new elections.[34] The constitution established a more difficult impeachment procedure also involving the Supreme Court and the Constitutional Court, Duma indictment, and Federation Council trial and conviction both by two-thirds votes of chamber memberships. This procedure guards against a repetition of the president's near impeachment by vote of the Congress of People's Deputies in March 1993.[35]

After the democrats' setback in the 1993 elections, the president accepted the resignations of some leading democrats, including Finance Minister Boris Fyodorov and Deputy Prime Minister Yegor Gaidar. Moving further away from his democratic base, the president came around to accepting parliament's amnesty of the August 1991 coup plotters, the May 1, 1993, rioters, and the leaders of the 1993 White House armed actions.[36]

Vladimir Shumeiko, speaker of the Federation Council, with the president's blessing, and Ivan Rybkin, speaker of the new Duma and then a member of the opposition Agrarian bloc, both tended to avoid confrontation with the president. The constitutionally weakened separation of powers further eroded when the president invited Speakers Rybkin and Shumeiko to be permanent (voting) members of the Security Council after the start of the war in Chechnya.[37] The war originated in Russia's new authoritarianism—the ill-fated mixture of freedom, anarchy, and massive nonaccountable executive power.

The president's office, with its staff of about 1,800, tightened its secretive grip on the country as far as it could reach. The office occupied the premises of the old Communist Party Central Committee and came to resemble that body as the shadow government of Russia.[38] The Security Council, formally only an advisory body to the president, mirrored the old party Politburo, once the single most powerful body in the Soviet Union.[39] "The presidential decision-making mechanism," Sergei Kovalyov complained in his letter of resignation as human rights commissioner, "has become almost as secretive as it was in the days of the CPSU Central Committee Politburo."[40] The Security Council included the president and heads of the military, security, intelligence, and foreign-policy agencies. Security agencies operated without public or parliamentary supervision. This power center of the president hemmed in the chief manager of the economy, Prime Minister Viktor Chernomyrdin, who had replaced Yegor Gaidar in the December 1992.[41]

The new authoritarianism of 1993–95 nevertheless presented contrasts between an almost nonaccountable civilian-military-security-police oligarchy in the executive and a relatively free and critical society. Russia's government tolerated sharp criticism and legal opposition to a degree untypical of authoritarian governments such as those of the previous regimes in Chile and Argentina, the present ones in Nigeria, Singapore, Armenia, Azerbaijan, Belarus under Lukashenka, Kazakhstan, Tajikistan, Turkmenistan, Uzbekistan, and numerous other countries, even so-called democratic Turkey.[42]

In the administration, unaccountable groups of former Communist bureaucratic insiders acted according to the principle (to paraphrase *The*

Communist Manifesto): "bureaucrats unite, you have nothing to lose but your old ideology; you have a world of riches to win." Their new authoritarianism, with its facade of democratic freedoms, sheltered corruption and lured Moscow into another disastrous war, this time civil war.

Chechnya

The president's close advisers, David Remnick reports, urged him to use an "iron hand" so as "to impress an electorate grown weary of chaos and cynical about the prospects for a liberal society. That was the party of war which had urged Yeltsin to bombard Chechnya."[43] During the "parade of sovereignties," the separatist movement sweeping the USSR in 1991, President Yeltsin of the Russian Republic had said to the regions: "Take as much sovereignty as you can swallow."[44] Chechnya went further than the rest. Its new president, former Soviet Air Force general Dzhokhar Dudayev, declared the independence of Chechen-Ingushetia (Ingushetia split off after that) on November 1, 1991. When the interior minister and parliament balked at President Yeltsin's attempt to use Russian troops to end this independence in 1992, the president ordered the troops withdrawn.[45]

Beginning in June 1994, President Yeltsin escalated a covert military campaign against Chechnya's president. Yeltsin acted through Chechen opponents to Dudayev in the anti-Dudayev Nadterechny Region in the northern part of Chechnya. Ironically, Nadterechny Region had lived in peace with the rest of Chechnya since Dudayev's coup and takeover in 1991. In August 1994, ostensibly opposition forces, but actually Russian planes, bombed a telephone station and the railway line linking Moscow and Baku. By November, the Russian government concluded that its ally in Chechnya needed help. But the troops and tanks dispatched covertly by Moscow met with stunning defeat and destruction at the hands of pro-Dudayev guerrillas, while troops supplied by Moscow's Chechnya allies dispersed to loot kiosks.[46]

President Yeltsin and his entourage of aides and "power ministers" ignored these setbacks. The prowar group created around the president an atmosphere of false optimism and heightened enmity toward Chechnya. He was encouraged and egged on by false expectations of a wave of Russian support for the war and by disinformation from the Federal Counterintelligence Service (FSK) and its head at the time, Sergei Stepashin.[47] Told by Defense Minister Andrei Grachev that the war would be over in "two or three days," the president failed to heed many public warnings that an open Russian attack would unite Chechens behind Dudayev, whether he was a criminal or not, and would lead to a protracted and bloody war.[48]

The administration neither consulted parliament nor heeded urgent warnings by civilians and military officers[49] that an attack on Chechnya would unite its people around Dudayev and lead to one more bloody encounter in the bitter two-hundred-year history of Russian–Chechen relations, which included the deportations in 1994 and a loss of a third of the Chechen population. One of the military critics, cashiered Deputy Defense Minister Colonel General Boris Gromov, had led the Soviet forces out of Afghanistan under Gorbachev. Said Gromov, "I am against methods which are incompatible with constitutional order and democracy." [50]

Interpretations differ as to whether Chechnya marked a new turn away from democracy, as Yeltsin's former supporters, including Yelena Bonner and Duma Deputy Shabad, believed,[51] or whether it extended a long-standing authoritarianism and ambition for power. Either way, in Deputy Shabad's words, "Authoritarian rule is already here. . . . They do not consult the Duma and consult only with some influential people. This is the typical authoritarian way." Yeltsin governed "by Presidential decree and through his cabalistic Security Council—whose core is a small circle of men from the 'power' ministries of defense, police and intelligence." [52]

Russian troops crossed the Chechnya border toward Grozny on December 10, 1994, and attacked it the next day. Three days later, *Trud* published Human Rights Commissioner Kovalyov's statement of December 8 decrying the lack of public accountability in government—"We've had enough of Bolshevik politics." Kovalyov not only warned against war but suggested conducting a referendum on Chechnya's independence—an idea the new Security Council Secretary (for a while), General Lebed, was to voice again after his appointment in June 1996.[53]

Defense Minister Grachev blasted Kovalyov as "an enemy of Russia, a traitor." Grachev depicted Duma deputy Sergei Yushenkov, chair of the Duma's Defense Committee, as "a vile toad who slanders the army, which gave him education, which gave him rank . . . a vile little toad, who defends the scoundrels who want to destroy Russia." Had they lived under a full-fledged authoritarian regime, Yushenkov, Kovalyov, and his group of monitors would have disappeared or been imprisoned, as Kovalyov had been years before. Rather, the president's chief of staff, Sergei Filatov, called these denunciations "unacceptable." [54] The relative freedom of criticism in the media also would have been unthinkable under Communism. But embattled media freedom did not compensate for the lack of executive accountability.

Kovalyov and other monitors saw the president as bound by his oath to the constitution and its general provisions, cited earlier, to guarantee and protect human rights. The president was not released from this duty because of the criminality, repression, arms buildup, and separatism associated with the rule of Chechen president Dzhokhar Dudayev during three years of de facto independence. None of that justified what former ambassador to the Soviet Union Jack Matlock characterized as the "ghastly error" of the attack on Chechnya, which was bound to entail massive civilian casualties. "The Russian military was ill-prepared and ill-suited for such a mission. . . . Throwing raw recruits into a battle with determined guerrilla fighters, who freely mix with civilians and often fire from civilian locations, was the height of folly. It should have been predicted that Russian soldiers would panic and fire indiscriminately, and, if they failed to take their objectives, would call in air strikes to do the job for them, whether or not the President has authorized them." Least of all did the president's chief motive, "to improve his political position," justify the attack.[55]

Yelena Bonner wrote the president that the least of causes for which Russian soldiers were fighting in Chechnya was "defending the country's territorial integrity and restoring constitutional order." In fact, they were fighting to defend, above all, the interests of "the military-industrial complex . . . , the army brass . . . , and our domestic oil magnates [in controlling the oil pipelines through Chechnya from the Caspian]—the interests of those for whom blood is cheaper than oil. This mafia has taken charge of the state and you have been outwitted."[56] The war starkly revealed the power of the executive to apply unrestrained force against a rebellious region without regard to democratic consultation or human rights. The government pressed on with its violations of the human rights set out by the constitution[57] and by its international agreements—one of which Russia signed just six days before the attack and in which Russia undertook to ensure that, on missions of internal security, "the armed forces will adopt necessary measures to avoid harm to civilians and their property."[58] Unremitting bombing and shelling during the following weeks leveled much of Grozny—private homes, public buildings, hospitals, and orphanages alike. Civilian deaths reached many thousands in the Grozny region alone, many of them Russians caught there with no place to go.[59]

The wanton killing then spread to the villages, creating hundreds of thousands of refugees and displaced persons, while the troops tried to keep journalists from reporting the carnage.[60] Russian troops were described as using indiscriminate and disproportionate force, mistreating and torturing detainees in "filtration points," massacring unarmed villagers, looting, and exhibiting undisciplined behavior.[61]

The U.S. State Department's report on human rights gave substantial coverage to humanitarian violations on both sides in the Chechnya War, which produced as many as "tens of thousands of civilians killed and some 500,000 people displaced." But it concluded that "Violations committed by Russian military forces occurred on a much greater scale than those of the Chechen separatists."[62] By the time he had negotiated the August 1996 cease-fire, General Lebed reported that 80,000 people had been killed and about 240,000 wounded.[63]

Before Lebed's breakthrough toward peace, the government had long ignored tentative moves toward peace that suggested something short of Chechen independence, as well as appeals from its own human rights commissioner and numerous other human rights advocates at home and abroad.[64] Pressing on with its campaign, the Russian government had spoken of its "liberation" of Grozny and its determination to disarm "illegal armed groupings."[65]

In June 1995 Chechen separatists took hostages during a raid on the southern Russian town of Budyonnovsk in order to force a settlement. Russian forces broke the July 1995 cease-fire that followed. The second attempt at hostage taking in the Dagestan town of Kizlyar ended with the Russian's flattening the hostage takers' refuge, the Dagestan village of Pervomayskaya, while the rebels got away. Russian forces soon violated another cease-fire declared by the president on March 31, 1996. Nothing seemed to deter the administration and the military from their stubborn and bloody pursuit of elusive victory at any price. It cannot be said that the "international community" tried hard to prevent this.

The Struggle for Human Rights and Free Expression

Two days after the publication of Kovalyov's statement on December 8, 1994 (cited above), he and his group showed up in Chechnya; five days after that they issued their appeal to the appropriate bodies of the United Nations, the OSCE, and the Council of Europe to persuade the Russian government to stop the bombardment of Grozny and its suburbs.[66] Various NGOs poured out denunciations and vain appeals to stop the bloodshed and obey the constitution.[67] During the Russian attacks, one witness, Ludmilla Thorne of Freedom House (New York), wrote in *Moskovskie novosti*, "thousands of civilians have been killed, wounded or have lost their homes. Hundreds of Russian and Chechen soldiers have also perished, and violations of international human rights covenant have occurred. The most basic of these are articles 20 and 22 of the Russian Constitution, which state that every citizen has a right to life and to freedom and personal inviolability."[68]

As human rights organizations put aside differences arising over the storming of parliament in 1993, seventy-nine of them signed an agreement "On Working Together in Defense of Peace and Freedom, Against Bloodshed in Chechnya."[69] The NGOs seemed very much alone at the time. The administration seemed accountable to nobody. The government failed to back Sergei Kovalyov, its human rights commissioner, when in March 1995 the Duma stripped him of the temporary title of Human Rights Ombudsman, pending a law establishing that office. In August 1994 the president had attempted to suppress the report of the Human Rights Commission headed by Kovalyov. Neither domestic nor foreign human rights organizations managed to change the president's mind about the war: The administration simply ignored their well-documented complaints against the administration's egregious violations of Russia's humanitarian obligations under rules protecting noncombatants during internal wars, and under numerous human rights treaties and declarations to which Russia was a party.[70]

It would take the Communist gains in the parliamentary elections of 1995, the presidential elections of 1996, and the Chechens' recapture of Grozny, to rekindle the peace process.[71] Meanwhile, abandoning hope in the administration, Kovalyov resigned as chair of the shell of the Human Rights Commission in January 1996 and turned to monitoring as a private citizen.[72] Nonetheless, the expressive freedoms he had championed continued their precarious existence.

The democrats lacked experience in building democratic coalitions and institutions; their talent lay in the use of words and in opposing. Their great achievement, during and after *perestroika*, has been the drafting and implementation of laws on freedom of the press, association, and conscience.[73] Although the law on freedom of assembly requires the permission of local authorities for public meetings and demonstrations, they seem to take place freely enough. Moscow authorities briefly detained members of the NGO "Memorial" for demonstrating against the Chechen war in front of the building housing the presidential administration; they were later released. Academic freedom continues to expand in Russia, though not without resistance on the part of reactionary education officials who linger in government.[74] Cultural exchanges have flourished despite the unconcealed enmity of the security services to foreign research and human rights organizations operating in or concerned with Russia.[75]

Russian troops harassed and killed journalists covering the war in Chechnya. Nevertheless, the media managed to produce wide and graphic coverage of the war and the debates it provoked.[76] The media, observed Katrina van den Heuvel, a journalist critical of Russian democracy, ran "harrowing reports on the Russian military's ineptness and brutality, the futile valor of poorly trained soldiers . . . , and Yeltsin's political opportunism in launching the war." Opposition to the war extended beyond human rights advocates to include the Committee of Soldiers' Mothers, "simple, poor women who took out loans to travel hundreds of miles to Russian military headquarters in Mozdok, where they demanded information about their sons; most learned nothing, but several actually managed to bring the boys home." Van den Heuvel heard reports of "antiwar demonstrations in provincial cities across Russia; in Ekaterinburg and Volgograd, women sat on the rails and blocked military convoys."[77] The coverage of the war stirred opposition to it and diminished the president's already low popularity ratings.

When the government imposed censorship during the crisis of October 1993, the affected newspapers published their editions with blank spaces. On the more positive side, President Yeltsin formed a Judicial Chamber for Mass Media Disputes arising out of claims of abuses of freedom by government authorities and by the media. Its practice, in many scores of cases studied by Frances Foster, has revealed a concern to achieve both a new lawfulness and a new professional ethic in media work and administration, under conditions of "freedom with problems."[78]

In the course of their work, the media have nurtured a wide public belief that a free press is preferable to a controlled one.[79] But, seen from the inside, freedom suffers from restraints and from lack of an ethic of freedom. The subsidies and government printing facilities on which some media depend remain a potential source of pressure. So does governmental retaliation. Resistance to such pressure has persisted. The prosecutor general charged the director of the satirical TV puppet program "Kukly" with tax evasion, illegal currency dealings, and insulting officials after he had depicted Yeltsin and Chernomyrdin puppets as tramps trying to get by on the minimum wage. The government later dropped the transparently false charges.[80]

Now the old fear is gone, writes Aleksei Simonov, head of the Glasnost Defense Foundation, but pressures continue and new grounds for fear arise. With subsidies to privately owned media ended, state monitoring of truth in advertising can be a way to pressure the papers with threats of fines. The fear of censorship under a Communist president caused the pro-democratic media to slip with ease into self-censorship and to slant its amount of coverage and its analysis to favor President Yeltsin over Gennady Zyuganov, candidate of the Russian Communist Party.

The Federation government has tolerated de facto administrative censorship in the provinces. Local authorities have an array of means to stifle criticism and objective reporting. To silence a critical newspaper, they can arrange to have it harassed by local agencies from the fire brigade to the tax auditor, to block the paper's account while inspecting its bank, to remove it from registration and take over its offices, and even to have the local registration office substitute another paper for the offending one— a paper with the same name and masthead, but with a compliant editorial policy. The two papers *Lyuberetskaia pravda* and *Sovetskaia kalmykia* found themselves supplanted by counterfeit publications and the prospect of a protracted legal case.

A paper can be taken to court for libel or for offending the honor and dignity of some local official, and not just in the provinces. The editor of the widely read Moscow paper *Izvestiia* has fought up to twenty-three such cases at a time. More than half the 1,200 journalists in the provinces questioned by the Glasnost Defense Foundation in a survey conducted at the end of 1994 stated that they had been the object of pressure or threats from the authorities or various political, commercial, and criminal groups.[81]

Outside the Law

During the two years studied by the Glasnost Defense Foundation, more than ten journalists were killed "either to prevent publication of material they had collected or in revenge for what they had already published." Threats against journalists and their families have come both from criminal groups and from corrupt law-enforcement agencies under the Ministry of the Interior. "Regional administrations and local militias [police] are frequently connected with suspect organizations and their treatment of journalists (especially those who write on corruption and irregular behavior by the militia) is essentially nothing short of criminal. The Glasnost Defense Fund has documented cases in many places including Vladivostok, Mordovia, Volgograd, Vologda and Voronezh."[82] Unresolved suspicions surround the killing of the son of Sergei Grigoriants, head of the Glasnost Foundation, by a hit-and-run driver in January 1996, and a beating attack on Grigoriants himself in March.[83]

Suspicions alighted on high-ranking army and security officers in the murder of Dmitry Kholodov, a twenty-seven-year-old investigative reporter with a reputation for fearlessness, on October 17, 1994. Kholodov had been in the process of exposing corruption among top army officers. He had been slated to testify in the Duma on corruption in the Russian armed forces before their final departure from East Germany. Kholodov was killed by a bomb in a briefcase he picked up after a tip-off by a security agent acquaintance who told Kholodov the case contained documents on military corruption. The mourning editors of Kholodov's newspaper, *Moskovskii komsomolets*, blamed the killing on the military and secret services. When then Minister of Defense Pavel Grachev tried to implicate organized crime, the bosses of several major crime syndicates telephoned the newspaper, disclaiming any involvement in Kholodov's killing. The government dismissed General Matvei Burlakov, former commandant in East Germany, but otherwise covered up any evidence of corruption. Meanwhile, threats and beatings involving investigative journalists continued.[84]

Yelena Bonner, once a Yeltsin supporter, saw a "prologue to the war" in the Kholodov murder and in the compliments the president paid Defense Minister Grachev immediately after the murder.[85] An occasion for renewed mourning came with the murder of the popular television personality Vladislav Listyev, the new executive director of Ostankino TV (ORTS). He was shot to death on March 1, 1995, by unknown assailants just after he had decided to eradicate the lucrative and corrupt practice of selling commercial TV time.[86] Oleg Poptsov, the independent-minded former director of the state ORT television station, said that he was dismissed not so much for his objectivity in broadcasting policy as for standing in the way of profits by opposing the move to put the ORT channel into partly private ownership.[87]

Organized crime and the corrupt officials who are in league with them

threaten Russia's democratic future and human rights by inhibiting investment, threatening reporters and lawmakers, draining off resources, and
discrediting democracy in the eyes of the public.[88] Business people and
bankers seem particularly vulnerable to extortion and murder. In one four-
year period, organized crime made ninety attempts on the lives of bankers
and their bodyguards alone, resulting in forty-seven deaths and many crippling injuries; virtually all of the crimes remain unsolved. Mobsters killed
seventeen people in Moscow in five days.[89]

Corruption extends into the government, parliament, and police to the
point where the gangs have had little to fear from law enforcement officials, whom they pay off.[90] Duma deputies have had shadowy and fatal
connections with organized crime. During 1994–95, mysterious assassins
killed four Duma deputies, contract style. Gangsters killed Deputy Sergei
Skorochkin in early 1995, apparently in revenge for his killing an organized
crime leader in 1994. In ten months, three Duma deputies with business
dealings were killed by mysterious assassins.[91]

Government inaction suggests complicity. Deputy Vitaly Savitsky, a
leader of the Christian Democratic Union, was expected to win a Duma
seat in the 1995 elections. He died eight days before the elections. A respected and prominent member of the Duma, Savitsky served as vice-chair
of the Committee on Social and Religious Organizations. Among his controversial actions had been his support for the repeal of a law that guaranteed legal immunity for Duma members. Savitsky died in a car borrowed,
with driver, through the good offices of then mayor of St. Petersburg,
Anatoly Sobchak, after Savitsky's car had broken down. Savitsky's driver
had twenty years' experience. He suddenly and inexplicably swerved left,
off his route, and into oncoming traffic, causing a collision in which Savitsky suffered massive wounds. Savitsky then lay unattended on the street
while the driver was rushed to a military hospital with relatively minor injuries; the driver was kept isolated and then later reported to have died
from "medical complications."[92]

Savitsky's "accident" calls to mind the mysterious traffic deaths of the
Stalin era and adds to a growing record of suspicious behavior by police
and prosecutorial and security agencies, who have exhibited a helpless in-
ability to solve any of the scores of murders of bankers and business people.
Responses to organized crime also pose a threat to human rights—be they
in the form of procedural shortcomings in arresting and processing suspects[93] or in the proliferation of armed private groups, including security
guards, in what the President's Commission has dubbed a "militarization
of society."[94]

Part of the nonaccountability in Russia's new authoritarianism comes
from the anarchic aspects of rule in Russia. The center has limited control over its own officials, organized crime, and regional governments. The
president authorized local governors to abolish the old local soviets after

the events of October 1993. Governors complied, setting up regional and city dumas (councils). But poor turnouts for local elections, and the lack of local constitutional frameworks for them, have undermined the dumas' legitimacy and effectiveness. Local governors tend to become authoritarian rulers of their regions.[95] The heads of regions, republics, and cities are ostensibly answerable to Moscow, but local officials are potentates in their own smaller domains, and they cut their own deals with local criminals. This reality may have serious consequences for rights to due process and freedom of expression and information.[96] "In towns dominated by a single industrial enterprise, the leaders of that enterprise have sufficient power to suppress investigative reporting and discussion of embarrassing topics, such as environmental pollution or privatization schemes benefiting management."[97]

Religion, Freedom, and Identity

Freedom of religion contributes to democratic pluralism—diversity within unity. As part of its consistent affirmation of ideological and organizational diversity, the Russian Constitution proclaims Russia to be a secular state in which "religious associations shall be separate from the state and shall be equal before the law," while a guarantee of freedom of conscience and religion entails "the right to profess individually or collectively any religion or not to profess any religion, and freely to choose, possess, and disseminate religious and other convictions and act in accordance with them." Religious life flourished, especially after the enactment of the December 1990 law that put all religions on an equal footing and provided for simple registration of religious groups. Churches and mosques and synagogues are being returned to their congregations after prolonged negotiations. Christian, Jewish, and Muslim community life is reviving. Religion helps satisfy a need for identity, and for spiritual faith.[98]

The Russian Orthodox Church retains a preeminent position. Its hierarchy tends to discourage parish outreach and social activism within the church. Its traditional closeness with the Russian state was symbolized by the participation of Patriarch Aleksy II in the president's inauguration.[99] Patriarch Aleksy's collaboration with the government appears to go back for decades, in his efforts, perhaps, to protect the church from further destruction under the Communists: The dissident priest Fr. Gleb Yakunin cites evidence that the Patriarch had been KGB agent "Drozdov," active within the church for thirty years as he moved up the hierarchy.[100]

The Orthodox Church is at once a confessional community, a pillar of statehood, and an arena for a liberal minority's struggle to make the church more inclusive in outlook and more socially active in the parishes. It has continued in its traditional role, expressing the Russian ethnic national identity especially in the times of insecurity following the breakup of the USSR and loss of Soviet identity.[101] Russians have been reclaiming not only the old place-names but also the Orthodox Church and its holidays. In 1991 the country officially celebrated Orthodox Christmas for the first time since the Bolshevik takeover in 1917. Churches that Stalin blew up have been rebuilt with funds from private and church sources.

People who equate identity with religion, however, may tend to increase their sense of distinctiveness from other ethnic groups. "The open incorporation of Orthodoxy into the Russian national identity," says Roman Szporluk, "not only further de-Sovietizes Russia, but further separates the Russians from other Soviet peoples who have their own cultural and religious legacies."[102] The merging of ethnic Russian identity and Orthodoxy has caused non-Orthodox Christians to wonder about the standing of their churches and led Russia's neighbors to wonder about a possible new Russian empire.[103]

A liberal minority of rights-oriented priests and lay persons among Russian Orthodox believers are working together toward greater parish outreach, more dialogue with other religions including Judaism, and the condemnation of anti-Semitism (see Chapter 10).

Draft legislation, opposed by the president, crops up regularly in the Duma, which would regulate and limit proselytizing by foreign "nonhistorical" religious groups such as the Mormons and Hare Krishna groups. Foreign religions have experienced restrictions on proselytizing at the local level. The constitutional right to conscientious objection remains unrealized in practice, beyond a scattered recognition in courts here and there.[104] Despite these infringments on constitutional freedoms, one may expect religious organizations to take an increasing social and political part in Russian life, both in the upholding and enforcement of human rights and in the formation of a civil society.

The People's Choice

The Chechnya war did not undermine democracy; rather, it resulted from democracy's decline. Yet the war also contributed to the beginning of a new democratic accountability. Several factors working together played a part in this turn of events, not least of which was the unpopularity of the war[105] and the growing antiwar activism of the Mothers of Russian Soldiers and of other groups.[106] This stirring replaced the public apathy of 1992–94.[107] Public opinion polls showed strong majorities in favor of peace talks, even though a majority of the Duma deputies declined to vote against the war.[108] Former President Gorbachev noted "the alienation between ruling regime and people, which has come to a head in the Chechen gamble, in this senseless, ruthless and devastating war that has trampled on the law, human rights and public opinion." Deteriorating social conditions for the majority of people augmented this alienation.[109] The Yeltsin administration's lies about the purported victorious and humanitarian campaigns in Chechnya also deepened the public's distrust of it.[110] The public and some regional heads shared the skepticism of highly placed critics not only about the administration's veracity, but also about its political motivations for launching the war when it did.[111]

Once President Yeltsin chose to hold the elections, against the advice of close aides, the war's unpopularity and his low poll ratings began to affect policy.[112] The president had to begin to respond to majority opinion. The second free Duma elections on December 17, 1995, confirmed the finding of "the fragmentation of democratic reform parties in Parliament and around Yeltsin, and the increasing influence of nationalist, agrarian and neo-Communist parties."[113] Yet the elections also marked a procedural step forward toward democracy, a step toward greater accountability.[114]

The Central Election Commission refused to register several parties—including former vice president and current adversary Aleksandr Rutskoi's "Derzhava" party and Grigory Yavlinsky's Yabloko party—on deadline technicalities, for the Duma elections. But the Supreme Court restored them to the ballot, amid some government cries of "foul." Voters calmly pored over the ballot, with its forty-three listed parties, in a relatively high turnout (65 percent compared with 38 percent in the U.S. congressional elections of 1994 and 49 percent in the U.S. presidential election of 1996). There was no noticeable intimidation by the militia, despite some concern about possible Chechen terrorism. Foreign observers gave the elections a passing grade as free and fair. In one sour note on camera, a militiaman in central Moscow told a reporter, "Yes, we are ordered to keep watch and keep the street clear of parked cars near the polling place and to 'check documents of persons with a Caucasus complexion.'" TV coverage of the election and incoming results seemed almost continuous on both ORT and NTV (independent television), as if indeed the national elections meant something.

Neither the cold winter weather nor the complexities of the ballots (in addition to the 43-party list ballot were the ballot for one of the 250 candidates elected from single-member constituencies and the ballot for provincial governor) prevented a high turnout, contrary to the expectations of many. Some marked their ballots on tables and shelves rather than in the too few curtained voting booths, but this did not affect the foreign observers' approval of the elections as fair and free—fair, that is, if one ignores attempts of the pro-Yeltsin "Our Home Is Russia" party to take advantage of an inside track on state television.

On party list voting for 225 of 450 seats, the Communist Party of the Russian Federation topped the balloting with 22.7 percent. An additional fifty-eight single-member constituency seats gave the CPRF a commanding 158 seats. Vladimir Zhirinovsky's Liberal Democratic Party got 11.4 percent and fifty-one seats; Chernomyrdin's group, Our Home Is Russia, received 10.3 percent and fifty-five seats in all; and Yabloko, the democratic reformist party led by Grigory Yavlinsky, received 6.9 percent and forty-five seats. The other thirty-nine parties, which failed to get the minimum 5 percent, needed to share in the party-list seats. Almost half the voters, 49.8 percent, voted for party lists that put no one in parliament. Of these, Women of Russia got the next highest vote: 4.7 percent and 3 seats.[115]

The war continued on its cruel course between the parliamentary and presidential elections. Russian troops barred humanitarian agencies such as the Red Cross from entering bombed villages to evacuate the wounded or even to distribute water. Security Service Chief General Mikhail Barsukov characterized the Chechen as capable of being "only a murderer, or at least a robber, or at least a thief."[116] The United States and other liberal democracies all but ignored Chechnya and continued to treat Yeltsin as though his ability to control inflation and lower deficits was all that counted, as though the war had caused no setbacks, and as though he meant the electoral ploys of the cease-fires of March 31 and May 27, 1996, to be taken seriously.

The Russian government seemed as unaccountable abroad for its actions in Chechnya as it was at home.[117] Yet they are events which, the Russian Human Rights Commission finds, "in the magnitude and severity of the human rights violations, in the sufferings of hundreds of thousands of Russian citizens, and in the brutalities perpetrated against the civilian population . . . are unparalleled since the era of mass political repressions in the USSR."[118] Human Rights Watch/Helsinki deplored the acceptance of Russia into full membership in the Council of Europe in February 1996 and criticized the reluctance of the international community "to maintain pressure on the Russian government to end the horrendous conduct of its troops and to hold abusive forces accountable . . . for their obligations under international humanitarian law." It also deplored the March 1996 IMF three-year loan to Russia of $10.2 billion, "without there being any attempt by member states to link such financial support to efforts to end Russian forces abusive conduct in the war in Chechnya."[119]

The 1995 election results had pushed Yeltsin to make at least a show of seeking peace, but Russian commanders quickly violated the cease-fire announced by the president on March 31. As presidential elections approached, the president rejected the advice of his close aide and head of security, General Aleksandr Korzhakov, and other pessimists to postpone elections.[120] Rather, Yeltsin recruited a new re-election team headed by his former chief privatizer, Anatoly Chubais, and mounted a vigorous, sophisticated, and well-funded campaign across the country. The president's Communist adversaries and others claim that his control of the state media and his influence with liberal independent media unfairly swung the elections in Yeltsin's favor. It could be argued that political pork played a part: Yeltsin owes his electoral success to such acts of business-subsidized government largesse as doubling pensions, promising to pay back wages to workers in state enterprises, and even gifts, such as cars and cash.[121]

In his quest to regain enough popularity to beat his chief rival, Gennady Zyuganov of the Communist Party of the Russian Federation, the president on May 27 concluded a surprise cease-fire agreement. He signed it in the Kremlin, together with Chechen President Zelimkhan Yandarbiyev, successor to Dzhokhar Dudayev, who had been killed, reportedly, in a missile attack on April 22.

The president's campaign staff and supporters also bankrolled the campaign of presidential hopeful General Alexandr I. Lebed. Lebed was a political amateur, Afghan war veteran, and former commander of the Russian 14th Army when it assisted separatist Slavs in the Transdniestrian region of Moldova. He had begun an outspoken opposition to the Chechnya war. In the first-round voting on June 16, the president won a narrow lead, with 35.1 percent, and 32 percent went to his nearest rival, Zyuganov. Lebed did very well, coming in third, with 14.7 percent of the vote from 11 million voters, far ahead of Yabloko's liberal economist, Grigory Yavlinsky, who received 7.4 percent, and Zhirinovsky, who captured only 5.84 percent. Two percent of the vote went to all the other candidates put together, including only 0.51 percent for Gorbachev. Only 1.54 percent voted against all candidates. The high turnout of 69.7 percent of registered voters exceeded 1993 levels by almost 40 percent and topped the 1995 level of about 65 percent.[122]

To ensure a victory after the first round, the president decreed that voting day be shifted from Sunday, July 7, to Wednesday, July 3, declaring it a holiday. In this way he aimed to collect the vote of his potential supporters who otherwise would be off to their dachas (summer cottages) and garden plots for the weekend. The president also boosted his electoral campaign by appointing General Lebed on June 18 to be the new secretary of the powerful Security Council, replacing Oleg Lobov.[123] The campaign efforts paid off with a wide victory margin for President Yeltsin—53.82 percent with 40,208,384 of the votes, to 40.3 percent for Gennady Zyuganov with 30,113,306 votes, and 4.83 percent voting against both candidates, in a high turnout of 68.89 percent.[124] About 70 percent of Lebed's voters and 80 percent of Yavlinsky's—12.2 million people—went over to Yeltsin, as those leaders had urged.[125] Yeltsin's support lay in the cities rather than the villages, among younger people rather than those over forty, and among the more educated of the electorate, those with college and secondary (high) school educations. Yeltsin's support among the young increased after he turned up on the video screen dancing at a rock concert in Volgograd.[126]

Democracy Restored?

Among the leading experts, Boris Kagarlitsky, a politically active Moscow sociologist, saw in the 1996 elections "no winners" and the same "passive majority who in 1937 had watched the repressions with indifference." For a hardly less pessimistic Peter Reddaway, the 1996 elections were a chance to reject the Communists in "a choice between two unattractive candidates."[127] At the other extreme, the *Washington Post* praised the "remarkable triumph of the Russian people" who, "despite all their suffering and shrugging off all predictions to the contrary . . . made history by advancing democracy in their country and by rejecting once and for all the false promises of the Communists."[128]

With the guarded optimism I share, Kennan Institute director Blair Ruble noted that, "with each election, Russian democracy's roots grow that much farther into the ground," though the situation in Russia had become more dangerous because of the president's disabilities, conflicts in his entourage, and "a disaffected forty percent of the electorate."[129] The seasoned election observer Michael Ochs concluded that "choosing government by ballot . . . appears to have become a part of Russian culture," while noting the unfairness of the government's access to state electronic media and its flouting of campaign finance rules, as well as authoritarian trends and human rights violations under Yeltsin.[130] Also close to my view is a British team's comment that the free election leaves democracy as "competitive but not consolidated," lacking the rule of law and executive accountability.[131]

The elections put Alexandr Lebed on the public scene. Yeltsin's isolation in hunting lodges and behind Kremlin walls would be harder as long as this gadfly was politicking. General Lebed's pushy peacemaking and tactless blasts against the military and civilian supporters of the war and his rivals in government annoyed many in high places and brought on his dismissal from office on October 17, 1996. But his persistence and outspokenness kept the peace process going against all odds, and seemed to shake up the administration. After the 1996 elections, Yeltsin dismissed leaders of his "war party" inner circle: Pavel Grachev (June 17), Deputy Prime Minister and Chief of Staff Oleg Soskovets (June 20), head of the Federal Security Service Mikhail Barsukov, and the head of Presidential Security Aleksandr Korzhakov, "in all probability, the second most powerful man in the country," according to Moscow political gossip.[132] On July 15, the president appointed Anatoly Chubais to replace Nikolai Yegorov as his chief of staff.[133]

A struggle began for the integrity and reform of the armed forces. General Lev Rokhlin, chair of the Duma's Defense Committee, condemned corruption and named names in high military places. The president soon appointed General Igor Rodionov, friend of General Lebed and the respected head of the General Staff Academy, to replace the discredited Pavel

Grachev as Minister of Defense—for how long remained to be seen.[134] If carried out, goals of reform in government and the military such as Lebed voiced could, in one Russian view, end the dangerous slide of the military into praetorian political involvement as an independent force. It could restore firm civilian control over the military and help bring the rule of law into civilian governance.[135]

The peace process took a step backward when Russian commanders in Chechnya began a violation of the May 27 cease-fire and follow-up agreement of June 10, with massive attacks on Chechen villages and strongholds beginning on July 7, four days after Yeltsin's electoral victory.[136] The rebels responded by attacking Grozny on August 6, 1996. Within two days Moscow's puppet Chechen leader, Doku Zavgayev, fled back to Moscow. The separatists were in control of Grozny and had raised the number of Russian troop fatalities in Chechnya by 600, to 3,826 dead, by the time of the inauguration of a very shaky Yeltsin on August 9. The leader of the Chechen raid on Grozny, Shamil Basayev, stated, "For 300 years they have killed us, and tried to erase us as a nation. To me that is the great humiliation for Russia. They have hungry miners they should be feeding." Basayev continued, "Why are they spending all their money destroying Chechnya?"[137] When General Lebed turned against the war and also asked that question publicly, peace became a possibility. As the debacle unfolded in Grozny, the president named General Lebed his special envoy to Chechnya, replacing the pro-war envoy Oleg Lobov. Lebed met with Chechen chief of staff and future president of the Chechen republic Aslan Maskhadov outside Grozny on August 11 and 14. Back from his August 11 visit, Lebed, horrified, exposed the Russian troops as "hungry, lice-ridden, and underclothed weaklings" who were in worse condition than the Russian partisans who had fought the Germans in World War II.[138] On August 14, Yeltsin gave Lebed sweeping powers to resolve the Chechen conflict and dissolved the Commission on the Crisis in Chechnya headed by Prime Minister Chernomyrdin.[139]

Despite the opposition of ground commanders, whose orders to counterattack Lebed canceled on the spot, and despite the president's aloofness and unwillingness to meet with Lebed, Lebed negotiated a cease-fire agreement with Maskhadov, a former Soviet colonel of artillery, in the town of Novye Atagi on August 22; both sides then began withdrawing fighters from Grozny. On August 31 Lebed signed a preliminary peace accord with the Chechen at Khasavyurt, Dagestan. Under the accord, Russian troops would leave Chechnya, but joint patrols would be left to keep order during the disengagement, and the Chechens were to disarm (which they did not).

Reflecting on Lebed's large role in ending the Chechnya bloodshed, one is reminded of an interview that academician Dmitry Likhachev gave in the fall of 1995: "A collective submits to force much more easily than an individual. An individual can be more decisive and independent. A general can become a national hero, but a parliament cannot."[140] Likhachev may not be always correct in this, but as the Chechnya war ground into its twenty-first month, only a war hero of unquestioned reputation and bravery had a chance to become a Russian national hero by turning war into nonwar, where the only sanctioned combat would be a soccer match between Russian and Chechen troops.

The Khasavyurt agreement raised questions that only time and politics in Russia and within Chechnya could answer. The basic question was how to reconcile the Russian political elite's insistence on Russian territorial integrity (an insistence not shared by the war and generally weary public) with the Chechen rebels' insistence on independence. The agreement built in a delay on resolving this issue by providing for a referendum to be held within five years, by late 2001—that is, after the next scheduled Russian parliamentary and presidential elections. After the president's dismissal of General Lebed from the government, Ivan Rybkin, Lebed's replacement as secretary of the Security Council and envoy to Chechnya, vowed and acted to back up the Khasavyurt accord. The president, recovering from his November 5 heart bypass operation, backed the peace by ordering the withdrawal from Chechnya of the remaining two brigades of about six thousand Russian troops.

The stability and quality of Russian democracy would depend on whether the peace process could reconcile Moscow's insistence on Russia's territorial integrity with the peace-plan provision for a referendum on Chechnya's future by December 31, 2001. Peace might fall apart over the makeup of the provisional government of Chechnya, or over Chechen demands for restitution and aid in reconstruction, or over the missing persons and prisoners held on both sides, or over questions of punishing torturers and war criminals guilty of various crimes against noncombatants in Chechnya; or it might depend on whether such common interests as the peace itself and the operation of the oil pipeline through Chechnya would help the agreement. Would the OSCE do more to back up the initiatives for peace, aid, and human rights of its Assistance Group in Chechnya?[141] Would the "international community" in any guise do more to assist and encourage the politically, socially, and strategically vital peace process?

Outside of Chechnya, Russian democracy proved sufficiently stable to deal constitutionally with President Yeltsin's incapacitation after the July 1996 elections, and to allow openness of information during and after his quintuple heart bypass operation by a team of Russian surgeons aided by U.S. and German specialists.

Conclusions

The deadlock of democracy in 1992–93 and the resulting new authoritarianism of 1993–95, with its sequel in the disastrous war in Chechnya, lent credence to deep pessimism, but the progress in freedom of expression and of religion gave reason for some optimism. Freedom of expression, however, came under threat from problems inherent in the media, abuses on the part of local authorities, and retaliatory violence by targets of media investigation. Religious life, incomparably freer than it had been up to 1988, showed signs of tension between "historic" religions and various sects, some long established in Russia, which opponents of "foreign" influences would like to see curbed.

A combination of circumstances, choices, and personalities brought Russia into a new phase of its struggle for human rights and democracy in the later 1990s. The two major circumstances were the Chechnya war catastrophe and the elections of 1995–96. One key event Russians chose to take the elections seriously, and without violence and intimidation outside of Chechnya. Yeltsin's choice to go ahead with elections, to ally himself with General Lebed, and to campaign vigorously with all—not always quite legal—media and financial stops pulled out, helped turn opinion around. Other crucial choices of the president included those to begin peace negotiations during the election campaign, to appoint Lebed to the leading security post in his administration, and to replace several of the "war party." Also key were Yeltsin's decision to make Lebed the special envoy to Chechnya, Russian field commander General Tikhomirov's decision to obey the cease-fire, and the Chechen leaders' decision to accept it.

General Lebed's personality made a difference, as did President Yeltsin's; for all his shortcomings as a democrat, Yeltsin did on occasion rise above the lingering imperialism and anxiety over status that beset his aides and got on with the peace. The circumstances, choices, and personalities cited here have brought a small degree of executive openness and accountability, and a more candid face-off between friends and foes of change in the military and civilian ranks. Just when complete pessimism about Russia seemed to be justified, the elections and peacemaking recounted here showed signs of gains in the struggle for human rights and democracy. The events of the 1990s support the premise voiced, sincerely or not, by President Yeltsin that "Authority in Russia will only be effective when it becomes open, understandable, and predictable."

Chapter 9
Russia: The Context of Freedom

> The costs and miscalculations of economic reform hurt the people materially and spiritually. The state's huge arrears in wage payments to blue- and white-collar workers, its nonfulfillment of other obligations to citizens, cause people to feel a justified discontent. Especially alarming is the violation of the constitutional principles and basic rights of citizens in the course of privatizing state property. Privatization often turns into theft of public property created by the toil of many generations.
>
> —Constitutional Court of the Russian Federation[1]

In his letter of resignation, Human Rights Commissioner Sergei Kovalyov told President Yeltsin, "Beginning at least late in 1993, you have consistently chosen not those decisions that would have strengthened the force of law in a democratic society, but those that revived the blind and inhuman might of the state machine which is above rights, the law, and individuals."[2] Kovalyov's criticism centered particularly on the president's complicity in violations of constitutionally proclaimed human rights: civil rights and due process of law; economic, social, and cultural rights; and rights of minorities to equality and self-determination within the Federation. These civil and economic-social rights provide the basic context for democratic rights and freedoms; to the extent that they remained endangered, so will Russia's democratic freedoms.

Endangered Civil Rights

Some nonbinding constitutions are merely facades for authoritarian rule through loopholes that bestow emergency powers, as occurred in the lapsed democracies of the "national security states" of Latin America up to the 1980s. Nonbinding, too, have been the programmatic or "ideological" constitutions of Communist countries.[3] The constitution began to become binding in the USSR when Mikhail Gorbachev linked significant governmental changes with changes in the constitution through duly enacted amendments.[4] But the constitution remained considerably detached from day-to-day politics, owing to the lack of legality in administration and law enforcement and to the weakness of judicial review.

The human rights provisions of the 1993 Russian Constitution were drawn up in reaction to the totalitarian past of "holy writ" law. For the first time, the constitution now forbids the imposition of a single ideology. It recognizes ideological and political pluralism in a multiparty system where all social organizations are equal before the law, and one may not be compelled to join any of them.[5] The constitution also bars the compulsory declaration of one's nationality (ethnicity) or opinion and beliefs, and forbids censorship.

New rights added to the constitution as a result of *perestroika* include cultural freedom; freedom of conscience and religious instruction; freedom of information (except for hate speech and state secrets); unhampered and equal access to public office; rights to protection against deprivation of citizenship and against impeding the choice of citizenship; the banning of exile from the country; the right to private property; the right to life; an end to the secrecy of normative acts; freedom of movement within the country and to enter and leave it; and freedom of domicile.[6] Individual rights may be limited for reasons of national security, public morality, or the rights of other citizens; but this may be done only by federal law, not by decrees or directives of the president.[7]

The Chechnya war and administrative practices in general reveal big gaps in such guarantees. The constitution provides for parliamentary supervision of rights and freedoms and the appointment of a parliamentary ombudsman for human rights.[8] However, parliament's dismissal of Sergei Kovalyov, the first holder of that post, in March 1995, left the efficacy of any future ombudsman in doubt.

In areas signifying some mixed gains for rights, the government in 1993 decriminalized consenting homosexual acts between men for the first time since Stalin made them a crime in 1934.[9] Gay and lesbian people were beginning to "come out." But the hazards of homophobic discrimination and harassment continued. Lesbianism has never been a crime. Still, some politically active lesbians might have found themselves committed to psychiatric hospitals against their will upon the request of relatives or acquaintances. Aside from their social impact, these anti-gay actions and social biases tended to delay democratic advocacy of gay rights in the public arena under the freedoms of expression and association.[10]

Russia retained the death penalty, as have most post-Communist states, the United States, South Africa, and many less developed countries. The government has eliminated the death penalty for economic crimes except counterfeiting, decriminalized a variety of former economic crimes associated with entrepreneurial activity, and left the death penalty in force for espionage, treason, and eleven violent crimes.[11] Another partial reform introduced a right of habeas corpus, the requirement for court approval of confinement, which existed in the previous constitution as amended in April 1992.[12] As of the mid-1990s, the courts were ordering releases of suspects in a little under one-fifth of the complaints, or about 3 percent of all arrests.[13] Courts here and there began to be guided by the constitution rather than by local bosses. In a few recorded cases, they affirmed the illegality of the outlawed and persistent residence permit system and found in favor of conscientious objectors to military service.[14]

Carried over from 1991–92 amendments was the right to jury trial "in cases provided for by federal law"[15] and in capital cases.[16] The right to trial by jury in felony cases first came to Russia with the judicial reforms of 1864. The Bolsheviks abolished jury trials in 1917. The Russian courts held their first jury trials after three-quarters of a century in late 1993, following a presidential decree of September 22, 1992, which ordered their experimental introduction. Where jury trials existed, they increased defendants' chances of realizing their human right to impartial justice, as a counterpoise to the powerful Procuracy (prosecutor's office). But funding setbacks and opposition in central and local government confined this reform to only nine regions, as of 1996. Every third defendant in those regions applied for a jury trial; there were 376 jury trials in 1995. Acquittal rates were about 20 percent, compared with 1 percent in nonjury trials. Obviously, jury trials reduced a defendant's chance of being deprived of life or freedom after trial by faulty justice. Lags persisted in organizing jurors' support services and stipends and in the training of judges. All in all, jury reform pales when compared with its pre-revolutionary forerunner.[17]

The case of Vil Mirzayanov blended old and new in criminal justice. In the old way, the Russian Procuracy brought charges of revealing state secrets against chemical engineer Vil Mirzayanov after he published an article stating that Russia continued to manufacture banned chemical weapons, and that officials in charge of this toxin making were diverting research funds into acquiring Mercedes cars and other goods. Mirzayanov was arrested in October 1992. In November he obtained his release from prison under the above-mentioned new procedure for court appeal of one's confinement. Following an investigation that lasted well over a year, the acting procurator general dropped charges in March 1994.[18] Mirzayanov successfully sued the Ministry of Defense (his former employer) and the Procuracy for damages. He won an award of 30 million rubles ($15,000). The defense ministry countersued, but dropped the suit in March 1995. This might have been the first time a court recognized an individual's right to compensation for the state's arbitrary action.[19] Meanwhile, however, Mirzoyanov had suffered owing to the grave lapses both in the application of the state secrecy laws and due process.

The general picture of justice was less favorable.[20] Another whistleblower, a retired naval captain, Aleksandr Nikitin, was arrested in 1996 and charged with treason for passing information about serious radioactive contamination by the Russian Northern Fleet to the Norwegian environmental organization Bellona. Nikitin's arrest and prosecution marked another survival of the government's use of secrecy laws and coercion to cover up mistakes, such as dangerously slipshod environmental protection.[21]

The 1996 report of the President's Human Rights Commission called secrecy one of "the critical problems in Russia."[22] In a disturbing example, the Ministry of Atomic Industry classified information about the amount of atomic wastes stored underground. It marked as "secret" annual inspection reports on the country's nuclear and radiation safety. The commission also gave ample evidence of the unlawful withholding of information from the media. Access to many government archives is closed or disappearing. The commission sees this as "a step toward a new alienation of society from its history."[23] There was essentially no effective legislative oversight of the powerful police and security agencies of surveillance and control.[24] Law enforcers and security agents ignored with impunity the rights to privacy constitutionally protected by the requirement of a court order to search homes and premises, tap phones, and open mail.[25]

Russia's courts remained overloaded, underequipped, and desperately short of funds. The number of judges remained at about 15,000 while caseloads grew by 16 percent a year, to 1,000,000 criminal cases in 1994–95. By then, civil cases (under family, tort, property, and related law) had soared to 2.5 million.[26] Russian authorities, including the president and human rights monitors, agreed that comprehensive reform projects were blocked by lack of resources and by the opposition of officials in the police, court administration, and Procuracy.[27] Trial benches of one professional and three lay judges, or a professional judge, remained susceptible to political pressure.[28]

The report of the Russian Human Rights Commission singled out for criticism President Yeltsin's Decree 1226 of June 14, 1994, "On Urgent Measures to Protect the Population against Gangsterism and Other Manifestations of Organized Crime." It was condemned in various other human rights reports as well. The decree opened to arbitrary police searches and seizures the accounts, homes, and offices of suspects and their relatives and cohabitants, without court orders or the presence of witnesses. It authorized the police to detain suspects for up to thirty days without formal charges or the sanction of a court or prosecutor—all in violation of constitutional and international human rights.[29] Some independent-minded judges began to invalidate the thirty-day detention orders.[30]

The findings of the mission of the Council of Europe visiting Russia in May–June 1994 accorded with reports by the U.S. State Department, Human Rights Watch, and the Russian Human Rights Commission under

Kovalyov. The mission noted considerable post-Communist progress in human rights and freedoms, but concluded that, when it comes to civil rights, "*in cases of conflict and confrontation between public authorities and individuals, and whenever protection by the State, including the courts, is required, the implementation of human rights is, to say the least, problematic.*"[31]

Some of the worst violations of civil rights occur in prisons. The government tolerates abominable, even deadly, prison conditions throughout the penal system, but especially in pretrial detention centers, the SIZOs.[32] By the later 1990s, 295,000 persons were crowded into 168 SIZOs that had been built to house only 81,000 people. In such conditions, prisoners have suffocated to death for lack of oxygen: eleven died from suffocation during six days in early July 1996 in the Novokuznetsk SIZO. Rates of tuberculosis infection were forty times higher than within the civilian population, among whom released prisoners spread the disease; there, the TB infection rate of 2 percent was twice the rate constituting an epidemic.

Owing to underfunding, correctional staff went unpaid for months. Suicides among staff personnel increased because of the desperate conditions. Yet the state failed to reduce the prison and labor camp population by extending bail for lesser and nonviolent offenders, an action that could have also lowered the infection rates among prisoners and their civilian contacts. Although the torture and suffering experienced by Valery Abramkin, head of the Moscow Center for Prison Reform, when he was a political prisoner were horrible, he found present conditions even more so:

all this torture was limited in time: minutes, hours, days, months. Now prisoners are being tortured for years. In 1994, when as a State Duma expert I happened to visit a common cell in the Butyrka prison, I felt a deadly horror and realized that the horror I had seen before was a mere trifle. . . . Since 1991, not only human rights organizations but authorities of the MVD GUIN [Corrections Administration of the Interior Ministry] and the Procuracy in charge of SIZOs appealed many times to state officials, urging them to take measures immediately to prevent a coming catastrophe. Those appeals concerned not only prisoners' rights, they also warned that SIZOs presented a threat to the whole country, a threat not less dangerous than crime itself.[33]

Crime rates leveled off by the mid-1990s. By then the penal population had reached the world's highest rate of incarceration—740 per 100,000 population, compared with 60 per 100,000 in tsarist Russia in the early twentieth century, and the rate of 72 per 100,000 in England and Wales.[34] Outside prisons, people at liberty were barricading themselves behind metal doors and locked cages that fenced off apartment house corridors. The President's Commission on Human Rights lamented "the militarization of society" in the proliferation of armed private groups and security guards.[35] The militarization added dangers while providing uncertain security for the rich and powerful. Contract killings claimed 560 victims in 1995 in mostly unsolved crimes, nearly half of them against businessmen and financiers; 450 victims were targeted in 1996 by the time eleven assassin's bullets struck down thirty-nine-year-old Paul E. Tatum, the first U.S. entrepreneur to die in this way. Tatum had been a partner (40%) in the Radisson-Slavyanskaya Hotel joint venture, along with the city of Moscow (50%) and the Radisson group (10%). At the time of his murder, Tatum had been in the midst of a dispute with the other partners over ownership of the hotel. His death cannot help but discourage foreign investors; it illustrates the apparent risks of doing business in Russia for foreigners already put off by Russia's corruption and uncertain framework of tax and contract law.[36]

Donald Barry's opinion on rule of law at the end of the Soviet period holds true for Russia years into independence: "on the one hand, some evidence of respect for legal and constitutional principles . . . on the other hand, a willingness to dispense with these principles in the interest of political necessity"[37]—but at high costs for economic reform and democracy.

Constitutionalism on Trial

Law in Russia, said the prominent jurist Aleksandr Maksimovich Yakovlev, was traditionally seen as an instrument of state coercion and control. The idea has not yet taken hold in Russia that law is a set of rules of behavior and definition of rights rather than a coercive means of control, and that laws limit state power. "Laws as norms are yet to become laws in life." The Procuracy, said Yakovlev, still plays conflicting roles as prosecutor and guardian of rights and due process. The Constitutional Court has limited authority to enforce a rule of law.[38]

Before independence, Russia moved to build on the precedent of the Soviet Constitutional Oversight Commission (see Chapter 4), which under Gorbachev had been a weak and short-lived but momentous step toward bringing government to account under the higher law of the USSR Constitution and international human rights.[39] The Russian parliament established the Constitutional Court of the Russian Federation in July 1991. It gave the court powers to review legislation for constitutionality on its own or upon other official initiative. The court also received authority to accept individuals' suits against patterns of administrative and judicial violations of constitutional rights. Parliament elected the first court, thirteen out of a full complement of fifteen judges, in October 1991,[40] and it began to issue opinions in January 1992.

The Constitutional Court used its authority to annul the president's merging, in November 1991, of the two police ministries—Interior and Security—as a violation of the separation of powers.[41] President Yeltsin's future antagonist, the court's chairman Valery Zor'kin, said that the president's retraction of the decree showed him to be a "law-governed president."[42] This accord between president and chairman soon gave way to enmity. Neither antagonist thereafter was noted for his consistent lawfulness of behavior.

The court recognized the constitutionality of Yeltsin's 1991 ban on the Communist parties at the same time that it recognized their right to have grass-roots organizations. The court referred questions of confiscated party property to the regular courts and refused to pass on the constitutionality of the CPSU as a question made moot by the party's collapse. The court's decision in the Communist Party case left its credibility largely intact in 1992.[43] Justice Ernest Ametistov said that the court viewed its decision as the best compromise under the circumstances.[44]

In late June 1993, Justice Ametistov heard the U.S. Supreme Court announce its decisions in Washington. "If only we had your problems," he said after the session. Back in Russia, his court, particularly its chair, had been siding with parliament in its deadlock with the president over economic policy.[45] This violated its mandate and Zor'kin's pledges to keep the court "above politics."[46] Deadlocked with the Ninth Special Session of the Russian Federation Congress of People's Deputies, the president on March 20, 1993, announced an impending emergency powers decree. Chairman Zor'kin improperly spoke out against Yeltsin in a press conference, and in the Congress of People's Deputies. Zor'kin then brought the case before the Constitutional Court, in illegal haste and on illegal substantive grounds, on the basis of a draft decree that had not been promulgated. After an overnight session on March 22–23, a majority of the court declared the emergency powers decree unconstitutional and annulled it.

The Constitutional Court retained some authority within central governmental institutions. It ruled that the "yes" votes in questions on the April 25, 1993, referendum concerning confidence in the president and support for his reforms were valid, although they fell short of a majority of registered voters. But the court declared invalid the vote for an early election of parliament because the vote majority did not reach a majority of registered voters.[47]

On September 21, 1993, the president addressed the nation to announce a decree dissolving parliament and calling for new elections and a new constitution. Two hours after the 8 P.M. broadcast, the Constitutional Court met; that same evening it annulled the president's decree as unconstitutional, on the grounds that it violated principles of the separation of powers, popular sovereignty, and supremacy of the constitution and of parliament as the "highest organ of state power." These violations, said the court, were grounds for suspending the president from office or removing him through impeachment procedures.[48] A minority of judges, already at loggerheads with Chairman Zor'kin over his politicizing of the court, wrote dissenting opinions on many grounds, including illegal prejudgment, hasty procedures, and lack of careful legal reasoning and attention to the constitutional principle of popular sovereignty and the people's will as expressed in the April referendum of confidence in the president and his policies. The court illegally preempted the authority of the Congress of People's Deputies to define the criminal basis for impeaching the president.[49]

The president responded by suspending the court in October. He had its statute rewritten to eliminate its authority to initiate the review of laws and treaties for constitutionality, and to exclude from its jurisdiction questions of the constitutionality of the government's actions, which was left to the still weak ordinary courts. Individuals and ordinary courts may not appeal to test the legality of presidential and governmental decrees. Yet decrees have been the main sources of abuses and of authoritarian governance.[50]

The president packed the court, enlarged to nineteen, in prolonged negotiations with the Federation Council over the six new justices. This took until February 1995, more than five months after the statutory time limit.[51] The court swore an oath "to obey only the Russian Federation Constitution, nothing and no one else,"[52] on February 13, 1995, and resumed work by electing its new chairman, the law professor and constitutional reform expert Vladimir Tumanov.[53]

The new version of the Constitutional Court operates under tighter inhibitions against political involvement than did its predecessor, the 1991 model.[54] For example, its statute bars justices from making public statements on matters that could be, are going to be, or are actually under examination by the Constitutional Court and otherwise seeks to protect the justices, as well as the court, from taint of outside influence or procedural violations.[55] Individual petitioners no longer have to exhaust all other remedies before turning to the Constitutional Court. Both regular courts and individual petitioners may appeal to test the constitutionality of laws only. The court has also lost its former right, and the right of its predecessor—the Soviet Committee of Constitutional Oversight—to initiate cases on its own.[56] The court has lost its right to issue advisory opinions on the constitutionality of legal norms and treaties on its own initiative. This it does only at the request of the presidents of the Russian Federation, Federation Council, and State Duma; legislative and executive organs of the Federation components, the Federation Supreme Court, and Supreme Arbitration Court; or one-fifth of the members of the Federation Council or deputies of the State Duma.[57]

As yet the Constitutional Court lacks adequate enforcement power to carry out its mission, under its new statute of July 1994, "to protect the foundations of the constitutional system and the basic rights and freedoms of the individual and the citizen, and . . . to ensure the supremacy and direct action of the Russian Federation Constitution on the entire territory of the Russian Federation."[58] For example, local governments continued the residence permit system (see below) despite being forbidden by law and a decision of the court, which found the permit rule to be an uncon-stitutional infringement on the right of free movement.[59]

During the more than year-long paralysis of judicial review, President Yeltsin launched the Chechen war. For the human rights community, the Chechnya case before the court became a "litmus test" of the court's guardianship of the constitutional rule of law and human rights.[60] The court began public hearings in the Chechnya case on July 11, 1995, after months of fighting in Chechnya had already inflicted enormous harm upon civilian lives, health, and property. The case originated with "in-quiries" from both houses of the Federal Assembly, the new parliament elected in December 1993. Presenting their case were three deputies who represented a group of deputies of the State Duma and three representa-tives of the Federation Council. The plaintiffs questioned the constitution-ality of President Yeltsin's decrees that launched the assault in Chechnya, and of a governmental directive that permitted the banning of undesirable people from the region and the rescinding of the accreditation of jour-nalists there. The government was represented by Deputy Prime Minister Sergei Shakhrai, Presidential Security Adviser Yury Baturin, and Doctor of Juridical Sciences Oleg Kutafin, rector of the Moscow State Academy of Law. Each side called in experts to give added testimony.[61]

Plaintiffs argued that: (1) the president decreed the attack secretly, in violation of the constitutional rule that normative acts affecting indi-vidual rights, freedoms, and obligations may not be implemented until published;[62] (2) the war decrees violated existing federal law by ordering the internal use of army troops; (3) the first war decree of November 30, No. 2137s (s for secret), declared a state of emergency without immediately informing the State Duma and Federation Council and without obtain-ing the latter's assent—a violation of the constitution; (4) although the decree was secretly repealed on December 11, the day the Russian forces attacked Grozny, it remained in effect de facto;[63] (5) the president vio-lated Article 55(3) of the constitution by establishing a state of emergency which, by its nature, abridged those rights and freedoms of the human being and the citizen which may be abridged only by federal law; (6) the president, though authorized to declare a state of emergency, violated the constitution by not immediately informing the Federation Council and State Duma, and receiving the confirmation of the Federation Council;[64] and (7) the "normative legal acts . . . resulted in massive violations of the unalienable constitutional rights and freedoms of citizens of the Russian Federation."[65]

Speaking for the government and the president, the respondents cited political urgency and expediency in situations of armed rebellion unde-fined by existing law as justification for the decrees and the attack. The president's national security adviser, Yury Baturin, told the court that by the end of 1994 the limitless corruption had gone so far that "further in-action would have violated the constitution." Deputy Prime Minister (and lawyer) Sergei Shakhrai argued that the president had acted out of necessity, as he was obligated and empowered to do under Article 80 of the constitution as guarantor of individual rights and Russia's sovereignty, security, and integrity. In this situation of threat to order, security, and national integrity, no appropriate legal definition of a state of emergency existed.[66]

After twenty days of hearings and deliberations, Chairman Tumanov delivered the ruling of the court on July 31, the day after the signing of the abortive cease-fire in Chechnya. The court found for the government on the main question of the constitutionality of Yeltsin's orders framing the Chechnya campaign, following basically the reasoning of the respondents. The president, said the court, was not obligated to declare a state of emergency for the military actions he ordered because "the law on the state of emergency is not designed for extraordinary situations like that in the Chechen Republic, where regular armed forces armed with state-of-the-art weapons oppose the federal authorities."[67]

To carry out his mandate to preserve the integrity of the Russian Federation, the president had to venture onto a legal terra incognita with his decrees. The court ruled that arguments based on the violations in Chechnya of Russia's human rights commitments under domestic and international law were irrelevant: The human rights violations were beyond the competence of the court. Also, it agreed with the respondents that the violations did not necessarily follow from the presidential and governmental decrees that launched the attack.[68] In its verdict, the court concealed the secrecy, and hence illegality, of key decrees by omitting the suffix "s" from their numbers. On the side of the rule of law, the court found governmental directive (*postanovlenie*) No. 1360 unconstitutional where it called for expelling certain categories of citizens from Chechnya and provided that troublesome journalists be deprived of their accreditation without a court hearing.[69]

The Constitutional Court heard the Chechnya case in a joint session of its two chambers. The verdict was divided, with eight dissenters, all of whom (of the eighteen who heard the case) were from the original bench of thirteen justices elected in 1991; the newly appointed justices went along with the verdict.[70] One of the government respondents, Yury Baturin, co-authored a constitutional comment that, alongside the new freedoms and democratization and building toward a rule-of-law state, "as a whole, the constitutional status of the individual is a long way from being fully and consistently realized. The situation in this sphere of life cannot be considered satisfactory."[71] The Chechnya case, and the war, ironically confirmed Baturin's comment.

Decisions of the Constitutional Court have upheld various civil and economic rights of individual petitioners where less than presidential authority was at stake. The court annulled a series of norms as unconstitutional violations of various individual rights, for example:

- the part of the Code of Criminal Procedure which stated that only persons already imprisoned can appeal their confinement in court, which violates the right of all persons to equality before the law;
- the part of the law on collective bargaining which bans strikes in an entire branch, such as civil aviation, as so broadly written that it violates the right to strike;
- the 1991 law on the rehabilitation of victims of political repression, which was unconstitutional in the part that excluded those who were under sixteen and not repressed but suffering indirectly from political repression when accompanying exiled parents, which violated rights to equal protection, court protection of their rights, and restitution for harm inflicted by official arbitrariness;
- the part of the law on the militia (police) under which a former head of a provincial internal affairs administration had his equal rights violated and suffered age discrimination because it permitted dismissals on pension of those who had reached pension age, regardless of their capacity to serve;
- upon petition of the Murom People's Court and individual citizens, the housing code clause that denied the right of an imprisoned person to hold an apartment for more than the usual absentee's limit of six months, because the clause violated the rights to equal protection, and housing, and protection against an unjustified curtailment of rights, and the rights not to be punished again for one crime.[72] These actions represent a creeping rule of law, significantly initiated at the grass roots of a nascent civil society.

Economic and Social Wrongs and the Imperial Legacy

The constitution commits the government of the Russian Federation to "the protection of people's labor and health, a guaranteed minimum wage, state support of the family, and invalids and senior citizens; the system of social services is developing, there are state pensions, grants, and other guarantees of social defense."[73] If that commitment were fulfilled, the resulting benefits would legitimize and nurture democracy.

Yelena Bonner, human rights champion and widow of Andrei Sakharov, noted that an essential condition for the consolidation of democracy will be the economic development that results in the formation of a private propertied class and a strong independent working class with interests different from those of the state bureaucracy. Instead of society being dependent on the state, "the state will be dependent on us. This will lead, first, to the emergence of a civil society and, second, to the establishment of the rule of law. The state will be subordinate to society and not the other way around."[74] In all these aspects of development the accountability of state to society still seems distant.

Economic and social rights remained far from realization as Russia approached the century's end. The President's Commission on Human Rights concluded, from citizen complaints and appeals, that "violations of social and economic rights and citizens' legitimate interests constitute the most widespread form of human rights abuse and are the main source of social tension."[75] The complaints made to local human rights NGOs (reviewed in Chapter 10), seem to confirm this. During the 1990s economic development brought stark contrasts between the elite made up of wealthy or comfortably well-off people and the third of the population who lived in poverty.[76] Many of the poor lacked the means even to bury their dead, while compatriots drove fleets of Mercedes.[77] The elderly were particularly hard hit. They had once helped their families by standing in line to purchase goods while their children worked; but the lines have disappeared — the plentiful goods are too expensive for many. So the elderly have become superfluous, and their pensions mean less than ever.[78]

Specialists at the Ministry of Social Security estimate that real income by the end of 1995 had dropped to 46 percent of what it was in 1991. Many people hung on by feeding themselves out of their own garden plots with potatoes, vegetables, and fruit, and with more meat and milk than they had produced in the past.[79] Teachers I met in the town of Uglich, north of Moscow, in 1996 had not been paid for months and lived by selling their crafts to tourists. School students in the village of Goritzi, farther north, could not afford to buy pens for school work or travel to where they could get them. Without their garden plots their families would probably starve. In well-supplied Moscow, the Metro passages and pedestrian underpasses sheltered women selling mewing kittens, scared puppies, combs, trinkets, American cigarettes at 45 cents a pack (in rubles), and loaves of bread. Gaunt mothers and children begged for pittances. Nearby, kiosks and shops sold cameras, tapes, videos, CDs, sneakers, perfume, clothes, liquor, food, and flowers — almost everything except bagels and Scotch tape. Around the corner a McDonald's did a brisk trade.

By the later 1990s the government had not yet reconciled (1) its efforts to hold down deficits and therefore to qualify for portions of its 10.2 billion IMF loan, with (2) the restoration of basic social safety nets and services. Economic outlooks clashed in the debate between partisans of less shock and more therapy[80] and supporters of shock first, therapy later.[81]

An effectively enforced and reasonable tax system would be a step toward government solvency and payment of back wages;[82] so would a drastic but unlikely cleanup of government corruption. However, tax problems, corruption, and bureaucracy alone do not explain why Russia's recession was deeper and longer-lasting than that of Eastern Europe. The economist

Vladimir Kontorovich has drawn attention to another reason for the lag: Russia's Communist imperialist legacy. As an impoverished great power, the Soviet Union saddled its society with an exceptionally high percentage of spending on the military-industrial complex. "Among the most costly components of the imperial legacy," says Kontorovich, "are the military industry, the Russian Far East, entanglements in the former republics."[83] That legacy's sad state foreshadowed humiliation and dangers: humiliation with failures and setbacks in Russia's space program—the failed Mars probe in 1996 and loss of its last military "spy" satellite in November 1996— and the dangers of nuclear technology proliferation, should nuclear scientists accept work in hitherto non-nuclear "rogue" countries. This latter danger was brought home by the suicide in October of Vladimir Nechai, head of Russia's Chelyabinsk-70 nuclear complex. Nechai shot himself in despair because the government had not paid his staff for months. Seemingly oblivious to the danger created by their neglect, government officials stayed away from Nechai's funeral. For Yabloko leader Grigory Yavlinsky, Nechai had revealed to everyone that, in Russia, "no one can guarantee the security of thermonuclear programs."[84]

Government corruption, failed tax revenues, and mismanagement did not spare the military, neither its hungry and unpaid troops nor its angry officers. A study conducted by the Conflict Studies Research Centre of the British army found the ill-housed, ill-clothed, and ill-trained Russian army was sick and approaching a crisis point. "Systemic failure and collapse are now imminent and will take place if something is not done." The Russian minister of defense told his interviewers that the Russian army was in its worst state since the 1920s. Duma deputy Sergei Yushenkov, an opponent of the war (the "toad" of Grachev's naming), said that "The Russian army takes one-fifth of the federal budget and we have no idea of how it is spent."[85]

Women's Human Rights

Neither *perestroika* nor independence served the cause of women's rights, except insofar as freedom allowed women to champion their own rights and interests (see Chapter 10). Anastasia Posadskaya, founding member of the Moscow Center for Gender Studies, noted "increasing violence against women, brought about by market 'reform': sexual harassment in the workplace, sexual exploitation of young women, street violence, growing domestic violence, unheard-of violence against older women with the goal of seizing their privatized homes. Then there are the problems of reproductive health and reproductive rights, particularly the limiting of access to free medical assistance, including childbirth and abortion. In addition, there are millions of refugee and migrant women, and women surrounded by military conflict."[86]

Due to the lack of legal restraints, unabashed sexism proliferated in the workplace. Women seeking work often had to trade on their femininity, and even on their sexuality. Those who would not play the role of the coquette might limit their opportunities in the new private-sector job market. Quite possibly with relief and even pleasure, women who dropped out of the economy reverted to their widely accepted role of keeper of the domestic hearth.

Women made up some 70 percent of the unemployed. Their wages, calculated as percentages of men's, fell by the mid-1990s from 70 to 40 percent, owing to glass ceilings in privatized economy and to general discrimination. Another source of hardship was the increase in the numbers of single mothers because of abandonment and divorce. The always high divorce rate climbed to over half the marriage rate. Divorces have always been initiated mainly by women in response to husbands' drunkenness, infidelity, indifference, or maltreatment.[87] Women have set up dozens of matrimonial agencies for Russian women seeking American husbands. One agency founder, Nina Vasilyeva, a successful office manager earning $1,300 a month in a French photo agency, said that among her clients American men have the reputation of being "more polite, they don't drink as much, and they accept responsibility for their families."[88]

The uncertainties and hardships of the economic transition lowered birthrates during the 1990s among already relatively infertile Russian women. "The market is killing babies, both those already born and those expected," said Moscow State University professor Boris Khodov.[89] Inadequate natal care was killing mothers. Maternity deaths were five times the U.S. rate, 25 times the rate in Scandinavia.[90] Because of failure in providing for full reproductive choice, abortions remained the main means of birth control, occurring at more than twice the rate of live births (more than four million registered abortions—and this is likely an understatement).[91] During the general economic and social breakdown, the number of children abandoned completely or left to state foster care by mothers rose year after year.[92] By the mid-1990s, shelters held more abandoned and orphaned children than they had during the World War II,[93] more homeless and refugees than at any time since that war—and this in the midst of others' consumption of more foreign luxuries than ever before.

Short Lives

Penny Morvant reminds us that demographic data are "a reflection of the well-being of the people and provide some indication of the social costs of the transition from communism to a market-oriented society."[94] Industrialized democracies top the list in life expectancy and infant survival (low mortality); next come the Eastern European democracies; below them come Russia and other newly independent states which rate just above the more prosperous developing countries of the third world in demographic indicators of well-being.[95] In Russia and other newly independent states, the stresses of everyday life, heavy smoking, heavier than ever drinking, bad diets, the legacy of catastrophic environmental pollution of air, land, water, and food, and accidents all take their toll. Rather than being able to mitigate these threats to life and health, already bad medical care has worsened for all but the well-to-do.

The strains on men's health show up in the startling differences between male and female longevity.[96] In Russia, men's life expectancy at birth fell from nearly 65, or 9.5 years shorter than women's in 1986–87, to a low of 57.3 years, or almost 14 years shorter than women's in 1995, and a reported 58.3 in 1996. This is the biggest gap in the world. Women's life expectancy, meanwhile, decreased by 3.5 years. Accidental and violent deaths, a high cause of male mortality, nearly doubled in seven years (1987–94) even as they decreased in the West. Behind this rise was the increase in violent crime, suicides, and auto fatality rates.[97]

As under the Communists, high levels of respiratory diseases and rising death rates occurred among children due to industrial pollution, in gross violation of the right to a safe and clean environment and to compensation for harm done by pollution.[98] Social issues such as children's health have tended to be ignored in favor of economic reform. The demographer Murray Feshbach warns that pollution may cost dearly in progress as well as in lives, as progress depends ultimately on people's productivity, which in turn depends on their health.[99] Other countries have an interest in Russia's environmental cleanup. These countries, too, suffer from the tremendous oil leaks in the vulnerable Russian Arctic environment, nuclear dumping at sea, and lax controls over nuclear materials and waste. Victor Menshikov, consultant to the Security Council's interdepartmental commission on environmental safety, deplores the loss of comprehensive interagency controls: "Russia is currently a time bomb for the whole world."[100]

Minority Rights

The 1993 constitution presents the Russian Federation and its "multinational people" as nothing less than a democratic community of equals who freely choose and express their ethnic identity.[101] The problem lies in bringing practice into closer conformity with principles by ending discrimination.

National extremism remains a divisive issue. The President Yeltsin strongly condemned fascism, though not specifically anti-Semitism, before parliament. He drew attention to the growing support for increasingly active fascist organizations. Numbers of extreme right-wing publications tripled to 150 between 1992 and 1995. Aleksandr Barshakov's Russian National Unity has its own publications, security forces, supportive priests, and commercial enterprises and branches in 350 cities. But the government does little or nothing to root out and prosecute violent groups.[102] State anti-Semitism of the Soviet days—so-called anti-Zionism—has faded, leaving anti-Semitism from below, led by nationalist groups such as Pamyat and some dissident intellectuals, including the mathematician Igor Shafarevich. Ethnic conflicts and biases affect many minority groups. Between 1993 and 1996 a Jewish cultural club was vandalized in Penza. Extremist thugs burned synagogues in Moscow and bombed others. They desecrated Jewish graves in St. Petersburg.[103] Still, a visit to the Orthodox synagogue on Lermontov Prospekt in June 1996 presented a different picture to that of 1987. The fear was gone; young Jews encountered at the synagogue said that they felt no fear. They talked of the five new Jewish schools and the new Jewish community organizations.

Local authorities have been deeply involved in the discrimination against people of Caucasian and Central Asian origin. Discrimination and attempted social cleansing by Cossack groups erupted in Krasnodar and Stavropol territories as refugees from fighting in the Caucasus poured in. It flared up in the aftermath of the "Moscow October" in 1993, during the anticrime campaign beginning the following year, and after the two bombings of Moscow trolleybuses in May 1996, which media and authorities widely attributed to Chechens. By then, political and media depictions and images of vicious conflict in Southern Ossetia and Nagorno-Karabakh had stirred up a fear of "persons of Caucasian complexion," be they Armenians, Chechens, Georgians, Azerbaijanis, or any other darker-skinned people from the Caucasus or Central Asia.[104] "With wide public support," the U.S. State Department reported, "law enforcement authorities targeted dark-complexioned people for harassment, arrest, and deportation from urban centers. According to Russian human rights monitors, some were dragged from automobiles in traffic, harassed, subject to extortion, and beaten in broad daylight on the streets."[105]

Unconstitutional and illegal limits on free movement compound the difficulties of targeted minorities. Stalin restored the internal passport system, a tsarist practice, in 1932, in order to restrict and control movement and tie peasants to their collective and state farms. The system continued under the governmental Statute on the Passport system of August 28, 1974, and persisted into the mid-1990s in violation of the freedom of movement affirmed in Russian law and the constitution.[106] Moscow, St. Petersburg, Volgograd, Saratov, cities in Siberia, and even in the far north used the system of residence permits (*propiski*) or its replacement, the registration system, to limit in-migration. They extracted huge fees from dark-skinned people picked up on the street and found to be lacking residence permits, and from organizations for each new employee registered.[107]

At the end of 1995, the Interior Ministry issued instructions to replace the permit system with a system of informative registration at a modest fee.

But the head of the Passport and Visa Department admitted that it lacked funding to administer the new system. Also, local shortages of funds and stubborn local resistance did not bode well for a rapid reform.[108]

Travel abroad has become less encumbered with red tape,[109] but not entry from abroad. The lack of a *propiska* (residence permit) is one of the reasons given by the Federal Migration Service for the denial of asylum to refugees and forced migrants (internally displaced persons and citizens fleeing back from abroad). Many of these people face uncertain futures and mixed receptions in Russia, owing both to lack of funds for needed assistance and to Russian authorities' violations of their own laws on refugees and forced migrants.[110]

Self-Determination

Aside from the problems of building toward democracy and a market economy, "the most serious challenge," in one informed Russian view, "is the problem of governing a multiethnic society within the framework of a single state."[111] Ethnic Russians face freedom's ordeal with the additional postimperial trauma of loss of identity as "elder brother" and "leading people" of the USSR. Nationalists play on nostalgia and issues of Russians' rights in the "near abroad" to undermine the government. They demand new leaders and more pressure on the near abroad in the name of "human rights."[112]

A necessary condition for the stability and democracy of the Russian Federation is the avoidance of either Russian national centrist or ethnic national separatist solutions. This would require uniting a diverse population of non-Russian and ethnic Russians—*russkie*—into a constitutionally proclaimed "multinational people." Fortunately for intergroup relations, integrationists failed to achieve their vision of Russia without politically significant ethnoterritorial boundaries.[113] The Russian government, despite its episodes and tolerance of discrimination, has rejected a narrow, ethnically Russian state exclusivity in favor of building a nation of multiethnic *rossiane.*

Russia is relatively homogeneous. The population of about 150 million is over 82 percent Russian. The next largest ethnic group, the Tatars, comprises about 4 percent of the population, and they are not seceding. Russia is ethnically complex, containing over a hundred ethnic groups that live scattered inside and outside their titular homelands.[114] Ethnic self-awareness was built up in part by the deliberate Soviet emphasis on ethnic group identities and ethnically named regions. These range from the Mordovian and Karelian republics in the western part of the former USSR to the Chechen Republic in the northern Caucasus and the republics of Sakha (Yakutia) and Buryatia in Eastern Siberia. As Communism collapsed, pollsters found that the public had difficulty forming an "awareness of the principles of the new Russian statehood. . . . What is Russia within the borders of the former RSFSR?"[115] The expression of the cultural and religious diversity of the peoples in Russia was no longer limited by a superimposed ideology. The rapid decompression toward freedom, and then independence, from Soviet authority released forces and declarations of ethnic minority self-assertion and grievances.[116]

Interethnic tensions persist in the Russian Federation. Independent Russia experienced its first interethnic war in 1992, when fighting erupted between Northern Ossetians, a Christian group of Caucasus mountain people, and the Muslim Ingush. Some Ingush wanted to return to Prigorodnyi District, once part of the Chechen-Ingush Autonomous Republic and home to Ingush before Stalin deported them in 1944, abolished the Chechen Ingush Republic, and transferred Prigorodnyi District to the Northern Ossetian Republic. After the restoration of the Chechen-Ingush Autonomous Soviet Socialist Republic (ASSR) in 1956, Ingush began returning to their homes, including Prigorodnyi District.[117]

The three Ingush-inhabited districts of what had been the Chechen-Ingush ASSR decided not to join the Chechens in embracing independence lest that jeopardize their claims to regain the Prigorodnyi region. The Russian Federation Supreme Soviet then formed the Republic of Ingushetia within the Federation. Tens of thousands of Southern Ossetian refugees fleeing from the fighting with the Gamsakhurdia government of Georgia to the south raised tensions. Scattered incidents of violence flared into armed Ingush–Ossetian conflict in Prigorodnyi District. An Ingush influx into former homelands of Prigorodnyi District in 1991–92 then led to armed conflict between Ingush and Northern Ossetians. Beginning on October 31, 1992, the conflict continued until Russia imposed a state of emergency on November 2 and sent in troops three days later.

Russians intervened purportedly as peacemakers, but they appeared to favor the Ossetians. More than 8,000 people had been wounded or killed and some 56,000 internal refugees uprooted, in both cases mainly Ingush. Seventeen Russian soldiers died. The conflict remained unresolved in the later 1990s.[118] During the ensuing cycle of states of emergency and temporary calm, unknown assailants killed the Russian temporary administrator, V. Polyanichko, and a Russian general and lieutenant. Anti-Russian feeling in Ingushetia flared up after Russian Cossacks joined Ossetians and others to block the entry of Ingush fighters in October–November 1992, causing 8,000 to 10,000 Russian-speakers to flee Ingushetia.[119]

Indigenous minorities resented the discrepancy between their higher educational attainments and the Russians' political dominance. The disappointed expectations of educated members of indigenous minorities fed sentiments of resentment against "them" and "their people" in "our republics."[120] The stakes were large. Upon independence, as now, the republics and autonomous regions covered nearly half of the Russian Federation.

They contain valuable resources, including much of Russia's oil, gold, diamonds, and minerals. All have sizable Russian populations—Russian majorities, in fact, in more than half of them. The minorities of Russia live as majorities in only eight of the thirty-two autonomous units named after ethnic groups.[121]

Late in 1991, the Chechens and Ingush joined other once-deported Muslim groups—Kabardins, Balkars, Karachais, Cherkess, Abkhazi, and others—to begin forming a Confederation of the Peoples of the Caucasus.[122] This move prompted fear among nationalist Russian constitution makers that autonomous Muslim areas such as those in the North Caucasus would follow the lead of Chechnya and seek independence.[123]

The constitution leaves a very flexible—one might say ill-defined—set of principles of federation. It asserts "the sovereignty of the Russian Federation over its entire territory . . . the integrity and inviolability of its territory."[124] On the other hand, it recognizes "the equality and self-determination of the peoples in the Russian Federation."[125] Attempts to reconcile these opposing principles continue in the ceaseless bargaining and maneuvering between Moscow and the eighty-nine "subjects of the Russian Federation." These consist of twenty-one republics named after the main minority group there and sixty-nine regional subjects in the form of oblasts (provinces), *krais* (more sparsely settled territories), major cities, and so on.

The 1993 constitution stripped republics of their formal "sovereignty," recognized in earlier drafts, and of the related right to have a separate republic citizenship. Unlike the territories, however, the republics retained rights to their own flag, state language, and constitution, whereas the regions could have only a charter. For regions and republics too, there was some possible solace in the existence of the Federation Council, made up of two representatives from each of the eighty-nine constituent entities—usually the legislative chairperson and the chief executive. That upper chamber, which together with the Duma makes up the Federal Assembly, had considerable powers, including the power to impeach, appoint judges and the prosecutor general, approve the president's decrees, declare martial law and states of emergency, and approve the use of armed forces.[126] Another inducement to republic leaders to accept the constitution has been the allowance of a very un-Soviet diversity in republic constitutions and forms of government,[127] as well as administrative and fiscal concessions in negotiations with Moscow.[128] The elections of regional governors have boosted local power without precluding various collaborative agreements with Moscow. One may expect regions and republics to play a large role in economic recovery.

Nizhny Novgorod Oblast, along the Volga, is relatively advanced in economic reform and strongly autonomist, though not apparently contemplating separation from Russia. Moscow makes its peace with resource-rich republics like Tatarstan by allowing it to get away with much lower rates of tax payments to Moscow than it allows to many much poorer provinces. Ethnic Russians tend to identify with their local regions out of economic self-interest, though not to the point of separatism. A real federal devolution of power exists for the first time in Russia, judging from the elections of independent-minded regional governors in late 1996 and their bargaining power with Moscow. The best guarantor of stable union will be continued democratization, economic reform, a sound currency, and economic integration through the market.[129]

The intensity of separatist sentiments has varied from republic to republic. Marjorie Balzer correctly placed Chechnya, in the North Caucasus region, and Tatarstan, in the Volga region, at the top of the list of secession-minded republics.[130] Chechnya and Tatarstan refused to sign the Federation Treaty with the other nineteen republics on March 31, 1992. The Tatar Republic disregarded the Constitutional Court's banning of a referendum on sovereignty; the referendum went ahead on March 21, 1992, as planned.[131] Chechnya had declared independence in November 1991. The Federation Treaty drafted in 1992 presented a broadly phrased blueprint for relations between Moscow and the subjects of the Russian Federation. The treaty was ratified as a separate part of the RF constitution on April 10, 1992. The treaty and the constitution left for further negotiations the federal division of powers in the protection of human rights, law enforcement, taxation, and control over property and resources, such as Yakutia's diamonds, gold, gas, and oil and Tiumen's large oil reserves.[132]

Russia seems unlikely to follow the Soviet Union into disintegration. The Federation government used both diplomacy and leverage through its control of oil pipelines to conclude a separate treaty with Tatarstan in February 1994, followed by similar treaties with Bashkortostan (the Bashkir republic southeast of Moscow) and Kabardino-Balkaria in the northern Caucasus. The compromise honored Tatarstan's demands for a separate agreement and certain rights to tax and control resources, conduct its own foreign economic relations, and retain its own flag, parliament, and constitution, while keeping intact the idea of the undivided sovereignty of the Russian Federation.[133] Recent polling on people's sense of separate ethnic and shared Russian identity, as well as the relatively wide public participation in the elections of 1995 and 1996 across the Federation outside of Chechnya, suggest that multiethnic nation-building has begun.[134] The Federation has lost considerable control over its parts;[135] but it is not disintegrating.[136]

Neither the integrationist melting pot nor the separatist solution of secession appears to be likely in most members of the Russian Federation, but this will depend on economic developments and future leadership. Two days after his heart bypass operation, President Yeltsin proclaimed November 7 (for decades the anniversary of the "Great October Socialist Revolution") to be, instead, the Day of Concord and Reconciliation. He also ordered the planning of a competition for monuments to commemorate "the victims of the Revolution, the Civil War, and political repressions," as well the drafting of proposals for the removal from government buildings and premises "anything that is at variance with the constitutional principle of ideological and political diversity"—presumably, Communist symbols such as hammers and sickles, red stars, busts and statues of Lenin, and the like.

As though to remind the government that one historic political community remained far off, the Communists rallied in Moscow and across Russia on November 7 to mark the revolutionary anniversary. Communist Gennady Zyuganov, leader of the coalition Patriotic Union of Russia, probably spoke truly when he said that "real, not merely declared, concord in Russian society can be achieved only when people are paid their wages on time and in full and when respect for the elderly and concern for children are shown through deeds."[137]

Conclusions

Civil rights, the rights to personal inviolability, privacy, and due process, have shown some progress since independence in the field of judicial reform. But the progress has been sporadic and underfunded. Because civil rights depend directly on the agencies of law enforcement and security, they have been more threatened than Russia's embattled freedoms. This is particularly true of police, security, and prosecutorial activities, prison conditions, and governmental secrecy.

The Constitutional Court has been chipping away at laws that violate the constitution and international human rights. But on big issues, such as Chechnya, it is hampered by the vagueness of the laws; the president's increased role in its selection and empowerment; and its limited jurisdiction, which excludes governmental acts as distinguished from actions and shields governmental and presidential decrees from suits by individual petitioners.

The fulfillment of economic and social rights lags behind incipient gains in economic development—in some ways, with greater impact on women, in others, for men, though affecting all except an elite of the rich and comfortably well-off. Economic development would be faster were it not for corruption, faulty management of tax policy, and the bloated expenditures on the legacies of imperialism. Extending beyond bribery, privileged takeovers, and embezzlement, corruption links up with pervasive organized crime and claims hundreds of victims annually among those who hold the key to the prospects for economic turnaround, to say nothing of the impact all this has on prospective investors at home and abroad. Russia's economic shortcomings and their attendant blows to human rights and well-being retard the building of democratic concord, legitimacy, and accountability.

The attempt to construct a national community across ethnic, regional, and class lines has a mixed record to date. Minorities from the Caucasus and Central Asia endure discrimination outside their homelands, and sometimes within them. Jews still face anti-Semitism from below. War against or within some regions accompanies treaty making with others. Regions and republics seek to work out balances of power and interest with Moscow as crucial factors in future recovery.

Constitutional proclamations of civil and economic rights, though violated, have marked a radical departure from the old constitutional principles, which held that rights were conditioned on serving the cause as defined by the ruling party. The change from an ideological to a formally binding constitution, from rights as means to rights as ends, will require a "long march" of struggle in order for it to be realized in practice. Meanwhile, the change provides leverage for human rights advocacy, to which I now turn.

Chapter 10
The Struggle Continues

It depends on each one of us. We cannot expect others to do it for us. If society, the people, will not demand respect for human rights, nobody else will.

—Ludmilla Alexeyeva[1]

[D]emocracy, as it is understood by millions of Russian citizens, consists precisely of a society that does not allow itself to be manipulated, [of] a people having the right to express their opinions and, through peaceful, legal paths, to protect their interests and the interests of the country if those in power cannot manage to do so.
—Organizing Committee of the All-Russian Antiwar Movement[2]

The New Advocacy

The present movement for human rights in Russia goes back to the mid-1960s. It was the first independent social movement in the Soviet Union after Stalin. The monitoring and demands for the release of political prisoners marked what Ludmilla Alexeyeva, the leading Russian chronicler of Soviet dissent, calls the "classical phase" of human rights activism. This aspect of its work continues. In it, the movement defends dissenters against repression and commemorates its victims. But the movement has also entered a new phase of active networking in addition to intense advocacy for economic, social and civil rights in local communities.[3]

Nongovernmental organizations exist to close the gap between government and people, said Viktor Kogan-Yasny, a Russian NGO activist. "The least we can do is to publish what we know, shed light on events, aid in finding peaceful methods of conflict resolution in society."[4] They serve also to empower people to call to account violators of their rights and to help remedy the violations.[5] NGOs carry out three essential functions of a civil society: protecting human rights; holding violators—mainly in government—accountable for their violations and interacting with government officials to correct them; and lobbying for desired policies and laws (a process still in its incipient stage).

Alexeyeva told a meeting of teachers of human rights in the Moscow region that, as yet, there is no comparison between Russian activism and that of the United States, with its thousands of organizations pressing authorities daily on rights issues. But "if we don't do the same thing, our rights will not be defended. It depends on each one of us. We cannot expect others to do it for us."[6] By mobilizing civic activism, Alexeyeva believes, the human rights movement will help to pull Russia into a stable democracy. The country she foresees is one that will not be dependent only on decisions made in the Kremlin, the president's office, parliament, and the other government institutions, but one in which the people, too, have an ongoing voice, as well as an electoral choice.[7] NGOs, Alexeyeva told the teachers in Moscow, explain people's rights to them and how to defend their rights by legal means. The new independent trade unions, with their some three million members in the Russian Federation, are mainly human rights organizations that serve to defend their members' rights to wages and other labor rights.[8]

This chapter surveys the human rights movement in the newly independent countries, the expansion of networking through cooperation in Russia, the work of nonprofit organizations, and problems of funding.

The Human Rights Movement

An NGO directory of "rights protecting organizations" published in late 1995 carries an incomplete listing of over two hundred NGOs and branch organizations scattered across the Commonwealth of Independent States, from Archangel in the northwest to Krasnoyarsk in eastern Siberia; from Baku in war-torn Azerbaijan to Bishkek in peaceful Kyrgyzstan. Their concerns include myriad issues of individuals' economic and social rights, consumers' rights, the rights of army recruits and their families, and those of prisoners, political detainees, hostages, children, women, the elderly, and refugees. The movement grew largely out of recent initiatives. Of the eighty NGOs that list registration dates, two-thirds registered between 1992 and 1995. The rest registered mainly in 1991–92. About one-third of the NGOs listed are outside Russia, in other CIS countries. There would be more were not several countries inhospitable to human rights NGOs, and were not the listings incomplete. A growing number of NGOs in Russia are registered outside Moscow and St. Petersburg.[9]

Group activities respond to particular local violations. The Azerbaijan National Committee of the Helsinki Citizens Assembly, registered with the head office in Prague since 1992, engages in the search for and protection of prisoners of war and hostages (in the fighting with Armenians). It gives humanitarian assistance to children, the elderly, and refugees. Some NGO groups in Armenia are organized by opposition parties to monitor elections.

As long as the Kazakh government permits it, the Almaty Helsinki Committee will continue "monitoring the fulfillment of human rights principles, civic freedoms, justice, security agencies, police, court and prison reform, the protection of private property, minority rights, equal opportunity and nondiscrimination, and Kazakhstan's fulfillment of international human rights obligations, lobbying for democratic reforms and the creation of an open, law-governed democratic society."[10] This mandate is typical of general human rights NGOs. Their mandates, broader than one finds for Western human rights, NGOs reflect the fact that each of the thinly spread Russian counterparts must do what would be done by several different NGOs in places where advocacy has had decades longer to develop.

Natalia Taubina, associate director of the Foundation for a Civil Society, which makes small grants to human rights NGOs across the country, pointed out that the main struggle against human rights violations has shifted from the center to the localities, where they address mainly economic and social rights. Even as the violations pile up, most outlying NGOs in Russia (and, it follows, in the other newly independent states) lack the formal structures and professional staffing of their Western counterparts. Their shortage of funds compels them to rely more heavily on volunteers than on professional, full-time advocates.[11]

Human rights education has become a priority. The Kazakhstan-American Bureau for Human Rights and Legality sponsors a television school on human rights, "You Have Rights." Human rights education is also one of the projects of the Association for Legal Development in Kazakhstan, and of NGOs in some other CIS countries. An internationally supported project for secondary school education in human rights in the Moscow region reached the pilot stage by 1996.[12] Quite a few NGOs in Ukraine, such as the Ukrainian Human Rights Center and Ukrainian Legal Foundation, are planning or issuing their own newspapers or newsletters. The Tomsk Center for Research on Human Rights in Eastern Siberia publishes the bulletin *Human Rights Violations*.[13]

"Memorial," one of the first groups to form during *perestroika*, is centered in Moscow and has a network of namesakes across Russia and in other CIS countries. Memorial began with the purpose of commemorating and listing the victims of Stalinist repression; it still carries on that work. Other NGOs, too, such as "Karta" (Charter) in Ryazan and "Sovest' " (Conscience) in Archangel, work to uncover the history of Stalinist repression, camps, and victims, or to assist victims of past repression. Memorial also monitors and helps individuals to protect their human rights and publishes and broadcasts human rights news, as in the "Vybor" (Choice) radio program of the Moscow Memorial Human Rights Center.[14]

Why has there been no truth commission, let alone criminal trials, to uncover the torturers, executioners, and informers? I was told, "It's a sensitive question."[15] No doubt. Agents and collaborators of the secret police numbered in the millions throughout society. Also, an inquiry into guilt might also cause archives to be shut and thus disrupt Memorial's important project of recording and commemorating the fates of the victims of the purges.[16]

A range of specialized NGOs in Russia and other CIS countries includes environmentalists. Five groups in St. Petersburg are involved in the rehabilitation of former prisoners and in giving them material and psychological assistance. Organizations concerned with the rights of children and youth look out for victims of war, including, in addition to children, hostages (Azerbaijan, Armenia), war veterans (Azerbaijan), and noncombatants (Azerbaijan). Other NGOs devote themselves to the rights of Russian-speaking minorities (in Azerbaijan, Kyrgyzstan, Cossacks from around Rostov-on-Don, and so on).

The rights of draftees and their families are championed by committees of soldiers' mothers both outside Russia (e.g., in Armenia) and in various Russian cities, including Moscow, Murmansk, and St. Petersburg. The Interregional Foundation for Mothers' Rights gives legal, material, and psychological support to families of soldiers who perished while in the armed services. The mothers have an uphill fight. Pending possible army reforms, the plight of army recruits was little better than that of detainees. They underwent brutal and often deadly hazing. The Mothers' Rights foundation estimated that 4,000 to 5,000 soldiers died from abuse or committed suicide in 1995. The army systematically concealed the causes of death from the parents of the victims.[17] The army recruited more soldiers than were required for military duties and sent them to work as virtual slave laborers on projects, such as laying pipelines, that profit oil and gas industries and foreign corporations.[18]

Other NGOs work with refugees, forced migrants, present political prisoners, and respond to abuses of the rights and security of journalists in Belarus and Russia. A few NGOs for women's rights are noted by the human rights NGO network, as is the women's organization of the Kola Peninsula based in Murmansk. Various NGOs promote the rights of invalids (Moscow); of persons seeking to defend their rights as plaintiffs and defendants, property owners, business people, and consumers; of people in third-world countries (the Moscow Committee for Democracy and Human Rights); of victims of psychiatric abuse or violence; of persons convicted of economic "crimes" and their rights to economic freedom (Moscow); of victims of cultural repression (Solzhenitsyn Foundation, Moscow); and of workers. Dozens of NGOs specializing in legal assistance render aid to the general population, children, refugees, and others, under both secular and religious auspices. More than 150 NGOs across Russia joined in a movement to demand the end of the war in Chechnya.[19]

A minority of priests and lay persons among Russian Orthodox believers promote parish outreach, inter-religious dialogue, and the condemnation of anti-Semitism. Dr. Vladimir Ilyushenko, a political scientist and Russian Orthodox believer, is president of the "Society for Cultural Rebirth" in the name of Aleksandr Men'. Father Aleksandr Men' was murdered on his way to his church, on October 9, 1990. The murder remains unsolved. Ilyushenko's society preserves Father Men's spirit of openness and communication among religions. Ilyushenko keeps in contact with the human rights movement.[20]

Networking

The human rights movement works and grows through networking. Networking has featured a tide of new initiatives since independence; cooperation locally and joint action with the NGOs in the network; the sharing of information on violations, laws, and techniques of advocacy; and the constant search for funding. The former director of Human Rights Watch/Helsinki in Moscow, Rachel Denber, has emphasized the importance of increased cooperation among groups in Russia, and the adoption of new communications technologies to assist in this cooperation among Russian NGOs and with the movement abroad.[21] The Moscow Research Center on Human Rights is a hub of such communication and networking among Russian human rights NGOs. The center is crowded into a cluster of rooms that one reaches by walking past worried-looking and shabbily dressed clients. "The Center," it says of itself, "is the first in the entire history of Russia whose work is devoted to the coordination and development of the country's human rights movement." It shares its quarters with a group of other NGOs.[22]

Sergei Smirnov and his assistants at the Moscow Center maintain communications with the far-flung network of human rights NGOs in the provinces, marked by pins on the wall map over Smirnov's desk, through their monthly bulletin and its e-mail version on Glasnet. As long as funds permit, the bulletin *Prava cheloveka v Rossii: Informatsionnaya set'* (Human Rights in Russia: Information Network) provides a record of growth in the range and sophistication of outreach and fund-raising. The Moscow Center began an informational human rights network in 1993 to link Russian human rights organizations. In order to further networking, the bulletin reported, the center resorts to seminars in networking itself, e-mail and other telecommunications, and the bulletin:

[It] extends organizational and technical help to rights-protecting groups, supplies legal and educational literature, supplies equipment and instruction on using computers and computer networks. Between March 1995 and February 1996, the Center conducted five seminars on the theme "The Personal Computer and Communication," with participants from twelve regions around the country. This organization obtained gear needed in their day-to-day work and the development of their communications. The series of sessions . . . opened in February–March 1996 with a seminar in St. Petersburg with the support of the Eurasia Foundation. It was meant to further deepen the technical and organizational skills of rights-protecting NGOs. We expect that the practical knowledge received by our colleagues in the provinces will help them to utilize the wide possibilities of telecommunications (in the first place, reliable and rapid electronic mail links, and also data available through Internet) in order to increase the effectiveness of their work.[23]

The five-day St. Petersburg seminar, one of a series, discussed electronic networking. It brought together eight men and four women advocates from the organizations of Soldiers' Mothers of St. Petersburg, Vladimir Province, and Chelyabinsk; general human rights advocacy organizations in Krasnodar Territory, Murmansk Province, Nizhnyi-Tagil, Penza Province, Perm Province, Kursk, and Ryazan; and Christians Against Torture and Child Slavery (Rostov-on-Don).[24]

The center bulletin contains instructions on when and how to appeal to the European Court on Human Rights in Strasbourg and how to draw up a grant proposal addressed to the Foundation for a Civil Society; it lists the addresses of foundations supporting rights protection. Of the foundations, twelve are funded from and mostly located in the United States; there is one in Japan, one in the UK, and one with the Council of Europe. The bulletin also includes sociological findings on problems that NGOs have in working with the mass media, such as inexperience or timidity. The information concludes with pointers on how to conduct a press conference. It mentions the resources available at the Russian-American Information and Press Center at the USA-Canada Institute, 2/3 Khlebnyi Lane, in cooperation with the Center on War, Peace, and Mass Media of New York University. The press center has also set up branches in various cities in the European and Siberian parts of Russia.[25]

The Central Black Earth Human Rights Center in Kursk reports that construction workers were cheated out of the apartments and the wages promised them for their work. The court cited various legally unfounded and fictitious pretexts not to try the case. It incorrectly ruled class action suits illegal and required that such suits should first go before a grievance committee at work—which does not exist.[26]

The press release (Russian, *press-reliz*) of the Soldiers' Mothers of St. Petersburg reprinted in the center bulletin carries the report of a typical case of a mother, Zinaida Egorovna, who sought evidence in the purported suicide by hanging of her eighteen-year-old draftee son. Her persistent inquiries revealed growing evidence that the military were covering up yet another brutal beating death by hazing. The bulletin reprinted a letter of conscript S. Ch. Velikoredchanin from Rostov-on-Don. It told of almost unbelievable brutality perpetrated against the writer and other conscripts serving in Chechnya. Soldiers awaiting replacement hid weapons of various kinds for sale to the Chechens. Corrupt officers looted furniture to take back with them from Chechnya; some of them told soldiers they could speed up their demobilization by bringing them a tape recorder or dual cassette player.[27]

The Committee of Soldiers' Mothers of Vladimir Province reported that the local election commission, in a decision upheld by the Provincial Court, denied the committee's candidate registration for the December 1995 election by invalidating needed signatures (on the ground that the year was missing from the required date) and delaying the return of the petition sheets. The committee had more luck interceding to get a telephone for the mother of a son who had died in the army in 1980 and who now needs a home phone for emergencies during the onset of her frequent heart attacks.[28]

The same bulletin issue carried a report from the Association of Prison Guardians of Serpukhov, a city of 140,000 about sixty miles due south of Moscow. A three-month seed-money grant from the Foundation for a Civil Society (Moscow Center) enabled the Serpukhov organization to help relatives of detained suspects. The advocates heard of cases where the police pressured suspects to sign waivers of their right to counsel and affidavits affirming the lie that they had been told regarding their right not to testify against themselves and to say nothing at all. The Serpukhov organization planned tort suits against authorities for damage to prisoners' health and other abuses, and suits claiming the unconstitutionality of legal norms issued locally and by the Federation. Serpukhov asked for help from "all regional human rights organizations" to help cover the legal costs of such suits.[29]

Toward a Civil Society: Perm

In the fall of 1994, members of the All-Russian "Memorial" Society, the party group Democratic Choice of Russia, and the Social Democratic Party of Russia decided to form the Center for Rights Protection in Perm, a city about 700 miles east-northeast of Moscow in the western Urals. It was registered on January 31, 1995, by the Justice Department of Perm Province. The Perm Center opened its doors to its first visitors in March. It recruited volunteer expert commissions and working groups, and has sponsored and assisted in the organization of several other local groups. The Perm Center's fifteen-page report on the first eleven months of its activities went out in print and on e-mail through the Moscow Center's bulletin. The Perm Center participates in seminars on communications and other practical matters organized by the Moscow Center. Aside from its own library, it has the donated services of the "Kodeks" electronic legal information retrieval service of the Perm-Kodeks Company.[30]

At report time, the Perm Center had about twenty individual members and a staff of five to ten who worked in two rooms in the Province Cultural-Business Building, equipped with telephones, computer, and copier. The Perm Center's mandate bars its acting in the name of any political organization or in the interests of any political or pressure group or state institution. The center's broad mandate is to defend people's political and civil, economic, social, and cultural human rights, "regardless of their political views, social status, nationality (ethnicity) and religion." That broad mandate resulted in contacts with numerous state and private organizations.[31] The center was setting up branches in rural areas, such as the village of Karagai, with the aid of small grants of about U.S. $1,000. The center used the local press, press conferences, round tables and radio and television broadcasts, as limited resources allowed, to help get out its message and move forward cases in which it had an interest. It also taught a human rights course in a local school.

In a sociological inquiry reported to Moscow, the center asked sample social groups: "Who has most violated your rights?" In all but one of eight social groups, officials of the bureaucracy topped the list in people's experience, followed by salespersons and militiamen (police officers). Politicians, tax inspectors, and physicians also showed some notoriety. The question "Who in your view can defend you at the present time?" evinced a consistently top score of "You yourself"—one-half of the respondents answered this in the social cross-section sample. Next-highest rated as likely defenders of their rights were NGO centers, for 20 percent of respondents. *All groups expressed the least confidence in the city Duma (council), city administration, trade unions, and political parties,* all of which scored very low—at most, 5 percent for the city administration among nonworking people such as pensioners. Judges and consumer groups fared considerably better. Private law offices, human rights NGOs, and one's employing enterprise got the best reviews. Substantial majorities of most social samples said that they would use the services of a rights-protecting center should the need for help arise.[32]

The center's first eleven months saw over 1,500 visitors presenting complaints and questions concerning their rights. In thirty-six cases of dispute over economic and social rights, the center became an active sponsor, obtaining remedies through the court in four cases, by settlement in seven cases, with six cases dropped for various reasons and others in various stages of progress.

In Case No. 002, the center represented students of the Urals branch of the All-Russian Academy of Painting, Sculpture, and Architecture in a successful suit to recover unpaid scholarships and for pain and suffering due to the abuses of the administration. Case No. 008 pitted the center against the Perm Province Youth Employment Exchange and the operator of a summer camp in Volgograd Province for unsanitary conditions and violations of child labor laws. The center got the children evacuated from the camp, held a press conference, prevailed on the local authorities to look into the situation there, and organized a meeting of parents of large families. After the center complained to the provincial Procuracy (prosecutor's office), a number of officials received reprimands. The Procuracy ordered the head of the Chief Administration of Education and the general director of the Youth and Student Employment Exchange to end the violations.

Case No. 010, Dima Matveev versus the Administration of Boarding School No. 126, rose from the mental and physical abuse of the boarding school's pupils. The case was conducted together with "Our Children" Parents Association and the Vetta Television Company. The center, which held a press conference with the participation of several adolescents, put on written notice the governor of Perm Province, the Chief Education Administration of Perm Province, and the Perm City Administration for Education and Science, and sent a complaint to the Procurator of Ordzhonikidze District. Staff members of the center reported for Vetta TV on their findings at the children's home. The City Committee for Education and Science investigated, and then fired, the director of the boarding school, sped up renovations and increased maintenance funds, and saw to it that hoarded study aids got to the children. The prosecutor refused to initiate a criminal case.[33]

The center helped prove a draftee physically unfit for the army; intervened to preserve the voluntary nature of tuition payments to a Kotov and Drozdov Commercial College; helped a conflicted family obtain separate housing; helped the "Memorial" Society prepare documents for a successful suit in the Russian Federation Constitutional Court against legislation denying inheritance to the grandchildren of purge victims (see above); and helped teachers of Karagai Village School No. 1 obtain their unpaid back wages through visits to the school, with an article in the newspaper *Permskie novosti*, and a complaint to the Procuracy. In the absence of laws defining the rights of children with Down's syndrome to special preschool programs, the center contacted local education and social welfare authorities and helped to form an Association of Parents of Children with Down's syndrome. The center also lobbied for passage of a local law lowering rents and utility costs for veterans in accordance with federal legislation.[34]

At issue in Perm, in order of diminishing frequency of cases, are: rights of investors, rights in the sphere of housing and privatization, labor rights, consumer's rights, medical care, the rights of purge victims and kin, rights to education, rights to land, rights of military conscripts, prisoners' rights, environmental issues, rights in marriage, and freedom of movement. These issues may not be typical for all regions, but they involve a broad cross section of local groups involved in advocacy and local improvements.

In May 1996, President Yeltsin appointed Vladimir Kartashkin to succeed Sergei Kovalyov as chairman of the Human Rights Commission. Kartashkin, an international law expert and professor, served between 1969 and 1985 as an expert in the UN Human Rights Department and then as legal consultant to the UN Secretary General. He participated effectively in the nongovernmental dialogue on human rights and the future that began in 1989 (see Chapter 4). Dr. Kartashkin's appointment prompted some skepticism at the time on the part of human rights monitors.[35] He wrote me a few months later that he had "worked very hard to set up the work of the commission in Moscow and create its bodies in all 89 subjects of the Russian Federation." He thought that the commission "will have a good future," but that "a lot has to be done to ensure better protection of human rights in Russia."[36] The Commission's contribution to their protection will depend on the autonomy and resources allocated to it, and on its relations with the public, NGOs, and officials of central and local government.

Human rights NGOs number many fewer than the estimated 40,000 to nearly 50,000 other nonprofit organizations (NPOs). NPOs include everything from schools to charitable and service organizations.[37] In less than a year, the Perm Center worked with thirty-six local organizations, among them not only human rights NGOs like Memorial, but also NPOs like the Barsyk Family Defense Foundation, in connection with problems of children's medical care and the foundation's tax obligations; the Association of Children with Down's Syndrome, helping it organize and register; the Guardianship Council (PTA) of School No. 12, on questions of tax obligations, fund-raising, giving lectures in the school, and role playing with people from the Children's Defense League; the Perm Association for the Blind, on tax matters and organizing an enterprise of the blind; the Society of Defrauded Investors and Shareholders of Perm Province, in pursuit of their lost deposits of hope; and the charities "Hospice" and "Diabetic Child."

Perm Center has worked in partnership with local civic and political organizations, including the Province Association of Psychiatrists and Physicians, on realizing rights to medical care; the office of Duma Deputy V. V. Pokhmelkin, which gave the center useful legal and political information; the Perm branch of the Russian Youth League; the club of Intellectual Games, on the protection of children's rights to education; the Perm Society for the Deaf; The Association of Parents of Invalid Children; the Perm Branch of the Russian Children's Fund; the "Hope" charitable foundation; the "Vita" organization of cancer victims; the Musical Society of Perm Province; and the Self-Government Council of Krym Village.

The communities served by the various NGOs featured here were organizing from below rather than above, the old way. NPOs lacked management skills and habits of spontaneous activism and cooperation, and worked on a shoestring—sometimes out of someone's apartment. The Antiwar Movement, a shifting coalition of Moscow NGO, attracted only small crowds to its demonstrations.[38]

Muslim Initiatives

Sometimes religious organizations join the network with urgent appeals. One such appeal called for support to stop the repression of independent Muslim mullahs and congregations in Uzbekistan. It referred to the disappearance of an independent cleric, Imam Sheikh Abdulavi Qori Mirzoev, and an associate, Ramazanbek Matkarimov, at Tashkent airport on August 29, 1995, when they were on the way to address an international Islamic conference in Moscow. In response to their disappearance, a consortium of Muslim religious, advocacy, and cultural groups placed a notice in the monthly bulletin of the Moscow Center for Research on Human Rights. The signers of the appeal claimed that eyewitnesses had seen the two travelers being detained by agents of the Uzbekistan Security Service. They asked for help from religious and secular organizations both in Russia and abroad to pressure the government of Uzbekistan to reveal the whereabouts of the kidnapped Muslims and to allow contact with them.[39]

The bulletin *Human Rights in Russia* carries a thoughtful and revealing analysis by the acting head of the Foundation for the Development of the Muslim Peoples (FDMP), G. A. Iskandyarov, on the subject of Muslim ethnic and religious rights in Russia. The FDMP began its existence as a legally recognized and protected entity with its registration in the summer of 1992. Its formation had the support of prominent spokespersons and eighteen Muslim groups in Moscow.

In response to the rampant prejudice against Muslim peoples, Iskandyarov points out that Muslims in Russia can trace the adoption of Islam by indigenous peoples of Russia back more than eleven centuries. He warns that it would be "dangerous to underestimate the role and importance of this faith, or of its layers of culture and outlook, when building a democratic Russia of the future." Recent "dramatic happenings" and the utterances of some "half-baked ideologues" reflect "old social prejudices, which multiply with dangerous rapidity, nurtured by the excesses of these times."

Iskandyarov recounts a history of bias—and biased history—on the Russians' part, beginning with the mistaken idea that Muslims were part of the Mongol invasion in the thirteenth century, when in fact the Mongols devastated indigenous Muslims in revenge for the latter's tenacious resistance in the Caucasus and Volga regions; indeed, their resistance protected Russian principalities from the Mongols for eight years. Volga Bulgars, not Mongols, are the sources of the Tatar ethnic culture. Tsarism brought centuries of colonization and forcible conversion to Orthodoxy. Later, the Soviet regime nearly liquidated the Muslim clergy and intellectual heritage. Since the time of Ivan the Terrible, Iskandyarov tells his Russian readers, the "image of the insidious enemy" has justified the "armed robbery" of the Muslim people. "How else to explain the crude plunders of Russian nationality policy which has shed rivers of Caucasian blood?"[40]

The lack of a firm policy for the coexistence and free development of ethnic groups during the rapid liberation from totalitarian repression, Iskandyarov says, has allowed leaders of certain groups like the Stavropol Cossacks (in southern Russia near the Caucasus) to commit all sorts of violations in the name of "national and/or religious rights" and to use nontitular minorities as scapegoats for the disasters befalling ordinary Russians. Iskandyarov urges the Russian Federation to restore peace and tranquillity through a consistent and resolute policy of minorities' equal rights and cultural and religious freedom. This, he says, should foster a sense of kinship among peoples who are now "simply cellmates." The "bottomless crater of the Caucasian war," state terrorism, which should be severely punished, the luxurious living of self-enriching officialdom, and the damaging rise in crime—all exact their costs in troubled regions and in society generally.[41] The FDMP, he says, seeks inclusivism, not separation of groups, in the spirit of the Koran, which says, "Allah created us different not to divide us but to distinguish us one from the other." The troubled times have prompted the FDMP to expand from charitable and cultural activities to "participat[ing] in building new social relations, based on principles of openness and democratism. Therefore we greet the idea of creating an international human rights network, we are grateful to its organizers and ready to become active participants."

The FDMP opened a branch on December 10, 1995, as the Ingushetia Information Center, in the city of Nazran', in the northern Caucasus zone of conflict between Christian Ossetians and Muslim Ingush over Ingush claims to land lost after the 1994 deportations. Managing the center were representatives of social organizations in Ingushetia: the "Almos" Women's Committee, the Chernobyl Union, the Council of Internationalist Fighters, the Union of the Deported, the Committee to Assist in the Search for Hostages and Missing Persons, the Union of Jurists, the Union of Cossack Formations of the Office of the Mufti, and the Orthodox Church. The means of community building specified in the Ingushetia Center's charter were at the same time an array of means for moving toward a civil society, including:

the propagation of achievements of democracy and progress; ideas of peace, intra-ethnic and interreligious accord; keeping track of citizens needing legal, material, and social support and giving support to them; ensuring social control and openness in the rendering of humanitarian assistance. The Ingushetia Information Center is called upon to help efforts of society in the normalization of the situation arising out of the Ossetian–Ingush and Chechen conflicts; to . . . develop citizens' social activism, and the mutual assistance and cooperation of the healthy forces of society.[42]

Practical sides of its work included "the training of local human rights advocates, providing decent telephone service, linking up with the computer network, etc." To help complete its equipment and keep it going, the center looked to "the beneficent help, cooperation, and support of the democratic community."[43]

Funding

Such help chronically fell short of minimal needs.[44] The NGO directory includes dozens of secular and religious charitable organizations. They work among the needy, the homeless, prisoners, victims of political repression, and refugees, in Moscow, St. Petersburg, throughout Russia and, no doubt, in other CIS countries. Most private charities seem to be funded by private donations from secular and religious sources.[45] But NPOs administering humanitarian aid from abroad find their programs undermined by cutoffs of foreign funds.

Charity has a proud history in Russia. In 1551, the Patriarch of the Russian Orthodox Church requested permission from the tsar to build old-age homes in Russia. In 1775, Catherine the Great formally decreed the establishment of private and public charities. The emancipation of the serfs in 1861 and the subsequent spurt in growth of the modern urban sector brought on a huge increase in the number of orphanages, hospitals, and aid agencies of all kinds run by nonstate charities.[46] Local governments provided other services.

Soviet Communist social cleansing liquidated private charities, along with all private NPOs. To fill the gaps left by state-funded social help programs, charity withdrew to the smaller spheres of workplace, friends, and relatives. But, Katherine Young notes, these informal help groups have broken down in Russia's "increasingly individualistic society." Once again, NPOs have become necessary beyond their means to fill the needs. New laws to regulate and protect charitable and nonprofit organizations gave them added protection but omitted the incentive to donors of tax-deductible contributions.[47] Until it is curbed, widespread tax evasion also would limit the incentive of tax deductibility, even if it existed.[48]

The dire poverty of the NGOs has naturally limited their work. A lack of funds forced the Perm Center for Rights Protection to curtail its publishing of self-help information on everything from suing in court to finding psychiatric help and exposing consumer fraud.[49] As a result, human rights NGOs and programs have been seeking support and cooperation from abroad. The Nizhni Novgorod Human Rights Association in the Volga region of central Russia publishes the newspaper *Pravozashchita* (Rights Protection) and runs a center for human rights assistance to the local population. The association reported having received funding from the U.S. Ford Foundation along with the Institute on Problems of a Civil Society in the

CIS (funded by TACIS of the European Union and the German International Society for Human Rights).[50] Various numbers of the Moscow Center's *Bulletin on Human Rights in Russia: Information Network* were published entirely with the support of foreign funding from the National Endowment for Democracy (U.S.), the Joyce Mertz-Gilmore Foundation (U.S.), the U.S. Agency for International Development, the Eurasia Foundation (U.S.), the Government of Switzerland's "Liberty" foundation, and, in the past, the Phare and TACIS programs of the European Union to support democratic society in Central and Eastern Europe, newly independent states, and Mongolia, the Westminster Foundation for Democracy (UK, 1994), and the Cultural Initiative Foundation (1995). The Moscow Center also received help—earmarked partly for the bulletin—from the Ministry of Foreign Affairs of Norway, and IREX, the International Research and Exchanges Board (U.S.). The American Development Foundation and the publisher "Human Rights" are acknowledged for their special attention and partnership in the project. The Moscow Center and several of its members have joint programs with, and receive funding from, foreign organizations;[51] but such funding is often for a limited time, as the listing of past donors above indicates.

The Moscow Center for Prison Reform compiled extensive findings on prison conditions and reform projects for the courts and corrections in their volume, *In Search of a Solution: Crime, Criminal Policy, and Prison Facilities in the Former Soviet Union*, which I have cited extensively. The book was underwritten by the Phare/TACIS Democracy Program of the European Union. The work of the Moscow Center for Prison Reform also received support from the European Human Rights Foundation in Belgium, the Jewish Community Development Fund/The Tides Foundation in the United States, the Open Society Institute in Moscow (funded by George Soros), and the Liberty Road Association in Switzerland. The center has cooperated with Penal Reform International (UK) and The Danish Center for Human Rights (Copenhagen). For its report, the center depended on materials from colleagues and NGOs in Russia, Kazakhstan, Belarus, and Azerbaijan; from various scholars in Russia; and from officials in Belarus and Moldova. The center received documents from listeners to the center's radio program "Oblaka" (Cloud), and from prisoners, penitentiary workers, and their families.

Ekspress-khronika, a weekly human rights newspaper with a circulation of 15,000, is edited by Aleksandr Podrabinek, formerly a human rights dissident and exile. It publishes stories and reports on human rights violations and gains from all over the former USSR. After shutting down for lack of funds, the paper revived with support from U.S. sources, including the Eurasia Foundation, the Henry M. Jackson Foundation, the National Endowment for Democracy, and the Open Society Institute.

Foreign cooperation also includes joint activities with local NGOs. Freedom House's office in Ukraine organizes and supports research, public-opinion polling, and funding of human rights NGOs. Its Moscow program sponsors radio and television programs and various forms of joint action with Russian NGOs, and assists in the organizing of the Sakharov Archive and Museum. Amnesty International maintains informational offices in Moscow, Moldova, and Ukraine. The AFL-CIO maintains a Free Trade Union Institute in Moscow. The Helsinki Citizens Assembly has a foreign link to Prague. The Azerbaijan group of the International Human Rights Association sends information to its central office in Frankfurt am Main. The Moscow Helsinki Group compiled the new directory of human rights NGOs in cooperation with Freedom House, with funding from USAID and the AID-funded Legal Consortium of ARD/Checchi in Washington.[52] *Monitoring* and *fandreising* have been adopted into the Russian vocabulary and world of human rights advocacy along with seminars on the writing of grant proposals, accounting, and networking among Russian human rights NGOs.[53]

Until more generous domestic funding appears, foreign grants are a lifeline for a great deal of NGO activity. But local donations to NGOs of money, resources, and services are increasing. Support of the Perm Center has come partly from abroad, from the U.S.-funded Human Rights Project Group (U.S. $6,986), and partly from the Russian-British joint enterprise "Perm Brewery Inc." Local contributors have included the Center Group Publishing Company, which donated publishing and printing services worth 500,000 rubles (then about U.S. $125) monthly from March to October 1995, or a total of 4,000,000 rubles (U.S. $1,000); the "Register" Society, which donated 3,000,000 rubles (U.S. $750) toward office and postal expenses from April to September 1995; and the Perm Council of the Union of Employees in Small and Medium Business, which gave 1,000,000 rubles (U.S. $250) a month from June 1995 to January 1996, totaling 8,000,000 rubles (about U.S. $2,000), to pay the salary of an attorney. Salaries for two more attorneys came from the Urals Agency for the Support of Small and Medium Enterprises. Duma Deputy V. V. Pkhmelkin gave 2,000,000 rubles (U.S. $500) and private entrepreneur V. V. Shavrin gave 1,000,000.[54]

The Fund for the Development of Muslim Peoples received help to open its branch in Ingushetia, both from abroad, through the MATRA Foundation of the Kingdom of the Netherlands and George Soros's Open Society Foundation, and from domestic donations from: the Democratic Russia movement, the Supreme Coordinating Center of the Religious Board of Russian Muslims, and a local entrepreneur, Akhmed Sagov. Mr. Sagov donated a two-story building, with office equipment, library, and lecture room.[55]

Doubtless, local organizations should be encouraged to find domestic sources of funding. But a precipitous drop in U.S. aid risks undoing the work of past assistance before it can be replaced by domestic sources. The annual U.S. aid budget to Russia dropped from $1.3 billion in 1994 to around $100 million by 1996. Less than 20 percent of this went to fund NPO work ranging from public education to mental health and environmental programs and publications. Yet the program of aid to NPOs has been praised as yielding "high impact at low cost." Galina Bodrenkova, director of Charity House in Moscow, has helped 250,000 people since 1991. Several of its eight programs received U.S. funding, including programs for distributing foreign-aid parcels. Like other NPOs, Charity House runs up against indifference or limited help on the part of authorities and public skepticism or ignorance.[56] Hard-pressed NPOs are faced with issues of how closely to cooperate with local authorities, who might supply potential solutions to some of their funding problems, without losing their independence. Aware of her difficulties but undaunted, Galina Bodrenkova told her interviewer: "Many people, especially the Communists, think we aren't ready for . . . a civil society. But I think that where people act for themselves to help others, that's already a civil society, if only on a small scale."[57] The work of human rights advocates and of numerous nonprofit organizations is widely passed over in political analyses of the post-Soviet states. Yet their work is a sign and condition of progress toward a democratic community.

Summing Up

Democratic Russia of the future continues to struggle with despotic Russia of the past, as Paul Milyukov saw in 1903. "An omnipotent bureaucracy" continues to defend the past, as it did in his day. In February 1991, nearly nine decades after Milyukov's remarks, Yuri Orlov, founder of the Moscow Helsinki Watch Group in 1976, saw the Russia of 1991 as locked in a "struggle between two programs: the program of the democrats and that of the reactionaries."[58] The outcome of that struggle is not predetermined in Russia or in other post-Soviet countries.

Russia's despots barred legal opposition and governmental accountability. As the country began to modernize, the autocrats regarded with suspicion any civic initiatives in society and local government. Nevertheless, a growing professional and commercial stratum committed itself to civic activism, public service, individual rights, democratization, and, later yet, parliamentary assertiveness in the face of a tenacious tsarist administration. The Provisional Government of 1917 that followed the fall of tsarism lost the race with the Bolsheviks, owing to the disaster of world war— but not by popular vote, and not before Russia had become, in Lenin's own words, and because of its curbs on repression, "the freest country in the world," on the verge of making a choice for democracy. The progress in reform and democratization in prerevolutionary Russia is too readily written off by some leading specialists.[59]

The Communists took over a free, though not yet democratic, country, and with their social and political cleansing made it the least free. They imposed by force the dependency principle of law and rights, just as the supremacy principle was taking hold. Stalin brutally wiped out the remnants of economic autonomy in farming and commerce, and professional autonomy in academia, literature, and the arts. His totalitarian political community gained a new legitimacy with its nationalism, its opportunities for advancement, and its victory in the Great Fatherland War.

The speed of the thaw that came after Stalin confirmed that he had not wiped out ideas of freedom and non-Party truths. The persistence of a creeping openness even as Brezhnev repressed the new human rights movement reflected the contradictions that George Kennan and Soviet dissidents had suggested existed between despotism and the creative initiatives needed for advanced development. Gorbachev's restructuring destructured Communist autocracy and, unintentionally, the USSR as well. But the gains in freedom he fostered carried over, unevenly, into the post-Soviet states, as did the entrenched, self-enriching bureaucracy and militarized imperial priorities. That mixed legacy caused economic recovery and democratization in the newly independent states to lag behind economic and political development in the less thoroughly communized Eastern European countries and the Soviet-occupied Baltic states.

Russian and Soviet absolutism broke down because of their own contradictions. The breakdowns came ever more rapidly over time—at first, after centuries, then decades, then years or even days. Democracy, on the other hand, has made a faltering and disorderly start. But dawning democracy has survived crises and setbacks in countries with a majority of the post-Soviet population and with diverse cultures and ties to the West.

Paradoxes have abounded in response to historic patterns, the contingencies of leadership, and the nature of the Soviet experience. The most Westernized and economically advanced Baltic states of Estonia and Latvia were also the most exclusive in their citizenship policy. Ukraine, one of the least economically recovered countries, became the most inclusive in its policies of citizenship and efforts at nation-building. Moldova stuck to democracy despite its internal conflict with the separatist and authoritarian Transdniestrian region. Christian, European Belarus fell behind Central Asian, nominally Muslim, and poverty-stricken Kyrgyzstan in the struggle for human rights and democracy. The war-torn Transcaucasus nurtured an emerging democracy, Georgia, and two authoritarian states where opposition and human rights advocacy, though harassed, were not yet extinguished. The most despotic states, in Central Asia, were also among the least economically developed: no paradox there.

Russia confounded doomsayers several times after independence. A well-known Russian analyst saw the high vote for opposition of the left and right in the parliamentary elections of 1995 as "an expression of sympathy not simply protest, of sympathy for old authoritarian Russia. . . . In fact the people did express their will: by democratic means to regain the right to live without free elections." [60] After President Yeltsin rejected his (later fired) aides' advice to postpone the 1996 elections, a clear majority of people voted not to turn back. Less pessimistically inclined Russian and U.S. observers took this as a good omen.

Among signs of democratization in Russia, as in other newly forming post-Soviet democracies, were the onset of businesslike relations between the executive and parliament, and the survival of embattled rights and freedoms of expression, information, and association. Civic development and a culture of law and rights were being nurtured by foreign and a growing domestic philanthropy, by democratically inclined media and educators, by the necessities of emerging market transactions, and by the network of advocates for the rights of army recruits, prisoners, hostages, consumers, women, children, and minorities, and for religious diversity, fair elections, environmental cleanup, and commemoration of the repressed past. Thousands of new nonprofit public-interest organizations strove to serve the needy.

The media and NGOs began to make local government accountable for its lapses and abuses, and to hold small-scale private swindlers to the rule of law. Nonprofit organizations began to draw local governments into the services for which both assumed responsibility. Still, the executives in most post-Soviet states retained great power and little accountability. This too was changing—for example, in the wake of twenty months of the Chechen war in Russia, and in battles in Ukraine over reforms and the new constitution.

The agenda of struggle for human rights and democracy in Russia and other democratizing post-Soviet countries includes the following actions and tests of progress:

1. continue the formation of multiparty systems and coalitions that close the door to demagogues as credible candidates;
2. curb threats to and pressures on independent media;
3. among other means of holding the political elites more accountable, continue to support the development of human rights NGOs and nonprofit organizations through increasing domestic sponsorship, favorable tax-deduction law, and cooperation, if possible, with the president's Human Rights Commission;
4. increase rather than decrease assistance to nonprofit organizations, and to crucial programs for education in human rights and the rule of law, as well as in the full story of Imperial Russian and Soviet history, urgently reversing the decline in public education;
5. speed up progress toward the rule of law and reduce threats to civil rights by also pressing on with military, police, and judicial reform,

the passage of a law on the constitutionally mandated human rights ombudsman, and the election of an objective and independent ombudsman;

6. build an efficient and socially just, regulated market economy as a material basis for democratic legitimacy and social counterweight to state power, and as a source of domestic support for the NGOs, by rooting out corruption step by step, collecting taxes due, and joining vigorously in the international effort to smash, or at least weaken, organized crime;

7. improve the legal framework and security for foreign investment in private enterprises in Russia (in 1996 such enterprises numbered the same in Russia as in Estonia, with one hundred times less population);

8. recruit a competent leadership that will reject costly imperialist priorities as the way to restore Russia's greatness while defending Russia's national interests in the "near abroad" and beyond;

9. continue to build a diverse national community across ethnic, regional, and class lines and live up to constitutional guarantees of minority equality and federal partnership, through negotiation and conflict resolution;

10. exercise restraint, within the limits of a reasonable conception of national interest, in Russia's relations with other post-Soviet states;

11. encourage countries abroad to join with Russia and the other post-Soviet states in efforts to expand cooperation and dialogue among equals, whether up in space or down here on troubled and endangered earth, for which Russia, a major polluter and strong but faltering democracy, can become a major benefactor in its contributions to international trade, enlightenment and science, environmental protection, and peacekeeping. But this means that all parties to cooperation must live up to the lofty language of constitutional and international commitments.

Nearly two centuries of freedom's ordeal and struggle in Russia and successor states have resulted neither in the triumph of democracy nor in despotism with demonstrated staying power in developing economies. The case for cultural relativism is not proven; nor is the case for simplistic universalism. The latter ignores the obvious ordeals of freedom: the need for democracy to adapt to particular cultures and circumstances; the struggle between the attitudes of a despotic past and a democratic future in countries that have long been deprived of freedom; the perils of discord and the tensions inherent in massive violations of economic and social human rights.

One can agree with Gorbachev's confident prediction that "a return to a totalitarian regime will not succeed," though there may be "a temporary rollback of democratic reforms and democratic processes."[61] Still one should view democratization not as an overnight panacea, but rather, as Max Weber described politics, as a complex and lengthy "slow boring of hard boards."[62] Natalia Taubina of the Moscow Foundation for an Open Society anticipates that democracy is taking hold in Russia, and that "this will not happen in ten years. The Communists ruled for seventy years, and it will take a long time to recover from that."[63] The whole tenor of this book agrees with the views of Natalia and a member of her grandparents' generation, academician Dmitry Likhachev. "My predictions are optimistic," he said. "Moses led his people through the desert for forty years, until several generations had passed. Those who have become accustomed to employing Stalinist or Brezhnevite methods must become extinct . . . these officials have to vanish at some point, in a natural way, without firing squads. And in their place will come a new youth."[64]

Notes

Introduction

1. On democracy's waves and reverse waves, see, e.g., Samuel P. Huntington, "Democracy's Third Wave," *Journal of Democracy* 2, no. 2 (Spring 1991): 12.

2. Adrian Karatnycky, "Democracies on the Rise, Democracies at Risk," *Freedom Review* (January–February 1995): 5–10.

3. Ibid.

4. Zbigniew Brzezinski, *Out of Control: Global Turmoil on the Eve of the 21st Century* (New York: St. Martin's Press, 1993), 7–18.

5. Human Rights Watch, *Slaughter among Neighbors: The Political Origins of Communal Violence* (New Haven, CT: Yale University Press, 1995).

6. Charles W. Kegley, Jr., and Eugene R. Wittkopf, *World Politics: Trend and Transformation*, 5th ed. (New York: St. Martin's Press, 1995).

7. Alexander Motyl, "Soviet Remnants," *Freedom Review* (January–February 1996): 30–34; Barbara Applebaum, "Nice Guys Finish Last," *Freedom Review* (January–February 1996): 24–30.

8. James R. Millar and Sharon L. Wolchik, eds., *The Social Legacy of Communism* (Cambridge and New York: Cambridge University Press, Woodrow Wilson Center Series, 1994). The members of a democratic political community, as conceived of here, share allegiance to a government that is accountable to them, enjoy human rights under the rule of law, and recognize responsibilities to one another and to the community. Nigel Ashford and Stephen Davies, eds., *A Dictionary of Conservative and Libertarian Thought* (London and New York, 1991), 41–42; Mary Anne Glendon, "Rights in Twentieth-Century Constitutions," in Amitai Etzioni, ed., *Rights and the Common Good: The Communitarian Perspective* (New York: St. Martin's Press, 1995), 27–36.

9. Karl Dietrich Bracher, *The German Dictatorship: The Origins, Structure and Effects of National Socialism* (New York/Washington: Praeger Publishers, 1971), 1–214.

10. Panel Discussion at the Harriman Institute, Columbia University, New York, December 8, 1995.

11. Lilia Shevtsova, "Russia's Post-Communist Politics: Revolution or Continuity?" in Gail W. Lapidus, ed., *The New Russia: Troubled Transformation* (Boulder, CO: Westview Press, 1995), 3–36; Robert Sharlet, "Post-Soviet Constitutionalism": Politics and Constitution-Making in Russia and Ukraine," in Michael Kraus and Donald D. Liebowitz, eds., *Russia and Eastern Europe after Communism* (Boulder, CO: Westview, 1996), 15–34.

12. Ken Jowitt, "The End of Leninism: The New World Disorder," *Journal of*

Democracy 2, no. 1 (1991): 13–14, 17–18; quotes from 18. See also Ken Jowitt, *New World Disorder: The Leninist Extinction* (Berkeley: University of California Press, 1992), 249–331.

13. Frederic J. Fleron, Jr., and Erik P. Hoffmann, "Post-Communist Studies and Political Science," in Frederic J. Fleron, Jr., and Erik P. Hoffmann, *Post-Communist Studies and Political Science: Methodology and Empirical Theory in Sovietology* (Boulder, CO: Westview Press, 1993), 382.

14. Larry Diamond and Marc E. Plattner, eds., *The Global Resurgence of Democracy*, 2d ed. (Baltimore: The Johns Hopkins University Press, 1996), passim; Peter Juviler and Bertram Gross, eds., with Vladimir Kartashkin and Elena Lukasheva, *Human Rights for the 21st Century* (Armonk, NY: M. E. Sharpe, 1993).

15. "X," [George Kennan], "The Sources of Soviet Conduct," *Foreign Affairs* (July 1947); reprinted in Philip E. Mosely, ed., *The Soviet Union 1922–1962: A Foreign Affairs Reader* (New York: Frederick A. Praeger, 1963), 169–85.

16. Aleksandr Proskury, *Union of Fraternal Nations* (Moscow: Novosti Publishers, 1982), 47.

17. Mancur Olson, "Dictatorship, Democracy, and Development," *American Political Science Review* 87, no. 3 (1993): 567–76; reprinted with abridged footnotes in Bernard E. Brown and Roy C. Macridis, *Comparative Politics: Notes and Readings* (Belmont, CA: Wadsworth Publishing Co., 1996), 368–80; quote from 379.

18. Robert D. Putnam, *Making Democracy Work: Civic Traditions in Modern Italy* (Princeton, NJ: Princeton University Press, 1993), 183–85; quotes on 183, 184. See also Andrew Nathan, "Will the Conception of Human Rights in China Necessarily Be the Same as the International Conception or Will It Be Substantially Different?" *Human Rights Tribune* 2, no. 2 (1991): 6.

19. An exemplar of this approach is Karen Dawisha and Bruce Parrott, *Russia and the New States of Eurasia: The Politics of Upheaval* (New York: Cambridge University Press, 1994); e.g., 123–60, 281–97. See also Chapter 1 of this book.

Chapter 1. Getting to Democracy

1. Baron de Montesquieu, *The Spirit of the Laws* (1748), excerpted in Walter Laqueur and Barry Rubin, *The Human Rights Reader*, 2d ed. (New York: Meridian Books, 1990), 60.

2. "The Bible points to the fact that human persons are endowed with freedom to choose"; Archbishop Desmond M. Tutu, "Preface," in John Witte, Jr., and Johan D. van der Vyver, *Religious Human Rights in Global Perspective: Religious Perspectives* (The Hague: Martinus Nijhoff, 1996), ix–xvi (quote from xi).

3. An exemplar of this multifactor approach is Karen Dawisha and Bruce Parrott, *Russia and the New States of Eurasia: The Politics of Upheaval* (New York: Cambridge University Press, 1994), 123–60, 281–97. On minority riots and their significance, see also: Donald L. Horowitz, *Ethnic Groups in Conflict* (Berkeley: University of California Press, 1985) and his "Democracy in Divided Societies: The Challenge of Ethnic Conflict," *Journal of Democracy* 4, no. 4 (1993): 19–38; Hurst Hannum, "The Limits of Sovereignty and Majority Rule: Minorities, Indigenous Peoples, and the Right to Autonomy," in Ellen Lutz, Hurst Hannum, and Kathryn J. Burke, *New Directions in Human Rights* (Philadelphia: University of Pennsylvania Press, 1989), 20–21; Peter Juviler, "Are Collective Rights Anti-Human?: Theories on Self-Determination and Practice in Soviet Successor States," *Netherlands Quarterly of Human Rights* 11, no. 3 (1993): 267–82.

4. Governmental accountability in a democracy is emphasized by Philippe C.

Schmitter and Terry Lynn Karl, "What Democracy Is . . . And Is Not," *Journal of Democracy* 2, no. 3 (1991): 76.

5. Philippe C. Schmitter points to contributions in new democracies of innovating leaders who may "jump stages" of evolution, and of interest groups. "Interest Systems and the Consolidation of Democracy," in Gary Marks and Larry Diamond, eds., *Reexamining Democracy: Essays in Honor of Seymour Martin Lipset* (Newbury Park, CA: Sage Publications, 1992), 157, 176.

6. Larry Diamond, "Introduction," in Larry Diamond, ed., *The Democratic Revolution* (New York: Freedom House, 1992), 7–8. Civil society, as Locke and Jefferson conceived it, made government its agent in the protection of the rights of its individual members; John Locke, *Second Treatise on Government*, ed. C. B. McPherson (Indianapolis: Hackett Publishing Co., 1980), 42–65. Democracy, in Robert Dahl's useful definition, is popular rule exercised through widely shared opportunities for participation and consent. A civil society is most likely to take advantage of those opportunities. See Peter Juviler, "Will Democracy Survive Freedom in the ex-USSR?" in the inaugural issue of *Demokratizatsiia* (Washington, D.C.) 1, no. 1 (1992): 73–81.

7. Larry Diamond, "Civil Society and the Struggle for Democracy," in Larry Diamond, ed., *The Democratic Revolution* (New York: Freedom House, 1992), 6–15; Robert A. Dahl, *A Preface to Democratic Theory* (Chicago: University of Chicago Press, 1956; Phoenix ed. 1963, reprinted 1965), esp. 63–89 ("Polyarchal Democracy").

8. Archie Brown and Jack Gray, *Political Culture and Political Change in Communist States*, 2d ed. (New York: Holmes and Meier, 1979); quote from Archie Brown, 1.

9. David Easton, *A Framework for Political Analysis* (Englewood Cliffs, NJ: Prentice-Hall, 1965).

10. Jonathan Schell, "The Uncertain Leviathan," *Atlantic Monthly* (August 1996): 70–78; Michael W. Foley and Bob Edwards, "The Paradox of Civil Society," *Journal of Democracy* 7, no. 3 (1996): 38–52.

11. E. E. Schattschneider, *The Semi-Sovereign People* (New York: Holt, Rinehart, and Winston, 1960).

12. Vaclav Havel address of February 7, 1990, as recorded in *Congressional Record —House*, February 21, 1990, H. Doc. 394. People's lives and rights are affected by governmental, corporate, and other interests that seem to be significantly beyond the reach of democratic controls and inputs. David Burnham, *Above the Law: Secret Deals, Political Fixes, and Other Misadventures of the U.S. Department of Justice* (New York: Scribner, 1996); Ellen Goodman, "Women Activists in a Hundred Countries," *Washington Post*, March 6, 1993; David C. Corton, *When Corporations Rule the World* (West Hartford, CT: Kumarian Press, 1995); Charles E. Lindblom, *Politics and Markets: The World's Political-Economic Systems* (New York: Basic Books, 1997); Charles S. Maier, "Democracy and Its Discontents," *Foreign Affairs* 72, no. 4 (1994): 48–64; David Schoenbrod, *Power without Responsibility: How Congress Abuses the People through Delegation* (New Haven, CT: Yale University Press, 1993); Richard Morin, "Tuned Out, Turned Off," *Washington Post National Weekly Edition*, February 5–11, 1996, 6–7; "Food and Hunger: How to Make a Pigeon Stew," and "Ten Facts You Should Know about Hunger," *Street News*, October 1990, 19.

13. Louis Henkin, *The Age of Rights* (New York: Columbia University Press, 1990).

14. Article 21: "1. Everyone has the right to take part in the government of his country, directly or through freely chosen representatives. 2. Everyone has the right to equal access to public service in his country. 3. The will of the people shall be the basis of the authority of government; this shall be expressed in periodic and genuine elections which shall be by universal and equal suffrage and shall be held by secret vote or by equivalent free voting procedures"; UDHR in the Center for the

Study of Human Rights, Columbia University, *Twenty-Five Human Rights Documents* (New York, 1994), 8. Secretary of State Warren Christopher: human rights "cannot be guaranteed except in countries where there is accountable democratic government"; conference "From Early Warning to Rebuilding: Human Rights Policy in the Post-Cold-War Era," Department of State, Washington, D.C., April 3, 1993. See also n. 22, below.

15. See, e.g., the 1990 *Document of the Copenhagen Meeting of the Conference on the Human Dimension of the CSCE* (Washington, D.C.: U.S. Commission on Security and Cooperation in Europe, June 1990); Boutros Boutros-Ghali, *Statement of the UN World Conference on Human Rights*, June 25, 1993 (United Nations, NY, 1993); Akwasi Aidoo, "Africa: Democracy Without Human Rights?" *Human Rights Quarterly* 15, no. 4 (1993): 703–15.

16. Boutros-Ghali, *Statement*, 8.

17. Hurst Hannum, *Autonomy, Sovereignty, and Self-Determination: The Accommodation of Conflicting Rights*, 2d ed. (Philadelphia: University of Pennsylvania Press, 1996); Peter Juviler, "Rethinking Rights without the Enemy," in Peter Juviler and Bertram Gross, eds., *Human Rights for the 21st Century* (Armonk, NY: M. E. Sharpe, 1993), 275–79.

18. Boutros-Ghali, *Statement*, 12.

19. Philip Alston, "The Legal Basis of the Right to Peace," *Peace Review* (Fall 1991): 23–27; Katerina Tomasevski, "The Right to Pace after the Cold War," *Peace Review* (Fall 1991): 14–22; Bertram Gross, "Power, Rights and Peace," *Peace Review* (Fall 1991): 3–8.

20. A safe and healthy environment is strongly implied by the right to health care in Article 25 of the UDHR, and even more so in Article 12 of the International Covenant on Economic, Social and Cultural Rights, Article 12, 2(b), which lists among the steps toward "the highest attainable standard of physical and mental health": "The improvement of all aspects of environmental and industrial hygiene." The right to a safe and healthy environment is recognized in the Draft Protocol Additional to the American Convention on Human Rights (1986), Article 12, in Blaustein, 576, and the Vienna Declaration, with its very weak statement in part I, Article 11, recognizing that toxic waste dumping "potentially constitutes a serious threat to the human rights of life and health of everyone."

21. Gregory H. Fox, "The Right to Political Participation in International Law," *Yale Journal of International Law* 17, no. 2 (1992): 539–607; UDHR, Articles 2–21, and corresponding articles of the 1966 International Covenant on Civil and Political Rights.

22. They remain vulnerable also as to their rights to freedom of movement and of citizenship. Articles 2–16 of the UDHR and corresponding articles of other international documents.

23. Aristotle, "On Democracy and Tyranny," in Roy C. Macridis and Bernard E. Brown, eds., *Comparative Politics: Notes and Readings*, 7th ed. (Pacific Grove, CA: Brooks Cole, 1990), 129; Juan J. Linz, "Transitions to Democracy," *The Washington Quarterly* (Summer 1990): 157. Polish former dissident and politician Vladislav Geremek agrees with the human rights theorist Jack Donnelly that, in Geremek's words, the principle of majority rule "must be tempered by the rule of law, by governmental checks and balances, and by the principle of respect for the rights of minorities" and "a commitment to . . . a respect for the dignity of the human being." Vladislav Geremek, "A Horizon of Hope and Fear," *Journal of Democracy* 4, no. 3 (1993): 105; Jack Donnelly, "Human Rights in the New World Order," *World Policy Journal* 9 (1992): 249–77; Jack Donnelly, *International Human Rights* (Boulder, CO: Westview Press, 1993), 145–52.

24. Sergei Zamoshkin, "Re-Reading the Criminal Code," *Moscow News*, no. 28, July 15–21, 1994, 13.

25. Erik P. Hoffmann, "Challenges to Viable Constitutionalism in Post-Soviet Russia," July 1994 draft of paper presented at Second International Conference, Committee on Viable Constitutionalism, Center for Legislative Development, State University of New York at Albany, March 17–20, 1994.

26. John N. Hazard, *Law and Social Change in the U.S.S.R.* (Toronto: The Carswell Company, 1953), 1–34; A. D. Radygin, *Reforma sobstvennosti v Rossii: na puti iz proshlogo v budushchee* (Moscow: Respublika, 1994), 13; Hiroshi Kimura, *Personal Property in the Soviet Union*, Vols. 1 and 2 (Tokyo, 1969–70); Larry Diamond, "Economic Development and Democracy Reconsidered," 93–139.

27. Henry Shue, *Basic Rights: Subsistence, Affluence, and U.S. Foreign Policy* (Princeton, NJ: Princeton University Press, 1980); Preambles, International Covenant on Civil and Political Rights and International Covenant on Economic, Social, and Cultural Rights, Center for the Study of Human Rights, Columbia University, in *Twenty-Five Human Rights Documents* (New York, 1994), 10–17.

28. "The Vienna Declaration and Programme of Action. Adapted 25 June 1993 by the World Conference on Human Rights," in *World Conference on Human Rights, Vienna, Austria, June 1993* (New York, UN DPI/1394-39399–August 1993-20M, 1993), Article I, section 8.

29. Larry Diamond cites abundant statistical evidence of a correlation between democracy and human development, more than exists with sheer growth or income as such. Democracies are likely to have a relatively high human development index—an index developed by the UN Development Program from figures on GNP, longevity, and literacy. "Economic Development and Democracy Reconsidered," in Gary Marks and Larry Diamond, eds., *Reexamining Democracy: Essays in Honor of Seymour Martin Lipset* (Newbury Park, CA: Sage Publications, 1992), 124–30.

30. The Vienna Declaration and Program of Action, part I, Articles 8, 10, 11, 25; part II, Article 36.

31. David E. Schmitt, *Violence in Northern Ireland: Ethnic Conflict and Radicalization in an International Setting* (Morristown, NJ: General Learning Press, 1974), 1–35.

32. For an introduction to conflicting views on nationalism, see Charles P. Cozic, ed., *Nationalism and Ethnic Conflict* (San Diego, CA: Greenwood Press, 1994). See also: Ernest Gellner, *Nations and Nationalism* (Ithaca, NY: Cornell University Press, 1983); Ted Robert Gurr and Barbara Harff, *Ethnic Conflict in World Politics* (Boulder, CO: Westview Press, 1994).

33. Kenneth Maxwell, "Spain's Transition to Democracy: A Model for Eastern Europe?"; Nils H. Wessel, ed., *The New Europe: Revolution in East–West Relations*, Proceedings of the Academy of Political Science (New York) 38, no. 1, 47–48; Robert A. Scalapino, "Democratizing Dragons: South Korea and Taiwan," *Journal of Democracy* 4, no. 3 (1993): 70–83.

34. UDHR, Article 1, in Human Rights Center, *Twenty-Five Documents*, 6.

35. Putnam, *Making Democracy Work*, 3.

36. Meeting of the delegation of the Lawyers Committee for Human Rights at the Institute of State and Law, Moscow, December 12–13, 1989, notes of Peter Juviler.

37. Demetrios Caraley, ed., *Presidential and Parliamentary Democracies: Which Work Best?* Special issue of *Political Science Quarterly* 109, no. 3 (1994).

38. Douglas Greenberg, Stanley N. Katz, Melanie Beth Oliviero, and Steven C. Wheatley, *Constitutionalism and Democracy: Transitions in the Contemporary World* (New York: Oxford University Press, 1993), xix.

39. Adamantia Pollis, "Human Rights in Liberal, Socialist, and Third World Perspective," in Richard Pierre Claude and Burns H. Weston, eds., *Human Rights in the*

World Community: Issues and Action, 2d ed. (Philadelphia: University of Pennsylvania Press, 1992), 146–56; Asmaron Legeese, "Human Rights in African Political Culture," in Kenneth W. Thompson, ed., *The Moral Imperatives of Human Rights: A World Survey* (Washington, D.C.: The University Press of America, 1980), 123–38.

40. Non-Western Nobel Prize winners who have espoused ideals of democracy and human rights include the late Andrei Sakharov; the Dalai Lama of Tibet; Daw Aung San Suu Kyi, democratic leader in Myanmar (Burma); Rigoberta Menchu, Mayan Indian champion of human rights in Guatemala; and Nelson Mandela of South Africa (jointly with then President de Clerk). See Aung San Suu Kyi, "Transcending the Class of Cultures: Freedom, Development, and Human Worth," *Journal of Democracy* 6, no. 2 (1995): 11–19; the Dalai Lama, *A Policy of Kindness* (Ithaca, NY: Snow Lion Publishers, 1990), 11–27. Advocates for human rights and rule of law work and sacrifice at the grass-roots level the world over, many without recognition. The Lawyers Committee for Human Rights, *The Persecution of Judges and Lawyers in 1993* (New York, 1994), annually; Lawrence Wechsler, "Sentries," *The New Yorker,* January 10, 1994, 71–74; Lawrence Wechsler, "Lost in Rwanda," *The New Yorker,* April 25, 1994, 42–45.

41. Adamantia Pollis, "Cultural Relativism Revisited: Through a State Prism," *Human Rights Quarterly* 18, no. 2 (1996): 316–44.

42. UDHR, Article 29; Henry Shue, "Negative Duties toward All, Positive Duties toward Some," in Juviler and Gross, *Human Rights for the 21st Century,* 266–74.

43. Adda B. Bozeman, "Human Rights in Western Thought," in Kenneth W. Thompson, ed., *The Moral Imperatives of Human Rights: A World Survey* (Washington, D.C.: University Press of America, 1980), 25–38.

44. Jeremy Waldron, ed., *Nonsense upon Stilts: Bentham, Burke and Marx on the Rights of Man* (London and New York: Methuen, 1987); Amartya Sen, born in India, on the contrary makes a case against utilitarianism and for human rights, in "Individual Freedom as a Social Commitment," *New York Review of Books,* June 14, 1990, 49–54; on Western diversity, see Louis Henkin, "Preface," in Louis Henkin and John Lawrence Hargrove, eds., *Human Rights: An Agenda for the Next Century* (Washington, D.C.: American Society of International Law, 1994), ix.

45. Thomas G. Weiss, David P. Forsythe, and Roger A. Coate, *The United Nations and Changing World Politics* (Boulder, CO: Westview Press, 1995), 106–11.

46. Quoted from Walter Laqueur and Barry Rubin, *Human Rights Reader,* 2d ed. (New York: Mentor Books, 1990), 156.

47. Dennis J. Driscoll, "The Development of Human Rights in International Law," in ibid., 41–56.

48. Louis Henkin and Albert Rosenthal, eds., *Constitutionalism and Rights: The Influence of the United States Constitution Abroad* (New York: Columbia University Press, 1990).

49. UDHR, Preamble and Article 1.

50. They cover spheres ranging from the rights of labor (first codified through the International Labor Organization founded in 1919); the rights of women and children; the status of refugees; the stand against torture or degrading treatment and punishment and religious intolerance; the rights of indigenous and tribal peoples; treatment of prisoners; prevention of racial discrimination, genocide, and torture; but not, or not yet, including the rights of homosexuals or the right to abortions. Connie de La Veda, "Using International Human Rights Law in Legal Services Cases," *Clearinghouse Review* (March 1941): 1243; Center for the Study of Human Rights, Columbia University, *Twenty-Five Human Rights Documents*; Michael Gigante, "Gay Rights: The Ongoing Struggle," in *Breakthrough* (Winter/Spring 1989): 56–59.

51. Vienna Declaration and Programme of Action (1993), Part I, Article 5; Ved P. Nanda and George W. Shepherd, Jr., "U.N. Conference Affirms Priority of Human Rights," *The Independent* [of the UNA-USA] (Fall 1993): 4; Weiss et al., *The United Nations and Changing World Politics*, 1–6, 103–24.

52. Samuel P. Huntington, *The Third Wave: Democratization in the Late Twentieth Century* (Norman and London: University of Oklahoma Press, 1993); "Democracy for the Long Haul," *Journal of Democracy* 7, no. 2 (1995): 3–13.

53. John Shattuck, Assistant Secretary of State: "A key to the development of democracy is the force of NGOs" for human rights. Conference "From Early Warning to Rebuilding: Human Rights Policy in the Post-Cold-War Era," Department of State, Washington, D.C., April 3, 1993.

54. *The Human Rights Internet HRI Reporter: A Listing of Organizations Concerned with Human Rights and Social Justice Worldwide* (Ottawa: Human Rights Internet, 1994); Lawyers Committee for Human Rights, *World Conference on Human Rights — The Establishment of the Right of Nongovernmental Human Rights Groups to Operate* (New York: Lawyers Committee for Human Rights, June 1993).

55. Ludmilla Alexeyeva, lecture on human rights education attended by the author at the Institute for Advanced Educational Training, Moscow, December 15, 1995.

Chapter 2. Changing Russia

1. Paul Milyukov, Crane Lectures for 1903, published as *Russia and Its Crisis* (Chicago: University of Chicago Press / London: T. Fisher Unwin, 1905), vii–viii.

2. Richard Sakwa, *Russian Politics and Society* (London/New York: Routledge, 1993), 393–95; quote from 394. On cultural determinism in Russia, see Peter Juviler, "Russia Turned Upside Down," in Peter Juviler and Bertram Gross, eds., with Vladimir Kartashkin and Elena Lukasheva, *Human Rights for the 21st Century* (Armonk, NY: M. E. Sharpe, 1993), 33–34. On the durability of despotism, see Bertram Wolfe, *Three Who Made a Revolution* (New York: Delta, 1964), 11–38. For a latter-day Slavophile rejection of Western rule of law and preference for a pre-Bolshevik, moderate authoritarianism, see, e.g., Aleksandr I. Solzhenitsyn, *Letter to the Soviet Leaders* (New York: Harper and Row, 1974); idem, Address at Harvard Commencement, *New York Times*, June 9, 1978. On Russian collectivism, see, e.g., Edward L. Keenan, "Human Rights in Soviet Political Culture," in Kenneth W. Thompson, ed., *The Moral Imperatives of Human Rights* (Washington, D.C.: University Press of America, 1990), 69–80.

3. Theodore Taranovski, "The Return to Normalcy: Commentary," in Theodore Taranovski, ed., *Reform in Modern Russian History: Progress or Cycle* (Washington, D.C./Cambridge: Woodrow Wilson Press and Cambridge University Press, 1995), 420. John McCormick omits altogether any mention of the February Revolution of 1917 which toppled the tsar through popular demonstrations and passes over the accomplishments of the Provisional Government, in his *Comparative Politics in Transition* (Belmont, CA: Wadsworth Publishing Co., 1995), 132–43.

4. Arkady Vaksberg, "Kakim dolzhno byt' pravovoe gosudarstvo?" *Literaturnaia gazeta,* June 8, 1988.

5. Juviler and Gross, *Human Rights for the 21st Century*, 28–31, 69–93.

6. Sakwa, *Russian Politics and Society*, 393.

7. Helene Carrere d'Encausse, *Confiscated Power: How Soviet Russia Really Works* (New York: Harper and Row, 1982), 7–10.

8. Neil B. Weissman, *Reform in Tsarist Russia: The State Bureaucracy and Local Gov-*

ernment 1900–1914 (New Brunswick, NJ: Rutgers University Press, 1981), 221–23; quote from 223.

9. Wolfe, *Three Who Made a Revolution*, 23.

10. Marquis de Custine, *The Empire of the Czar: A Journey Through Eternal Russia* (New York: Doubleday Anchor Books, 1989), 183.

11. B. H. Sumner, *Peter the Great and the Emergence of Russia* (London: English Universities Press, 1950); Robert K. Massie, *Peter the Great: His Life and World* (New York: Alfred A. Knopf, 1980).

12. Michael Karpovich, *Imperial Russia, 1801–1917* (New York: Holt, Rinehart, and Winston, 1932; reprint, 1961), 13.

13. Nicholas V. Riasanovsky, *A History of Russia*, 4th ed. (Oxford/New York: Oxford University Press, 1984), 248, 254–64.

14. A. N. Radishchev, *Puteshestvie iz" Peterburga v" Moskvu*, introduction by Vladimir Burtsev" (Paris: Librairie Russe et Français L. Dodstein, 1921); Thomas Riha, ed., *Readings in Russian Civilization*, vol. 2, rev. ed. (Chicago: University of Chicago Press, 1969), 266–79; quote from 269.

15. Riha, *Readings in Russian Civilization*, 261–66; quote from 278.

16. Michael T. Florinsky, *Russia: A History and an Interpretation*, vol. 2 (New York: Macmillan, 1953), 696–97.

17. Custine, *The Empire of the Czar*, 139.

18. Riha, *Readings in Russian Civilization*, 303–14.

19. Riasanovsky, *A History of Russia*, 324.

20. W. Bruce Lincoln, *The Great Reforms: Autocracy, Bureaucracy, and the Politics of Change in Imperial Russia* (DeKalb: Northern Illinois University Press, 1990), 33. Uvarov, quoted in Riasanovsky, *A History of Russia*, 324.

21. W. E. Mosse, *Alexander II and the Modernization of Russia* (London: English Universities Press, 1958).

22. Arthur Mendel, "On Interpreting the Fate of Imperial Russia," in Theofanis George Stavrou, ed., *Russia under the Last Tsar* (Minneapolis: University of Minnesota Press, 1969), 24–25.

23. Riasanovsky, *A History of Russia*, 433, 454.

24. Ibid., 413–15.

25. Mendel, "On Interpreting the Fate of Imperial Russia," 13–41, particularly 24–26.

26. Louis Fischer, *The Life of Lenin* (New York: Harper Colophon Books, 1965), 1–92.

27. V. I. Lenin, *Chto Delat'* [What is to be done; written Fall 1901–February 1902], *Polnoe sobranie sochinenii*, 5th ed. vol. 6 (Moscow: Gosudarstvennoe izdatel'stvo politicheskoi literatury, 1959), 3–190; David Shub, *Lenin*, rev. ed. (Baltimore: Pelican Books), 13–90.

28. Isaac Deutscher, *The Prophet Armed: Trotsky, 1879–1921* (New York: Oxford University Press, 1954), 89.

29. Susan Eva Heuman, "Socialist Conception of Human Rights: A Model from Prerevolutionary Russia," in Adamantia Pollis and Peter Schwab, eds., *Human Rights: Cultural and Historical Perspectives* (New York: Praeger Publishers, 1978), 44–59; George Fischer, *Russian Liberalism: From Gentry to Intelligentsia* (Cambridge, MA: Harvard University Press, 1958); Boris Elkin, "The Russian Intelligentsia on the Eve of the Revolution," in Richard Pipes, ed., *The Russian Intelligentsia* (New York: Columbia University Press, 1961), 32–46.

30. W. Bruce Lincoln, *The Great Reforms*, 195.

31. Ibid., 191–92, 195; quote from 195–96, citing A. P. Chekhov, *Anton Chekhov's*

Life and Thought: Selected Letters and Commentary, trans. Michael H. Heim and Simon Karlinsky (Berkeley: University of California Press, 1975), 176.

32. Mendel, "On Interpreting the Fate of Imperial Russia, 19, 20–21.

33. Lincoln, *The Great Reforms,* passim.

34. Quotes from Bernard Pares, *A History of Russia,* rev. ed. (London: Jonathan Cape, 1947), 459; Florinsky, *Russia: A History and an Interpretation,* 1147.

35. Olga Crisp and Linda Edmondson, eds., *Civil Rights in Imperial Russia* (Oxford: Clarendon Press, 1989), vi–vii.

36. Evgenii Skripilev, "Individual Rights before October 1917: A Russian Perspective," in Juviler and Gross, eds., *Human Rights for the 21st Century,* 69–81; Susan Heuman, "Prerevolutionary New Thinking," in Juviler and Gross, eds., 82–93.

37. Quoted in Linda Edmondson, "Was There a Movement for Civil Rights in Russia in 1905?" in Crisp and Edmondson, 267–68.

38. The Union of Liberation had brought together Russians across lines of estate, class, education, and experience—from veterans of decades of administrative and political activity in the zemstvos to young freelance writers. Donald W. Treadgold, "Russian Radical Thought, 1894–1917," in Theofanis Stavrou, ed., *Russia Under the Last Tsar* (Minneapolis: University of Minnesota Press, 1969), 81–85.

39. William G. Rosenberg, "The Zemstvo in 1917 and Its Fate under Bolshevik Rule," in Terence Emmons and Wayne S. Vucinich, eds., *The Zemstvo in Russia: An Experiment in Local Self-Government* (New York: Cambridge University Press, 1982), 383–421; Terence Emmons, "The Zemstvo in Historical Perspective," in Emmons and Vucinich, eds., 425–26, 441; Thomas Riha, "Constitutional Developments in Russia," in Stavrou, *Russia Under the Last Tsar,* 89. The Union of Liberation joined with the Union of Zemstvo-Constitutionalists to form the Constitutional-Democratic Party.

40. Mendel, "On Interpreting the Fate of Imperial Russia," 20; Kermit E. McKenzie, "Zemstvo Organization and Role within the Administrative Structure," in Emmons and Vucinich, eds., 31–78.

41. ". . . the leading advocates of this idea were the majority of the Tver committee," who declared their aim to be "to replace the former patriarchal ties . . . with new ones, with ties of social benefit and mutual interest, and in the name of this significant principle, to unite equally all inhabitants of the region." Emmons, "The Zemstvo in Historical Perspective," 435, quoting from his *The Russian Landed Gentry and the Peasant Emancipation of 1861* (Cambridge: Cambridge University Press, 1968), 136.

42. Riasanovsky, *A History of Russia,* 423. On the even more restricted municipal duma franchise and the annulled elections of 217 mayors and members of municipal boards in 318 towns, 1910–14, see Thomas Riha, "Constitutional Developments in Russia," 89; Sergei Witte, *Samoderzhavie i Zemstvo* (St. Petersburg, 1908), quoted in Riha, 88.

43. Rosenberg, "The Zemstvo in 1917 and Its Fate under Bolshevik Rule," in Emmons and Vucinich, eds., 383–421; Emmons, "The Zemstvo in Historical Perspective," in Emmons and Vucinich, eds., 425–26 and 441–43; Thomas Fallows, "The Zemstvo and the Bureaucracy, 1890–1914," in Emmons and Vucinich, eds., 177–242. The election law of 1890 reduced peasant participation and made elections indirect from district to county assemblies. William Gleason, "The All-Russian Union of Zemstvos and World War I," in Emmons and Vucinich, eds., 365–82.

44. Each estate of nobles, merchants, townspeople, and peasants, had its specified privileges and obligations. Skripilev, "Individual Rights before October 1917," 69–70.

45. Emmons, "The Zemstvo in Historical Perspective," 435–36; see also Riasanovsky, *A History of Russia,* 305–7.

46. Lincoln, *The Great Reforms,* 196–201.

47. Jeffrey Brooks, "The Zemstvo and the Education of the People," in Emmons and Vucinich, eds., 243–78; Nancy M. Frieden, "The Politics of Zemstvo Medicine," in Emmons and Vucinich, eds., 315–42; Robert E. Johnson, "Liberal Professionals and Professional Liberals: The Zemstvo Statisticians and Their Work," in Emmons and Vucinich, eds., 343–64; Samuel C. Ramer, "The Zemstvo and Public Health," in Emmons and Vucinich, eds., 279–314.

48. The provincial assembly of the Tver' gentry in 1862 renounced its gentry privileges. It demanded the convocation of a constituent assembly representing the entire people to establish a new order in Russia. Emmons, "The Zemstvo in Historical Perspective," in Emmons and Vucinich, eds., 434–36.

49. John D. Klier, "The Concept of 'Jewish Emancipation' in a Russian Context," in Crisp and Edmondson, eds., 140. The Basic Law (Constitution) of 1906, together with the judicial reforms of 1864, recognized in principle an impressive list of rights to freedom and due process. The government violated its own laws; no effective appeal against its violations existed. William E. Butler, "Civil Rights in Russia: Legal Standards in Gestation," in Crisp and Edmondson, eds., 1–12; Richard E. Wortman, *The Development of Russian Legal Consciousness* (Chicago: University of Chicago Press, 1976). On the half-free press under censorship, see Caspar Ferenczi, "Freedom of the Press under the Old Regime, 1905–1914," in Crisp and Edmondson, eds., 191–214.

50. Riha, "Constitutional Developments in Russia," 102–5; quote from 102.

51. The Emperor sacked two ministers of war for excessive cooperation with the Duma. In 1909 he forbade the new minister, Sukhomlinov, to appear in the Duma. The Duma could not legislate on railway rates, tariffs, or the price of vodka, or on 74 percent of the budget of the Ministry of the Interior, 64 percent of the Ministry of Education, and 35 percent of the Ministry of War. It controlled 52 percent of the budget in 1907 (ibid., 100–1, 103–4).

52. Ibid., 97–98, quote on 98 from *Vestnik Partii Narodnoi Svobody* (St. Petersburg), June 21, 1907.

53. The tsar appointed half; extremely restricted suffrage packed the rest of the State Council with supporters. Its vetoes stopped a bill legalizing the *volost* (regional) zemstvos; a bill broadening the Duma's budgetary rights; most of the legislation increasing religious freeom for the Old Believers and for those seeking to change their faith; and a bill on criminal penalties for excesses of lower officials, including police officials. Emmons, "The Zemstvo in Historical Perspective," 439; Riha, "Constitutional Developments in Russia," 106.

54. Riha, "Constitutional Developments in Russia," 94–95.

55. Nineteen percent of the Third Duma deputies were peasants, compared with 39 percent in the First Duma; 44 percent were nobles rising to 51 percent in the Fourth Duma elected in September 1912), compared with 25 percent in the First Duma (ibid., 93, 96, 108).

56. Ibid., 97–98, 107; quote from 113.

57. Mendel, "On Interpreting the Fate of Imperial Russia," 22–27; quotes from 23, 27. See also George Kennan, "The Breakdown of the Tsarist Autocracy," in Richard Pipes, ed., *Revolutionary Russia* (Cambridge, MA: Harvard University Press, 1967), 1–15.

58. Raphael R. Abramovitch, *The Soviet Revolution, 1917–1939* (New York: International Universities Press, 1962), 1–6.

59. Literacy increased from 27.8 to 40.2 percent between 1897 and 1914 (Riha, "Constitutional Developments in Russia," 99).

60. Weissman, *Reform in Tsarist Russia*, 226.

61. Riha, "Constitutional Developments in Russia," 88; quote from 93.

62. Lincoln, *The Great Reforms*, 158.

63. Weissman, *Reform in Tsarist Russia*, 228.

64. Donald W. Treadgold, *Twentieth Century Russia*, 8th ed. (Boulder, CO: Westview Press, 1995), 98–100.

65. Riasanovsky, *A History of Russia*, 377.

66. V. I. Stoliarchuk, *A. F. Koni i ego okhruzhenie* (Moscow: Iuridicheskaia literatura, 1990).

67. Robert Paul Browder and Alexander F. Kerensky, eds., *The Provisional Government, 1917: Documents*, 3 vols. (Stanford, CA: Hoover Institution, 1961), 1: 191–242 ("Justice and Law Enforcement").

68. Marc Raeff, *Understanding Imperial Russia* (New York: Columbia University Press, 1984), 218.

69. S. A. Smith, "Workers and Civil Rights in Tsarist Russia," in Crisp and Edmondson, eds., 164.

70. Local elected courts (justice of the peace courts and peasant courts) tried cases of petty disputes and misdemeanors. Some children's courts modeled on the pioneering U.S. children's court of Cook County, Illinois, also functioned. Appointed general courts tried larger disputes and felonies in over one hundred circuit courts, before juries for criminal cases, with appeals to about fourteen judicial chambers. Both tracks, local and general courts, ended in the Governing Senate as a supreme court. Samuel Kucherov, *Courts, Trials, and Lawyers under the Last Three Tsars* (New York: Frederick A. Praeger, 1953); Peter Juviler, *Revolutionary Law and Order: Politics and Social Change in the USSR* (New York: Free Press, 1976), 4–12.

71. Emmons, "The Zemstvo in Historical Perspective," 431.

72. Sakwa, *Russian Politics and Society*, 394–95.

73. Leonard Schapiro, *The Communist Party of the Soviet Union*, 2d ed. (New York: Vintage Books, 1971), 161–65.

74. H. J. White, "Civil Rights and the Provisional Government," in Crisp and Edmondson, eds., 287–312; S. A. Smith, "Workers and Civil Rights in Tsarist Russia, 1899–1917," 145–70.

75. Decree on Peace, November 8, 1917; Decree on Land, November 8, 1917; Decree organizing the Council of People's Commissars, in Meisel and Kozera, *Materials for the Study of the Soviet System* (Ann Arbor: George Wahr Publishing Co., 1950), 15–22.

76. Oliver Radky, *Elections to the Russian Constituent Assembly of 1917* (Cambridge, MA: Harvard University Press, 1950), 13–22; Riasanovsky, *A History of Russia*, 477; Treadgold, *Twentieth Century Russia*, 121–23.

77. Abramovitz, *The Soviet Revolution*, 1.

78. Mendel, "On Interpreting the Fate of Imperial Russia," 15–17.

79. Mikhail Heller and Aleksandr Nekrich, *Utopia in Power: The History of the Soviet Union from 1917 to the Present* (New York: Summit Books, 1986), 11.

Chapter 3. The Contradictions of Communism

1. Rosa Luxemburg, "The Russian Revolution," in Bertram D. Wolfe, ed., *The Russian Revolution and Leninism or Marxism* (Ann Arbor: University of Michigan Press, 1961), 71.

2. Donald W. Treadgold, *Twentieth Century Russia*, 8th ed. (Boulder, CO: Westview Press, 1995), 112–55. Under the Treaty of Brest Litovsk, Russia lost 1,300,000 square miles of territory containing 62 million people, including Poland, and lands soon regained by force of arms: most of the Ukraine, Byelorussia, and land in the south Caucasus.

3. Mikhail Voslensky, *Nomenklatura: The Soviet Ruling Class*, preface by Milovan Djilas (Garden City, NY: Doubleday, 1984).

4. Early on, the dictatorship of the party had left room for considerable dispute within the leadership. They had debated seizing power, forming a broad coalition after takeover (rejected), introducing concessions to private trade and farming under what came to be called the NEP (New Economic Policy), whether to give trade unions full freedom of bargaining (they did not), and whether to allow continuation of organized party factions (they did not, passing in 1921 Lenin's resolution banning organized factions, which Stalin later used on his way to dictatorship). Robert Vincent Daniels, *The Conscience of the Revolution: Communist Opposition in Soviet Russia* (Cambridge, MA: Harvard University Press, 1960).

5. V. I. Lenin, "Proletarian Revolution and the Renegade Kautsky" (October–November 1918), excerpted in Robert C. Tucker, ed., *The Lenin Anthology*, 2d ed. (New York: W. W. Norton, 1975), 465, 469.

6. According to Pobiedonostsev: "In a Democracy, the real rulers are the dexterous manipulators of votes. . . . The history of mankind bears witness that the most necessary and fruitful reforms—the most durable measures—emanated from the supreme will of statesmen, or from a minority enlightened by lofty ideas and deep knowledge, and that, on the contrary, the extension of the representative principle is accompanied by the abasement of political ideas." Konstantin Pobiedonostsev, *Reflections of a Russian Statesman* (London: Grant Richards, 1898), excerpted in Thomas Riha, ed., *Reading in Russian Civilization*, vol. 2, rev. ed. (Chicago: University of Chicago Press, 1969), 391.

7. Quoted often, including in Leonard Schapiro, *The Communist Party of the Soviet Union*, 2d ed. (New York: Vintage Books, 1971), 288.

8. Moshe Lewin, *Lenin's Last Struggle* (New York: Pantheon Books, 1968).

9. Rosa Luxemburg, *The Russian Revolution*, 35–38, 71–71; quote on 71.

10. John N. Hazard, *Communists and Their Law: A Search for the Common Core of the Legal Systems of the Marxian Socialist States* (Chicago/London: University of Chicago Press, 1969), 69, 521, 525; quotes on 521.

11. The RSFSR Constitution of 1918, chap. 5, in Aryeh L. Unger, *Constitutional Development in the USSR: A Guide to the Soviet Constitutions* (New York: Pica Press, 1982), 27–29. The 1924 Constitution for the new Union of Soviet Socialist Republics formed on December 30, 1922, omitted a bill of rights, leaving that to the constitutions of the union republics.

12. The new populist facade of justice included the participation of legally equal but in fact subordinate lay judges flanking the trial judge. My friends these "people's assessors" call "nodders." Other devices included politically controlled "elections" of judges to trial courts; relatively informal procedures and rules of evidence; public participation as accusers or defenders; and "visiting sessions" for the workplace show trials of thieves, hooligans, etc. Robert Sharlet, "The Communist Party and the Administration of Justice in the USSR," in Donald B. Barry, F. J. M.

Feldbrugge, George Ginsburgs, and Peter B. Maggs, eds., *Soviet Law after Stalin, Part III: Soviet Institutions and the Administration of Law* (Alphen aan den Rijn, Netherlands, and Germantown, MD: Sijthoff and Noordhoff, 1979), 321–92; Peter Juviler, "Mass Education and Justice in Soviet Courts: The Visiting Sessions," *Soviet Studies* 18, no. 4 (April 1967): 494–509; R. D. Rakhunov, *Vyezdnaia sessiia suda* (Moscow: Iurizdat, 1968).

13. Bolshevik dismantling and political expediency brought conflict with jurists of the old school, including even some radical jurists like the Left Socialist Revolutionary I. N. Shteinberg, briefly *Narkomiust* (People's Commissar of Justice) during the coalition of Left SR's and Bolsheviks from December 1917 to March 1918. John N. Hazard, *Settling Disputes in Soviet Society* (New York: Columbia University Press, 1960); Peter Juviler, "Justice and the Judicial System, 1917–1921," in George Jackson and Robert Devlin, eds., *Dictionary of the Russian Revolution* (New York: Greenwood Press, 1989), 258–91. On the withering away of crime, state, and law under Communism, see V. I. Lenin, *Gosudarstvo i revolutsiia: Uchenie marksizma o gosudarstve i zadachi proletariata v revoliutsii* [State and revolution: Marxist theory of the state and the tasks of the proletariat in the Revolution] (August–September 1917), in *Polnoe sobranie sochinenii*, 5th ed. vol. 33 (Moscow: Gosudarstvennoe izdatel'stvo politicheskoi literatury, 1962), 3–120.

14. "When the state will be proletarian, when it will be a machine for proletarian violence against the bourgeoisie, then we are unconditionally for strong state power and centralism." V. I. Lenin, *Uderzhat li bolsheviki gosudarstvennuiu vlast'?* [Will the Bolsheviks retain state power?] (end of September 14–October 1917), in V. I. Lenin, *Polnoe sobranie sochinenii* (1962), 34:318.

15. Quoted in Peter Juviler, *Revolutionary Law and Order: Politics and Social Change in the USSR* (New York: The Free Press, 1976), 24, from Alexander Dallin and George W. Breslauer, *Political Terror in Communist Systems* (Stanford, CA: Stanford University Press, 1970), 10.

16. "The power of the police and gendarmerie passed into the hands of the Communist usurpers, who, instead of giving the people freedom, instilled in them fear of falling into the torture chambers of the Cheka, which in horrors far exceed the gendarme administration of the tsarist regime." Translated from the original, dated March 8, 1921, as reprinted in "Pravda o Kronstadte" (1921) by Paul Avrich, in *Kronstadt 1921* (Princeton, NJ: Princeton University Press, 1970), 241.

17. H. Kent Geiger, *The Family in Soviet Russia* (Cambridge, MA: Harvard University Press, 1968).

18. Lenin pushed through, over opposition, a decree of January 14, 1918, raising the minimum age of juvenile criminal liability from ten to seventeen. But as crimes by *besprizornye* (homeless street children) mounted, the Bolsheviks retreated from the principle of "no courts or prisons for children." The minimum age of criminal liability was lowered from seventeen to fourteen in 1919 (Juviler, *Revolutionary Law and Order*, 276, n. 22). On homelessness and communes etc., see V. L. Shveitser and S. M. Shabalova, eds., *Besprizornye v trudovikh kommunakh: Praktika raboty s trudnymi det'mi: sbornik statei i materialov* (Moscow, 1926); James Bowen, *Soviet Education: Anton Makarenko and the Years of Experiment* (Madison: University of Wisconsin Press, 1965); "Besprizornost' v SSSR," *Bol'shaia sovetskaia entsiklopediia*, 1st ed., vol. 5 (Moscow, 1927); G. Daian, "Vtoroi psikhonevrologicheskii s"ezd (okonchanie)," *Krasnaia nov'*, no. 5 (1924), 227; and see note 21.

19. James H. Meisel and Edward S. Kozera, *Materials for the Study of the Soviet System* (Ann Arbor, MI: George Wahr Publishing Co., 1950), passim; Juviler, *Revolutionary Law and Order*, 15–38; Rudolf Schlesinger, ed., *The Family in the U.S.S.R.: Documents and Readings* (London: Routledge & Kegan Paul, 1949), 30–171.

20. Wendy Z. Goldman, *Women, the State, and Revolution: Soviet Family Policy and Social Life, 1917–1936* (New York: Cambridge University Press, 1993).

21. Peter H. Juviler, "Contradictions of Revolution: Juvenile Crime and Rehabilitation," in Abbott Gleason, Peter Kenez, and Richard Stites, eds., *Bolshevik Culture: Experiment and Order in the Russian Revolution* (Bloomington: Indiana University Press, 1985), 261–78; and see note 17.

22. Richard Pipes, *The Formation of the Soviet Union* (Cambridge, MA: Harvard University Press, 1954).

23. Merle Fainsod, *How Russia Is Ruled*, 2d ed. (Cambridge, MA: Harvard University Press, 1963), 132–75; Schapiro, *The Communist Party of the Soviet Union*, 217–89.

24. Stalin later inserted this thesis into a piece published early in 1924. Robert C. Tucker, *Stalin as Revolutionary, 1879–1929* (New York: W. W. Norton, 1973), 377–88; Joseph Stalin, "Problems of Leninism," in *Leninism*, translated from the 1926 edition by Eden and Cedar Paul, vol. 1 (London: Modern Books Ltd., 1928; 2d impression, 1932), 52–63.

25. Stephen F. Cohen, *Bukharin and the Bolshevik Revolution: A Political Biography, 1888–1938* (New York: Alfred A. Knopf, 1973).

26. It transcended in its reach and sweep the regimes of his two models, Ivan the Terrible and Peter the Great. Isaac Deutscher, *Stalin: A Political Biography* (New York: Vintage Books, 1960).

27. "The highest development of state power with the object of preparing the conditions for the withering away of state power—such is the Marxist formula. Is this 'contradictory'? Yes, it is 'contradictory.' But this contradiction is bound up with life, and it fully reflects Marxist dialectics." J. V. Stalin, "Political Report of the C.C. to the XVI Congress of the CPSU (B)," in *Works* (Moscow, 1955), 12:381.

28. Roy Medvedev, *Let History Judge: The Origins and Consequences of Stalinism*, rev. ed. (New York: Columbia University Press, 1989), 92–248.

29. Juviler, *Revolutionary Law and Order*, 55.

30. Stalin cited the absence of capitalist property and "antagonistic classes" to justify continuing the monopoly of the Communist Party. In the USSR, democracy was not "for the propertied majority" but "for the toilers, that is democracy for all." They lived in a "voluntary union," as the constitution contained the right of secession, though "not a single republic would want to secede from the USSR." J. V. Stalin, "O proekte konstitutsii Soiuza SSR," in *I. V. Stalin Sochineniia*, ed. Robert H. McNeal, vol. 1(16) (Stanford: The Hoover Institute on War, Revolution, and Peace, 1967), 177, 164–65, 171.

31. This caused, in one estimate, 19 million deaths by shooting, torture, and inhumane conditions in labor camps, in addition to the more than 20 million who had died during collectivization and the deportations and famine of 1930–32 (and 16 million during the civil war and the famine of 1921–22)—totaling about double the deaths caused by the Nazi invaders. Anton Antonov-Ovseenko, *The Time of Stalin: Portrait of a Tyranny* (New York: Harper and Row, 1981), 213. (See also note 28 and Conquest, *The Great Terror*, 699–713; Juviler, *Revolutionary Law and Order*, 64, 202 n. 135). Among the "enemies of the people" were chance victims rounded up to fill quotas for camp labor (a group of gypsies pitching camp in the town square, or the woman who went to the Novocherkassk NKVD [secret police] office to ask what was to be done about a nursing infant left behind by her neighbor who had been arrested by the NKVD; after a two-hour wait, she was arrested too). Juviler, 63.

32. Pashukanis argued against P. I. Stuchka's theory of a new "proletarian law." Such views brought Pashukanis, first fame and dominance in legal scholarship, but then, in the 1930s, criticism and doom. Andrei Vyshinsky, purge trial prosecutor as well as Prosecutor General of the USSR, became Pashukanis's successor

as legal doyen. P. I. Stuchka et al., *Soviet Legal Philosophy*, trans. Hugh W. Babb, intro. by John N. Hazard (Cambridge: Harvard University Press, 1951), 17–69; Piers Beirne and Robert Sharlet, eds., *Pashukanis: Selected Writings on Marxism and Law*, trans. Peter B. Maggs, foreword by John N. Hazard (New York: Academic Press, 1980); Andrei Y. Vyshinsky, *The Law of the Soviet State*, trans. Hugh W. Babb, intro. by John N. Hazard (New York: Macmillan, 1948); E. B. Pashukanis, *Izbrannye proizvedeniia po obshchei teorii prava i gosudarstva*, ed. V. N. Kudriavtsev et al. (Moscow: Izdatel'stvo Nauka, 1980).

33. Robert Conquest, *The Nation Killers: The Soviet Deportation of Nationalities* (New York: Macmillan, 1970).

34. W. H. Chamberlin, *Russia's Iron Age* (London: Gerald Duckworth, 1935).

35. Fainsod, *How Russia Is Ruled*, 131–502.

36. Moshe Lewin, *The Gorbachev Phenomenon*, 2d ed. (Berkeley: University of California Press, 1990), 177–79.

37. J. V. Stalin, "The Tasks of Business Executives" (1931), in *Works* (Moscow, 1955), 13:43 ("capture" not "storm" in text).

38. Dina Kaminskaya, *Final Judgment: My Life as a Soviet Defense Attorney* (New York: Simon and Schuster, 1982), 11–36; Vera S. Dunham, *In Stalin's Time: Middle-Class Values in Soviet Fiction* (New York: Cambridge University Press, 1976); Andrei Sakharov, *Vospominaniia* (New York: Izdatel'stvo imeni Chekhova, 1990); Lev Kopelev, *The Education of a True Believer* (New York: Harper and Row, 1978).

39. Adam Ulam, *Stalin*, expanded ed. (Boston: Beacon Press, 1989), 536–615.

40. Peter Juviler, "Family Reforms on the Road to Communism," in Peter Juviler and Henry Morton, eds., *Soviet Policy-Making: Studies of Communism in Transition* (New York: Praeger and London: Pall Mall, 1967), 29–60; "Forword," Yuri I. Luryi, *Soviet Family Law* (Buffalo, NY: William S. Hein and Co., 1980), i–vi; H. Kent Geiger, *The Family in Soviet Russia* (Cambridge, MA: Harvard University Press, 1968).

41. Peter H. Juviler, "The Soviet Family in Post-Stalin Perspective," in Stephen Cohen et al., eds., *The Soviet Union since Stalin* (Bloomington: Indiana University Press, 1980), 229–30.

42. Abram Tertz [Andrei Sinyavsky], *On Socialist Realism* (New York: Pantheon Books, 1960); Treadgold, *Twentieth Century Russia*, 321–36.

43. Vladimir Voinovich, *The Anti-Soviet Soviet Union* (New York: Harcourt Brace Jovanovich, 1985), 316.

44. Juviler, *Revolutionary Law and Order*, 47–53.

45. Medvedev, *Let History Judge*, 786.

46. Carol R. Saivetz and Sheila Levin Woods, eds., *August 12, 1952: The Night of the Murdered Poets* (New York: National Conference on Soviet Jewry, 1972).

47. Dina Kaminskaya, *Final Judgment: My Life as a Soviet Defense Attorney* (New York: Simon & Schuster, 1982), 41; Ulam, *Stalin*, 700–739; Medvedev, *Let History Judge*, 802–7; Conquest, *The Great Terror*, 663–64; Fainsod, *How Russia Is Ruled*, 446–47.

48. Leo Gruliow, ed., *Current Soviet Policies* (New York: Praeger, 1953), 251.

49. Ibid., 255, 259–60. The Supreme Soviet (parliament) convoked on March 16 stood in equal silent tribute to Stalin and to the late president of Czechoslovakia, Klement Gottwald.

50. Merle Fainsod removed terror as "the lynchpin of totalitarianism" from the second edition of his classic, *How Russia Is Ruled* (Cambridge, MA: Harvard University Press, 1963), 447–48.

51. Peter Juviler, *Revolutionary Law and Order Politics and Social Change in the USSR* (New York: The Free Press, 1976), 69–71; Gruliow, *Current Soviet Policies*, 258–59; Fainsod, *How Russia Is Ruled* (1963), 449.

52. The speech was leaked to the outside world on June 4, 1956, and issued by the

State Department. Bertram D. Wolfe, ed., *Khrushchev and Stalin's Ghost: Text, Background and Meaning of Khrushchev's Secret Report to the Twentieth Congress on the Night of February 24–25, 1956* (New York: Praeger, 1957); compare with the milder critiques in the official record of the congress from which this report was missing, *XX S"ezd Kommunisticheskoi Partii Sovetskogo Soiuza: Stenograficheskii Otchet*, 2 vols. (Moscow: Gosudarstvennoe izdatel'stvo politicheskoi literatury, 1956). Khrushchev's open central committee report, Mikoyan's speech, and the secret speech are all available in Leo Gruliow, ed., *Current Soviet Policies: II. The Documentary Record of the 20th Communist Party Congress and Its Aftermath* (New York: Praeger, 1957), 29–63, 80–89, 172–89.

53. China had raised questions as to whether it was Stalin or the system which spawned terror. It cited the "Polish October" (1956) of national communist dissent under Vladislaw Gomulka; the Hungarian Revolution by Communist Imre Nagy; Palmiro Togliatti's doctrine of polycentrism; the movement toward a liberalized "eurocommunism"; later, the premature "Prague Spring" of 1968; and disillusionment among communists and fellow-travelers worldwide. Meanwhile, the Soviet quest for influence and profitable trade in the third world continued. Russian Institute, Columbia University, *The Anti-Stalin Campaign and International Communism* (New York: Columbia University Press, 1956); Zbigniew K. Brzezinski, *The Soviet Bloc: Unity and Conflict*, rev. ed. (New York: Praeger, 1961); Alvin Z. Rubinstein, ed., *The Foreign Policy of the Soviet Union*, 3d ed. (New York: Random House, 1972); Andrzej Korbonski and Francis Fukuyama, eds., *The Soviet Union and the Third World: The Last Three Decades* (Ithaca, NY: Cornell University Press, 1987); Elizabeth Valkenier, *The Soviet Union and the Third World: An Economic Bind* (New York: Praeger, 1983).

54. *XXII S"ezd Kommunisticheskoi Partii Sovetskogo Soiuza: Stenograficheskii Otchet*, vol. 3 (Moscow: Gospolitizdat, 1962), 121.

55. Yevgeny Yevtushenko, "Nasledniki Stalina" [Stalin's heirs], my translation from the Russian text in *The Poetry of Yevgeny Yevtushenko 1955–1965*, trans. and intro. by George Reavey (New York: October House, 1965), 160.

56. Helene Carrere D'Encausse, *Confiscated Power: How Soviet Russia Really Works* (New York: Harper and Row, 1980), 139–46.

57. Ludmilla Alexeyeva, *Soviet Dissent: Movements for National, Religious and Human Rights* (Middletown, CT: Wesleyan University Press, 1985), 3–4; Peter H. Juviler, "Communist Morality and Soviet Youth," *Problems of Communism* 10, no. 3 (1961): 16–24; Lev Kopelev, *To Be Preserved Forever* (Philadelphia and New York: J. B. Lippincott, 1977); Raisa Orlova, *Vospominaniia o neproshedshchem vremeni* (Moscow: Izdatel'stvo sovetsko-britanskog o sovmestnogo predpriatiia slovo, 1993).

58. Joshua Rubenstein, *Soviet Dissidents: Their Struggle for Human Rights*, 2d ed. (Boston: Beacon Press, 1985), 1–5.

59. Peter Juviler, "Family Reforms on the Road to Communism," in Peter Juviler and Henry Morton, eds., *Soviet Policy Making: Studies of Communism in Transition* (New York: Praeger, 1967), 29–60.

60. Anatoly Marchenko, *My Testimony* (New York: Dutton, 1969), xvii (Max Hayward in introduction), 3, passim. Marchenko died in camp in 1986.

61. Two students typed and distributed, on November 7 or 8, 1956, eight or nine copies of a leaflet protesting the bloodshed by Soviet troops putting down the revolution. The KGB arrested them in March 1957, and a court convicted them in July and sent them to labor camp for "hooliganism" under Article 206 of the Criminal Code. "Istoriia odnoi kompanii: Otryvki iz vospominanii Vladimira Kuznestsova," *Ekspress khronika*, April 12, 1996.

62. James H. Billington: *The Icon and the Axe: An Interpretive History of Russian Culture* (New York: Knopf, 1958), 551–52.

63. Peter Juviler, "Law and the Delinquent Family: Reproduction and Upbringing," in Donald D. Barry, George Ginsburgs, and Peter B. Maggs, eds., *Soviet Law after Stalin: Part II. Social Engineering through Law* (Alphen aan den Rijn: Sijthoff & Noordhoff, 1978), 221–28, and "Soviet Marxism and Family Law," *Columbia Journal of Transnational Law* 23, no. 2 (1985): 385–400.

64. Peter Juviler, "Whom the State Has Joined: Conjugal Ties in Soviet Law," in Donald D. Barry, George Ginsburgs, and Peter B. Maggs, eds., *Soviet Law after Stalin: Part I. The Citizen and the State in Contemporary Soviet Law* (Leyden: A. W. Sijthoff, 1977), 129; S. Kulaeva, "Novye sovetskie prazdniki i obriady—vazhnyi faktor komunnistichekogo vospitaniia grazhdan," *Sovetskaia iustitsiia*, no. 11 (1981), 4–8; V. G. Sinitsyn, ed., *Nashi Prazdniki: Sovetskie obshchegosudarstvnnye, trudovye, voinskie, molodezhnye i semeino-bytovye prazdniki, obriady, ritualy* (Moscow: Politizdat, 1977); V. A. Zots, ed., *Traditsii, obriady, sovremennost'* (Kiev: Politizdat Ukrainy, 1983).

65. Religious belief seemed on the rise. Ethel Dunn and Stephen Dunn, "Religion as an Instrument of Culture Change: The Problem of the Sects in the Soviet Union," *Slavic Review* 23, no. 3 (1964): 459–78; Ivan D. London and Nikolai P. Poltoratzky, "Contemporary Religious Sentiment in the Soviet Union," *Psychological Reports*, Supplement 3 (1957): 113–30. I remember reading Komsomol (Communist Youth League) letters of condemnation and hearing about the expulsion of worshipers when I was attending Moscow University for the first time in 1958–59.

66. Telford Taylor, with Alan Dershowitz and George Fletcher, *Courts of Terror: Soviet Criminal Justice and Jewish Emigration* (New York: Vintage Books, 1976); "Economic Crimes in the Soviet Union," *Journal of the International Commission of Jurists* 5, no. 1 (special issue) (1964): 1–47.

67. *Mezhvuzovskoe nauchnoe soveshchanie na temu: "Dal'neishee razvitie sovetskoi demokratii i ukreplenie sotsialitichekoi zakonnosti: teksty dokladov i tezisy nauchnykh soobshchenii. Sektsiia ugolvnogo protsessa; sektsiia ugolovnogo i ispravitel'nogo-trudovogo prava; sektsiia grazhdanogo protsessa* (Moscow, 1958).

68. George Feifer, *Justice in Moscow* (New York: Simon & Schuster, 1964); Peter Juviler, "Marriage and Divorce," *Survey*, no. 48 (1963): 104–17.

69. Kaminskaya, *Final Judgment*, 51–137.

70. Juviler, *Revolutionary Law and Order*, 70–74; M. S. Strogovich, *Pravo obviniaemogo na zashchitu i prezumptsiia nevinovnosti* (Moscow: Nauka, 1984).

71. USSR Academy of Sciences, *Ot sotsialisticheskoi gosudarstvennosti k kommunisticheskomu obshchestvennomu samoupravleniiu* (Moscow: Akademiia Nauk, 1960); A. Sokolov, *Uchastie trudiashchikhsia v okhrane sovetskogo obshchestvennogo poriadka* (Moscow: Iurizdat, 1962); Ts. A. Iampol'skaia, *Obshchestvennye organizatsii i razvitie sotsialisticheskoi gosudarstvennosti* (Moscow: Iurizdat, 1965); S. Zhilinskii, *Rol' KPSS v ukreplenii zakonnosti na sovremennom etape* (Moscow: Mysl', 1977).

72. The thaw's refreezing and the Brodsky case are summed up in Joshua Rubenstein, *Soviet Dissidents: Their Struggle for Human Rights*, 2d ed. (Boston: Beacon Press, 1985), 5–30.

73. Khrushchev had Pasternak's novel *Dr. Zhivago* banned and ordered him to refuse his Nobel Prize for Literature after Feltrinelli published it in Italy in 1957. Ludmilla Alexeyeva, *Soviet Dissent: Contemporary Movements for National, Religious and Human Rights* (Middletown, CT: Wesleyan University Press, 1985), 4–5.

74. Rubenstein, *Soviet Dissidents*, 10–13.

75. Alexeyeva, *Soviet Dissent*, 4–5.

76. Rubenstein, *Soviet Dissidents*, 28–29, 17–23.

77. Ludmilla Alexeyeva and Paul Goldberg, *The Thaw Generation: Coming of Age in the Post-Stalin Era* (Pittsburgh, PA: University of Pittsburgh Press, 1993), 105.

78. Adam Ulam, *Stalin: The Man and His Era*, 2d ed. (Boston: Beacon Press, 1989), ix.

79. Moshe Lewin, *The Gorbachev Phenomenon*, 2d ed. (Berkeley: University of California Press, 1990), 182.

80. *Pravda*, November 3, 1987.

81. Articles 125, 126, 1936 constitution, in S. S. Studenikin, *Istoriia sovetskoi konstitutsii (v dokumentakh) 1917–1956*, 744; Unger, *Constitutional Development in the USSR*, 156.

82. Julia Wishnevsky, "The Rise of Dissidence in the Brezhnev Era," *Radio Liberty Report*, 453/82 (November 15, 1982), 2–8; Juviler, *Revolutionary Law and Order*, 85–115.

83. Max Hayward, trans. and ed., *On Trial: The Soviet State versus "Abram Tertz" and "Nikolai Arzhak,"* 2d ed. (New York: Harper and Row, 1967); Pavel Litvinov, comp., Peter Reddaway, ed., *The Trial of the Four: The Case of Galanskov, Ginzburg, Dobrovolsky and Lashkova* (New York: Viking Press, 1971).

84. Wishnevsky, "The Rise of Dissidence in the Brezhnev Era," 5.

85. Alexeyeva, *Soviet Dissent*; Abraham Brumberg, *In Quest of Justice: Protest and Dissent in the Soviet Union Today* (New York: Praeger, 1970); Valery Chalidze, *To Defend These Rights: Human Rights in the Soviet Union* (New York: Random House, 1974); *The Chornovil Papers* (New York: McGraw-Hill, 1968); Stephen H. Cohen, ed., *An End to Silence: Uncensored Opinion in the Soviet Union* (New York: Norton, 1982); Helsinki Watch, *Ten Years Later: Violations of the Helsinki Accords* (New York: Helsinki Watch Committee, 1985), 151–299; Michael Meerson-Aksenov and Boris Shragin, eds., *The Political, Social and Religious Thought of Russian 'Samizdat'—An Anthology* (Belmont, MA: Nordland, 1977); Mihaylo Osadchy, *Cataract* (New York: Harcourt Brace Jovanovich, 1976); Peter Reddaway, trans. and ed., *Uncensored Russia: Protest and Dissent in the Soviet Union* (New York: American Heritage Press, 1972); Rudolf L. Tokes, ed., *Dissent in the USSR: Politics, Ideology, and People* (Baltimore: The Johns Hopkins University Press, 1975).

86. Tatyana Mamonova, *Zhenshchina i Rossiia: Al'manakh* (1979), translated as *Women and Russia: Feminist Writings from the Soviet Union* (Boston: Beacon Press, 1984); Rubenstein, *Soviet Dissidents*, 262, 265–66.

87. Rubenstein, *Soviet Dissidents*, 122–25; P. G. Grigorenko, *The Grigorenko Papers: Writings by General P. G. Grigorenko and Documents in His Case* (Boulder, CO: Westview Press, 1973); Petro G. Grigorenko, *Memoirs* (New York: W. W. Norton, 1982); *Prisoners of Conscience in the USSR: Their Treatment and Condition*, 2d ed. (London: Amnesty International, 1980); Sidney Bloch and Peter Reddaway, *Psychiatric Terror: How Soviet Psychiatry Is Used to Suppress Dissent* (New York: Basic Books, 1977); Walter Reich, "The World of Soviet Psychiatry," *New York Times Magazine*, January 30, 1983, 20–26, 50.

88. Amnesty International, *Prisoners of Conscience in the USSR*, 14–17.

89. Andrei Sakharov, "Progress, Coexistence and Intellectual Freedom" (June 1968), "Manifesto II" (March 1970), "Memorandum" (March 5, 1971), and "Postscript to Memorandum," in Andrei D. Sakharov, *Sakharov Speaks* (New York: Vintage Books, 1974), 56–158.

90. Andrei D. Sakharov, *Vospominaniia* (New York: Izdatel'stva imeni Chekhova, 1990), and *Gor'kii, Moskva, dalee vesde* (New York: Izdatel'stvo imeni Chekhova, 1990); Wishnevsky, "The Rise of Dissidence in the Brezhnev Era," 4–6; Rubinstein, *Soviet Dissidents*, passim.

91. Theodore H. Friedgut, "Soviet Anti-Zionism and Anti-Semitism: Another

Cycle," Research Paper No. 54, Soviet and East European Research Center, Hebrew University of Jerusalem; Zvi Gitelman, *The Jewish Religion in the USSR* (Synagogue Council of America, 1971); "Soviet Jews Speak," *Jews in Eastern Europe*, vol. 5, no. 1 (1972); *Anti-Semitic Propaganda: Evidence from Books, Press and Radio* (London: Institute for Jewish Affairs, 1978); V. A. Semeniuk, *Sovremennyi sionism* (Minsk: Belarus', 1986); R. M. Brodsky and O. Ya. Krassivsky, *Istinnoe litso sionisma* (Lvov: Kameniar, 1983).

92. Rubinstein, *Soviet Dissidents*, passim.

93. Wishnevsky, "The Rise of Dissidence in the Brezhnev Era," 4.

94. Rubinstein, *Soviet Dissidents*, 235.

95. Ibid., 274.

96. Peter Meyer, "The International Bill: A Brief History," in Paul Williams, ed., *The International Bill of Rights* (Glen Ellen, CA: Entwhistle Books, 1981), xxx–xxxi.

97. President Kennedy's assassination on November 23, 1963, Nikita Khrushchev's replacement by Brezhnev on October 14, 1964, and the onset of the Vietnam War, interrupted a resumed course toward arms reduction begun by the three-environment test-ban agreement in 1963. Raymond Garthoff, *Detente and Confrontation: America–Soviet Relations from Nixon to Reagan* (Washington, D.C.: The Brookings Institution, 1985); Erik P. Hoffmann and Frederick J. Fleron, Jr., eds., *The Conduct of Soviet Foreign Policy* (New York: Aldine, 1980); Adam Ulam, *Expansion and Coexistence: The History of Soviet Foreign Policy, 1917–67* (New York: Praeger, 1968), and *Dangerous Relations: The Soviet Union in World Politics, 1970–1982* (New York: Oxford University Press, 1983); Marshall D. Shulman, ed., *East–West Tensions in the Third World* (New York: W. W. Norton, 1986); N. S. Khrushchev, *K pobede v mirnom sorevnovanii s kapitalizmom* (Moscow: Gospolitizdat, 1959); V. V. Zagladin, *Revoliutsionnyi protsess: obshchee i osobennoe* (Moscow: Mysl', 1981).

98. Donald R. Shanor, *Behind the Lines: The Private War against Soviet Censorship* (New York: St. Martin's Press, 1985).

99. *Conference on Security and Cooperation in Europe: Final Act, Helsinki, 1975. The Department of State Bulletin Reprint*; William Korey, "Helsinki, Human Rights, and the Gorbachev Style," *Ethics & International Affairs* 1 (1987): 113–33; Craig R. Whitney, "The Legacy of Helsinki," *The New York Times*, November 19, 1990.

100. William Korey, *The Promises We Keep: Human Rights, the Helsinki Process and American Foreign Policy* (New York: St. Martin's Press, 1993), 1–25.

101. Leonid Brezhnev reporting on the draft 1977 constitution to the USSR Supreme Soviet, *Pravda*, October 5, 1977.

102. Adam Ulam, *Dangerous Relations: The Soviet Union in World Politics* (New York: Oxford University Press, 1983); Dmitri K. Simes, "Human Rights and Detente," in Grayson Kirk and Nils H. Wessell, eds., *The Soviet Threat: Myths and Realities* (New York: The Academy of Political Science, 1978), 135–47; Peter H. Juviler and Hannah J. Zawadzka, "Detente and Soviet Domestic Politics," in Kirk and Wessell, eds., 158–67; Robbin F. Laird and Erik P. Hoffmann, eds., *Soviet Foreign Policy in a Changing World* (New York: Aldine, 1986).

103. *Konstitutsiia (osnovnoi zakon) Soiuza Sovetskikh Ssotialisticheskikh Respublik* (Moscow: Izvestiia, 1988).

104. Victor Zaslavsky, *The Neo-Stalinist State* (Armonk, NY: M. E. Sharpe, 1982).

105. Louis Fischer, *Fifty Years of Soviet Communism* (New York: Popular Books, 1968), 120–22.

106. Author's notes, June 4, 1974.

107. Peter Juviler and Hannah J. Zawadzka, "Detente and Soviet Domestic Politics," in Kirk and Wessel, eds., *The Soviet Threat*, 158–67; quote on 166.

108. V. G. Kalenskii, *Gosudarstvo kak ob"ekt sotsiologicheskogo analiza* (Moscow: Iur-

izdat, 1977); G. V. Osipov and Ia. Shchepanskii, eds., *Sotsial'nye problemy truda i proizvodstva* (Moscow: Mysl', and Warsaw: Ksiazka i Wieda, 1969).

109. "Not all traits of the urban way of life conform to ideals of socialism and communism. The negative sides of city life include survivals of the past such as people's isolation in their dwelling places, limited neighborliness and communication, increased pollution of the air and water supplies, noise, estrangement of humans from nature, etc." E. S. Demidenko, *Demograficheskie problemy i perspektivy bol'shikh gorodov* (Moscow: Statistika, 1960), 66.

110. O. N. Ianitskii, *Urbanizatsiia, nauchno-tekhnicheskaia revoliutsiia i rabochii klass* (Moscow: Nauka, 1971); Evelina Karlovna Vasil'eva, *The Young People of Leningrad: School and Work Options and Attitudes* (translated from the Russian) (White Plains, NY: International Arts and Sciences Press, 1976).

111. A. G. Kharchev and M. C. Matskovskii, *Sovremennaia sem'ia* (Moscow: Statistika, 1978).

112. Peter Juviler, *Revolutionary Law and Order*, 123–67. Its sociological study resumed, after a hiatus of some thirty years, with the work of A. A. Gertsenzon, summed up in *Ugolovnoe pravo i sotsiologiia* (Moscow: Iurizdat, 1970), and continued in the work of N. V. Kudriavtsev, e.g., *Prichiny pravonarushenii* (Moscow: Nauka, 1976); A. M. Yakovlev, *Teoriia kriminologii i sotsial'naia praktika* (Moscow: Nauka, 1985); and others.

113. See, e.g., G. A. Prudenskii, *Vremia i trud* (Moscow, Mysl', 1965); Gl. G. Bliakhman, A. G. Zdravomyslov, and O. I. Shkaratan, *Dvizhenie rabochei sily na promyshlennykh predpriatiakh* (Moscow: Ekonomika, 1965); A. G. Kharchev and S. I. Golod, *Professional'naia rabota zhenshchin i sem'ia* (Leningrad: Nauka, 1971); A. A. Gordon and E. V. Zdravomyslov, *Chelovek posle raboty: Sotsial'nye problemy byta i vnerabochego vremeni*, 2 vols. (Moscow: Nauka, 1972); V. F. Bukin and E. F. Karavaev, eds., *Nauchno-tekhnicheskaia revoliutsiia i lichnost'* (Leningrad: Izd. Leningradskogo Universiteta, 1982).

114. M. V. Kurman and I. V. Lebedinskii, *Naselenie bol'shogo sotsialisticheskogo goroda* (Moscow: Statistika, 1968), 3. On demographic policies and debates, see John F. Beseneres, *Socialist Population Politics: The Political Implications of Demographic Trends in the USSR and Eastern Europe* (White Plains, NY: M. E. Sharpe, 1980); Peter Juviler, "The Family in the Soviet System," Paper No. 306, *The Carl Beck Papers in Russian and East European Studies* (University of Pittsburgh, 1984).

115. Thane Gustafson, *Reform in Soviet Politics: Lessons of Recent Policies on Land and Water* (Cambridge: Cambridge University Press, 1981).

116. Juviler and Zawadzka, "Detente and Soviet Domestic Politics," 158–67.

117. H. Gordon Skilling and Franklyn Griffiths, eds., *Interest Groups in Soviet Politics* (Princeton, NJ: Princeton University Press, 1971); Timothy J. Colton, *The Dilemma of Reform in the Soviet Union*, rev. and expanded ed. (New York: Council on Foreign Relations, 1986).

118. N. A. Tolokontsev and G. M. Romanenkova, *Demografiia i ekologiia krupnogo goroda* (Leningrad: Nauka, 1980), and *Okruzhaiushchaia sreda i narodonaselenie* (Moscow: Finansy i Statistika, 1981).

119. "The Urban Family and the Soviet State: Emerging Contours of a Demographic Policy," in Henry W. Morton and Robert C. Stuart, eds., *The Contemporary Soviet City* (Armonk, NY: M. E. Sharpe, 1984), 84–112; M. S. Bednyi, *Mediko-demograficheskoe izuchenie narodonaseleniia* (Moscow: Statistika, 1979).

120. Boris Komarov, *Unichtozhenie prirody: Obostrenenie ekologichekogo krizisa v SSSR* (Frankfurt/Main: Posev, 1978), is more frank than the officially published work of Ia. I. Rubin, *Dom nash zemnoi: Nauchno-tekhnichekii progress i razvitie obshchestva* (Minsk: Belarus, 1981).

121. Colton, *The Dilemma of Reform in the Soviet Union.*

122. Seweryn Bialer, *The Soviet Paradox: External Expansion, Internal Decline* (New York: Alfred A. Knopf, 1986).

123. *Ten Years Later: Violations of the Helsinki Accords* (New York: Helsinki Watch, 1985), 152–53.

124. Lewin, *The Gorbachev Phenomenon*; quotes from 157, 158.

125. "X" [George Kennan], "The Sources of Soviet Conduct," *Foreign Affairs* (July 1947), reprinted in Philip E. Mosely, ed., *The Soviet Union 1922–1962: A Foreign Affairs Reader,* 169–85; Geoffrey Hosking, *The Awakening of the Soviet Union,* 2d ed. (Cambridge, MA: Harvard University Press, 1991), 1–20.

126. S. Frederick Starr, "Soviet Union: A Civil Society," *Foreign Policy,* no. 70 (Spring 1988), 26–41; quote from 27.

127. Lewin, *The Gorbachev Phenomenon,* 175.

128. "Certainly the young *revoltes* were more certain of what they were against than of what they favored" (Billington, *The Icon and the Axe,* 583).

129. 1977 Constitution of the USSR, *Konstitutsiia (osnovnoi zakon) Soiuza Sovetskikh Sotsialisticheskikh Respublik* (Moscow: Iuridicheska ia literatura, 1978), Articles 6, 39, 50, and 51.

130. Solzhenitsyn, *Letter to the Soviet Leaders* (New York: Harper & Row, 1974); Andrei Amal'rik, *Will the Soviet Union Survive until 1984?* (New York: Harper & Row, 1970).

131. Geoffrey Hosking, *The Awakening of the Soviet Union,* enlarged ed. (Cambridge, MA: Harvard University Press, 1991), 1–20, 55–81; quote from 5 (emphasis added).

132. Theodore H. Von Laue, "Problems of Industrialization," in Theofanis George Stavrou, *Russia Under the Last Tsar* (Minneapolis: University of Minnesota Press, 1969), 117–53, quote on 151; and Von Laue's *Why Lenin? Why Stalin?* (Philadelphia/New York: Lippincott, 1964).

133. Roy Medvedev, *On Socialist Democracy* (New York: Knopf, 1975), xv, xix; Ken Coates, ed., *Detente and Socialist Democracy: A Discussion with Roy Medvedev* (New York: Monad Press, 1976), 18–19 (as reprinted from *Dissent,* no. 83, January 1973).

Chapter 4. Restructuring Rights

1. M. S. Gorbachev, General Secretary's Report to the 28th CPSU Congress, *Pravda,* July 3, 1990.

2. Thomas Riha, "Constitutional Developments in Russia," in Theofanis George Stavrou, ed., *Russia Under the Last Tsar* (Minneapolis: University of Minnesota Press, 1969), 114, quoting from *Russian Review* (London) 3, no. 1 (1914): 152.

3. Timothy Colton, *Dilemmas of Reform in the Soviet Union,* 2d ed. (New York: Council on Foreign Relations, 1986), 68–116.

4. Nikolai Zlobin, "Humor as Political Protest," *Demokratizatsiya* 4, no. 2 (1996): 226.

5. M. S. Gorbachev, *Perestroika i novoe myshlenie dlia nashei strany i dlia vsego mira* (Moscow: Izd. Politicheskoi Literatury, 1988), 28. See also speeches in *Pravda,* July 15, 1987, and February 19, 1988.

6. Don Oberdorfer, *The Turn: From Cold War to a New Era: The United States and the Soviet Union, 1983–1990* (New York: Poseidon Press, 1991), 299–300.

7. Mary McCauley, *Soviet Politics, 1917–1991* (New York: Oxford University Press, 1992), 109; Peter Reddaway, "Empire on the Brink, *New York Review of Books,* Jan. 31, 1991, 7–9; Yury Afanasyev, "The Coming Dictatorship," *New York Review of Books,* Jan. 31, 1991, 36–39.

8. Stephen F. Cohen, editorial, *New York Times*, March 11, 1991; Jerry Hough, "Gorbachev's Endgame," *World Policy Journal* 7, no. 4 (Fall 1990): 638–72.

9. Robert C. Nelson, "Nobel Laureate in Literature Talks of Glasnost in Soviet Society," *Christian Science Monitor*, October 23, 1987.

10. Vyacheslav Maslennikov, "Legal Duties and Responsibilities of the Individual," in V. Kudriavtsev, ed., *Rights of the Individual in Soviet Society* (Moscow: Iurizdat, 1986), 91. See also I. Lediakh and G. Mal'tsev, "The Crisis of the Bourgeois Conception of Human Rights," in Kudriavtsev, ed., 124–47; D. A. Kerimov and G. V. Mal'tsev, *Politika—delo kazhdogo* (Moscow: Politizdat, 1986), 20–26; D. A. Kerimov and V. M. Chkhikvadze, eds., with V. A. Kartashkin and E. A. Lukasheva, *Problemy prav cheloveka v sovremennoi ideologicheskoi bor'be* (Moscow: Izdatel'stvo politicheskoi literatury, 1986), 15–66; on the "state of the whole people" (*obshchenarodnoe gosudarstvo*) and use of the constitutional definition of rights "to nurture the individual of the communist society," see L. D. Voevodin, *Iuridichekie garantii konsitutsionnykh prav i svobod lichnosti v sotsialisticheskom obshchestve* (Moscow: Izdatel'stvo Moskovskogo universiteta, 1987), 43; B. N. Topornin (later director of the Soviet and then Russian Institute of State and Law into the 1990s), *Obshchie nachala teorii sotsialisticheskoi konstitutsii* (Moscow: Nauka, 1986).

11. V. M. Savitsky, "Pravosudie i perestroika," *Sovetskoe gosudarstvo i pravo*, no. 9 (1987), 29–35. The supposed watchdog of legality, the USSR Prosecutor's Office, had been an unreliable guardian of justice. Party decree on procuratorial supervision of June 4, 1987, "V Ts K," *Pravda*, June 19, 1987.

12. Andrei Sakharov, in "Actors in the Drama Speak Out" panel at public meeting of the U.S.–Soviet Dialogue on Human Rights and the future, Berkeley, California, August 11, 1989, in Peter Juviler and Bertram Gross, eds., with Vladimir Kartashkin and Elena Lukasheva, *Human Rights for the 21st Century* (Armonk, NY: M. E. Sharpe, 1993), 19.

13. Boris Shragin, "The Human Rights Movement: An Introduction," in M. Meerson-Aksenov and Boris Shragin, eds., *The Political, Social and Religious Thought of 'Samizdat'* (Belmont, MA: Nordlund, 1977), 179–80.

14. Yury Kudriavtsev, the author of anonymous articles on reform in *Kommunist*, told me that the party leadership meant the articles to be taken seriously (interview, Moscow, June 8, 1998); Peter Juviler, "Law and Individual Rights in the USSR: The Shifting Political Ground," in Albert J. Schmidt, ed., *The Impact of Perestroika on Soviet Law* (Dordrecht/Boston/London: Martinus Nijhoff, 1990) 107–32.

15. "Iuridicheskaia nauka i praktika v usloviiakh perestroiki," *Kommunist*, no. 14 (1987): 42–43, 45, 50.

16. Yury Kudriavtsev, "We Learn Democracy: Restructuring and Human Rights," *Nedelia*, October 19–25, 1987; condensed in *Current Digest of the Soviet Press* 39, no. 42 (1987): 7.

17. V. S. Vereschetin and R. A. Miullerson, "Mezhdunarodnoe pravo, osheinik dlia mezhdunarodnykh otnoshenii ili normativnoe vyrazhenie obshchechelevecheskikh tsennostei?" in Iu. M. Baturin, ed., *Puls' reforma: Iuristy i politologi razmyshliaiut* (Moscow: Progress, 1989), 303–15.

18. *On Speaking Terms: An Unprecedented Human Rights Mission to the Soviet Union (January 25–31, 1988)* (Vienna: International Helsinki Federation for Human Rights, 1988). Soviet UN delegate Aleksandr Khodakov welcomed NGO criticism of certain governments, including the Soviet, as "not such a bad thing" as long as it was "well grounded" and not politicized (*United Nations, Committee on NGO's, 495th Meeting, Press Release NGO/158*, 23 January 1989, p. 3). Amnesty International's book on the death penalty was translated and published in the USSR and excerpted in

the journal *Soviet State and Law*, no. 12 (1989), with a laudatory introduction by death penalty opponent Dr. Sofia Kelina.

19. On old thinking, see V. M. Chkhikvadze and E. A. Lukasheva, *Sotsialisticheskaia kontseptsiia prav cheloveka* (Moscow: Nauka, 1986); on new thinking, see Elena Lukasheva, "Witness to Upheaval," "Human Rights: A Time for Hard Decisions," and, with Vladimir Kudriavtsev, "Postcommunist New Thinking on Human Rights," in Juviler and Gross, eds., *Human Rights for the 21st Century*, 7–9, 56–68, 94–102.

20. V. O. Mushinskii, "Pravovoe gosudarstvo i pravoponimanie," *Sovetskoe gosudarstvo i pravo*, no. 2 (1990): 21–27.

21. V. M. Chkhikvadze, in "Actors in the Drama Speak Out," in Juviler and Gross, eds., 17.

22. Peter Juviler, "The Drive for Discipline: Andropov Makes His Mark," *Soviet Union* 11, pt. 3 (1984): 296–300.

23. Ibid., 64, 105; Larry Martz et al., "A Hard Bargain," and "Vowing To Fight On" (Sakharov–Bonner interview), *Newsweek*, January 5, 1987, 12–18.

24. Peter Juviler, "Prospects for Perestroika: New Goals, Old Interests," in Peter Juviler and Hiroshi Kimura, eds., *Gorbachev's Reforms: U.S. and Japanese Assessments* (Hawthorne, NY: Aldine de Gruyter, 1988), 31–32.

25. Jack F. Matlock, *Autopsy on an Empire: The American Ambassador's Account of the Collapse of the Soviet Union* (New York: Random House, 1995), 119.

26. *Sovetskaia rossiia*, March 13, 1988; rebuttal in *Pravda*, April 5, 1995, cited in Matlock, *Autopsy on an Empire*, 119–21.

27. Asked on a Leningrad TV panel broadcast in June 1988, "May you print all you want in your paper?" an editor of *Izvestiia* answered, "No, we may not. (*applause*)"; Peter Juviler, "Memorandum to Allen Kassof, Director, IREX, on ACLS/Academy exchange visit 5/19–6/19 1988," August 3, 1988.

28. "The 19th All-Union CPSU Conference: Foreign Policy and Diplomacy. Report by Member of the Politburo of the CPSU Central Committee, Minister of Foreign Affairs of the USSR Eduard Shevardnadze at the Scientific and Practical Conference of the USSR Ministry of Foreign Affairs," July 25, 1988, *International Affairs* (Moscow), no. 10 (1988): 3–34.

29. Alexander Dallin, "Gorbachev's Foreign Policy and the 'New Political Thinking' in the Soviet Union," in Juviler and Kimura, eds., *Gorbachev's Reforms*, 97–113.

30. Gorbachev UN speech of December 7, 1988, *Pravda*, December 8, 1988; Paul Lewis, "Soviets to Accept World Court Role in Human Rights," *New York Times*, March 9, 1989.

31. *Concluding Document of the Vienna Follow-Up Meeting* (Washington, D.C.: U.S. Commission on Security and Cooperation in Europe, January 1989), 6, 34–35. The Soviet Union joined the U.S. in having a division on human rights and humanitarian affairs in the Foreign Ministry. David K. Shipler, "Dateline USSR: On the Human Rights Track," *Foreign Policy*, no. 75 (1989): 172.

32. *Document of the Copenhagen Meeting* (Washington, D.C., Commission on Security and Cooperation in Europe, 1990), Article 39.

33. Alexander Bessmertnykh, First Deputy Minister of Foreign Affairs, " 'International Affairs' Guest Club: Five Meetings with Our Laureates," *International Affairs* (May 1989): 3–9.

34. Andrei Grachev, "Poslevoennyi mir i prava cheloveka," *Novoe vremia*, special supplement (December 1988), 3–5; Gail Warshofsky Lapidus, "Gorbachev's Agenda: Domestic Reforms and Foreign Policy Reassessments," in Juviler and Kimura, eds., *Gorbachev's Reforms*, 1–20.

35. Yuri F. Orlov, "Memorandum: The Meaning of Gorbachev's Reforms," January 31, 1988.

36. An authoritative study of CSCE's progress and problems into 1992 is William Korey, *The Promises We Keep: Human Rights, the Helsinki Process and American Foreign Policy* (New York: St. Martin's Press, 1993).

37. I wrote about this in "Introduction," and "Prospects for Perestroika: New Goals, Old Interests," in Juviler and Kimura, eds., *Gorbachev's Reforms*, x–xviii, 21–47.

38. Donald W. Treadgold, *Twentieth Century Russia*, 8th ed. (Boulder, CO: Westview Press, 1995), 414.

39. *Pravda*, July 15, 1987.

40. Mary McCauley, *Soviet Politics, 1917–1991*, 89–106.

41. Interviews with Professors Georgy Barabashev and Avgust Mishin, Moscow, March 1989.

42. Geoffry Hosking, *The Awakening of the Soviet Union*, 2d ed. (Cambridge, MA: Harvard University Press, 1991), 163–69.

43. Quote from Yelena Bonner in "Actors in the Drama Speak Out," U.S.–Soviet Dialogue on Human Rights and the Future, Berkeley, California, August 11, 1989, Juviler and Gross, 18–19. See also Antonina Bouis, "Watching the Soviet Congress on TV," *Soros Foundation Newsletter* 1, no. 3 (1989).

44. He called for an end to the legal political monopoly of the Communist Party several times in 1989. Sakharov, in "Actors in the Drama Speak Out," 22.

45. Richard Sakwa, *Russian Politics and Society* (London/New York: Routledge, 1993), 4.

46. Decree of April 8, 1989, *Pravda*, April 11, 1989, providing punishment from three to ten years or stiff fines for "advocating the overthrow or betrayal of the Soviet state and social system or changing it by means contravening the Soviet Constitution"; Law of July 11, 1989, FBIS-SOV, August 4, 1989, 29.

47. Law on Press and Other Mass Media of June 12, 1990, in *Vedomosti S"ezda Narodnykh Deputatov SSSR i Verkhovnogo Soveta SSSR*, no. 26, (June 12, 1990): item 492. Yuri Baturin, Vladimir Entin, and Mikhail Fedotov, "*Glasnost'* Struggles: An Insider's Account," *Meeting Report*, Kennan Institute for Advanced Russian Studies, June 11, 1990; Law on Freedom of Conscience and Religious Organizations, October 1, 1990, *Vedomosti*, no. 41 (1990), item 813; Law on Public Association, October 9, 1990, *Vedomosti*, no. 42 (1990), item 839; Peter Juviler, "Human Rights after Perestroika: Progress and Perils," *The Harriman Institute Forum* 4, no. 6 (June 1991): 2.

48. Denied USSR registration under pressure from the Union of Soviet Writers, which wanted control, the editors of *Literaturnaia gazeta* turned to the Russian Republic Mass Media Ministry, which registered it, with the independent-minded editors as founder-owners. Levon Grigorian, "New Soviet Law on Mass Media: More Problems of Implementation," draft paper of December 9, 1990; Vera Tolz, "Recent Attempts to Curb Glasnost'," *Radio Liberty Report*, March 1, 1990, 1–5.

49. Cronid Liubarsky, *USSR News Briefs*, no. 1, January 31, 1991.

50. *Vedomosti Verkhovnogo Soveta SSSR*, no. 22, items 391–92, May 21, 1990.

51. Department of State, *Country Reports on Human Rights Practices for 1991* (Washington, D.C.: Government Printing Office, Department of State, 1992), 1281–82.

52. Ernest Ametistov, report, New York City, Lawyers Committee for Human Rights, and Patterson, Belknap, Webb, and Tyler, September 27, 1990.

53. S. E. Kurginian et al., *Postperestroika: Kontseptual'naia model' razvitiia nashego obshchesta, politicheskikh partii i obshchestvennykh organizatsii* (Moscow, 1990); my interview with Dmitri Piskunov, director, and Sergei Kara-Murza, historian of science,

Analytical Center for Problems of Socio-Economy and Science-Technology Development," New York, May 1991; "Soiuznyi Dogovor: Zhiznesposobnost' strany i prava cheloveka," *Politika*, no. 3 (April 1991); Victor Yasman, "Elite Think Tank Prepares 'Post-*Perestroika*' Strategy," *Radio Liberty Report* 3, no. 21 (1990): 1–6; Elizabeth Teague, "The 'Soiuz' Group," *Radio Liberty Report* 3, no. 20 (1990): 16–21.

54. Matlock, *Autopsy on an Empire*, 429–32.

55. Speech to administrators and war and labor veterans, Mogilev Province, *Izvestiia*, March 2, 1991.

56. *Izvestiia*, March 1, 1991.

57. Juviler, "Human Rights after Perestroika," 1; Matlock, *Autopsy on an Empire*, 318–21, 561–62.

58. Afanasyev, "The Coming Dictatorship," quote from 38.

59. Between 1985 and 1991 Soviet troops and OMON special forces of the Ministry of the Interior left more than 200 demonstrators dead in five republics, to say nothing of numerous injuries and arrests. "Patterns of Violence: Lithuania Is Latest Example of Soviet Army's Use of Lethal Force," *News from Helsinki Watch*, January 25, 1991; *Human Rights Watch World Report 1991* (New York, 1991), 388–91. On mild U.S. responses, Lawyers Committee for Human Rights, *Critique: Review of the U.S. Department of State's Country Reports on Human Rights Practices 1991* (New York, 1992), 391–402.

60. Lawyers Committee for Human Rights, *Critique*, 1992, 392.

61. Julia Wishnevsky, "The 'Law-Based State,' Soviet Style," *Radio Liberty Report*, March 8, 1991, 1–2; Lawyers Committee for Human Rights, *Critique*, 1992, 392–93.

62. The prosecutor general denied Soviet troop responsibility for the killings while KGB and army officers detained investigators of a dissident officer group, Shield, and beat up two of them. Shield reported credible documentary evidence of a plan to overthrow the Baltic governments. It had been approved by the Politburo, of which Gorbachev was a member; Lawyers Committee for Human Rights, *Critique*, 1992, 393. Gorbachev's declaration, *Izvestiia*, January 23, 1991; Colonel Viktor Alksnis, Tokyo TV, FBIS-SOV-91-025, 63–64; Jeri Laber, "The Baltic Revolt," *New York Review of Books*, March 28, 1991, 60–64.

63. Soviet special forces attacked, destroyed, or closed thirty customs posts placed by Estonia, Latvia, and Lithuania as expressions of their sovereignty. At least eight customs and police officers were killed in the July 1991 attacks. Interior Minister Pugo (later a suicide, after the failed coup plot) denied OMON involvement; President Gorbachev denied prior knowledge. Lawyers Committee for Human Rights, *Critique*, 1992, 394.

64. *Moskovskie novosti*, no. 9 (1991).

65. It received legislative backing in a 1987 complaint law that was so weak as to be stillborn. A 1989 replacement only slightly improved on the 1987 law. *Vedomosti Verkhovnogo Soveta SSSR*, no. 22 (1989), item 416, law of November 2, 1989.

66. *Vedomosti Verkhovnogo Soveta SSSR*, no. 29 (1989), item 572, law of December 23, 1989, article 21, part 3.

67. Juviler, "Human Rights after Perestroika," 3, 6. The first published finding of the COC was on noncompliance with human rights standards and the constitution of a number of laws banning the court hearing of labor disputes in certain professions. *Vedomosti Verkhovnogo Soveta SSSR*, no. 23 (1990), items 418 and 421.

68. Igor Petrukhin, *Vam nuzhen advokat . . .* , (Moscow: Izdatel'stvo gruppa "Progress," 1993).

69. Eugene Huskey, "Between Citizen and State: The Soviet Bar (Advokatura) Under Gorbachev," *Columbia Journal of Transnational Law* 28, 1 (1990): 95–116; Peter Juviler, "Secret Justice and Personal Rights," in Richard M. Buxbaum and Kathryn

Hendley, eds., *The Soviet Sobranie of Laws* (Berkeley: University of California, Institute of International and Area Studies, 1991), 156–72; Juviler, article on the imprisonment, mistreatment, prison writings, and death in December 1986 of Anatoly Marchenko, in "Iz istorii sovremennosti: 'Zhivi kak vse,'" *Ogoniok*, no. 40 (1989), 16–19; Helsinki Watch, *Overview: Prisons and Jails in the Helsinki Countries, Prepared for the Moscow Conference on the Human Dimension,* September 1991; *Perestroika i prava cheloveka,* special supplement to *Novoe vremia,* December 1988; *Amnesty International Report,* 1985, 1986, 1987, 1988; D. J. Peterson, "The Zone, 1989: The Soviet Penal System Under Perestroika," *Radio Liberty Report* 1, no. 37 (1989): 1–6.

70. *Human Rights Watch World Report 1990,* 391–93; Catherine Fitzpatrick, "Psychiatric Abuse in the Soviet Union," *News from Helsinki Watch,* May 1990; Juviler, "Human Rights after Perestroika," 3; "List of Political Prisoners in the USSR as of 30 October 1990," Cronid Liubarsky, *USSR News Brief: Human Rights,* no. 1 (1991): 8. The figure of 157 prisoners is cited from Liubarsky's estimate in Lawyers Committee for Human Rights, *Critique,* 1992, 401. Andrei Mikhlin, "Zapret pytok: Pravo osuzhdennykh k lisheniiu svobody na gumannoe obrashchenie," *Novoe vremia* supplement, December 1988, 16–17; Viktor Kogan in *Sovetskaia iustitsiia,* no. 3 (1988); 12–13; no. 7, 26–27; no. 19, 21–22. The decree of January 26, 1991, on "Economic Sabotage," and a law of May 16 gave the KGB powers of warrantless search and surveillance. Lawyers Committee for Human Rights, *Critique,* 1991, 395–96.

71. Peter Juviler, "The Soviet Declaration of Individual Rights: The Last Act of the Old Union," in *The Parker School Bulletin on Soviet and East European Law* 2, no. 8 (October 1991): 3–4. On the death penalty, see Lawyers Committee for Human Rights, *Critique,* 1992, 400.

72. "I hypothesize that the undermining of the monopoly over media and ideology" was a crucial transformation that set off "a chain reaction that eroded the regime's reliance on coercion and the Communist Party's organizational prerogatives." Rasma Karklins, "Explaining Regime Change in the Soviet Union," *Europe-Asia Studies* 46, no. 1 (1994): 34–35 and 39–41.

73. Robert Sharlet, "Party and Public Ideals in Conflict: Constitutionalism and Civil Rights in the USSR," *Cornell International Law Journal* 23, no. 2 (1990): 341–62; *From Below: Independent Peace and Environmental Movements in Eastern Europe and the USSR* (New York: Helsinki Watch, 1987), 99–178; Geoffry Hosking, *The Awakening of the Soviet Union,* 55–81.

74. Lawyers Committee for Human Rights, *Critique,* 1992, 396–97; Jeff Trimble, "Snubbing People Power: Gorbachev's Show of Force Backfires . . . ," *U.S. News & World Report,* April 8, 1991, 38–40.

75. Talk at Harriman Institute, Columbia University, October 9, 1990.

76. Moshe Lewin, *The Gorbachev Phenomenon,* 2d ed. (Berkeley: University of California Press, 1990), 166.

77. McCauley, *Soviet Politics, 1917–1921,* 120–21.

78. Hosking, *The Awakening of the Soviet Union,* 14.

79. Riha, "Constitutional Developments in Russia," 115–16, quoting Philip E. Mosely, "1930–1932: Some Vignettes of Soviet Life," *Survey* (London), no. 60 (April 1965): 54.

80. Quoted in Bill Keller, "Soviets Adopt Emergency Plan to Center Power in Gorbachev and Leaders of the Republics," *New York Times,* November 18, 1990.

81. "Perestroika, Lenin, Sotsializm," *Sovetskaia iustitsiia,* no. 8 (April 1990): 2, 4; Anatoly Rybakov on hatred in "Children of the Arbat in 1937," *Moscow News,* no. 35, September 9–16, 1990, 16; A. N. Yakovlev, "'Sindrom vraga,': Anatomiia sotsial'noi bolezni," *Literaturnaia gazeta,* no. 7, February 14, 1990, 10.

82. "Respect for public law and order and common human moral values is going, and the atmosphere of an absolute power vacuum and irresponsibility is setting in. Discipline is plummeting, as is production; the crime rate is zooming." Elena Lukasheva, "Human Rights: A Time for Hard Decisions," in Juviler and Gross, eds., 60. Dr. Lukasheva's colleague and another dialogue participant, human rights specialist Vladimir Kartashkin, said to me in the spring of 1995 that Russia will have no replacements in human rights study; the young lawyers are interested in business law. A professor in the Institute of International Relations and wife of a Constitutional Court justice told me in Moscow in June 1990 that her students were much more interested in international economics and business law than they were in international law and relations, once the most popular subjects.

83. Igor Seliunin, "Istoki," *Novyi mir*, no. 5 (1988): 162–89; talk with Dr. Viktor Aleksandrov, Moscow, June 1988; Peter Juviler, "Memorandum to Allen Kassof, Director of IREX" (1988).

84. Marshall I. Goldman, "Soviet Energy Runs Out of Gas," *Current History* 89, no. 549 (1990): 313–16, 335–36; *What Went Wrong with Perestroika*, 2d ed. (New York: W. W. Norton, 1992).

85. A. V. Naumov, "Ugolovnyi zakon v usloviiakh perekhoda k rynochnoi ekonomike," *Sovetskoe gosudarstvo i pravo*, no. 2 (1991): 33; Vasily Petrovich Trushin, USSR Deputy Interior Minister, at October 22, 1990, session of USSR Supreme Soviet, Moscow TV service, FBIS-SOV-90-205, 39. "Most often persons convicted for private enterprise," wrote the jurist Dr. Naumov, "are persons who have set up various workshops within socialist enterprises, and auxiliary shops to produce scarce goods. Incidentally, often one finds in the defendant's dock, clever organizers of production whose enterprise found no place in the rigidly centralized planned economy of the administrative-command system." A. V. Naumov, "Perexod k rynku i ugolovnyi zakon," *Izvestiia*, October 28, 1990.

86. Judith Record McKinney, "Confusion in Soviet Economic Reform," *Current History* 89, no. 549 (1990): 317–20 and 342–43.

87. Peter Juviler, "Presidential Power and Presidential Character," *Soviet Union* 16, nos. 2–3 (1991): 245–55.

88. S. Shatalin et al., "Message," *Komsomolskaia pravda*, November 4, 1990, FBIS-SOV-90-214, 56–58. On guidelines: "Osnovnye napravleniia po stabilizatsii narodnogo khoziaistva i perexodu k rynochnomu ekonomike," *Pravda*, October 18, 1990; *Izvestiia*, October 27, 1990. M. S. Gorbachev, "Ob osnovnykh napravleniiakh po stabilizatsii narodnogo khoziaistva i perexodu k rynochnomu ekonomike" (address to USSR Supreme Soviet), *Pravda* and *Izvestiia*, October 19, 1990; T. Zaslavskaya, L. Kosals, and R. Rybkina, "Ekonomicheskoi svobode—garantii," *Izvestiia*, October 25, 1990.

89. Stanislav Kondrashev, "Shto my s etogo imeem," *Izvestiia*, October 31, 1990; Alexei Pushkov, "What Can We Expect from the USA: The Level of Soviet–U.S. Cooperation Depends Solely on the Success of Soviet Internal Political and Economic Reform," *Moscow News*, no. 26 (1990): 12; Padma Desai, "Aiding Moscow: The Quid Pro Quo Approach," letter to the *New York Times*, May 28, 1991. Henning Christophersen, the European Community's commissioner for economic affairs, said: "There must be a very clear reform program that can be monitored, clear targets that can be achieved. Otherwise it is impossible to get members of the Community to agree to large-scale aid." *New York Times*, June 6, 1991.

90. Matlock, *Autopsy on an Empire*, 523–59, 559–62, 648–65.

91. Universal Declaration of Human Rights, Article 25. See also International Covenant on Economic Social and Cultural Rights, Article 11. Center for the

Study of Human Rights, Columbia University, *Twenty-Five Human Rights Documents* (New York, 1994), 8–9, 12–13; Marat Baglai, "Sotsial'noekonomicheskie prava: oslabliaiutsia garantii?" *Novoe vremia supplement*, no. 12 (December 1988).

92. Yuri Levada, "Social Barometer: Hopes, Doubts, Faith," *Moscow News*, no. 25 (1990): 4.

93. Juviler, "Human Rights after Perestroika," 5.

94. Daniel Sneider, "Rival Demonstrations Hit Moscow," *Christian Science Monitor*, November 8, 1990.

95. J. V. Stalin, "O proekte konstitutsii Soiuza SSR," in Robert H. McNeal, ed., *I. V. Stalin Sochineniia*, vol. 1 (16) (Stanford: The Hoover Institute on War, Revolution and Peace, 1967), 171.

96. Roman Szporluk, "The Imperial Legacy and Soviet Nationalities," in Lubomyr Hajda and Mark Beissinger, eds., *The Nationalities Factor in Soviet Politics and Society* (Boulder, CO: Westview Press, 1990), 9–10.

97. Peter Reddaway wrote on the triple political, economic, and ethnic loss of legitimacy, in "The End of Empire," *New York Review of Books*, November 7, 1991, 53–59.

98. Part of the Fourth Army in Nagorno-Karabakh joined with Azerbaijan special force units in "Operation Ring" during forced deportations of Armenians from villages in the disputed region. *Human Rights Watch World Report 1992*, 530–32, 534–37; Hosking, *The Awakening of the Soviet Union*, 89–91; *Report of the Delegation of the First International Andrei D. Sakharov Congress of the Visit to the Shaumian District, 5 September 1991*; The Andrei Sakharov Foundation, *Report of a Delegation to Nagorno-Karabakh 3–8 January 1992*. The blockade's fuel crisis shut down factories, curtailed transport and winter heating, and nearly stranded our group of referendum monitors at the Yerevan airport in September 1991.

99. Rasma Karklins, *Ethnic Relations in the USSR* (Boston: Allen & Unwin, 1986); Michael Rywkin, *Moscow's Moslem Challenge: Soviet Central Asia* (Armonk, NY: M. E. Sharpe, 1982); Helene Carrere D'Encausse, *Confiscated Power: How Soviet Russia Really Works* (New York: Harper & Row, 1982), 279–80, 298–301; Andrei Amalrik, *Will the Soviet Union Survive Until 1984?* (New York: Harper & Row, 1970), 44–67; G. Ch. Guseinov, "Menshinstva v post-imperskom mire," *Korni* (Riga), no. 2, (December 1991): 2; Alexander Motyl, *Will the Non-Russians Rebel?: State, Ethnicity and Stability in the USSR* (Ithaca, NY: Cornell University Press, 1987), 1–52, 124–70; Alexander Motyl, *Sovietology Rationality, Nationality* (New York: Columbia University Press, 1990).

100. Algiras Prazauskas, "National Problems of Renovated Socialism," in *The Revolution Continues: Soviet Society in the Conditions of Restructuring* (Moscow: Social Sciences Today Editorial Board, Nauka Publishers, 1989), 202. Thanks to Frank Bonilla.

101. Vladimir Socor, "Moldova Proclaims Independence, Commences Secession from the USSR," *RFE/RL Report on the USSR*, no. 42 (1991): 21.

102. The immediate cause of demonstrations was the replacement of the First Secretary, a Kazakh, Dinmukhamed Kunaev, by a Russian outsider, Gennady Kolbin. Jeri Laber, "Stalin's Dumping Ground," *New York Review of Books*, October 11, 1990, 50–53. See also *Human Rights Watch, World Report 1992* (New York, 1992), 527. The most detailed substantiations of long-standing grievances and violations by Soviet troops and police through excessive force and violations of due process in mass arrests appeared in V. A. Ponomarev and S. Dzhukeeva, *Dokumenty i materialy o sobytiiakh 1986 goda v Kazakhstane* (Moscow: Panorama, 1993), and *Alma-Ata 1986: Kniga-Khronika* (Alma-Ata: Altyn Orda, 1991).

103. Talk by Dr. Jennifer Leaning, Physicians for Human Rights, Helsinki Watch Committee, New York, June 7, 1989; *"Bloody Sunday": Trauma in Tbilisi* (Boston:

Physicians for Human Rights, 1990); Celestine Bohlen, "Military Gas Used in Soviet Georgia," *New York Times*, May 25, 1989; Elena Bonner, "The Shame of Armenia," *New York Review of Books*, October 11, 1990, 39–40.

104. Otto Latsis, "Who Wanted This War?" *Moscow Times*, January 15, 1995, 42; Estonian declaration and Law of November 16, 1988, *Sovetskaia estoniia*, November 18, 1988; the center's negative response appeared in *Pravda*, November 28, 1988; Joel Aav, "Estonian Parliament Does Not Shrink Back," *Supplement to the Estonian Kodumaa Weekly*, December 14, 1988; for the declaration of state sovereignty of the Byelorussian SSR, July 27, 1990, see *Argumenty i fakty*, no. 31, August 4–10, 1990, 1–2; interview with Armenian President Ter-Petrossian, trans. from *Berliner Zeitung*, August 28, 1990, in FBIS-SOV-90-170, 55–56.

105. Matlock, *Autopsy on an Empire*, 511–12.

106. Peter Reddaway, "The End of the Empire," 53–59.

107. Hurst Hannum, *Autonomy, Sovereignty, and Self-Determination: The Accommodation of Conflicting Rights*, 2d ed. (Philadelphia: University of Pennsylvania Press, 1996); idem, "The Limits of Sovereignty and Majority Rule: Minorities, Indigenous Peoples, and the Right to Autonomy," in Ellen Lutz, Hurst Hannum, and Kathryn J. Burke, *New Directions in Human Rights* (Philadelphia: University of Pennsylvania Press, 1989), 20–21; Peter Juviler, "Are Collective Rights Anti-Human?: Theories on Self-Determination and Practice in Soviet Successor States," *Netherlands Quarterly of Human Rights* 11, no. 3 (1993): 267–82.

108. Douglas Sanders, "Collective Rights," *Human Rights Quarterly* 13, no. 3 (1991): 375.

109. "Po-novomu osmyslit' funktsii i rol' partii v obshchestve," *Pravda*, July 21, 1989.

110. Matlock, *Autopsy on an Empire*, 578–604.

111. Yelena Bonner speaking in at the Association of the Bar of the City of New York, October 22, 1991.

112. *Country Reports*, 1992, 1267.

113. For analysis of the coup and breakup, see Matlock, *Autopsy on an Empire*, 578–647; McCauley, *Soviet Politics, 1917–1991*, 107–19.

114. Martha Brill Olcott, "The Slide into Disunion," *Current History* 90 (1991): 338. Henry Huttenbach, "Managing a Federation of Multiethnic Republics," *Nationalities Papers* 19, no. 1 (1991): 26–32; Peter Juviler, "Getting to Yes on Self-Determination," *Nationalities Papers* 19, no. 1 (1991): 32–36; Jack F. Matlock, Jr., *Autopsy on an Empire*, passim.

115. Eduard Shevardnadze, "No One Can Isolate Us Save Ourselves: Self-Isolation Is the Ultimate Danger," *Slavic Review* 51, no. 1 (1992): 118, and his interview with Fyodor Burlatsky, *Literaturnaia gazeta*, April 10, 1991, FBIS-SOV-91-071, 31.

116. There was a minimum of 85 percent support for the independence of Ukraine in the December 1991 referendum. Jaroslaw Matyuniuk, "Ukrainian Independence and Territorial Integrity," *RFE/RL Research Report*, March 27, 1992, 65.

117. Matlock, *Autopsy on an Empire*, 636–37; Peter Juviler, "The Soviet Declaration of Individual Rights: The Last Act of the Old Union," in *The Parker School Bulletin on Soviet and East European Law* 2, no. 8 (1991): 3–4.

118. Stephen F. Cohen, "The Friends and Foes of Change: Reformism and Conservatism in the Soviet Union," in Stephen F. Cohen, Alexander Rabinowitch, and Robert Sharlet, eds., *The Soviet Union since Stalin* (Bloomington: Indiana University Press, 1980), 11–31.

119. "Boris Alone," *The New Yorker*, October 18, 1993, 6.

Chapter 5. Free at Last? Democracy in the Newly Independent States

1. Igor Greenwald, "A Chameleon Shows His Jeffersonian Side," *Christian Science Monitor*, March 28, 1996.

2. Larry Diamond calls democracies that have significant lacks in human rights beyond electoral rights themselves "electoral democracies." I prefer the Freedom House term, "partly free democracies," as more accurately conveying the varied mixes of rights that may exist beyond electoral rights in democracies of partly free countries. Larry Diamond, "Is the Third Wave Over?" *Journal of Democracy* 7, no. 3 (1996): 21–24. Adrian Karatnycky, "Democracy and Despotism: Bipolarism Renewed?" *Freedom Review* 27, no. 1 (1996): 5–7, quotes from 6; "Table of Independent Countries: Comparative Measures of Freedom," *Freedom Review* 27, no. 1 (1996): 16–17. Figures for 1997 are from *Freedom Review* 28, no. 1 (1997): 3–11.

3. The Freedom House methodology of rating is explained in Karatnycky, "Democracy and Despotism," 11–15. Countries scoring an average of 1–2.5 on political rights and civil liberties, on the basis of total raw scores, are rated as free; 3–5 as partly free; and 5.5–7 as not free. Free countries rate high both in "political freedoms" (free and fair elections of representatives who have a decisive voice over public policy)—raw scores on which ratings are based are compiled on the basis of eight political rights guaranteeing electoral participation and intragovernmental accountability to elected representatives—and "civil liberties": thirteen rights that underpin electoral participation and are essential for accountability to the electorate between elections. This broad array of empowering rights includes those to expression, assembly, association, etc.; civil rights to due process and personal inviolability; and rights to economic and social freedoms and equality.

4. The basis for these calculations (for the democracy proportion, excluding stateless persons under Estonian and Latvian citizenship law [see Chapter 6] and persons in separatist areas not under central authority) are population figures (in millions): Russian Federation, 150; Estonia, 1.6 (with about 28 percent stateless); Latvia, 2.7 (with about one-third stateless); Lithuania, 3.8; Belarus, 10.4; Ukraine, 51.9; Moldova (with 600,000 estimated in separatist Transdniestria), 4.4; Armenia, 3.5; Azerbaijan, 7.6; Georgia, 5.6 (with an estimated 10 percent excluded); Kazakhstan, 17.2; Kyrgyzstan, 4.6; Tajikistan, 5.6; Turkmenistan, 3.9; Uzbekistan, 21.6. All population figures are taken from William A. Dando, Lawrence A. Boenigk, and Ford D. Bond, *Russia and the Independent Nations of the Former U.S.S.R.: Geofacts and Maps* (Dubuque, IA: Wm. C. Brown Communications, 1996), 3–4, 13, 15, 19, 23, 25, 29, 35, 37, 41, 45, 47, 51, 53, 57.

5. Timothy J. Colton, "Politics," in Timothy J. Colton and Robert Legvold, eds., *After the Soviet Union: From Empire to Nations* (New York: W. W. Norton & Company, 1992), 22.

6. This survey is based on *Amnesty International Report 1996* (New York, 1996) and editions for 1993–95; Department of State, *Country Reports on Human Rights Practices for 1995* (Washington, D.C.: Government Printing Office, 1996), and years 1993–95; *Human Rights Watch World Report 1996* (New York, 1996) and the years 1993–95.

7. Paige Sullivan, "Former Soviet Union: Ballots, Bullets and Barricades," *Freedom in the World, 1993–1994* (New York: Freedom House, 1994), 59.

8. Human Rights Watch/Helsinki, *The Commonwealth of Independent States . . . ,* 10–12; *Amnesty International Report 1995* (New York, 1995); ibid., 1993, 56–60, 64, 126–27, 133–34, 178, 185–86, 210–11, 247–48, 277–78, 293, 296–97, 305–6; *Human Rights Watch World Report, 1993* (New York: Human Rights Watch, 1993), 228–52; *Human Rights in Turkmenistan* (New York: Helsinki Watch, July 1993); *Human Rights*

in Uzbekistan (New York: Helsinki Watch, May 1993); U.S. Department of State, *Country Reports on Human Rights Practices for 1992* (Washington, D.C.: Government Printing Office, 1993), passim; Interlegal Research Center, *Human Rights,* March 1992.

9. Ariel Cohen, Crime Without Punishment," *Journal of Democracy* 6, no. 2 (1995): 38.

10. Applebaum, "Nice Guys Finish Last," 24–30; quote from 27.

11. "In the fragile states of the FSU, most people are too busy eking out a meager existence and too resentful of the poverty and chaos they see around them every day to think about democratic ideals, civic responsibilities, the fine points of market economics, or local politics." Sullivan, "Former Soviet Union," 59.

12. Many people have lost what they once enjoyed of human rights to an adequate standard of living, education, health care, food, clothing, and shelter, and to a cultural life as recognized in the UDHR, articles 22–27, in Center for the Study of Human Rights, Columbia University, *Twenty-Five Human Rights Documents* (New York, 1994), 8–9.

13. Peter Juviler, "No End of a Problem: *Perestroika* for the Family?" in Anthony Jones, Walter D. Connor, and David E. Powell, eds., *Soviet Social Problems* (Boulder, CO: Westview Press, 1991), 194–212; Anastasiya Posadskaya, "Women as the Objects and Motive Force for Change in Our Time," and Zoya Khotkina, "Women in the Labor Market: Yesterday, Today and Tomorrow," both in Anastasiya Posadskaya, ed., *Women in Russia: A New Era in Russian Feminism* (London/New York: Verso, 1994), 8–13, 85–108.

14. Henry R. Huttenbach, "From Suppressed to Suppressor: Religious Freedom after Communism," *Association for the Study of Nationalities: Analysis of Current Events,* year 7, no. 10 (1996), 2–3. This issue of limits on proselytizing preoccupied an OSCE conference attended by representatives of 47 member countries, 2 international organizations, and 87 NGOs. Karen Lord, "Conference on Religious Liberty held in Warsaw, 16–19 April 1996," *CSCE Digest* 19, no. 5 (1996): 5, 8. On proselytizing laws and bans, see below under Armenia, Azerbaijan, Belarus, Moldova, Ukraine, and Uzbekistan.

15. See Article 2(2) and 10 of the UDHR, Article 26 of the International Covenant on Civil and Political Rights, on equality; Article 27 of the Covenant on Civil and Political Rights, on rights to cultural identity of members of minority groups.

16. Human Rights Watch/Helsinki, *The Commonwealth of Independent States: Refugees and Internally Displaced Persons in Armenia, Azerbaijan, Georgia, The Russian Federation, and Tajikistan,* vol. 8, no. 7(D) (New York, May 1996); Kazakhstan, a country of 17 million people, experienced a rising outflow of non-Kazakhs into the mid-1990s. V. Ponomarev, *Central Asia Papers Issue No. 1: The Demographic Situation in Kazakhstan* (Moscow: "Panorama," 1995), passim; Douglas Stanglin and Victoria Pope, "Desperate Trips at the End of Empire," *U.S. News & World Report,* April 11, 1994, 40–42; Helsinki Watch, *Punished Peoples of the Soviet Union: The Continuing Legacy of Stalin's Deportations* (New York, 1991).

17. *Forced Migration Monitor,* no. 12 (July 1996), 1–3.

18. For background, see, e.g., Peter J. S. Duncan, "Ukraine and the Ukrainians," in Graham Smith, ed., *The Nationalities Question in the Post-Soviet States,* 2d ed. (London/New York: Longmans, 1996), 188–209; Alfred A. Reich, "Transcarpathia's Hungarian Minority and the Autonomy Issue," *RFE/RL,* no. 6 (1992), 17–23.

19. The nuclear meltdown at Chernobyl was preceded by other less publicized but equally dire nuclear accidents. These placed children and young adults especially at risk. Every mother of a child in Ukraine, regardless of her ethnic origin,

had an interest in establishing a state in which she would have a say about her children's future. "News of Note Across the Region: Ukraine. Dealing with Chernobyl," *Transition,* September 8, 1995, 29–30.

20. *Rukh: The Popular Movement of Ukraine for Restructuring—Program and Charter* (Kiev, 1989).

21. *Meeting Report,* Kennan Institute for Advanced Russian Studies, April 16, 1992.

22. By 1996, they had all been shipped to Russia for destruction, with U.S. assistance, under terms of nonproliferation agreements signed by the United States and Russia with Ukraine, Belarus, and Kazakhstan. At a ceremony of June 4, 1996, top defense officials of Ukraine, Russia, and the United States sprinkled sunflower seeds on a field where silos had once housed not cattle feed but nuclear missiles. Jane Perlez, "Sunflower Seeds Replace Ukraine's Old Missile Sites," *New York Times,* June 5, 1996.

23. It defined *sovereignty* as "supremacy, independence, fullness and indivisibility of the republic within the boundary of its territory, and its independence and sovereignty in international relations." *The Supreme Rada of the Ukrainian SSR: Declaration of the State Sovereignty of Ukraine,* Kiev, July 16, 1990 (in Ukrainian and English).

24. *Freedom in the World: Political Rights & Civil Liberties, 1991–1992* (New York: Freedom House, 1992), 454.

25. Ibid., 460.

26. *Country Reports,* 1995, 1022–23.

27. Dando, Boenigk, and Bond, *Russia and the Independent Nations of the Former U.S.S.R.,* 25.

28. Orest Daychakiwsky, "Anniversary of Chernobyl Nuclear Disaster Focus of Hearing," *CSCE Digest* 19, no. 5 (1996): 4.

29. Anders Aslund, "Ukraine's Resurrection," *American Foreign Policy Interests* (National Committee on American Foreign Policy) 17, no. 3 (1995): 13.

30. Findings in this part have been checked against *Country Reports,* 1996, 1085–93.

31. *Country Reports,* 1995, 1020.

32. *Amnesty International Report, 1996,* 307.

33. "Religion, Nationalism, and Intolerance—Ukraine's Millennium of Strife," *In Brief* (United States Institute of Peace), no. 32 (1991): 1–4, quotes on 2, 3; see also Jane Perlez, "Catholics Can Worship, But Not Always in Church," *New York Times,* June 18, 1994. The bitterness turned to violence when the police broke up a procession of supporters of the Autocephalous Church as they attempted to bury the remains of their Patriarch Volodymyr in the pavement of the (Russian) Orthodox Cathedral of St. Sophia. Lida Poletz, "Ukraine's Religious Standoff Makes Unlikely Political Allies," *Christian Science Monitor,* July 21, 1995.

34. A law of December 23, 1993, limits proselytizing by stating that "foreign clergy and other representatives of nonnative religious organizations" may preach and carry on other canonical activities "only in those religious organizations which invited them to Ukraine and with the official approval of the government body that registered the statutes and the articles of the pertinent religious organizations." *Country Reports,* 1995, 1021.

35. Robert Cullen, "Report from Ukraine," *The New Yorker,* January 27, 1992, 53–57; Roman Solchanyk, "Ukrainian–Russian Confrontation over the Crimea," *RFE/RL Report,* no. 8, 1992, 26–30; Serge Schmemann, "Ukraine Facing the High Costs of Democracy," *New York Times,* November 6, 1992.

36. Threats loomed of possible civil war, joined by pro-Tatar intervention by the Confederation of Mountain Peoples of the Caucasus, an alliance of autonomous republics within Russia, with the breakaway republic of Chechnya, since then en-

gulfed and devastated by the Russian government attack on it in 1994–95. The Confederation was already involved in the fighting against Georgian forces in Ab-khazia. Aleksandr Pilat, "For Tatars, Paradise Is No Paradise," *Golos Ukrainy*, October 2, 1992 (complete text), and "Hell in Krasny Rai [Red paradise]," *Golos Ukrainy*, October 3, 1992 (excerpts); "Civil War in the Crimea?—Krasny Rai Has Become Hell for the Crimean Tatars. The Majlis May Announce Mobilization," *Nezavisimaia gazeta*, October 3, 1992 (excerpts); "Whose Side Will Kiev Take—The Confrontation in the Crimea Builds," *Nezavisimaia gazeta*, October 6 (condensed text); Aleksandr Pilat, "The Situation Is Strained to the Limit," *Nezavisimaia gazeta*, October 8, in *Current Digest of the Soviet Press* 44, no. 40 (1992): 17–19.

37. *The Economist*, March 25, 1995, 58, and April 8, 1995, 45.

38. *Country Reports*, 1995, 1017.

39. "Recommendations of Participants of the Parliamentary Hearings on the Status of Women in Ukraine," Organizational Committee and the Parliamentary Commission on Human Rights, Rights of National Minorities, and Interethnic Relations, July 1995. Quoted in Martha Bohachevsky-Chomiak, "Women: Changing Roles. Practical Concerns and Political Protest in Post-Soviet Ukraine," *Transition*, September 8, 1995, 12–17, at 16; "News of Note Across the Region: Ukraine. Dealing with Chernobyl," *Transition*, September 8, 1995, 29–30. Women's organizations included: the Ukrainian Committee of Soldiers' Mothers, Zhinocha Hromada [Women's Community]; the Committee of Families with Many Children; the "Mother-86" group of mothers of children born around the time of the Chernobyl disaster; and the more official Union of Women of Ukraine.

40. Vladimir Skachko, "Parliament Readies Appropriate Measures" and "Leonid Kuchma Thanks Deputies and Cancels Referendum," *Sevodnya*, June 28 and 29, 1996; condensed text in *Current Digest of the Post-Soviet Press* 48, no. 26 (1996): 24–25.

41. Anders Aslund, "Eurasia Letter: Ukraine's Turnaround," *Foreign Policy*, no. 100 (1995), 125–43. On the legislative showdown, polls on the president and Rada, and security issues, see Chrystyna Lapychak, "Showdown Yields Political Reform," *Transition* 1, no. 13 (July 28, 1995): 3–8; Jaroslaw Martyniuk, "The Shifting Political Landscape," *Transition*, 9–11; Ustina Markus, "Foreign Policy as a Security Tool," *Transition*, 12–17.

42. *The Economist*, September 2, 1995, 48–49; Zenovia Socor, "No Middle Ground? On the Difficulties of Crafting a Consensus in Ukraine," in special issue of *The Harriman Review*, "Peoples, Nations, Identities: The Russian–Ukrainian Encounter" (Spring 1996): 57–61. Hungary had $13 billion in foreign investments by the mid-1990s; Ukraine, with five times its population, had all of $700 million. Jane Perlez, "Despite U.S. Hope and Help, Ukraine's Star Fades," *New York Times*, June 27, 1996.

43. George Zarycky, "Along Russia's Rim: The Challenges of Statehood," *Freedom Review* 27, no. 1 (1996): 34–43.

44. The G-7 (Group of Seven) industrial countries pledged $4 billion, conditioned on Ukraine's commitment to reform, and came through with half. The International Monetary Fund, World Bank, Russia, and Turkmenistan raised loan assistance to a total of $5.3 billion by mid-1996. The U.S. European Union and Japan furnish additional modest bilateral aid without conditions. Information in this paragraph, except where noted, is based on Anders Aslund, "Give Ukraine a Break," *New York Times*, August 8, 1996.

45. Zarycky, "Along Russia's Rim," 37.

46. Dando, Boenigk, and Bond, *Russia and the Independent Nations of the Former U.S.S.R.*, 29.

47. Text of declaration in Charles S. Furtado, Jr., and Andrea Chandler, eds., *Perestroika in the Soviet Republics: Documents on the National Question* (Boulder, CO: Westview Press, 1992), 308–9.

48. Jonathan Eyal and Graham Smith, "Moldova and the Moldovans," in Smith, ed., *The Nationalities Question in Post-Soviet States*, 223–44.

49. Both the constitution's Article 32 and the new press law ban "contesting or defaming the State and the people." Article 41 of the constitution declares unconstitutional political parties that "militate against political pluralism, the principles of the rule of law, or of the sovereignty, independence, and territorial integrity of the republic of Moldova." Except where otherwise noted, information on human rights in Moldova is based on *Country Reports*, 1996, 949–55; quote from 953.

50. Text of letter by Mircea Snegur, n.d., in FBIS-SOV-92-071, April 13, 1992.

51. Vladimir Solonar', "Russofony i Romanisty," *Novoe vremia*, no. 37, 1991, 8; Bruce Seymore II, *The Access Guide to Ethnic Conflicts in Europe and the Former Soviet Union* (Washington, D.C.: Access, 1994), 53.

52. Eyal and Smith, "Moldova and the Moldovans," 241.

53. Interview with Deputy Vladimir Solonar' of the Moldovan Supreme Council, Moscow, September 17, 1991. As it turned out, by 1992 Moldovan public opinion, as well as a multiethnic parliamentary majority including part of the Moldovan Popular Front, had turned against union with Romania. In July 1992, a revamped Moldovan "government of national consensus" affirmed its commitment to equal rights of all, regardless of ethnicity. Moldova cracked down on the Communist Party and confiscated its property, including *Sovetskaya Moldava*. The newspaper's assets, which included the largest printing press in Moldova, the government transferred to the new pro-Moldovan daily, *Nezavisimaia Moldava*. Vladimir Socor, "Moldavia Defies Soviet Coup, Removes Vestiges of Communism," *RFE/RL Research Reports*, no. 38 (1991), 21.

54. *Human Rights Watch World Report 1992*, 538–39; Vladimir Solonar', "Nenavist' i strakh na raznykh beregakh," *Novoe vremia*, no. 14, 1992, 18. As violence escalated, Transdniestrians' appeals for help to Russia and Ukraine remained unanswered except by intruding Cossacks and the army and nationalists, such as Vice President Rutskoi, who supported Transdniestrian independence. Valery Vyzhutovich, "Rossiiskaia vlast' ne osuzhdaet agressiiu," *Izvestiia*, March 10, 1992.

55. The army played an ambiguous role. It supplied arms to the rebels at the very least. Also, it intervened to help stop the fighting. "Moldova: Yes, a Country," *The Economist*, August 26, 1995, 43–45; Eyal and Smith, "Moldova and the Moldovans, 241; Alina Pastiu, "Human Rights and Power Politics: An Analysis of the Conflict between the Moldovan Government and the DMR Authorities," unpublished paper, Columbia University, 1993.

56. FBIS-SOV-92-071, 13 April 1992, 50, 54.

57. Secession in case of Moldovan unification with Romania was supported on April 8 by a resolution of the 6th Russian Congress of People's Deputies, to the displeasure of Moldovan leaders. FBIS-SOV-92-069, 9 April 1992, 57; -072, 14 April, 52; -073, 15 April, 51; -078, 22 April, 38. See also *Country Reports*, 1993, 847; Karen Dawisha and Bruce Parrott, *Russia and the New States of Eurasia: The Politics of Upheaval* (New York: Cambridge University Press, 1994), 146; Vladimir Socor, "Dniester Involvement in the Moscow Rebellion," *REF/RL Report*, vol. 2, no. 46, November 19, 1993, 25–32. Svetlana Gamova, "Population of Left Bank Endorses Course Aimed at Independence for the Region," *Sevodnya*, December 24, 1996, *CDPSP*, 48, no. 51 (1996): 20; Natalya Kalashnikova, "It's Hard To Be Independent of Leftist Comrades," *Kommersant-Daily*, December 3, 1996, *CDPSP*, 48, no. 49 (1996): 20.

58. *Country Reports*, 1996, 950–52, 954.

59. Estimates for 1995, "Moldova: Yes, a Country," *The Economist*, August 26, 1995, 43–44.

60. Zarycky, "Along Russia's Rim," 37.

61. Information based on *Country Reports*, 1996, 862–69; *Human Rights Watch World Report 1996*, 217–19; and other sources where cited.

62. Dando, Boenigk, and Ford, *Russia and the Independent Nations of the Former U.S.S.R.*, 41.

63. "Conflict in Georgia," *Helsinki Watch*, no. 33 (1991): 16; Commission on Security and Cooperation in Europe, *Staff Delegation Trip Report on Moscow, Georgia, Moldova and Belarus, June 25–July 4, 1992* (Washington, D.C., August 1992).

64. Zarycky, "Along Russia's Rim," 38.

65. Ibid., 35. Atrocities by Abkhazy included beatings, expulsions, the murder of as many as 800 Georgians through 1994, along with frequent rapes in front of victims' families, torture, and the burning to death of victims in front of the families. The atrocities continued after 1994. "In the village of Kvemo Bargebi," according to one report, "the Ochamchira unit of the Abkhaz militia beat prisoners with rods, burned them with knives and bayonets, stabbed them, and set their bodies on fire. Most of the 28 persons killed the militia had tortured to death. Despite an OSCE mission, and Russian peacekeeping troops along the war zone border, the perpetrators of these and other crimes against humanity remain unpunished." *Country Reports*, 1996, 864. *Amnesty International Report 1996*, 156–57, reports 13 Georgian civilian men, women, and children killed—10 after horrible torture—in the Gali district, and 35 others beaten and tortured.

66. "Jewish Life in the Republic of Georgia," *The WJC Report* 20, no. 2 (1996): 12.

67. Zarycky, Along Russia's Rim," 38–39.

68. Ibid., 39.

69. Authorities had allotted thirty-two hectares of land from an Uzbek-held collective farm to build houses for the Kyrgyz. Representatives of the Kyrgyzstan parliament and of President Akayev recognized this improper transfer and spoke of joint efforts with Uzbekistan to avert future outbreaks (meetings in New York, May 5 and 6, 1992). The ensuing protest and riot claimed 230 lives, with 91 more missing. The Kyrgyz government responded with emergency aid, enforcement measures, and talks between Presidents Karimov of Uzbekistan and Akayev of Kyrgyzstan, to head off violence and settle grievances (meeting with Beksultan B. Ishimov, Chairman, Committee on Defense, National Security and Crime Prevention, Parliament of Kyrgyzstan; Timurbek O. Kenenbaev, Committee on Legislation, Parliament of Kyrgyzstan; and Leonid I. Levitin, Legal Adviser to President Akayev of Kyrgyzstan, at Patterson Belknap, Webb, and Tyler, New York City, under the auspices of the Scott Horton and Sakharov Foundation, May 5, 1991).

70. Greenwald, "A Chameleon Shows His Jeffersonian Side," *Christian Science Monitor*, March 8, 1996.

71. Paige Sullivan, "Former Soviet Union: Ballots, Bullets and Barricades," *Freedom in the World: The Annual Survey of Political Rights and Civil Liberties, 1993–1994* (New York: Freedom House, 1994), 67.

72. The government uses a broadly limiting list of forbidden topics in the press law of 1992. It obtained a court order to shut down the parliament's newspaper, *Svobodnye gory*, alleging that it published "deliberately distorted information aimed at discrediting the President, circulating material which violates ethical norms, and deliberately insulting leaders of foreign states and their symbols, thus significantly damaging the interests and integrity of the state and threatening its stability." The law on media of 1992 adds to familiar proscriptions on pro-war and inflammatory, bigoted material, items like the desecration of national norms, ethics, and the

propagation of "false information as well as violations of the privacy and dignity of individuals." *Country Reports*, 1995, 866.

73. Akylbek Kydyrov, "So Says Askar Akayev, the Republic's President," *Nezavisimaya gazeta*, February 24, 1995, condensed in *Current Digest of the Post-Soviet Press* 47, no. 9 (1995): 15.

74. The flaws included the deregistration of three out of six opposition candidates on a court challenge of nominating signatures. Losers complained (as they did in Russia in 1996) that the president dominated the state-run media in violation of equal time rules. The election was marred by the arrest of two opposition campaign workers just prior to it, on charges, which they and their colleagues deny, of possessing leaflets slandering the president. This and other information on Kyrgyzstan is based on *Country Reports*, 1996, 916–22; *Human Rights Watch World Report 1997*, 226–27; Naryn Arp, "More Repressive Moves Against Kyrgyz Opposition," *Transitions* 3, no. 3, February 2, 1997, 48–49.

75. The government closed the parliamentary newspaper, *Svobodnye gory* (Free mountains) and the insert, *Politika*, in 1994. In 1995 the editor-in-chief of the newspaper *Res Publika*, Tamara Sydykova, and her deputy, Tamara Slashcheva, received prison sentences of eighteen months for criminal libel. On July 11, the president commuted them to release on the prisoners' own recognizance, and under the same criminal law forbade them to practice journalism. The prosecutor's office interrogated Slashcheva in connection with an article in support of Kubanychbek Apas. Dr. Apas, a surgeon, could find no decent job after he published two articles criticizing President Akayev, for which he too faced prosecution for criminal libel. The council on the mass media created by the president appears to have had a chilling effect on all but the boldest journalists. *Human Rights Watch World Report 1996*, 223–24.

76. *Country Reports*, 1996, 916, 919–20; quote on 920.

77. Interview with Timurbek Kananbaev, October 1993, Columbia University and Association of the Bar of the City of New York.

78. The president has acknowledged that discrimination is a factor in the departure of Russian-speakers. He postponed the adoption of Kyrygz as the official language until 2005 and made Russian the official working language in science and technical fields.

79. Interview with Deputy Kaneabaev; meeting with him and the other two representatives mentioned in note 69, as well as Ambassador Atabekov (that day accredited to the UN), New York City, May 6, 1992.

80. Farid Sultanov, "Russia Becomes Second Official Language," *Nezavisimaya gazeta*, July 1, 1996; condensed in *Current Digest of the Post-Soviet Press* 48, no. 26 (1996): 24; hereafter *CDPSP*.

81. "Citizens have the constitutional right to effect a peaceful change of government but do not have the ability to do so. The government has maintained its hold on power by means of two one-sided referendums, the closure of two newspapers, the manipulation of the parliament's closure, and a series of presidential decrees." *Country Reports*, 1995, 867.

82. *Amnesty International Report 1996*, 204.

83. Karatnycky, "Democracy and Despotism," 6.

Chapter 6. Varieties of Authoritarianism

1. Alexis de Tocqueville, *Democracy in America* (1848), 12th ed., trans. George Lawrence, ed. J. P. Mayer (New York: Doubleday Anchor Books, 1969), 239.

2. Peter Juviler, "Human Rights After Perestroika: Progress and Perils," *The Harriman Institute Forum* 4, no. 6 (June 1991): 1–10; quotes on 7.

3. "Table of Independent Countries: Comparative Measures of Freedom," *Freedom Review* 27, no. 1 (1996): 16–17.

4. Larry Diamond, "Is the Third Wave Over?" *Journal of Democracy* 7, no. 3 (1996): 25.

5. Orest Deychakiwsky, "Anniversary of Chernobyl Nuclear Disaster Focus of Hearing," *CSCE Digest* 19, no. 5 (1966): 1–3; Michael Specter, "10 Years later, Chernobyl Still Kills in Belarus," *New York Times*, March 31, 1996.

6. Peter Ford, "A Favorite Battleground for Invaders Now Finds Freedom Tough to Bear," *Christian Science Monitor*, April 11, 1996.

7. For example, in the run-up to the December 10 round, parliament speaker Myacheslav Grib tried to broadcast a message urging people to get out and vote. Denied air time on state television, Grib attempted to broadcast the message via two independent Russian television stations. But the Ministry of Communications shut down these stations' transmitters "for repairs." Department of State, *Country Reports on Human Rights Practices for 1995* (Washington, D.C.: U.S. Government Printing Office, 1996); hereinafter, *Country Reports*, 1996, 783.

8. *Country Reports*, 1996, 785.

9. This section is based on *Country Reports*, 1996, 780–87, and other sources noted.

10. *Amnesty International Report 1996*, 91.

11. Orest Deychakiwsky, "Commissioners Take Stand on Human rights in Belarus," *CSCE Digest* 19, no. 5 (1966): 2; *Amnesty International Report 1996*, 91; "Boris Yeltsin Offers Aleksandr Lukashenko De Facto Unification of Russia and Belarus," *Nezavisimaya gazeta*, January 14, 1997, *CDPSP* 49, no. 2 (1997): 7–9.

12. "Belarus Dissidents Seek U.S. Asylum," *New York Times*, August 1, 1996.

13. Ustina Markus, "Lukashenka's Victory," *Transition* 1, no. 14 (1995): 75–78.

14. Orest Deychakiwsky, "Belarus and Russia Agree to Form Political Union," *CSCE Digest* 19, no. 4 (1996): 2.

15. Only religious organizations already registered in Belarus may invite foreign clergy. Another rule aimed against the Catholic Church requires bishops to receive permission from the State Committee on Religious Affairs before transferring a foreign priest to another parish.

16. George Zarycky, "Along Russia's Rim: The Challenges of Statehood," *Freedom Review* 27, no. 1 (1996): 38.

17. *Country Reports*, 1995, 780.

18. *Freedom in the World: The Annual Survey of Political Rights and Civil Liberties 1994–1995* (New York: Freedom House, 1995), 109; Edmund M. Herzig, "Armenia and the Armenians," in Graham Smith, ed., *The Nationalities Question in the Post-Soviet States*, 2d ed. (London and New York: Longman, 1996), 248–56.

19. U.S. Commission on Security and Cooperation in Europe, *Report on Armenia's Parliamentary Election and Constitutional Referendum July 5, 1995* (Washington, D.C., 1995), 3–5; the politically over-optimistic but legally informative article by Elizabeth R. Defeis, "Constitution Building in Armenia: A Nation Once Again," *The Parker School Journal of East European Law* 2, no. 2 (1995): 153–200. Zarycky terms the Armenian presidency "the strongest in the OSCE," with its power to dissolve parliament, appoint and dismiss the prime minister, appoint all judges and members of the Constitutional Court, and declare martial law. Zarycky, "Along Russia's Rim," 42.

20. Zarycky, "Along Russia's Rim," 42.

21. Ibid., 39.

22. Information on Armenia is based on: *Country Reports*, 1996, 761–72; Commission on Security and Cooperation in Europe, *Report on Armenia's Parliamentary Election and Constitutional Referendum July 5, 1995* (Washington, D.C., 1995); *Human Rights Watch World Report 1996* (New York, 1996), 197–99, quote from 198; *Amnesty International Report 1996* (New York, 1996), 78–80; and other sources where noted.

23. *Amnesty International Report 1996*, 80.

24. *Country Reports*, 1996, 765.

25. Military police jailers of nine men confined for two weeks during a raid told the detainees that they were merely following orders (*Human Rights Watch World Report 1996*, 198). In April 1995, a group of about 25 men, some in uniform, some using iron bars, beat up 19 Hare Krishna devotees in their temple. Police at a local precinct house told one victim bleeding from a head wound that they were busy— he should come back later. An investigator allegedly told the man, "the case could not lead to any prosecutions, as those responsible were linked with the Ministry of Defense." *Amnesty International Report 1996*, 79.

26. William A. Dando, Lawrence A. Boenigk, and Ford D. Bond, *Russia and the Independent Nations of the Former U.S.S.R.: Geofacts and Maps* (Dubuque, IA: Wm. C. Brown Communications, 1996), 35.

27. *Country Reports*, 1996, 767.

28. Steve Levine, "Safety Fears Fail to Deter Armenians on A-Plant," *New York Times*, October 24, 1995; Henry R. Huttenbach, "The Emptying of Armenia," *Association for the Study of Nationalities: Analysis of Current Events*, Year 7, no. 8 (1996), 2–3.

29. Zarycky, "Along Russia's Rim," 42.

30. Ibid., 38.

31. *Country Reports*, 1995, 789, 792.

32. *Bloodshed in the Caucasus: Indiscriminate Bombing and Shelling by Azerbaijani Forces in Nagorno Karabakh* (New York: Helsinki Watch, July 1993); *Country Reports*, 1995, 780, 789–91; *Freedom in the World: The Annual Survey of Political Rights and Civil Liberties*, 117–21.

33. *Country Reports*, 1995, 789.

34. Information on Azerbaijan is based on *Country Reports*, 1996, 772–80; *Human Rights Watch World Report 1996*, 199–201; *Freedom in the World*, 117–21; and other sources noted.

35. Zarycky, "Around Russia's Rim," 25.

36. *Country Reports*, 1996, 773.

37. Four from the Popular Front, 4 from the Party of National Independence, 1 from the Musavat party. Michael Ochs, "Commission Staff Evaluates Azerbaijan Political Situation," *CSCE Digest* 19, no. 6 (1996): 13.

38. Zarycky, "Around Russia's Rim," 42.

39. Ochs, "Commission Staff Evaluates Azerbaijan Situation," 14.

40. *Amnesty International Report 1996*, 84–85.

41. *Amnesty International Report 1996*, 84.

42. *Country Reports*, 1996, 775.

43. Ibid., 773.

44. Ochs, "Commission Staff Evaluates Azerbaijan Situation," 12, 15.

45. *Freedom in the World: The Annual Survey of Political Rights and Civil Liberties, 1993–1994* (New York, 1994), 134.

46. Shafiqul Islam, "Capitalism on the Silk Route?" *Current History* 93, no. 582 (1995): 155–59.

47. Interview of Dr. T. Saidbayev conducted by A. Portansky, "Rossii ne grozit islamskaia revoliutsiia," *Izvestiia*, November 28, 1991.

48. Murray Feshbach, *Ecological Disaster: Cleaning up the Hidden Legacy of the Soviet Regime* (New York: Twentieth Century Fund Press, 1995), 53–78.

49. Referring to President Nabiyev's yielding place to an Islamic–nationalist–democratic coalition in 1992, followed by civil war, President Askar Akayev said: "Had they a different president in Tajikistan, there would be peace, there wouldn't be a half-million refugees, there wouldn't be so much blood spilled, so many problems. Nabiyev turned out to be a weak-willed man. He stepped aside." Igor Greenwald, "Being President Isn't Enough for these Ex-Soviet Leaders," *Christian Science Monitor*, March 28, 1996. "We have many believers in the republic," said Turkmen First Secretary Gapurov, hence the need to keep in mind the broadcasts from Iran on Islamic themes, the "propagation of Islam," seeking "to influence the nationalist struggle and to undermine the ideological and political unity of the Soviet people." Helene Carrere D'Encausse, *Confiscated Power: How Soviet Russia Really Works* (New York: Harper & Row, 1982), 305.

50. Graham E. Fuller, "Central Asia: The Quest for Identity," *Current History* 93, no. 582 (1994): 143–49; Martha Brill Olcott, "Central Asia's Islamic Awakening," *Current History* 93, no. 582 (1994): 149–54; James Chavin, "Central Asia: A Primer," *Current History* 93, no. 582 (1994): 160–63; Patrick Conway, "Kazakhstan: Land of Opportunity," *Current History* 93, no. 582 (1994): 164–68.

51. T. Saidbaev, "Rossii ne grozit islamskaia revoliutsiia," *Izvestiia*, November 28, 1991; "The President of the Islamic Center: There Should Be No Privileged Religion," *Pravda*, December 3, 1991, condensed in *The Current Digest of the Soviet Press* 43, no. 48 (1991): 13; Andrei Polonsky, "Islam in the USSR: Its Way of Life and Politics," *Khristianskaia demokratiia*, bulletin of the Christian Democrat International in Eastern Europe, no. 15 (September–October 1991): 14–23.

52. The growth of Algerian and other North African fundamentalist ideologies occurs in the context of the corruption and failures of the once bright promise of Algerian revolutionary socialism. Lamis Andoni, "Arabs Foresee Declining Prospects for Democracy," *Christian Science Monitor*, January 23, 1992; Youssief M. Ibrahim, "Algerians, Angry with the Past, Divide Over Their Future," *New York Times*, January 19, 1992; Jill Smolowe, "An Alarming No Vote: The Fundamentalists' Big Gain Is More a Protest against Socialist Rule Than a Mandate for an Islamic Republic," *Time*, January 13, 1992, 28; Mamoun Fandy, "Islamic Victory in Algeria Is a Harbinger," *Christian Science Monitor*, January 9, 1992.

53. Fuller, "Central Asia: The Quest for Identity," 147.

54. The 67-seat lower house, the Majilis, is directly elected. The upper house, the Senate, has 47 seats filled by indirect elections, most seats uncontested by the province and city assemblies, and 7 appointed by the president. They met first in January 1996. Zarycky, "Around Russia's Rim," 43.

55. Information on Kazakhstan comes from *Human Rights Watch World Report 1996*, 221–22; *Country Reports*, 1966, 907–16; and other sources noted.

56. *Country Reports*, 1996, 910–11.

57. Igor Greenwald, "Ex-Soviet States Stay Soviet on Rights," *Christian Science Monitor*, March 25, 1996.

58. *Country Reports*, 1996, 911. In December 1994, Human Rights Watch reports, "Justice Ministry Order No. 31 rescinded the registration of all Russian organizations and community groups in Kazakhstan" on the grounds that their ethnic exclusivity violated the constitution. This meant that they could not conduct public business, hold public meetings and conferences, or have bank accounts. *Human Rights Watch World Reprot 1995*, 213.

59. Zarycky, "Along Russia's Rim," 35; *Forced Migration Monitor*, no. 10 (March 1996): 2; *Country Reports*, 1996, 914.

60. *Country Reports*, 1996, 909–10.

61. Ibid., 914.

62. Ibid., 1995, 860.

63. *Transition* 2, no. 3 (1996): 63–64; *Country Reports*, 1996, 911.

64. *Amnesty International Report 1996*, 195.

65. Adrian Karatnycky, "Democracy and Despotism: Bipolarism Renewed?" *Freedom Review* 27, no. 1 (1966): 5.

66. Information on Tajikistan comes from *Country Reports*, 1996, 1049–60; *Human Rights Watch World Report 1996*, 236–38; and other sources noted.

67. Anthony Richter, "Springtime in Tajikistan," *World Policy Journal* 11, no. 2 (1994): 81–86; quote on 84.

68. Richter, "Springtime in Tajikistan," 81–82.

69. John Kampfner, "Russia Adopts Its Own 'Monroe Doctrine,'" *Moscow News*, August 6, 1993, 1, 4.

70. Richter, "Springtime in Tajikistan," 81; Shahrbanou Tadjbakhsh, "The Bloody Path of Change: The Case of Post-Soviet Tajikistan," *Harriman Institute Forum* 6, no. 11 (1993): 1–10, estimates casualties at 40,000 to 80,000. According to Dr. Albert Beninashvili of the Italian Institute of Near and Far East Studies and Dust Mohammed Dust of the Tajik democratic opposition, speaking during a course I taught in the spring of 1993, the death toll was then over 20,000 and the number of persons displaced and dispossessed by the violence was over 500,000 — the worst of all the violence and violations in post-Soviet states. *Human Rights Watch World Report 1995*, 225, put the toll at 20,000 to 50,000, with more than 500,000 displaced persons.

71. *Human Rights Watch World Report 1995*, 226; *Human Rights Watch World Report 1996*, quote from 236; *Country Reports*, 1996, 1049–50.

72. *Country Reports*, 1996, 933; Human Rights Watch/Helsinki, *Return to Tajikistan: Continued Regional and Ethnic Tensions* (New York) 7, no. 9 (May 1995); *Country Reports*, 1996, 1051.

73. Richter, "Springtime in Tajikistan," 84–86.

74. *Human Rights Watch World Report 1996*, 237–38.

75. Karatnycky, "Democracy and Despotism," 9.

76. Zarycky, "Along Russia's Rim," 42.

77. This account on Turkmenistan is based on *Country Reports*, 1996, 1079–84; *Human Rights Watch World Report 1996*, 245–47, quote from 245; and on other sources noted.

78. *Country Reports*, 1996, 1083; "Saparmurad Niyazov: Central Asian Strongman," *Transition* 1, no. 14 (1995): 74; Dando, Boenigk, and Bond, *Russia and the Independent Nations of the Former U.S.S.R.*, 53.

79. *Human Rights Watch World Report 1996*, 246. *Amnesty International Report 1996*, 304, reports that Ishonov's body bore marks of a severe beating, inflicted on him allegedly "to force him to name the organizers of the demonstration."

80. This section is based on *Country Reports*, 1996, 1110–17; *Human Rights Watch World Report 1996* (New York, 1996), 247–50; *Amnesty International Report 1996*, 317–19; Human Rights Watch/Helsinki, *Uzbekistan: Persistent Human Rights Violations and Prospects for Improvement* 8, no. 5 (d) (1966); Dando, Boenigk, and Bond, *Russia and the Other Independent Nations of the Former U.S.S.R.*, 57; and other sources noted. Quotes are from Human Rights Watch/Helsinki, *Uzbekistan*, 2, 4.

81. Human Rights Watch/Helsinki, *Uzbekistan*, 24–25, 35–37.

82. *Human Rights Watch World Report 1996*, 249.

83. *Amnesty International Report 1996*, 318. After their release, the women insisted

that they had consented, because tests revealed that one of the fetuses was dead, the other malformed. *Country Reports*, 1996, 1111–12.

84. Human Rights Watch/Helsinki, *Uzbekistan*, 7–12; quote on 7.

85. Ibid., 2–6.

86. *Country Reports*, 1996, 1111, 1127.

87. Human Rights Watch/Helsinki, *Uzbekistan*, 2.

88. Zarycky, "Along Russia's Rim," 34–35; quote from 34.

89. Evgenii Krutikov, "Rossiiskie voennye bazy v strankakh SNG—ostatki prezhnei roskoshi," *Novoe vremia*, no. 29 (1996): 18–19.

90. Zarycky, "Along Russia's Rim," 34–35.

91. Igor Greenwald, "Buffeted by Big Powers, Central Asia Gravitates Closer to Russia's Orbit: Central Asia Wooed by East and West," *Christian Science Monitor*, March 19, 1996, 7.

92. Van Z. Krikorian, "Sisyphus' Oil: Pipelines and Politics in the Caspian Basin," *CIS Law Notes*, December 1995, 1–7. When the key is found to "[u]nlocking the oil wealth of the Caspian" and to the future of "the unfortunate Azerbaijan, . . . it could well turn out to be in Russian hands" ("Caspian Oil: Of Pipedreams and Hubble-Bubbles," *The Economist*, March 25, 1995, 59–60; quote on 59). In June 1994, Almaty accused Russia of cutting off most of the country's oil exports to lever an equity share in the giant Karachagnak gas field and rich Tengiz oil field. Gasprom got a share of the deal with the Western companies, and a way opened to have the gas shipped through Russian pipelines. Zarycky, "Along Russia's Rim," 36.

93. Zarycky, "Along Russia's Rim," 35, 42.

94. *Report: Kennan Institute for Advanced Russian Studies—Multi-lateralism in Central Asia*, vol. 13, no. 10 (1996).

95. Fuller, "Central Asia: The Quest for Identity," 145–49.

96. Both quotes are from Greenwald, "Ex-Soviet States Stay Soviet on Rights."

97. S. V. R. Nasr, "Democracy and Islamic Revivalism," *Political Science Quarterly* 110, no. 2 (1995): 261–86; quote from 263, 285.

98. Zarycky, "Along Russia's Rim," 36, 43.

Chapter 7. Democracy for Whom? The Baltic States

1. Transcribed by the author, June 17, 1988.

2. See Chapter 1 and Donald L. Horowitz, *Ethnic Groups in Conflict* (Berkeley: University of California Press, 1985); Jack Donnelly, *International Human Rights* (Boulder, CO: Westview Press, 1993), 145–55; Donald L. Horowitz, "Democracy in Divided Societies: The Challenge of Ethnic Conflict," *Journal of Democracy* 4, no. 4 (1993): 19–38; Mark N. Katz, "Nationalism and the Legacy of Empire," *Current History* 93, no. 585 (October 1994): 327–31.

3. Graham Smith, "The Ethnic Democracy Thesis and the Citizenship Question in Estonia and Latvia," *Nationalities Papers* 24, no. 2 (1996): 199–216, quote on 200, from S. Smootha and T. Hanf, "The Diverse Modes of Conflict Regulation in Deeply Divided Societies," in A. Smith, ed., *Ethnicity and Nationalism*, 32.

4. Anatol Lieven, *The Baltic Revolution: Estonia, Latvia, Lithuania, and the Path to Independence*, 2d ed. (New Haven, CT: Yale University Press, 1994).

5. An estimated 100,000 of 475,000 Russians automatically retained Estonian citizenship. *Situation of Human Rights in Estonia and Latvia. Report of the Secretary-General*, UN General Assembly, 48th Session, A/48/511, October 26, 1993, section 21; Maarje Joeste et al., eds., *Eesti A & O* (Tallinn: Eesti Entsuklpeediakirjastus,

1993), 96, cited in Andrus Park, "Ethnicity and Independence: The Case of Estonia in Comparative Perspective," *Europe-Asia Studies* 46, no. 1 (1994): 71.

6. Dzintra Bungs, "Recent Demographic Changes in Latvia," *RFE/RL Research Report* 2, no. 50 (1993): 44–50. The percentage of Latvians increased to 54 percent in a population of 2.7 million. (*Country Reports*, 1995, 873). In Estonia 3.1 percent are Ukrainians, 1.7 percent Belarusians, 1.1 percent Finns; 0.3 percent Jews; the rest are Latvians, Germans, Tatars, Poles, Lithuanians, (0.9 percent). Park, "Ethnicity and Independence," 71.

7. *Country Reports*, 1994, 947; Commission on Security and Cooperation in Europe, *Human Rights and Democratization in Latvia* (Washington, D.C., September 1993), 4.

8. "Russian-speakers" according to the 1989 census include 906,000 Russians, 120,000 Belarusians (4 percent), 92,000 Ukrainians (3 percent), 60,000 Poles (2 percent), 35,000 Lithuanians (1 percent), 23,000 Jews (0.9 percent). ibid.

9. Park, "Ethnicity and Independence," 71.

10. In the early 1970s, 81 percent of non-Estonians and 55 percent of Estonians living in urban areas occupied "the more prestigious state-subsidized low-rent flats with central heating, bathroom and other similar amenities" (ibid., 78).

11. Interviews with Tiiu Pohl, Tallinn, June 1988 and October 1991, and New York City, September–November 1996; with Dr. Iuris Prikulis, Riga, October 1991; and with other Estonians and Latvians in those cities, as well as acquaintances in Vilnius, October 1991. On housing, also, Villu Kand, "Estonia: A Year of Challenges," *RFE/RL Research Report* 3, no. 1 (1994): 93.

12. In Estonia, with its 62 percent ethnic Estonian population, 78 percent of the votes cast favored independence in the referendum of March 3, 1991. *Situation of Human Rights in Estonia and Latvia: Report of the Secretary-General*, UN General Assembly, 48th Session, A/48/511, October 26, 1993, section 21.

13. Lieven, *The Baltic Revolution*, 219–27.

14. Demands included "economic self-management," "sovereignty," control over the environment and educational programs, condemnation of past repressions, Estonian as state language, democratization, and a socialist state based on rule of law. *Sovetskaia Estoniia*, June 18, 1988.

15. It held its ground when Gorbachev and the USSR Supreme Soviet declared the veto legislation unconstitutional, therefore null and void. Estonian declaration and Law of November 16, 1988, *Sovetskaia Estoniia*, November 18, 1988; center's response in *Pravda*, November 28, 1988; Joel Aav, "Estonian Parliament Does Not Shrink Back," *Supplement to the Estonian Koumaa Weekly*, December 14, 1988.

16. Supporters of these groups were a minority of under 30 percent of non-Estonians polled in April 1989. A majority of Estonians wanted an independent Estonia; a majority of non-Estonians wanted the republic's status not to be changed, not even to a sovereign republic in a Soviet confederation. Toomas Ilves, "Estonian Poll on Independence, Political Parties," *Radio Liberty Report on the USSR* 1, no. 22 (1989): 14–16.

17. Discussions with Russian and Estonian reformers at the Dialogue on Human Rights and the Future, of which I was co-organizer, University of California, Berkeley, California, August 1989.

18. Lieven, *The Baltic Revolution*, 227–44.

19. Villu Kand, "Estonia: A Year of Challenges," *RFE/RL Research Report* 3, no. 1 (1994): 92; FBIS-SOV-93-093, 15; Saulius Girnius, "Lithuania: Former Communists Fail to Solve Problems," *RFE/RL Research Report* 3, no. 1 (1994): 101.

20. Information on human rights and democratization in the Baltic republics

is based on *Country Reports*, 1996, 849–55, 922–29, 932–37; *Country Reports*, 1995, 802–7, 870–75, 878–83, and other sources where noted.

21. Juan Linz and Alfred Stepan, "Toward Consolidated Democracies," *Journal of Democracy* 7, no. 3 (1996): 14–33.

22. It replaced Ruutel with Lennart Meri and confirmed Mart Laar as the first post-Soviet prime minister. Council of Europe, Parliamentary Assembly, *Information Report on the Elections in Estonia (20 September 1992)*, Addendum I, 7.

23. Karen Dawisha and Bruce Parrott, *Russia and the New States of Eurasia: The Politics of Upheaval* (New York: Cambridge University Press, 1994), 143–44; John Taht, "Estonia Proves Itself," *Transition* 3, no. 2 (1997): 24.

24. Rumors circulated of a possible Sajudis coup before the elections of October and November. But democracy held, and Parliament approved the new president's nominee for prime minister. *AI Concerns in Europe*, November 1992–April 1993, 22; Saulius Gurnius, "The Baltic States," *REF/RL Report* 3, no. 16 (1994): 6. On 1996, see Saulius Girnius, "The Political Pendulum Swings Back in Lithuania," *Transition* 3, no. 2 (1997): 20, and "A Year of Consolidation in Latvia," *Transition* 3, no. 2 (1997): 22.

25. The Estonian constitution, directly enforceable in the courts, contains a recognition of the equal, universally recognized human rights of all persons and the precedence of international treaties over conflicting domestic legislation (*Constitution of the Republic of Estonia*, Articles 3, 8–55, 123). The government reaffirmed to the United Nations its commitments to equal rights and cultural autonomy under international and domestic law on November 30, 1993. UN General Assembly, 48th Session, Third Committee, A/C.3/48/19, November 30, 1993. "Situation of Human Rights in Estonia and Latvia: Letter Dated 29 November 1993 from the Permanent Representative of Latvia to the United Nations addressed to the Secretary General," signed Alvars Baumanis, 3, 4. See also Commission on Security and Cooperation in Europe, *Human Rights and Democratization in Estonia* (Washington, D.C., September 1993), 2–7, 10; Human Rights Watch, *Human Rights Watch World Report 1994* (New York, 1994), 225–26; Commission on Security and Cooperation in Europe, *Human Rights and Democratization in Latvia*, 10–26; *Country Reports*, 1994, 948–49.

26. The "traditional" communities are Latin Rite Catholics, Greek Rite Catholics, Evangelical Lutherans, Evangelical Reformers, Orthodox, Old Believers, Jews, Sunni Muslims, and Karaites. *Country Reports*, 1996, 934.

27. The prosecutor's office detained the former first secretary of the Latvian Communist Party, Alfred Rubiks, from his arrest on August 23, 1991, right after the attempted coup in Moscow, on charges of alleged participation in the conspiracies directed against the Latvian state. "Prosecutor on Release of Rubiks," Moscow BALTFAX 3 December 92, FBIS-SOV-92-235; "Rubiks Refuses to Testify," Riga Radio, August 27, 92, FBIS-SOV-92-168. He remained in jail in violation of an accused person's rights to due process, among them the rights under Article 9, part 3, of the International Covenant on Civil and Political Rights, which states that "anyone arrested or detained on a criminal charge shall be . . . entitled to trial within a reasonable time or to release." *Country Reports*, 1994, 948; Commission on Security and Cooperation in Europe, *Human Rights and Democratization in Latvia*, 10–11.

28. Riga Radio, May 8, 1995, FBIS-SOV-089, 96.

29. See *Country Reports*, 1995 and 1996, cited in note 20 above, and Peter Juviler, "Estonia," "Latvia," and "Lithuania," *Critique: Review of the Department of State's Country Reports on Human Rights Practices for 1993* (New York: Lawyers Committee for Human Rights, 1994), 105–12, 207–13, 224–29.

30. *Country Reports*, 1996, 849–50.

31. Call by German Environmental Minister to improve safety standards at the power plant, noted in Hamburg DPA, April 16, 1993, FBIS-SOV-93-074, 89; "Firm Suspected of Radioactive Land Shipping," *Respublika*, November 11, 1993, FBIS-SOV-93-225, 75; "Security Increased at Ignalina Power Station," Vilnius Radio, November 11, 1994, and "Plant Threatened by Crime Families," Moscow ITAR-TASS, November 12, 1995, FBIS-SOV-94-219, 55.

32. Girnius, "The Baltic States," 102; Saulius Girnius, "Lithuanian Democratic Labor Party in Trouble," *REF/RL Research Report* 2, no. 24 (1993): 17–18; Vadim Dubnov, " 'Vilniusskaia brigada' protiv 'Respubliki,' " *Novoe vremia*, no. 47 (November 1994): 17; "Respublika's Editor Shot, Killed Outside Home," Radio Vilnius, October 12, 1993, FBIS-SOV-93-198, 59–60; "Seimas Deputy Chairman's Reaction," Radio Vilnius, October 12, 1993, ibid., 60; "Seimas Leader Views Results of Preventive Detention Law," *Respublika*, September 21, 1993, FBIS-SOV-93-202, 89–90; "Reflections on Organized Crime Prevention," November 3 statement of Council of the Movement for National Progress, *Respublika*, November 11, 1992, FBIS-SOV-93-227, 105–6; report of police supposition of contract killing, arrest of a suspect Igor Akhremov, purportedly of the "Vilnius Brigade," in December. *International PEN, Half-Yearly Case List to 31 January 1994* (1994), 53.

33. *Country Reports*, 1996, 934.

34. Ibid., 933.

35. Ibid., 934.

36. See, e.g., Radio Vilnius, BNS, October 14, 1993, FBIS-SOV-93-199, 103; and economic analysis in *Tiesa*, November 18, 1993, FBIS-SOV-93-235, 73.

37. *Country Reports*, 1993, 960–61.

38. *Country Reports*, 1996, 853–54.

39. *Amnesty International Report 1993* (New York, 1993), 126–27, 197–98, 194–95; *Amnesty International Report 1994* (New York, 1994), 129, 192–93, 200.

40. George Zarycky, "Along Russia's Rim: The Challenges of Statehood," *Freedom Review* 27, no. 1 (1996): 36–37; quote from 36.

41. After the August 1991 coup attempt in Moscow, the Estonian government banned the pro-Communist and pro-Moscow organizations: the Council of Workers Collectives, the Intermovement, and the Communist Party of the Soviet Union. Local government councils of Narva, Khotla-Jarve, and Sillamae were dissolved. New elections held on October 20, 1991, returned the ousted leaders to office in Narva and Sillamae, and most of them in Khotla-Jarve (Park, "Ethnicity and Independence," 80). The Latvians also banned several pro-Soviet organizations: the Latvian Union for the Protection of the Rights of Veterans, the Association of Russian Citizens, and the Union of Communists. "Russian Envoy Protests Banning of Organizations," Moscow ITAR-TASS, October 11, 1993, in FBIS-93-198, 59.

42. Dismissals extended to council officials in the Russian-settled town of Sneckus near the nuclear power plant the Russians were brought in to run. The government ordered the suspension of the councils for six months to a year and approved the government's replacement of their leadership with appointed governors and their staffs. Commission on Security and Cooperation in Europe, *Minority Rights: Problems, Parameters and Patterns in the CSCE Context* (Washington, D.C., 1991), 101–8.

43. Deputy Czieslaw Okinczyc said that the council chairmen kept in touch with Moscow and supported the coup, but why create sympathy for them by taking it out on the councils as a whole, and illegally, without prior parliamentary investigation? Okinczyc, a supporter of the drive for independence by Sajudis, the Lithuanian Popular Front, felt betrayed by the move. Deputy Zbigniew Baltsievic, editor of the leading Polish-language newspaper, asked: could the government not have found at least one competent Pole among the 300,000 persons of Polish descent to staff

its takeover of the councils in its "nationalist coup"? Interviews, Vilnius, October 7 and 8, 1991, respectively.

44. Interview, Vilnius, October 8, 1991.

45. Roger Peterson, report to "Conference on Soviet Cultural Studies," Columbia University, April 10, 1992.

46. In a population of 3,751,000, and smaller proportions of Belarusians, Jews, and others. Girnius, "Lithuania," 100.

47. Girnius, "The Baltic States," 5.

48. The new law recognized as citizens those who had been citizens of Lithuania before June 15, 1940, and their children and grandchildren; those who became residents from January 9, 1919, to June 15, 1940, and their children and grandchildren, so long as they were residing in Lithuania on December 10, 1991; and children born in Lithuania to stateless parents. Lithuania also recognizes dual citizenship of Lithuanian emigrés. Republic of Lithuania, Law on Citizenship, December 10, 1991, in effect December 11, 1991; Supreme Council of the Republic of Lithuania, *Resolution on the Procedure for Implementing the Republic of Lithuania Law on Citizenship*, July 10, 1991. Emigré and exiled former Lithuanian citizens living abroad, and their children, gained the right to apply for Lithuanian citizenship, even if they were already citizens of another country, under a 1993 amendment to citizenship legislation. "Seimas Approves Amendments on Citizenship Claims," Vilnius BNS, December 7, 1993, FBIS-SOV-93-234, 73.

49. The 1991 law requires a residency of ten years, knowledge of spoken and written Lithuanian, knowledge of the basic provisions of the constitution of Lithuania, being stateless (and not ex-Soviet) or renouncing citizenship in another state, and taking an oath of allegiance to the republic.

50. Boris Tsilevich, "Etnopoliticheskii konflikt v post-sovetskom prostranstve: Baltiiskii variant," received from Joan Dawson, Newfoundland Legal Aid Commission, July 28, 1994.

51. Interview with former Latvian Supreme Soviet Deputy Alex Grigorievs, November 24, 1994, and his "The Baltic Predicament," received December 1, 1994. In Lithuania, ethnic Russians, the largest minority, voted actively in the 1992 elections, and by a large majority for the winning opposition Lithuanian Democratic Labor Party. Girnius, "The Baltic States," 5.

52. R. I. Kulik, *Zakon o grazhdanstve SSSR* (Moscow: Iurizdat, 1980), 33, and "Zakon Soiuza Sovetskikh Sotsialitichekikh Respublik o grazhdanstve SSSR," Articles 1 and 2, in Kulik, 85; Christopher Osakwe, "Equal Protection under Soviet Constitutional System," in T. Koopmans, ed., *Constitutional Protection of Equality* (Leiden: A. W. Sijthoff, 1975), 177. On percentages, see *Country Reports*, 1996, 926.

53. Research Directorate Documentation, Information and Research Branch, Immigration and Refugee Board, *Estonia: Ethnic Minorities* (Ottawa, 1992), 4.

54. The 1992 legislation restored the 1938 citizenship law on the principle of legal continuity from the Estonian Republic founded on February 24, 1918. Helsinki Watch, *Integrating Estonia's Non-Citizen Minority* (New York, October 1993), 6. The language requirement for naturalization was eased for persons born before 1930 and for the disabled; it was waived for persons who received primary, secondary, or higher education in the Estonian language or had a certificate of employment-related language competence at one of the two top levels. Certified alcoholics, drug addicts, and persons without earned incomes need not have applied.

Exemptions are granted in recognition of "particularly valuable service to the national defense or society of the Republic of Estonia, or who are widely known for their talents, knowledge or work," and for stateless persons with at least ten years residence in Estonia who were not formerly Soviet citizens. Ministry of Foreign Affairs Estonia Informpress, *Estonian Law of Citizenship; Law on Citizenship of 1938, English translation, as amended December 11, 1939, reinstated by resolution of November 6, 1991; amending enabling resolution of the Supreme Council (previous parliament) of February 26, 1992*, Articles 1, 3–6, 15; *Country Reports*, 1995, 802. About 34,000 noncitizens had applied through the Congress of Estonia (Park, "Ethnicity and Independence," 73).

55. Press and Information Department, Ministry of Foreign Affairs, Estonia, *Law on Citizenship, January 31, 1995*, Article 6.

56. *Law on Citizenship* (1995), Articles 8, 9.

57. Foreign military retirees married to Estonians for five years are exempted from the ban. Human Rights Watch/Helsinki has objected to exclusions as violations of due process and of protection against double jeopardy.

58. Commission for Security and Cooperation in Europe, *Human Rights and Democratization in Estonia*, 12.

59. *Country Reports*, 1996, 854.

60. Funding for Russian schools continued after independence, for one of every three school pupils and for a majority of pupils in Tallinn ("Estonian Ministry of Education," December 1992, faxed by the Estonian Foreign Ministry, February 14, 1993). An ethnic minority making up more than half the local population has the right to local government in their language (*Constitution of Estonia*, Article 52, section 2; *Law on Language of March 6, 1995* [unofficial translation of the Ministry of Foreign Affairs], Articles 10, 11, 28; *Law of February 1, 1989*, together with the decree on its application, of July 14, 1989). Consumers have the right to information and service in Estonian (Language Law [1995], Article 16).

61. *Law On Aliens, adopted by the Parliament of Estonia on 8 July 1993.* Seven forbidden categories, such as addicts and convicted felons and various collaborators in the occupation regime, are spelled out in Article 13 (4). Aliens residing in Estonia originally had until July 12, 1995, to obtain passports issued by the country of which they are citizens or Estonian-issued aliens' passports. The government subsequent to the passage of the revised 1993 Law on Aliens interpreted it to grant only temporary, three-year residence permits. On military pensioners, see *Country Reports*, 1996, 851.

62. Commission on Security and Cooperation in Europe, *Report on the March 5, 1995 Parliamentary Election and the status of Non-Citizens: Tallinn and Northeast Estonia* (Washington, D.C., 1995), 3. A law of July 3, 1995 extended the July 12, 1995, deadline for three years, as 100,000 of 400,000 alien residence had not yet applied. *Estonia Today*, July 12, 1995; "Amendments to the Law on Aliens," Estonian Radio, Tallinn, January 9, 1996; BBC Summary of World Broadcasts, January 10, 1996; *Estonia Today*, December 12, 1995.

63. Helsinki Watch, *Integrating Estonia's Non-Citizen Minority*, 2.

64. *Constitution of Estonia*, Article 32, part 3. Noncitizens may not participate in privatization of state enterprises as individuals or as members of a corporate body with preponderant noncitizen ownership (Helsinki Watch, *Integrating Estonia's Non-Citizen Minority*, 15). Only citizens could own land until an amendment of April 15, 1993, permitted the sale of land to foreigners (Park, "Ethnicity and Independence," 79).

65. As in much of Europe, and as under international law, Baltic law does not protect a right to expression inciting to racial, national, or religious hatred or propaganda of war. Girnius, "The Baltic States," 7. On minorities, e.g., in Estonia, see Article 3 (2) of text of *Law on Cultural Autonomy for National Minorities*; English translation released November 16, 1993. FBIS-SOV-93-225, 70.

66. If they want to leave, they may take their possessions out of the country

without paying the usual excise tax. Kristina Oyuland, delegate of Estonia to the Council of Europe and deputy to the Estonian Parliament, talk given at the Carnegie Endowment for International Peace, Moscow, seminar on "Rights of Nations and Human Rights," December 14, 1995.

67. Citizenship is required to vote in national elections. Estonian Ministry of Foreign Affairs, *How the Riigikogu Is Elected* and *Republic of Estonia: Riigikogu Electoral Law*, April 6, 1992, with amendments and supplements approved by the Supreme Council on June 18, 1992 (unofficial translation). Alien residents' right of association includes joining nonprofit associations or leagues to articulate immigrants' concerns and demands. Republic of Estonia, *Riigikogu Electoral Law*, Article 2, Article 20 (3); *Constitution of Estonia*, Articles 48, 156. The earliest date by which aliens might receive citizenship through naturalization was April 1, 1993, after the voting for the new Constitution and parliament.

68. The new prime minister in 1995, Tit Vahi (briefly prime minister in 1992), headed a coalition vowing to pay more attention to the needs of pensioners, farmers, etc., and soundly trounced the Fatherland Party, victors in 1992, which barely received the 5 percent of the vote required to place members in Parliament. On the 1995 election, see "Estonia's Government Is Ousted in Voting Signaling a Slower Reform," *New York Times*, March 7, 1995, 10; see also Tallinn Radio, March 31, 1995, FBIS-SOV-95-063, 72.

69. *Human Rights Watch World Report 1994*, 215.

70. Park, "Ethnicity and Independence," 73, 75.

71. Paige Sullivan, "Former Soviet Union: Ballots, Bullets and Barricades," in *Freedom in the World: The Annual Survey of Political Rights and Civil Liberties, 1993–1994* (New York: Freedom House, 1994), 67.

72. Interview with Aleksei Semyonov and Hanon Barabaner, cochairmen of the Russian Democratic Movement, Tallinn, October 1991; Russian-speaking activists continue to claim that the law excludes the immigrants from citizenship, eventually perhaps even from the country. Commission on Security and Cooperation in Europe (1995), 6–7.

73. Commission on Security and Cooperation in Europe, *Report on the March 5, 1955 Parliamentary Election*, 3; Smith, "The Ethnic Democracy Thesis," 206.

74. "Constitutional Law on the Rights and Obligations of a Citizen and a Person," December 10, 1991, section 3, in *About the Republic of Latvia*, 47–53.

75. *Republic of Latvia Supreme Council Resolution "On the renewal of Republic of Latvia citizens' rights and fundamental principles of naturalization,"* October 15, 1991.

76. *Human Rights Watch World Report 1994*, 225. Tallinn BNS 14 September 1993, FBIS-SOV-93-177, 87, gives a figure of 35%.

77. Ilze Arklina, "Latvia Will Remove Quotas from Citizenship Draft Law," *Baltic Observer*, March 17–23, 1994, 4. Alternate drafts submitted to Parliament in 1993 were even more exclusionary than was the Latvia's Way draft with quotas. *Republic of Latvia, Citizenship Law.* "*Summary of Three Proposed Legislative Acts on Citizenship (Naturalization) submitted to the Republic of Latvia 5th Saeima on September 23, 1993.* Admission of Latvia to the Council of Europe was deferred in the fall of 1993, pending passage of a citizenship law. *Izvestiia*, November 26, 1993; trans. in FBIS-SOV-93-227, 100.

78. Vladislavs Podniaks and Foreign Minister Valdis Birkavs, on Riga NEAKTA-RIGA CINA, March 1, 1995, FBIS-SOV-95-077-S, 77.

79. *Republic of Latvia Law on Citizenship, Adopted by the Saeima on June 21, 1994, with amendments adopted on July 22, 1994 (after the State President's resubmission). Submitted to the State President for his signature and official publication.* Courtesy Latvian Mission to the United Nations.

80. Nils Muznieks, "Non-Citizens in Latvia," *Human Rights and Civil Society* (International Helsinki Federation) 2, no. 2 (1996): 1. This government figure is higher than the quarter of noncitizen speakers of Latvian reported in the 1989 census. *Human Rights Watch World Report 1992*, 507–8.

81. The law reads: "A person can be granted [not *shall* be granted] the citizenship of Latvia." The required "command of the Latvian language" is proficiency in reading, writing, and speaking at an "everyday level," as defined by the Cabinet of Ministers. "The procedure for testing the knowledge of the basic principles of the Republic of Latvia Satsversme (Constitution) and the Constitutional Law . . . , the national Anthem, and the history of Latvia shall be determined by regulations issued by the Cabinet of Ministers." This, too, leaves room for governmental arbitrariness in composing and grading tests. Exempted from the language exam are only persons who have completed general education in a school with Latvian as the language of instruction and category 1 invalids. *Republic of Latvia Law on Citizenship*, Article 10, 12(1–5), 19. On appeal and oversight, see *Country Reports*, 1995, 873.

82. Finding of July 1995, quoted in Muznieks, "Non-Citizens in Latvia," 2.

83. "Constitutional Law on the Rights and Obligations of a Citizen and a Person," December 10, 1991, in *About the Republic of Latvia*, 47–53.

84. Muznieks, "Non-Citizens in Latvia," 1–2.

85. UN General Assembly, 49th Session, A/49/57, January 3, 1994. *Situation of Human Rights in Estonia and Latvia. Letter dated 30 December 1993 from the Permanent Representative of the Russian Federation to the United Nations addressed to the Secretary-General*, signed Y. Vorontsov, 2.

86. *Country Reports*, 1994, 951.

87. At least 70 percent of private broadcasts must be in Latvian. Prime-time television broadcasts must be 40 percent Latvian in origin. Foreign capital may not exceed 20 percent of the capital underwriting electronic media. *Country Reports*, 1996, 924.

88. The league holds meetings and acts as an advocacy group for noncitizens. *Country Reports*, 1995, 872.

89. The beating of reporter Nikolai Gudants, and a shot through the house door of a colleague on the newspaper *SM Segodnya* several days later, seemed to be connected with the publication in the Latvian-language paper *Atmoda* of a list of Russian "enemies of Latvian independence," including former Komsomol and party workers, and members of Interfront (the organization of Russian-speakers opposed to independence). Report of Tatiana Turchina, from Riga, in *Ekspress-khronika*, June 9–16, 1994, 5.

90. Noncitizens long faced the arbitrary and illegal denial of rights to register as permanent residents by the wayward Department of Immigration and Citizenship despite annulments of its decisions by Latvian courts. Helsinki Watch, "Violations by the Latvian Department of Citizenship and Immigration," vol. 5, issue 19 (New York: Helsinki Watch, October 1993), 6. *Human Rights Watch World Report 1994*, 225. After international furor, the government replaced the head of the Department of Immigration and Citizenship with his hardly less implicated deputy. *Country Reports*, 1994, 950, and 1996, 926.

91. Boris Tsilevich and Alexander Ruchkovsky, "Difference in Status and Rights between Citizens and Permanent Residents (Non-Citizens) of Latvia," December 28, 1994; translated and supplied by Alex Grigorievs. See also Commission on Security and Cooperation in Europe, *Human Rights and Democratization in Latvia*, 18; *Country Reports*, 1994, 951.

92. Latvia makes Latvian the official state language, with "constitutional rights of the residents of other nationalities to use their native language or other lan-

guages." *Republic of Latvia, Law on Amendments and Additions to the Language law of the Latvia Soviet Socialist Republic,* revision of law of May 5, 1989, dated March 31, 1992, Preamble Articles 1, 2. Public and private employees must be able to speak Latvian to the extent necessary "to perform their professional responsibilities." Ibid., Articles 4–9.

93. Alex Grigorievs, "The Baltic States: Citizenship, Minorities, and Human Rights," paper presented at the Mid-Atlantic Slavic Conference, AAASS, March 18, 1995, 2.

94. Meeting of Foreign Minister Manitski and members of the Estonian diplomatic corps with Michael Posner, executive director, and other members and consultants of the Lawyers Committee for Human Rights (including the author) and Helsinki Watch, at the Estonian Mission to the UN, September 30, 1992; Park, "Ethnicity and Independence," 73. Citizenship and language requirements, including the required bilingualism in public governance and commerce, medicine, and the police are essential for the preservation of the Latvian ethnic nation, said Dr. Prikulis of the Latvian Academy of Sciences in my interviews with him in Riga, October 1991, and New York City, April 1992. As in Estonia, language law was not stringently applied. *Country Reports,* 1994, 951; 1996, 928.

95. "National Minorities," in Commission on Security and Cooperation in Europe, *Human Rights and Democratization in Latvia,* 13–14.

96. "President Ulmanis Addresses UN General Assembly," Riga, Riga Radio network, trans. in FBIS-SOV-93-189, 39.

97. Interviews, Riga, October 5, 1991; interview with deputy Einars Cilinckis, an environmentalist, who saw a need not for expulsion or exclusion from citizenship but for legal measures like the residence requirement and language laws to guarantee the survival of the Latvian nation. Cilinckis interview, Riga, October 4, 1991.

98. Aliens who are out of the immigrant mainstream, such as orphans, automatically receive citizenship (*Republic of Latvia Law on Citizenship,* Articles 2, 3). Other exceptions to naturalization requirements may be granted to individuals on the basis of ethnic descent, pre-occupation residence and, upon resolution of the Saeima, to persons rendering "outstanding services" to Latvia (Article 13).

99. This held true for the eligible foreigners as long as they applied by July 1, 1995. *Republic of Latvia Law on Citizenship,* "Transitional Provisions," paragraph 1.

100. Former Latvian Supreme Soviet Deputy Alex Grigorievs, personal communication to the author, November 24, 1994, and Grigorievs, "The Baltic Predicament," paper received December 1, 1994. In Lithuania, ethnic Russians, the largest non-Lithuanian minority, participated actively in the elections of 1992. A large majority voted for the opposition (and winning party), the Lithuanian Democratic Labor Party (Girnius, "The Baltic States," 5). Currents of immigrant support for independence and radical Estonian nationalist opposition to citizenship for immigrants were discussed in the author's interviews with former deputy Peet Kask, March 1994. Peet Kask, "National Radicalization in Estonia: Legislation on Citizenship and Related Issues," *Nationalities Papers* 22, no. 2 (Fall 1994): 379–93, gives an overall analysis and an insider's history of the formation of policy toward immigrant minorities and the factors of power, as well as identity, involved.

101. Boris Tsilevich, "Etnopoliticheskii konflikt v post-sovetskom prostranstve: Baltiiskii variant," sent by Joan Dawson, Newfoundland Legal Aid Commission, July 28, 1994, 6–8, 10–13; quotes on 8.

102. Research Directorate Documentation, Information and Research Branch, Immigration and Refugee Board, *Estonia: Ethnic Minorities,* 4; Park, "Ethnicity and Independence," 76–77; Commission on Security and Cooperation in Europe,

Human Rights and Democratization in Latvia, 5. A small minority of Russians have sought Russian citizenship. *Batun: Baltic Chronology,* December 2, 1992, p. 2; and see n. 91 above.

103. Sergei Kovalyov, head of the Human Rights Committee of the former Supreme Soviet, saw the Estonian policies as intended to pressure Russian speakers to leave, humiliating them and denying them their dignity, in violation of Articles 6 and 15 of the UDHR and ICCPR Articles 2, 25, 26 concerning a person's rights to nondiscrimination, to equality before the law, to the vote, and to democratic participation ("The Situation of Human Rights . . . , sections 87–88, etc.). Frank J. Prial, "Yeltsin Asks U.N. to Help Russians in the Baltic," *New York Times,* November 8, 1992; "Gorbunovs Expresses Concern over Yeltsin's Remarks," Moscow BALTFAX, 5 April 1993, in FBIS-SOV-93-064, 83.

104. Article 15. 1. Everyone has the right to a nationality. 2. No one shall be arbitrarily deprived of his nationality nor denied the right to change his nationality.

105. "Whether a person has or has not the nationality of a particular state," says Paul Weis, "is a question to be determined exclusively in accordance with the law of that state." Paul Weis, *Nationality and Statelessness in International Law,* 2d rev. ed. (The Netherlands: Sijthoff & Noordhoff, 1979), 239–45; excerpted in Anthony D'Amato, ed., *International Law Anthology* (Cincinnati, OH: Anderson Publishing Co., 1994), 182–83. "Decisions about citizenship are an internal matter for each individual state. This is an accepted principle of international law." It was considered by the International Court of Justice in 1955, in the case of Liechtenstein vs. Guatemala. A quote from the court's decision is particularly instructive: "international law leaves it for each state to lay down the rules governing the grant of its nationality." Former Latvian Supreme Court Justice Guido Zembrino, speech at University of Michigan, 1993; I thank Mara Bolis for this source. See also Edward Lawson, (then) Under-Secretary-General for Human Rights, United Nations, *Encyclopedia of Human Rights,* with a foreword by Jan Martenson (New York: Taylor and Francis, 1991), 1135.

106. Various bans in the Baltic republics that apply to former security agents, convicted criminals, persons without steady legal incomes, drug addicts, alcoholics, and persons infected with especially dangerous diseases have been questioned under human rights standards. See, e.g., *Critique: Review of the Department of State Country Reports on Human Rights Practices for 1993* (New York: Lawyers Committee for Human Rights, 1994), 108, 212, 226–27; *Country Reports,* 1996, 852, 926. Quote is from Marina Sergeyeva, "Estonia's Russians Decide to Learn Estonian: Fewer and Fewer Want to Obtain Russian Citizenship," *Kommersant-Daily,* January 31, 1997, *CDPSP,* 49, no. 5, 20–21. On the Council of Europe decision, see Marina Sergeyeva, "Human Rights Situation Is Fine in Estonia: Russia Isn't Happy with This Decision," *Kommersant-Daily,* February 1, 1997, *CDPSP,* 49, no. 5, 20.

107. Helsinki Watch, "Integrating Estonia's Non-Citizen Minority," October 1993, 2 (quote), 12.

108. ICCPR Article 24 (3). "Situation of Human Rights . . . ," section 89, 91. The date of entry into force of the ICCPR for Estonia was January 21, 1992.

109. Latvia has become a party to the convention. *Human Rights: International Instruments. Chart of Ratifications as at 31 December 1993* (New York and Geneva: United Nations, 1994), 6–7. The convention reads, in part: "*Article 1.* A Contracting State shall grant its nationality to a person born in its territory who would otherwise be stateless. Such nationality shall be granted: a. at birth, by operation of law, or b. upon application" under specified conditions, including (Article 2d) that the person concerned has always been stateless—which is true for young children. The Convention on the Reduction of Statelessness (1954, in force 1975); reprinted in

Albert P. Blaustein, Roger S. Clark, and Jay A. Sigler, eds., *Human Rights Sourcebook* (New York: Paragon House Publishers, 1987), 153–63.

110. President Guntis Ulmanis said about 90 percent do. *Moscow News*, no. 17, May 5–11, 1995, 4.

111. Russia, most of whose troops had withdrawn by 1994, could stir up trouble in the name of solidarity with Russian compatriots in the Baltic. Going into the later 1990s, Lithuania has cause for anxiety because of a dependency on Russian oil and Russia's transit rights across Lithuania to its enclave of Kaliningrad, with its 150,000 troops. Russia could try to churn the waters in response to Estonia's claim that its border with Russia violates the border agreement of 1920 under the Soviet–Estonian Treaty of Tartu. Russian troops have remained in Latvia at the Skrunda antiballistic missile early-warning center. Zarycky, "Along Russia's Rim," 36.

112. *Country Reports*, 1995, 802, 805, 870, 873–74; "The Situation of Human Rights . . . ," section 36; CSCE, *Minority Rights*, 16, 23–24.

113. *Situation of Human Rights in Estonia and Latvia: Report of the Secretary-General*, sections 15, 36, 48–49; quote from section 15.

114. CSCE, *Minority Rights: Problems, Parameters and Patterns in the CSCE Context*, 33–34; Helsinki Watch, "Integrating . . . , 18, 27–28.

115. *Human Rights Watch World Report 1994*, 215; *Country Reports*, 1996, 853.

116. Conceding instructional inadequacies, representatives of the Estonian government have cited lack of funds as one reason for the deficiencies in the program of Estonian language training. Meeting with representatives of the Estonian government, including then Foreign Minister Jaan Manitski, September 30, 1992. See also *Country Reports*, 1996, 852–53.

117. The round table was formed by President Meri on June 25, 1993. The assembly was organized at a founding congress on January 30, 1993. The Representative Assembly, made up of delegates from various political and social groups, is a virtual political party. It fielded candidates in the October 17, 1993, elections to local government councils. Saulius Girnius, "Extremism in the Baltic States," *RFE/RL* 3, no. 16 (April 22, 1994): 6–7.

118. Tsilevich, "Etnopoliticheskii konflikt v post-sovetskom prostranstve: baltiiskii variant," 10–13.

119. *Moscow News*, no. 17, May 5–11, 1995, 4.

Chapter 8. Russia's Third Try

1. Boris Yeltsin, President's address to the National Assembly, Moscow Russian Television Network, February 16, 1995, FBIS-SOV-95-032, 8.

2. Sergei Kovalyov, "Open Letter to B. Yeltsin," *Izvestiia*, January 24, 1996, FBIS-SOV-96-016, 31, 32.

3. "Toska po poriadku," *Novoe vremia*, no. 31 (1996): 6.

4. Ludmilla Alexeyeva, talk at the Advanced Educational Training Institute, Moscow Province, December 15, 1995; interview, Moscow, December 18, 1995. On the conflict between reaction and reform, see Lilia Shevtsova, "Russia's Post-Communist Politics: Revolution or Continuity?" in Gail W. Lapidus, ed., *The New Russia: Troubled Transformation* (Boulder, CO: Westview Press, 1995), 5–36.

5. Michael McFaul, "Why Russia's Politics Matter," *Foreign Affairs* 74, no. 1 (1995): 87–99, and his "Russia: Transition without Consolidation," *Freedom Review* 28, no. 1 (1997): 30–49. Stephen F. Cohen has been one of the pessimists, seeing Russia as gripped by irrationality, authoritarian tradition and corruption, xenophobia, and elements of the unpredictable. Former Ambassador to the USSR Jack Matlock has been a lesser pessimist, inclined to look also to pragmatic imperatives of reform

as factors making democratization at least possible. Panel discussion at Columbia University, December 8, 1995.

6. Robert Sharlet, "Citizen and State under Gorbachev and Yeltsin," in Stephen White, Alex Pravda, and Zvi Gitelman, eds., *Developments in Russian and Post-Soviet Politics* (Durham, NC: Duke University Press, 1994), 109–28.

7. Julia Wishnevsky, "Anti-Democratic Tendencies in Russian Policy-Making," *RFE/RL Research Report* 1, no. 45 (1992): 21–25.

8. "Witch Hunt in Russian Parliament," *Moscow News*, August 6, 1993, 4; Vadim Bakatin, "Why Was Russia's Security Minister 'Retired'?" *Moscow News*, August 6, 1993, 2; Ruslan Khasbulatov, on the issue as one of preserving the separation of powers against presidential tendencies toward dictatorship, in his *Vlast': Razmyshleniia spikera* (Moscow: Tsentr Delovoi Informatsii, 1992). "Although principles of the separation of powers are proclaimed," writes Dr. Guliev, "in fact state structures struggle for fully unified power. . . . Our Supreme Soviet tries to do everything itself," turning out amateurish and self-contradictory laws. V. Guliev, "Rossii—nadezhnye vlastnye struktury," *Sovetskaia iustitsiia*, nos. 23–24 (1992): 6; Alexander Rahr, "Russia: The Struggle for Power Continues," *REF/RL Report* 2, no. 6 (1993): 5.

9. *Konstitutsiia (osnovnoi zakon) Rossiiskoi Federatsii*, with amendments as of December 10, 1992 (Moscow: Izdanie Verkhovnogo Sovieta Rossiiskoi Federatsii, "Izvestiia," March 1993), Articles 104, 121(1–11).

10. Robert Sharlet, "Chief Justice as Judicial Politician," *East European Constitutional Review* 2, no. 2 (1993): 34.

11. Olga Sirodoeva, a graduate of the Moscow University Law Faculty class of 1992, told me that, in her view, the public voted in the referendum for the lesser of available evils. Polling signs of the president's declining popularity supported the assumptions of this young Russian who is not yet sure of democracy in her country. Between 1989 and 1992, the vote for Mikhail Gorbachev as "personality of the year" fell from 44 to 1 percent. For Yeltsin, it was 19 percent in 1989, 44 percent in 1990, but down to 17 percent by 1992. Yury Levada, "Tired of Politics: The Electorate in 1993," *Moscow News*, July 23, 1993, 3.

12. A majority of 58.7 percent voted "yes" to the question "Do you have confidence in Russian President Yeltsin?," instead of the "no" vote expected by Yeltsin's parliamentary foes. On the question "Do you approve of the social policy pursued by the Russian president and the government of the Russian Federation since 1992?," the public voted "yes" by a majority of 53 percent. On the question "Do you think it is necessary to hold early elections of the president of the Russian Federation?," 49.4 percent voted "yes" as compared with the 67.2 percent who voted "yes" for "early elections of people's deputies of the Russian Federation." Moscow Itar-Tass, May 5, 1993, FBIS-SOV-93-085, 27.

13. Drafts of constitutions: "Proekt (vnesen Prezidentom Rossiiskoi Federatsii: Konstitutsiia (osnovnoi zakon) Rossiiskoi Federatsii," *Rossiiskaia gazeta*, June 24, 1993, 9–12; "Proekt (vnesen gruppoi narodnykh deputatov Rossiiskoi federatsii: Konstitutsiia Rossiiskoi Sovetskoi Federatsii," *Rossiiskaia gazeta*, June 24, 1993, 12–14. "After the new wave of 'sovereignization' when certain *oblasts* [provinces] have declared themselves republics or are on the way to this, it is difficult to agree on the section of the draft constitution on the federative structure." On republics' desire to retain sovereign status and regions' to gain it, see: Sergei Shakhrai, "Our Society Is Losing the Instinct for Self-Preservation," *Rossiiskie vesti*, July 17, 1993, FBIS-SOV-93-137, 15; "Rumyantsev on the Remaining Differences in Constitutional Drafts," *Rossiiskaia gazeta*, August 10, 1993, FBIS-SOV-154, 22–23; Vera Tolz, "Republics and Regions Unhappy about the Draft Constitution," *RFE/RL News Briefs*, July 12–16, 1993, 1; Ann Sheehy, "Amur Oblast Declares Itself a Republic," *REF/RL News Briefs*,

July 19–23, 1993. The draft lost support also at the hands of local politicians who sided with parliament against the president on the issue of the separation of powers at the center. Robert Sharlet, "The Prospects for Federalism in Russian Constitutional Politics," *Publius: The Journal of Federalism* 24, no. 2 (1994): 120–21.

14. Sharlet, "Citizen and State under Gorbachev and Yeltsin," 118–20.

15. I have heard that Elena Bonner and others urged Yeltsin to do this. "The Congress of People's Deputies of the Russian Federation is made up primarily of deputies whose electoral campaigns in 1990 had been promoted by the Communist Party." Alexander Rahr, "The First Year of Russian Independence," *RFE/RL Report* 2, no. 1 (1993): 53.

16. Lilia Shevtsova, "Russia's Post-Communist Politics: Revolution or Continuity?" in Gail W. Lapidus, ed., *The New Russia: Troubled Transformation* (Boulder, CO: Westview Press, 1995), 22–23. The rumors, of course, go back a few years. Author's interview with Russian lawyer Tatiana Ostakhova on August 21, 1992, New York City; Marina Shakina, "Lovushka dlia vsekh," *Novoe vremia*, no. 32, 1993, 4–6.

17. Robert Sharlet, "Citizen and State under Gorbachev and Yeltsin," 121, 126.

18. Gorbachev condemned the September decree as unconstitutional. Later he asked: "Is it really support of democracy in Russia when parliament gets shot up in October 1993 and CNN shows all of America what the government is doing here and at that moment we hear the response of the president of the United States: 'It seems nothing terrible has happened?'" Mikhail Gorbachev, interview with Fred Coleman and Alan Cooperman, *U.S. News & World Report*, February 13, 1995, 65.

19. Sharlet, "The Prospects for Federalism," 121–22; Elena Bonner, "Indian Summer of Communism: Observations of an Amateur," *World Policy Journal* 11, no. 2 (1994): 21; Sergei Kovalyov, "Open Letter to B. Yeltsin," 31; Julia Wishnevsky, "Liberal Opposition Emerging In Russia?" *REF/RL Report* 2, no. 44 (1993): 5–11. Ambassador Jack Matlock believes that violence started with leaders in the White House who sent armed irregulars out against buildings (panel discussion at Columbia University, December 8, 1995). A *Moscow News* poll of 860 Muskovites showed that 92 percent held either Rutskoi or Khasbulatov responsible for the violence of October 3–4, and 78 percent considered the use of troops justified. *Moscow News*, October 8, 1993, 1.

20. The democrats had agreed to the party-list system for half the Duma seats (the other half were elected in winner-take-all district voting). That gave the Communists and candidates of the Liberal Democrat Party (LDP) the advantage of name recognition, contributing to the democrats' setback. Serge Schmemann, "Russian Election: Some Rah-Rah, No Sis-Boom-Bah," *New York Times*, December 3, 1993.

21. *Konstitutsiia Rossiiskoi Federatsii: Constitution of the Russian Federation* (bilingual text; Moscow: Iuridicheskaia Literatura, 1994), Article 95; hereafter *Konstitutsiia RF*.

22. Antti Korkeakivi, "A Modern Day Tsar? Presidential Power and Human Rights in the Russian Federation," *Journal of Constitutional Law in Eastern and Central Europe* 2, no. 76 [*sic*] (1995): 100.

23. Komissiia po pravam cheloveka pri Prezidente Rossiiskoi Federatsii, *Doklad o sobliudenii prav cheloveka i grazhdanina v Rossiiskoi Federatsii za 1993 god* (Moscow, 1994), 29–30; hereafter Komissiia po pravam cheloveka, *Doklad*.

24. Robert Sharlet, "Citizen and State under Gorbachev and Yeltsin," 123.

25. V. Isakov, "Tricks Carried Out by Election Riggers," *Sovetskaia Rossiia*, April 4, 1995, in FBIS-SOV-95-006, 22–23.

26. *Konstitutsiia RF*, Article 2.

27. Ibid., Articles 15(4), 17(1). The incorporation occurred in 1991 and 1992. The 1993 constitution omitted the 1992 bill's mention of individuals' rights "to appeal to international organs protecting human rights and freedoms if they are refused

protection of their rights in all jurisdictions established under federal law." Peter Juviler, "The Soviet Declaration of Individual Rights: The Last Act of the Old Union," *Parker School Bulletin of Soviet and East European Law* 2, no. 8 (1991): 3–4; "Deklaratsiia prav i svobod cheloveka i grazhdanina," November 22, 1991, *Vedomosti S"ezda Narodnykh Deputatov RSFSR i Verkhovnogo Soveta RSFSR*, no. 52, item 1865; amendments rewriting chapters 5 and 6 of the 1978 RSFSR constitution confirming formal recognition of and deference to universal standards of the international laws of human rights: chapter 5, "Human and Citizens' Rights and Freedoms," and a new chapter 6, "Obligations of Citizens of the Russian Federation." The 1992 Russian bill of rights affirmed the principle that "human rights and freedoms belong to individuals from birth" and that "Generally recognized international norms relating to human rights have precedence over laws of the Russian Federation and directly create rights and obligations of citizens of the Russian Federation." Article 32, Amending law of April 21, 1992, *Vedomosti*, 1992, no. 20, item 1084, and *Konstitutsiia (osnovnoi zakon) Rossiiskoi Federatsii-Rossii* (Moscow: Izdanie Verkhovnogo Soveta Rossiiskoi Federatsii, 1992).

28. *Konstitutsiia RF*, Article 13(1–5).

29. Ibid., Article 10.

30. Ibid., Article 80(2).

31. Korkeakivi, "A Modern Day Tsar?"; Erik P. Hoffmann, "Challenges to Viable Constitutionalism in Post-Soviet Russia," *Harriman Review* 7, nos. 10–12 (1994): 19, 37–40; *Konstitutsiia RF*, Articles 1–16.

32. Deputy Anatoly Shabad, lecture sponsored by the Lawyers Committee on Human Rights, at Patterson, Belknap, Webb & Tyler, New York City, February 3, 1995; Vera Tolz, "The Shifting Sands of Stabilization," *Transition*, February 15, 1995, 5–7.

33. *Konstitutsiia RF*, Articles 111(4), 117(1, 2).

34. Ibid., Article 117(3, 4).

35. Ibid., Article 93(1, 2).

36. Nikolai Troitsky, "The Duma Remits the Sins of All Branches of Power," *Megapolis-Express*, no. 9, March 2, 1994, in *CDPSP* 46, no. 8 (1994): 3–4.

37. Ilya Bulavinov, "Changes in the Makeup of the Security Council: The Speakers Will Advise the President on a Regular Basis," *Kommersant*, January 11, 1995, in *CDPSP* 47, no. 3 (1995): 19.

38. Alan Cooperman, Sander Thoenes, and Fred Coleman, "A Long Road to Reform," *U.S. News & World Report*, February 27, 1995, 59–60; Marc Champion, "Letter from the Editor," *The Moscow Times*, January 29, 1995, 5.

39. Korkeakivi, "A Modern Day Czar?" 90; Thomas de Waal, "Critics Say Security Council Wields Power of a Politburo," *The Moscow Times*, January 22, 1995, 14–15.

40. Kovalyov, "Open Letter to B. Yeltsin," 32.

41. Mikhail Sokolov, "All Power to the Security Council—A Brief History of a Consultative Body," *Sevodnia*, January 12, 1993, 3, in *CDPSP* 47, no. 3 (1995): 19–20; Council of Europe, Parliamentary Assembly, Bureau of the Assembly, *Report on the Conformity of the Legal Order of the Russian Federation with Council of Europe Standards*, Strasbourg, October 7, 1994, courtesy of Antti Korkeakivi, Lawyers Committee for Human Rights, 35–39 (hereafter Council of Europe, *Report*); Alessandra Stanley, "Breathing Life Back Into the K.G.B.," *New York Times*, August 4, 1995; Sander Thoenes and Alan Cooperman, "Yeltsin's Eyes and Ears," *U.S. News & World Report*, August 7, 1995, 36–39.

42. On Turkey, see *Country Reports*, 1996, 1060–78. On authoritarian governments: Samuel P. Huntington, "Social and Institutional Dynamics of One-Party Systems," in Samuel P. Huntington and Clement H. Moore, eds., *Authoritarian Poli-*

tics in Modern Society (New York: Basic Books, 1970), 3–45; Clement H. Moore, "The Single Party as Source of Legitimacy," in Huntington and Moore, eds., 48–72; Rod Hague, Martin Harrop, and Shaun Breslin, *Political Science: A Comparative Introduction* (New York: St. Martin's Press, 1992), 458.

43. David Remnick, "Letter from Moscow: The Tycoon and the Kremlin," *The New Yorker*, February 20 and 27, 1995, 124.

44. Deputy Shabad lecture (see note 32).

45. John Colarusso, "Chechnya: The War without Winners," *Current History* 94, no. 594 (1995): 329–36.

46. The Russian servicemen's presence was to remain a secret. The minister of defense asserted that Russian prisoners were not in the Russian army, leading Dudayev to treat them as criminals. The chairman of the Parliamentary Defense Committee, Yushenkov, was prepared to recognize the POWs as Russian servicemen and obtained their release (Deputy Shabad lecture).

47. The Federal Security Agency (FSK) told Yeltsin that "Dudayev had a small force, Chechens would not support him, they were nothing but gangsters; we must save Chechnya from a gang of criminals" (Deputy Shabad lecture). See also "Aktual'noe interv'iu," with FSK head Sergei Stepashin, by Aleksandr Prasolov, *Argumenty i fakty*, no. 5, February 1995, 1–2.

48. Otto Latsis (member of the Presidential Advisory Council and political commentator for *Izvestiia*), "Who Wanted This War?" *The Moscow Times*, January 15, 1995, 42. According to Duma Deputy Shabad, the FSK fed Yeltsin "fantastic lies" about Dudayev and his regime, including his alleged role in fraudulent-type transfers to Chechnya. "All these 'facts' were used to justify what happened later" (Deputy Shabad lecture).

49. Statement by Vladimir Shumeiko, speaker of the Federation Council, Moscow Radio, December 5, 1994, and Interfax, December 5, 1994, in FBIS-SOV-94-234, 22; Boris Fyodorov, leader of the Liberal Democratic Union, Interfax, December 5, 1994, in FBS-SOV-94-234, 22–23; Deputy Defense Minister Gromov, Moscow NTV, December 5, 1994, ibid., 23; Inna Yermolova, deputy to the State Duma and chair of the Republic Party, Ostankino Television First Channel and Orbita Networks, December 4, 1994, in FBS-SOV-94-234, 23–24. Arrival of Deputies Grigory Yavlinsky and Sergei Yushenkov in Chechnya to take the place of Russian POWs taken during covertly supported opposition attacks on Dudayev, Ostankino First Television Channel, December 6, 1994, in FBS-SOV-94-234, 24–25; Otto Latsis, member of the Presidential Advisory Council, political commentator for *Izvestiia*, "Who Wanted This War?" *The Moscow Times*, January 15, 1995, 42.

50. Boris Gromov, "Chechnya Plans Kept from Deputy Defense Minister (interview with Aleksandr Zhilin)," *Moscow News*, January 13–19, 1995, 1, 3; quote on 3.

51. "The Russian–Chechen war is a clear demarcation, a defining point in the Russian government's turn away from democracy." The people whom Yeltsin did not let come to power in August 1991 "have conquered Russia and you." Elena Bonner, "A Letter to Boris Nikolaevich Yeltsin," December 28, 1994, trans. Catherine Fitzpatrick, *New York Review of Books*, February 2, 1995, 44; Katrina van den Heuvel: "The War in Chechnya is not an aberration. It has exposed the real nature of the Yeltsin regime behind its facade of 'reform'—one of economic and political polarization, impoverishment, rampant corruption and official contempt for democracy and Constitutionalism." Katrina van den Heuvel, "Letter from Moscow: Yeltsin Survives; Will Democracy?" *The Nation*, February 27, 1995, 270–72.

52. Deputy Shabad lecture.

53. Sergei Kovalyov, statement of December 8, 1994, *Trud*, December 14, 1994; translated and circulated by Edward Kline, Human Rights Projects Group.

54. Thomas de Waal, "Grachev Remarks Provoke Outrage," *The Moscow Times*, January 29, 1995, 11–12.

55. Enthusiastically received by an assembly of clan leaders in August 1991, Dudayev took over the government in an armed coup and declared Chechnya's independence. Yeltsin subsequently withdrew reinforcements, perhaps missing an opportunity to end the challenge to Moscow, for then Dudayev rapidly built up arms by bartering, buying, or stealing them from the Soviet troops. A traffic in arms and drugs easily evaded President Yeltsin's ineffective blockade (Jack Matlock, "The Chechnya Tragedy," *New York Review of Books*, February 16, 1995, 4). Dudayev, Deputy Shabad noted, was deeply implicated in wide repression. He dissolved the republic's Supreme Court and destroyed the system of law enforcement with its Procuracy and investigative branches, falling back on traditional institutions and creating a climate of fear. But that did not justify the war (Deputy Shabad lecture).

56. Elena Bonner, "A Letter to Boris Nikolaevich Yeltsin."

57. Derogations (exceptions) from human rights commitments may be made only in a state of emergency, according to the International Covenant on Civil and Political Rights; *Konstitutsiia RF*, Article 102, requires approval of a state of emergency by the upper house of parliament, the Federation Council. See also Michael Posner, Executive Director, Lawyers Committee for Human Rights, "Letter to President Boris N. Yeltsin," January 12, 1995.

58. Five days after signing edict No. 2137s of November 30, 1994 (see below), initiating preparations for the Chechnya campaign and ordering a state of emergency in Chechnya, President Yeltsin signed, at the Budapest meeting of the OSCE on December 5, an agreement on the "Code of Behavior Concerning Military-Political Aspects of Security." Point 36 of the OSCE agreement committed signatories to observe constitutional procedures and enforce safeguards when despatching armed forces on missions of internal security, "under the effective control of constitutionally established organs and in accordance with the principles of the rule of law." Only as much force as necessary should be used, and "the armed forces will adopt necessary measures to avoid harm to civilians and their property" (K. Lyubarsky, "V ozhidanii verdikta," *Novoe vremia*, no. 30 [July 1995]: 9). By sending in 40,000 troops, Russia also violated the OSCE agreement to notify other European countries when it moves more than 9,000 troops or 250 tanks. Other agreements that Russia violated include the Geneva Convention of 1949 and the Second Protocol of 1977 on rights and protection of noncombatants, and several articles of the International Covenant on Civil and Political Rights, including Article 6, affirming individuals' right to life. Ludmilla Thorne, "Prestuplenie Dudaeva—ne opravdanie dlia Moskvy," *Moskovskie novosti*, January 22–29, 1995, 1; *Country Reports*, 1995, 2.

59. "The bombs are indifferent to race, indifferent to sex, indifferent to age, indifferent to religion—they kill all. People are in the cellars together without water, heat, or food, 150,000 of them, Chechens and Russians . . ." (Deputy Shabad lecture).

60. Vladimir Yemalyanenko and Dmitry Ukhlin, "Zapiski iz mertvogo goroda," *Moskovskie novosti*, January 13–19, 1995, 1–2; Lidia Grafova, president of the Coordinating Committee to Help Refugees and Forced Migrants, "Esli Sergei Kovalyov spasaet chest' Rossii, neuzheli Gosduma ne spacaet emu zhizn'?" *Trud*, December 24, 1994; the Fund for the Defense of Glasnost's reaction to "numerous cases of maltreatment and persecution of Russian and foreign journalists by Russian military"; Bonner, "A Letter to Boris Nikolaevich Yeltsin."

61. Kronid Lyubarsky, "Prestuplenie bez nakazaniia," *Novoe vremia*, no. 11 (March 1995): 10–13; "Samashki Massacre Shows Grim Reality of War," *Moscow News*, no. 15,

April 21–27, 1995, 1–2; U.S. Congress, *Crisis in Chechnya: Hearings before the Commission on Security and Cooperation in Europe*, 104th Congress, 1st sess., January 19 and 27, 1995 (Washington, D.C.: Government Printing Office, 1995); ibid., *Crisis in Chechnya: Hearings before the Commission on Security and Cooperation in Europe*, 104th Congress, 1st sess., May 1, 1995; Stephen Blank, "Anti-Democratic Forces Consolidate in Russia," *Meeting Report, Kennan Institute for Advanced Russian Studies*, vol. 12, no. 14 (1995).

62. *Country Reports on Human Rights Practices for 1995* (Washington, D.C.: Government Printing Office, 1996), 989; hereafter *Country Reports*, 1996.

63. Michael R. Gordon, "Chechnya Toll Is Far Higher, 80,000 Dead, Lebed Asserts," *New York Times*, September 4, 1996.

64. Foreign Minister Ichkeria Iosef Shamssedin of the Chechen Republic told a correspondent in Grozny that Chechnya was prepared to enter the Commonwealth of Independent States and to form a confederacy with Russia. Compatriots vowed to fight on in guerrilla warfare. Nikita Gololobov, "Davai ukroem detei v gorakh," *Nezavisimaia gazeta*, December 12, 1994 (international issue, January–February 1995), 9; Valery Batuev, "Dudaeva 'sdelali' Moskva i oppositsiia," *Argumenty i fakty*, no. 5 (February 1995): 3; Jane Ormrod, "North Caucasus: Fragmentation or Federation," in Ian Bremmer and Ray Taras, eds., *Nation and Politics in the Soviet Successor States* (New York: Cambridge University Press, 1993), 156–57.

65. *Country Reports*, 1995, 940.

66. Sergei Kovalyov, Appeal to the International Community to Press for Peace Talks in Chechnya," December 21, 1994; via Edward Kline, Human Rights Projects Group, courtesy Scott Horton, Esq.

67. S. Kovalyov, open letter to President Yeltsin from Grozny, dated December 20, 1994, depicting the carnage and pointing to the war's threat to "the constitutional order of Russia," cosigned by V. Borshchev of the Yabloko faction, M. Molostvov of Russia's Choice Faction, L. Petrovsky of the Communist Party Faction, and O. Orlov of the Memorial Society (and an expert on the President's Human Rights Commission). Copy to Edward Kline, Human Rights Project Group; courtesy Scott Horton, Esq. The Fund for the Defense of Glasnost' reacted to "numerous cases of maltreatment and persecution of Russian and foreign journalists by Russian military"; Posner, "Letter to President Boris N. Yeltsin," January 12, 1995 (copies to seven Russian officials; President Dzhokar Dudayev; three U.S. officials, including Secretary of State Warren Christopher; and Miguel Angel Martinez, President, Council of Europe Parliamentary Assembly); Human Rights Watch/Helsinki, *Russia: Three Months of War in Chechnya*, vol. 7, no. 6 (1995).

68. Ludmilla Thorne, "Prestuplenie Dudaeva—ne opravdanie dlia Moskvy," *Moskovskie Novosti*, January 22–29, 1995, 1, and "Invasion Violates Rights," *Moscow News*, January 27–February 2, 1994, 1; *Country Reports*, 1995, 934, 940. Derogations (exceptions, abrogations) from human rights may be made only in a state of emergency, according to the ICCPR and Article 56 of the Russian Federation Constitution. Article 102 requires approval of a state of emergency by the upper house of parliament, the Federation Council (Michael Posner, "Letter to Boris N. Yeltsin"). Deputy Shabad watched the initial attack on Grozny from the Presidential Palace, under heavy bombardment, on January 1. He stayed long enough on Railroad Square to count thirty burned-out Russian tanks (there were more, but shelling forced him to leave) and to smell the burning flesh of their operators. He believes Chechen claims of high Russian losses to be correct (Deputy Shabad, lecture).

69. "Soglashenie 'O sovmestnykh deistviiakh v zashchitu mira i svobody, protiv krovoprolitiia v Chechne,'" *Ekspress khronika*, February 3, 1995, 1.

70. Human Rights Watch/Helsinki, *Russia: Partisan War in Chechnya on the Eve of the WW II Commemoration*, vol. 7, no. 8 (1995).

71. Marshall Ingwerson, "Yeltsin Deal for Chechens May Buy Time for Peace," *Christian Science Monitor*, April 4, 1996; "Russia: CPRF Criticized Government Policy on Chechnya," "Interview with Leonid Avanchenko, member of the Communist Party of the Russian Federation, member of the State Duma, and chairman of the parliamentary committee for regional policies." *Berlin Neues Deutschland* (in German), January 30, 1996, 2, FBIS-SOV-96-023, 4–5.

72. Sergei Kovalyov, "Open Letter to B. Yeltsin"; Chadwick R. Gore, "Kovalyov Establishes Human Rights Institute," *CSCE Digest*, 20, no. 1 (January 1977): 3.

73. Matlock, "The Chechnya Tragedy," 5.

74. Council of Europe, *Report*, 1994, 28.

75. The charges of complicity with foreign, especially U.S., intelligence services remind one of the antiforeign suspicion and denunciations by Vladimir Kryuchkov, erstwhile KGB head and coup plotter under Gorbachev. "Document: The FCS Is Concerned about the Activity of American Researchers in Russia. From a Report by the Federal Counterintelligence Service," in *On the US Special Services' Use of American Political Science and Sociology Centers, Universities, Nongovernmental Foundations and Public Organizations for Intelligence Activity and Subversion in Russia, Nezavisimaia gazeta*, January 10, 1995, in *CDPSP*, vol. 47, no. 3–5.

76. On coverage, e.g., see V. Rasskazov, "Ptentsy gnezda Gracheva," *Argumenty i fakty*, no. 4 (1995), 1–2; Sergei Kovalyov reports that the Russian government "continually hindered the activity of correspondents in the war zone . . . and force has been used to interfere with reporters, [including] instances of mistreatment, death threats and confiscation of material." *Country Reports*, 1995, 940.

77. Katrina van den Heuvel, "Letter from Moscow: Yeltsin Survives; Will Democracy?" *The Nation*, February 27, 1995, 270–72; quote on 270.

78. The tribunal was set up by presidential decree on December 31, 1993, as a body with broad jurisdiction but limited enforcement powers. Frances H. Foster, "Freedom with Problems: The Russian *Judicial Chamber* on Mass Media," *The Parker School Journal of East European Law* 3, no. 2 (1996): 141–74. The Judicial Chamber took the side of press freedoms during the Chechnya conflict. Korkeakivi, "A Modern Day Czar?" 99.

79. A poll of 4,000 respondents by the All-Russian Institute of Public Opinion and Market Research in October 1994 showed 62 percent in favor of media covering events from their own viewpoint; 10 percent responded that media should stick to the position of the authorities; and 28 percent remained uncertain. *Moscow News*, November 19, 1993, 2.

80. Lack of funding temporarily closed down *Ekspress-khronika*, a weekly paper noted for its coverage of human rights (A. Podrabinek, editorial, *Ekspress-khronika*, February 17, 1995, 1). On attempted pressure, see: L. Bershidsky, "Kremlin Lets Up in Siege of Media," *The Moscow Times*, January 29, 1995, 13; Yelena Dmitriyeva, "An Attempt at Censorship," *Moscow News*, July 23, 1993, 2; reports of Aleksandra Lugovskaya, *Izvestiia*, July 16, 1993, and Dmitry Volkov, *Sevodnia*, July 6, 1993, in *CDPSP*, vol. 44, no. 28, 32; Vera Tolz in *RFE/RL Report* 1, no. 39, (1992): 4–9; and S. Coudenhove, "In 'Kukly' Revenge, NTV Savages Prosecutor," *The Moscow Times*, August 17, 1995, 17.

81. Aleksei Simonov, "Censorship Yesterday, Today, Tomorrow," *Index on Censorship* 25, no. 3 (1996): 59–64; quote from 60.

82. Ibid., 62–63; quote on 62.

83. "The FSB's reported refusal to question the only witness to the January 22 murder of Timufei Grigoriants, son of Sergei Grigoriants, a long-time dissident

who monitors the FSB . . . , strongly suggests it was involved in the murder." *Human Rights Watch World Report 1996*, 229.

84. *Country Reports*, 1995, 940–41. Grigory Yavlinsky, once a president's adviser and head of the "Yabloko" faction, said bitterly that Kholodov's killing "shows what the future holds for people who speak the truth here." Oleg Kalugin, a former KGB general, opined that "The government is filled with mafia people. Unfortunately this is the reality of our country." Stephen Kinzer, "Thousands in Moscow Mourn Journalist Killed in Blast," *New York Times*, October 21, 1995.

85. Elena Bonner, "A Letter to Boris Nikolaevich Yeltsin."

86. Steven Erlanger, "Russian Journalist Is Slain; Profits May Be the Motive," *New York Times*, March 2, 1995; Alessandra Stanley, "Celebrity's Killing Stirs Talk of Intrigue in Russia," *New York Times*, March 3, 1995.

87. Oleg Poptsov, "Capital Television," *Index on Censorship* 25, no. 3 (1996): 64–65.

88. Philip Taubman, "Anarchy in Russia: One Kind of Fear Gives Way to Another," *New York Times*, March 12, 1995; Mikhail Gorbachev, "Stability without Democracy? 5; *Obshchaya gazeta*, July 13–19, 1995, FBIS-SOV-95-169-S, 2. Seventy to 80 percent of private businesses had paid 10–20 percent of their profits to organized crime as of early in 1994. *Critique: Review of the U.S. Department of State's Country Reports on Human Rights Practices for 1994* (New York, 1995), 194; hereafter, *Critique*, 1995.

89. M. Taibbi, "Kivelidi Honored by Colleagues," *The Moscow Times*, August 20, 1995, 16; M. Gulyayev and K. Perminova, "Bankers Fight Back after Murder," *The Moscow Times*, August 13, 1995, 10–12. The victims of the five-day carnage ranged from a retired major heading a private security company to an assistant director of a dry-cleaning company, a bodyguard, and gangland figures. M. Taibbi, "Gangland-Style Murders Claim 17 People in Five Days," *The Moscow Times*, August 13, 1995, 12.

90. M. Taibbi, "Chaos Reigns in Notorious Cases," *The Moscow Times*, August 13, 1995, 13; Penny Morvant, "War on Organized Crime and Corruption," *Transition*, February 15, 1995, 32–36; *Critique*, 1995, 196.

91. "Skorochkin's Murder Was a Bellwether," *The Moscow Times*, February 12, 1995, 14; *Country Reports*, 1996, 991.

92. "CSCE Editorial: Death in St. Petersburg: Accident, or Old-Style Revenge?" *CSCE Digest* (Washington, D.C.), March 1995, 2.

93. *Country Reports*, 1996, 994.

94. Report of the President's Commission, *On the Observance of the Rights of Man and Citizen in the Russian Federation (1994–1995). Approved at the February 5, 1996, Session of the Commission*, 57–60; courtesy of Antti Korkeakivi, Lawyers Committee for Human Rights; hereafter, Report of the President's Commission, 1996.

95. McFaul, "Why Russia's Politics Matter," 97.

96. Sergei Shishkin, political consultant and professor of law from Irkutsk, lecture, April 7, 1995, New York City.

97. *Country Reports*, 1995, 940.

98. *Konstitutsiia RF*, Articles 14, 28; *Country Reports*, 1996, 1001; Edith Coron, "Russia's Religious Revival," *Christian Science Monitor*, November 25, 1996, 9–11.

99. The decision to allow the Patriarch to speak for all "traditional" religions and their exclusion from the same participation constitutes a violation of Article 14 of the Russian Federation Constitution, which declares that "The Russian Federation is a secular state. . . . Religious organizations are separate from the state and equal before the law." Fr. Gleb Yakunin, "Gosudarstvo dolzhno ostavat'sia svetskim," *Ekspress-khronika*, August 16, 1996, 1; *Konstitutsiia RF*, Article 14(1, 2).

100. Yakunin also accuses the Patriarch of helping to instill "totalitarian ways"

into the church's self-interested, self-enriching hierarchy. Fr. Gleb Yakunin, "'Vy prevatili khram v dom torguiushchikh': Otkrytoe obrashchenie k patriarkhu Aleksiiu Vtoromu (A. M. Ridigeru)," *Express khronika* May 17, 1996, 1.

101. Peter Juviler, "Making Up for Lost Choice: The Shaping of Ethnic Identity in the Post-Soviet States," in James R. Millar and Sharon L. Wolchik, eds., *The Social Legacies of Communism* (Cambridge and New York: Cambridge University Press, Woodrow Wilson Center Series, 1994), 31–55. Nearly three-quarters of Russians polled after independence would then, they said, still vote for a renewed USSR. Of Russians polled, 72 percent supported the idea of the restoration of the USSR as a union of sovereign states linked at least economically and politically. A plurality of 45 percent also agreed to military union. Boris Grushin, "Nazad, k SSSR?" *Novoe vremia*, 14, 1992, 19.

102. Roman Szporluk, "The Imperial Legacy and Soviet Nationalities," in Lubomyr Hajda and Mark Beissinger, eds., *The Nationalities Factor in Soviet Politics and Society* (Boulder, CO: Westview Press, 1990), 15. See also Serge Schmemann, "Spirit of Christmas Calls Again to Russians," *New York Times*, January 8, 1992; photo shows a beaming Boris Yeltsin, who "says he is not a believer but respects religious traditions," shaking hands with Patriarch Aleksy II at a service on Russian Orthodox Christmas.

103. Dmitry Radyshevskii, "Reporting on Religion in Russia," *Kennan Institute Meeting Report*, January 13, 1992. "Statement to the Moscow CSCE Conference on the Human Dimension Presented by the World Conference on Soviet Jewry, Va'ad Confederation of Jewish Organizations and Communities (USSR)," September 17, 1991.

104. *Country Reports*, 1996, 1001.

105. Polling revealed regional differences—for example, strong antiwar majorities in Moscow, St. Petersburg, and Ivanovo (a textile center with a heavily female work force); quite negative in Krasnodar; and shading off to 50–50 in Kostroma and majorities in favor of the government's actions in Rostov-on-the Don and Stavropol. Nikolai Petrov, "The Regions Are Not Keeping Silent," *Nezavisimaia gazeta*, January 20, 1995, in *CDPSP* 47, no. 3 (1995): 15–16.

106. Between December 17 and January 20, 1994–95, an all-Russia survey of 1,335 respondents showed that those opposed to sending Russian troops into Chechnya rose from 63 to 71 percent; 74 percent thought it unfair to put on trial servicemen who refused to participate in the military operation in Chechnya, while 11 percent thought it fair; 47 percent agreed that the Russian army was fighting "gangster formations" there, whereas 21 percent saw the war as being "waged against the Chechen people." Survey: "The Majority of Russia's People Are Against Putting Military Men Who Refuse to Serve (in Chechnya) on Trial," *Sevodnia*, January 28, 1995, 3, in *CDPSP* 47, no. 4 (1995): 12. On civic activity, see "A Report from Interlegal USA, Inc. on Recognizing the Third Sector: A Russia–USA Conference held in Moscow May 19–21, 1993" (New York: Interlegal USA, 1993).

107. Deputy Shabad, lecture, February 3, 1995; Vera Tolz, "The Shifting Sands of Stabilization," 5–7.

108. "Deputies: There Turned Out to Be More Militarists in the Duma Than One Had Thought," *Kommersant*, January 24, 1995, in *CDPSP*, vol. 47, no. 4, 12.

109. M. Gorbachev, "Stability without Democracy?" *Moscow News*, June 2–8, 1995, 5.

110. Frances H. Foster, "Information and the Problem of Democracy: The Russian Experience," *American Journal of Comparative Law* 44, no. 2 (1996): 243–91.

111. "Vtoroe poslanie k rossiianam," *Novoe vremia*, no. 8 (1995): 4; "Dvuglavye orly vstrechaiutsia tol'ko v geral'dike," ibid., 6–7.

112. The president netted an 8 percent favorable rating, and a net minus 58 percent (i.e., those favoring minus those condemning), while his critic Sergei Kovalyov netted plus 7 (plus 28 and minus 21), and Zhirinovsky, minus 40 (plus 3 and minus 43) of 1,341 respondents in an all-Russia survey by the Public Opinion Foundation, "Survey: The People of Russia on the Chechen War," *Sevodnia*, January 19, 1995, in *CDPSP* 47, no. 3 (1995): 17. In the poll, 66 percent were against, and 21 percent for sending Russian troops into Chechnya. See also Kronid Lyubarsky, "'My vse gliadim v Napoleony . . .' Rol' vypolnena. Prepochtia sokhranit' vlast' liuboi tsenoi, prezident obrek sebia na porazhenie," *Novoe vremia*, no. 7 (1995), 16–18; Alexander Konovalov, "Russia's Creeping Coup," *The Moscow Times*, January 22, 1995, 34; Yegor Gaidar interview, *The Guardian*, February 24, 1995, FBIS-SOV-95-037, 15–16; Tolz, "The Shifting Sands of Stabilization," 8.

113. *Critique*, 1995, 192.

114. Central Election Commission of the Russian Federation. List of Deputies elected to the Russian Federation State Duma, *Rossiiskaia gazeta*, January 6, 1996, FBIS-SOV-96-021-S.

115. Michael McFaul, "The Vanishing Center," *Journal of Democracy* 7, no. 2 (1996): 92; John Finerty, "Communists Prevail in Russian Duma Elections," *CSCE Digest*, February 1996, 1, 8.

116. Greg Hansen, "Chechnya: Everyone Knows, No One Acts," *Christian Science Monitor*, April 30, 1996; quote from William Odom and Peter Reddaway, "Yeltsin's False Truce," *New York Times*, April 3, 1996.

117. *Human Rights Watch World Report 1996*, 232–33; in line with most U.S. policy, the State Department report on human rights fails to single out the Russian president's responsibility for the war and its atrocities. The report cites "Russia," "Russian military forces," or "Russian forces," and only once "government forces," as violators in the attack on Chechnya. It leaves unmentioned the responsibility of the president and the conservative cabal of security, police, and military officials that surrounds him in Moscow. *Country Reports*, 1996, 991, 998.

118. Report of the President's Commission on Human Rights, 1996, 15; *Country Reports*, 1996, 998–99.

119. Human Rights Watch/Helsinki, *Russia (Chechnya and Dagestan): Caught in the Crossfire: Civilians in Gudermes and Pervomayskoe* 8, no. 3 (D) (1996): 2. See also Human Rights Watch/Helsinki, *Russian Federation: A Review of the Compliance of the Russian Federation with Council of Europe Commitments and Other Human Rights Obligations on the First Anniversary of Its Accession to the Council of Europe* (New York: Human Rights Watch, 9, no. 3[D], February 1997).

120. Chechnya: Dead or Alive," *The Economist*, April 27, 1996, 54; quote from "Russian Limbo," *The Nation*, May 27, 1996, 5; "Prognoz generala Korzhakova," *Izvestiia*, May 7, 1996, 1; quote from Alessandra Stanley, "Yeltsin Declares Election in Russia Won't Be Put Off," *New York Times*, May 7, 1996.

121. Daniel Treisman, "Why Yeltsin Won," *Foreign Affairs* 75, no. 5 (1996): 54–77. See also Michael R. Gordon, "The Russian Bank Is Told by Yeltsin to Release Funds," *New York Times*, June 7, 1996; Michael R. Gordon, "Huge Russian Company [Gazprom] Is Biggest Yeltsin Backer," *New York Times*, June 30, 1996; Marshall Ingwerson, "Yeltsin Creates a Post-Poll Mess by Pledging Thrift, Doling Cash," *Christian Science Monitor*, June 5, 1996; Peter Ford, "In Russia's Heartland, Yeltsin Pitches a Defensive Message," *Christian Science Monitor*, June 11, 1996.

122. Reports of the Central Election Commission, *Rossiiskaia gazeta*, June 18, 20, 22, 1996, 1.

123. Teimurz Mamaladze, "Gracheva—v otstavku. Lebeda—v Kreml'. Eltsina—v prezidenty," *Izvestiia*, June 19, 1996, 1.

124. Report of the Central Election Commission summarized in *Nezavisimaia gazeta*, July 10, 1996, *CSPSP* 48, no. 27 (1996): 1.

125. Dmitry Oreshkin and Vladimir Kozlov, "One President, Two Countries," *Sevodnia*, July 10, *CDPSP* 48, no. 27 (1996): 7.

126. Yury Levada, "Za mesiats do vyborov: Koalatsii vse eshche net," *Izvestiia*, May 14, 1996, 2. Reports in *Kommersant*, July 5, 1996, and *Sevodnia*, July 4; *Sevodnia*, July 10; *Obshchaia gazeta*, July 4, *Pravda*, July 9, *CDPSP* 48, no. 27 (1996): 5–9.

127. John Finerty, "Commission Holds Russian Elections Hearing," *CSCE Digest* 19, no. 7 (1996): 6; Boris Kagarlitsky, "Russia Chooses—and Looses," *Current History* 95, no. 603 (November 1996): 305–10.

128. "The Vote in Russia," *Washington Post*, July 4, 1996; "A Victory for Russian Democracy." The *New York Times* extolled their "stoic patience and enduring hope," which kept them from voting in a Communist or fascist (*New York Times*, July 4, 1996).

129. Finerty, "Commission Holds Russian Elections Hearing," 6.

130. Michael Ochs, "Russia's Presidential Election," *CSCE Digest* 19, no. 8 (1996): 5.

131. Stephen White, Richard Rose, and Ian McAlister, *How Russia Votes* (Chatham, NJ: Chatham House Publishers, 1996), 242, 269.

132. Marc Champion, "Letter from the Editor," *The Moscow Times*, January 29, 1995, 5; Thomas de Waal, "Korzhakov Runs Secret Think Tank, Report Says," *The Moscow Times*, January 29, 1995, 18; "How Events in Moscow Developed on June 19–20, 1996," *Izvestiia*, June 21, 1996, *CDPSP* 48, no. 25 (1996): 9–10.

133. *Nezavisimaia gazeta*, July 16, 1996, *CDPSP* 48, no. 28 (1996): 1–2.

134. Michael R. Gordon, "Key Russian Legislator Accuses Leading Military Officers of Graft," *New York Times*, July 9, 1996; Peter Ford, "Yeltsin Taps Reformer to Revive Russia's Army," *Christian Science Monitor*, July 7, 1996.

135. Nikolai Efimov, "Armiia, obshchestvo, reformy," *Svobodnaia mysl'*, no. 9 (1995), 32–43; trans. in *Government and Politics* 34, no. 3 (1996): 6–22.

136. A June 10 agreement with the Chechen chief of state, Aslan Maskhadov, signed in the North Caucasus city of Naran, Ingushetia, included the trade-off of a Russian withdrawal for Chechen disarmament. Peter Rutland, "A Fragile Peace," *Transition* 2, no. 23 (1996): 49.

137. Alessandra Stanley, "Chechen Rebel Says Forces Will Pull Out of Capital," *New York Times*, August 9, 1996; Michael Specter, "Chechen Rebel Leader Savors Triumph in a Shattered City," *New York Times*, August 16, 1996.

138. John Thornhill, "The Humiliating Chechen War Has Highlighted Russia's Need to Rebuild Its Army as a Modern Fighting Force," *The Financial Times*, August 16, 1993, 11.

139. "Chechnya. Est' li shans zakonchit' voiny?" *Ekspress-khronika*, August 16, 1996, 1; Alessandra Stanley, "Yeltsin Security Aide Denounces the Russian War Effort in Chechnya," and "Yeltsin Gives Free Rein to End Fighting in Chechnya," *New York Times*, August 13 and 15, 1996.

140. Dmitry Likhachev, "O proshlom i buduiuschem Rossii," interview with Natal'ia Zhelnorova, *Argumenty i fakty*, October 23, 1995, trans. in *Russian Politics and Law* 34, no. 4 (1996): 81. "Largely because of Lebed's personal intervention and aggressive shuttle diplomacy," Lee Hockstader noted, "the possibility of peace in Chechnya has been nudged to the top of the government agenda for the first time in more than a year" ("Keeping the Kremlin Off Balance," *Washington Post National Weekly Edition*, September 21–28, 1996, 15).

141. "Russian, Meeting Chechens, Vows to Honor Pact," *New York Times*, October 28, 1996; Michael R. Gordon, "Yeltsin Orders Withdrawal of Troops in Chech-

nya," *New York Times*, November 24, 1996; Rutland, "A Fragile Peace," 49–50; Human Rights Watch/Helsinki, "Russia/Chechnya: Report to the 1996 OSCE Review Conference," vol. 8, no. 16 (D), November 1996.

Chapter 9. Russia: The Context of Freedom

1. *Vedomosti*, no. 27, 1992, item 1572; David Satter, "The Failure of Russian Reformers," *Wall Street Journal*, May 13, 1996.

2. Sergei Kovalyov, "Open Letter to B. Yeltsin," *Izvestiia*, January 24, 1996, in FBIS-SOV-96-016, 31, 32.

3. "With the Soviet Constitution of 1918," writes Said Amir Arjomand, "we witness the advent of a new genre, the ideological constitution, whose central goal is not the limitation of government but the transformation of society according to a revolutionary ideology." Said Amir Arjomand, "Constitutions and the Struggle for Political Order: A Study in the Modernization of Political Traditions," *Archives of European Sociology* 23 (1992): 42–46; quote on 46. I thank Dr. Stanley Katz for pointing me toward this source.

4. Robert Sharlet, "The Prospects for Federalism in Russian Constitutional Politics," *Publius: The Journal of Federalism* 24, no. 2 (1994): 116–17.

5. *Konstitutsiia Rossiiskoi Federatsii* (Moscow: Iuridicheskaia literatura, 1994), Articles 13, 30(2); hereafter *Konstitutsiia RF*.

6. Ibid., Articles 26(1), 29(3, 5), and on individual rights, Articles 17–54, 60–61.

7. Ibid., Article 55(3).

8. Ibid., Article 103(e).

9. Council of Europe, Parliamentary Assembly, Bureau of the Assembly, *Report on the Conformity of the Legal Order of the Russian Federation with Council of Europe Standards*, Strasbourg, October 7, 1994, 33–34 (hereafter Council of Europe, *Report*); on homosexuality: *Ugolovnyi kodeks Rossiiskoi Federatsii*, 2 vols. (St. Petersburg: Severozapad, 1994), Article 121.

10. State Department, *Country Reports on Human Rights Practices for 1994* (Washington, D.C.: U.S. Government Printing Office, 1995), 936; hereafter *Country Reports*.

11. Council of Europe, *Report*, 33–34.

12. *Ugolovnyi-protsessual'nyi kodeks RSFSR* (*sic*), amended as of December 1, 1995 (Moscow: Iurist, 1996), Article 220(2).

13. Valery Abramkin, Rachel Denber, Richard Schimpf, and Clare Hughes, eds., *In Search of a Solution: Crime, Criminal Policy and Prison Facilities in the Former Soviet Union* (Moscow: Center for Prison Reform, 1996), 80.

14. Antti Korkeakivi, *Justice Delayed: The Russian Constitutional Court and Human Rights* (New York: The Lawyers Committee on Human Rights, 1995), 13–14.

15. *Konstitutsiia RF*, Articles 47(2), 123.

16. Ibid., Article 120.

17. Of the first 127 jury trials (for 218 people), 67 percent were for aggravated homicide, 13 percent for rape, and 20 percent for bribery, economic crimes, and grave vehicular crimes. Abramkin et al., *In Search of a Solution*, 82–86. On prerevolutionary juries, see S. M. Kazantsev, ed., *Sud prisiazhnykh v Possli gromkie ugolovnye protsessy 1864–1917 gg.* (Leningrad: Lenizdat, 1991).

18. *Country Reports*, 1993, 888. Sergei Mostovchchikov, "Mirzayanov Case Dismissed for Lack of the Elements of a Crime," *Izvestiia*, March 12, 1994, in *CDPSP*, vol. 46, no. 10, (1994) 19–20.

19. *Country Reports*, 1995, 938–39; 1996, 996.

20. *Country Reports*, 1996, 994.

21. Michael R. Gordon, "In Russia, Whistle-Blowing Can Still Be Treason," *New York Times*, November 28, 1996.

22. *On the Observance of the Rights of Man and Citizen in the Russian Federation (1994–1995): Report of the President's Commission on Human Rights*, Moscow, approved at the February 5, 1996, Session of the Commission, (trans. of the Lawyer's Committee for Human Rights), 39; hereafter *Report of the President's Commission on Human Rights*, 1996.

23. *Report of the President's Commission on Human Rights*, 1996, 44–49; quote on 49.

24. These are the Federal Security Service, which seems to be regaining the powers of the old KGB, and the Ministry of the Interior (MVD), which runs the police, prisons, and internal security troops. *Country Reports*, 1996, 989.

25. *Konstitutsiia RF*, Articles 23, 25; *Country Reports*, 1995, 939; Council of Europe, *Report*, 35–39.

26. Abramkin et al., *In Search of a Solution*, 86.

27. Ibid., 73–89. The president said that the courts were "experiencing a profound crisis." "President's Address: Boris Yeltsin, Speech to the National Assembly," Moscow Russian Television Network, February 16, 1995, FBIS-SOV-95-032, 8.

28. *Country Reports*, 1995, 938; 1996, 996.

29. Komissiia po pravam cheloveka pri Prezidente Rossiiskoi Federatsii, *Doklad o sobliudenii prav cheloveka i grazhdanina v Rossiiskoi Federatsii za 1993 god* (Moscow, 1994), 16–20; (hereafter Komissiia po pravam cheloveka, *Doklad*); Kronid Lyubarsky, "Grazhdane pered litsom proizvola, 7–11; and Antti Korkeakivi, "A Modern Day Czar? Presidential Power and Human Rights in the Russian Federation," *Journal of Constitutional Law in Eastern and Central Europe* 2, no. 76 (*sic*), 101–09.

30. "Russian Law: Groping Ahead," *The Economist*, September 2, 1995, 42–43, 48.

31. Council of Europe, *Report*, 6, 7, 84–85; emphasis added.

32. Komissiia po pravam cheloveka, *Doklad*, 16–20; Kronid Lyubarsky, "Grazhdane pered litsom proizvole," *Novoe vremia*, no. 31 (August 1994): 7–11. Information is corroborated in, e.g., *Country Reports*, 1995, 937; *Amnesty International Report 1995*, 247–49.

33. Abramkin et al., *In Search of a Solution*, xi–xxiii, 55–72; quote from xvi. See also Vladimir Rudnev, "Kriminal'noe zarazhenie," *Podmoskovnye izvestiia*," July 14, 1993, 3.

34. Abramkin et al., xi–xxiii, 55–72; graphs on xx–xxi, 103.

35. *Report of the President's Commission on Human Rights*, 1996, 57–60.

36. "Is It Safe to Do Business in Russia?" *Russia Review*, December 2, 1996, 12.

37. Donald D. Barry, *Toward the "Rule of Law" in Russia? Political and Legal Reforms in the Transition Period* (Armonk, NY: M. E. Sharpe), xxiv.

38. Aleksandr M. Yakovlev, lecture at the Carnegie Endowment for International Peace, Moscow, December 14, 1995.

39. Donald D. Barry, "Constitutional Politics: The Russian Constitutional Court as a New Kind of Institution," paper prepared for conference on "Russian and America: From Rivalry to Reconciliation," University of Pennsylvania, February 18–19, 1993, 10–16.

40. "O Konstitutsionnom Sude RSFSR," Law of 12 July 1991, *Vedomosti*, no. 30, item 1017, 1991. Articles 163(3), 165, 165[1] in the 1978 constitution. *Konstitutsiia (osnovnoi zakon) Rossiiskoi Federatsii-Rossii* (Moscow: Izdanie Verkhovnogo Soveta Rossiiskoi Federatsii, 1992).

41. On a parliamentary complaint, the Constitutional Court on January 14, 1992, annulled as unconstitutional President Yeltsin's Decree No. 289 merging the Ministry of Security (successor to the KGB) with the Ministry of Internal Affairs (police,

prison guards and correctional institutions, internal security Special Force troops, fire fighting, and cartography) of the RSFSR into a single Ministry of Security and Internal Affairs. Valery Rudnev, "Konstitutsionnyi Sud otmenil Ukaz B. El'tsina o sozdanii MVD: Reshenie eto—okonchatel'noe. Obzhalovaniiu—ne podlezhit," *Izvestiia*, January 15, 1992.

42. "Valery Zor'kin: Glavnaia nasha zadacha—zashchitit' konstitutsionnyi stroi," *Sovetskaia iustitsiia*, nos. 7–8, April 1992, 18.

43. Barry, "Constitutional Politics," 31. See also Carla Thorson, "The Fate of the Communist Party in Russia," *RFE/RL Report* 1, no. 37, (1992): 1–6.

44. Interview with Justice Ernest Ametistov, Moscow, December 1992.

45. Olga Berezhnaya, "Deputies Intend to Hold Back Privatization," *Moscow News*, July 23, 1993, 1, 6.

46. "Valery Zor'kin: Glavnaia nasha zadacha," 18–20; Barry, 31–35; quote from 31.

47. Robert Sharlet, "Chief Justice as Judicial Politician," *East European Constitutional Review* 2, no. 2 (1993): 31–36. In the opinion of Judge Ametistov, one of three dissenting judges out of the bench of thirteen (a fourth judge then in the hospital later joined the dissenters), the court violated the Russian Federation Constitution through, among other things: (1) the chairman's comments to press and parliament before and during court examination of the issue, anticipating the finding; (2) issuing its finding on the basis of a draft decree not yet in effect; (3) procedural irregularities including inadequate notice of the session. Justice Ernest Ametistov, writing in *CIS Law Notes*, April 1993, 1–4.

48. "Zakliuchenie konstitutsionnogo suda Rossiiskoi Federatsii 21 sentiabria 1993 goda," *Vestnik Konstitutsionnogo Suda Rossiiskoi Federatsii*, no. 6 (1994), 40; hereafter *Vestnik KSRF*. Decision on the decree "On Step-by-Step Constitutional Reform in the Russian Federation."

49. *Vestnik KSRF*, no. 6 (1994), opinions of Justices E. Ametistov (41–45), V. O. Luchin (45–46), N. V. Vitruk (46–49), A. L. Kononov (50–53), and T. G. Morshchakova (54–56).

50. 1994 Law on the Constitutional Court, Articles 97–98. The situation can be said to resemble that of Soviet times, when thousands of executive decrees, according to William Butler, were "one of the key foundations of the authoritarianism of the Soviet legal system" (William E. Butler, "Justice in Russia: Soviet Law and Russian History," *Emory Law Journal* 42 [1993]: 433, 443; quoted in Korkeakivi, *Justice Delayed: The Russian Constitutional Court and Human Rights*, 13–14; quote on 14). The Russian Constitutional Court examines, in cases referred to it, the constitutionality of laws and other normative acts of the Russian Federation and the constitutions and charters of the Federation components, and their normative acts on matters of Federation or joint Federation–component jurisdiction, as well as international treaties not yet in force and treaties between the Federation and its components, or among the components. The Constitutional Court also resolves disputes over the competence of top governmental organs within and between the Federation and component governments; it gives binding interpretations of the constitution at the request of the presidents of the Federation, Federation Council, and State Duma, the government (Council of Ministers), and legislatures of Federation components (1994 Law on the Constitutional Court, Articles 105–6). Its consent on procedures is now required for an impeachment of the president to go forward (1994 Law on the Constitutional Court, Chapters 11, 15).

51. Federal Constitutional Law on the Constitutional Court of the Russian Federation, July 21, 1994, *Vestnik KSRF*, no. 1 (1995). On elections to the court, see the

1994 Law, Articles 4, 9; on structure, Article 20; elections of its chair, vice chair, and justice secretary, Article 23; chambers and sessions, Articles 20–22, Section 5, Transitional Provisions, parts 2, 3.

52. 1994 Law on the Constitutional Court, Article 10.

53. "Vstat'! Sud idet!" *Novoe vremia,* no. 29 (1995), 8; "Russia: Rights Arrive," *The Economist,* February 18, 1995, 51.

54. "O Konstitutsionnom Sude RSFSR," Law of 12 July 1991, *Vedomosti,* No. 30, item 1017, 1991. The present Russian Federation Constitution was amended to include reference to the Constitutional Court and outline its authority. *Konstitutsiia RF,* Article 125.

55. Law of 1994 on the Constitutional Court, Article 11 on public statements; Articles 12–15, 17–19 on terms, material support, irremovability, immunity, self-disciplining and resignation of justices; Article 29 on judicial independence; Articles 30–35 on openness, adversarial procedures, equal rights of parties; see also Articles 29–32, 42–70. Under a new requirement, a fifth of Duma deputies is required to initiate a case. The term of the chair is shortened from life to three years, his powers reduced, and his removal as Chair by the rest of the court possible, as not previously, in cases of laxity or abuse of office. The retirement age of the original thirteen justices is raised from sixty-five to seventy. But for the six new justices, the term is only twelve years. This limited term would seem to make the court more rather than less subject to political pressures and changes (1994 Law on the Constitutional Court, Article 12).

56. 1991 Law on the Constitutional Court, Article 74.

57. Ibid., Articles 3, 36, 84; Chapter 10 (on treaties); *Konstitutsiia RF,* Article 125 (2).

58. 1994 Law on the Constitutional Court, Article 3.

59. *Vestnik KSRF,* nos. 2–3 (1995), 37.

60. Said Deputy Shabad, "Each explosion should be given criminal content. . . . The whole situation is unconstitutional." Shabad visited Shali village two hours after the Russians had bombed its operating marketplace. The procurator general did not reply when Shabad suggested an investigation into this criminal act. Anatoly Shabad, lecture sponsored by the Lawyers Committee on Human Rights, New York, Patterson, Belknap, Webb & Tyler, February 3, 1995. Kronid Lyubarsky, "V ozhidanii verdikta," *Novoe vremia,* no. 30 (1995), 8.

61. "Postanovlenie Konstitutsionnogo suda Rossiiskoi Federatsiii," July 31, 1995, *Vestnik KSRF,* no. 5 (1995), 4 (hereafter, "Postanovlenie Konstitutsionnogo suda"); V. Rudnev, "Chechnya Case Being Heard," *Izvestiia,* July 11, 1995, FBIS-SOV-95-132, 11.

62. This summary, except where otherwise noted, is based on the text of the inquiry of the Federation Council, *Zapros Soviets Federatsii Federal'nogo Sobraniia Rossiiskoi Federatsiii . . . , Rossiiskoi biulleten' po pravam cheloveka* (Moscow: Human Rights Project Group), no. 6 (1995), 57–60.

63. Deputy Givi Yakovlev, representing the Federation Council before the court, stated that, on February 28, 1995, Defense Minister Pavel Grachev, at a meeting of top commanders of the Russian army, referred six times to the supposedly repealed edict and not once to the verdict repealing it. Lyubarsky, "V ozhidanii verdikta," 9.

64. *Zapros,* part 3; testimony of Federation Council Deputy Elena Mizulina, cited in Lyubarsky, "V ozhidanii verdikta," 11; *Konstitutsiia RF,* Articles 88, 102(c).

65. The constitutional rights violated, the "inquiry" stated, included the rights to life (*Konstitutsiia RF,* Article 20[1]); to freedom and personal inviolability (Article 25); to inviolability of the home (Article 25); to freedom of movement and choice

of place of residence (Article 27 [1]); to state protection of citizens' private property (Article 35[2,3]); to protection from arbitrary derivation of one's dwelling place (Article 40); and to protection of health and to medical assistance (Article 41[1]). *Zapros*, 7–9, quotation from point 1.

66. Lyubarsky, "V ozhidanii verdikta," 9–10; *Rossiiskaia gazeta*, July 12, 1995, FBIS-SOV-95-134, 18; Sergei Shakhrai, closing speech, *Rossiiskie vesti*, July 20, 1995, FBIS-SOV-95-144-S, 14; ITAR-TASS, July 11, 1995, FBIS-SOV-95-133, 14; L. Bershidsky, "Court Prepares to Rule on Chechnya Decrees," *The Moscow Times*, July 23, 1995, 13. *Konstitutsiia RF*, Article 80: "The President of the Russian Federation is the guarantor of the Constitution of the Russian Federation, of the rights and freedoms of the individual and the citizen. According to procedures established by the Constitution of the Russian Federation, he adopts measures to safeguard the sovereignty of the Russian Federation, its independence and integrity."

67. *Vestnik KSRF*, 9.

68. *Vestnik KSRF*, Lyubarsky, "Shemyakin sud," *Novoe vremia*, no. 32 (August 1995): 8–10; *Konstitutsiia RF*, Articles 52, 53, and 80.

69. Decrees 2137s and 2169s. The court held that because "decree No. 2137" of November 30, 1994 (ordering a state of emergency), had been repealed by decree No. 2169 of December 11, 1994, the court could drop it from the case, in accordance with the discretion noted in its statute. Court reasoning and decisions on the decrees, *Vestnik KSRF*, 6–18; see also Lyubarsky, "Shemyakin sud," 8–9; 1994 Law on the Constitutional Court, Article 43.

70. Lyubarsky, "Shemyakin sud," 8. The dissents followed the arguments of the plaintiffs making the inquiry, except for Justice Ernest Ametistov's dissent. It questioned the court's taking up the case in the first place, as the decrees were not normative and therefore were outside the court's jurisdiction. Dissents of Justices A. M. Ametistov, N. V. Vitruk, G. A. Gadzhiev, V. D. Zor'kin, A. L. Kononov, V. O. Luchin, T. G. Morshchakova, and B. S. Ebseev, in *Vestnik KSRF*, 20–64. Interview with Justice Ametistov, Moscow, December 22, 1995.

71. Respondent Yury Baturin had previously coauthored a commentary on the constitution. The book highlighted Article 2, which proclaims that human rights and freedoms are "the supreme value. Their recognition, observance, and protection are the obligation of the state." B. N. Topornin, Yu. M. Baturin, and V. G. Orekhov, eds., *Konstitutsiia Rossiiskoi Federatsii: Kommentarii* (Moscow: Iuridicheskaia literatura, 1994); quotes from 17 (endnote) and 25.

72. Decision of May 3, 1995, *Vestnik KSRF*, nos. 2–3 (1995), 39–44; decision of May 17, 1995, ibid., 45–50; decision of May 23, ibid., 51–56; decision of June 6, ibid., 57–62; decision of June 23, ibid., 73–79.

73. *Konstitutsiia RF*, Article 7(3).

74. Elena Bonner, "Indian Summer of Communism: Observations of an Amateur," *World Policy Journal* 11, no. 2 (1994): 19–25.

75. Other estimates hold that 53 million people, or 36 percent of the population, "cannot meet their minimum needs," even while managers continue to pay themselves high salaries. Industrial accidents and occupational diseases, under loose governmental occupational health and safety regulations, have killed, injured, or maimed more than a million workers in four years. "Report of the President's Commission," 72–75; quote from 75.

76. *Country Reports*, 1996, 989.

77. "Getting Richer, Getting Poorer," *The Economist*, February 6, 1993, 52.

78. Interview with Irina Paikecheva, lawyer and activist from Murmansk, Moscow, December 16, 1995.

79. Viktor Zaslavsky, "From Redistribution to Marketization: Social and Attitudinal Change in Post-Soviet Russia," in Gail Lapidus, ed., *Russia: Troubled Transformation* (Boulder, CO: Westview Press, 1995), 136.

80. G. Yavlinsky, *Ekonomika Rossii: Nasledstvo i vozmozhnosti* (Moscow: EPItsentr, 1995); *Reformy dlia bol'shinstva* (Moscow: Ob"edinenie "Yabloko," 1995).

81. Yegor Gaidar, *Zapiski iz zala* (Moscow: Izdatel'stvo "Evrasia," 1995). See also "Russia: Not Working," *The Economist*, November 20, 1993, 57–58; Marshall I. Goldman, "Is This Any Way To Create a Market Economy?" *Current History* 94, no. 594 (October 1995): 305–10; Anders Aslund, "The Russian Road to the Market," *Current History* 94, no. 594 (October 1995): 311–16.

82. Aleksei Arbatov, lecture at preelection meeting, Precinct No. 1, Moscow, December 15, 1995; Liam Halligan (economic expert with the Russian-European Center for Economic Policy in Moscow, contributor to *The Economist*), "How Russia Will Thrive," *Russian Review*, September 9, 1996, 9.

83. Vladimir Kontorovich, "Imperial Legacy and the Transformation of the Russian Economy," *Transition* 2, no. 17 (1996): 22–25, 64; quote from 22.

84. Grigory A. Yavlinsky, "Death of a Scientist," *New York Times*, November 15, 1996.

85. "Trusting Russia's Army—To Be Weak," *The Economist*, October 26, 1996, 60; John Thornhill, "The Humiliating Chechen War Has Highlighted Russia's Need to Rebuild Its Army as a Modern Fighting Force," *The Financial Times*, August 16, 1993, 11.

86. *The Nation*, September 11, 1995, 231. For details on women's status and rights and the emerging women's movement, see Anastasia Posadskaya, *Women in Russia: A New Era in Russian Feminism* (London/New York: Verso, 1994).

87. "Women: Victims—or Agents of Change?" A series of articles in *Transition* 1, no. 16 (1995): 2–28; Nadezhda Azhgikhina, "Will Russia Become the Capital of World Feminism?" *Demokratizatsiia* 3, no. 3 (1995): 243–51; Mary I. Dakin, "Women and Employment Policy in Contemporary Russia," *Demokratizatsiia* 3, no. 3 (1995): 252–61.

88. Alessandra Stanley, "Russian Mothers, From All Walks, Walk Alone," *New York Times*, October 21, 1995.

89. Penny Morvant, "Alarm Over Falling Life Expectancy," *Transition* 1, no. 19 (1995): 40–41; quote on 41.

90. Andrei Baiduzhy, "Demographic Catastrophe Has Become a Reality," *Nezavisimaia gazeta*, February 2, 1994, in *CDPSP* 46, no. 5 (1994): 18–19.

91. One-third of all girls in Moscow under the age of seventeen have been pregnant. Dmitry Frolov, "Bureaucrats Show Concern for Multiplying the Nation," *Sevodnia*, March 10, 1994, in *CDPSP* 46, no. 10 (1994): 16.

92. The number rose from 50,000 in 1990 to an estimated 125,000 in 1995, for a total of about half a million and rising. Genine Babakian, "Alarming Rise in Orphaned Children," *The Moscow Times*, October 22, 1995, 13.

93. Yelena Yershova, founder and director, Gaia Women's Center, lecture at United Methodist Office for the UN, New York, February 13, 1995.

94. Morvant, "Alarm Over Falling Life Expectancy," 40.

95. Ibid., 40–45, 72; Murray Feshbach, *Ecological Disaster: Cleaning Up the Hidden Legacy of the Soviet Regime* (New York: The Twentieth Century Fund Press, 1995); Mike Edwards, "Lethal Legacy: Pollution in the Former U.S.S.R.," and "Chernobyl: Living with the Monster," *National Geographic* 186, no. 2 (1994): 70–99, 100–15; "Health in Eastern Europe: Out of the Ward," *The Economist*, August 3, 1996, 45–46.

96. *The World's Women 1995: Trends and Statistics* (New York: United Nations, 1995), 84–85, 88, 99–103.

97. Unnatural deaths in Russia leaped from 137.6 per 100,000 population in 1986 to 227.9 in 1993. Morvant, "Alarm Over Falling Life Expectancy," 40–44. See also, on 1996, Yevgeny Andreev, "One People, Two Populations," *Moskovskie novosti* no. 1 (1997), *CDPSP*, 49, no. 1 (1997), 3.

98. *Konstitutsiia RF*, Article 42.

99. Morvant, "Alarm Over Falling Life Expectancy," 45, 72.

100. Dmitry Kukanov and Natalya Timashova, "Will Russia's Nuclear Umbrella Be Left without Proper Supervision?" *Izvestiia*, September 16, 1995, 1–2, in *CDPSP* 47, no. 37 (1995): 23.

101. *Konstitutsiia RF*, Articles 1–13, 19, 26; quote from Article 2.

102. President's address, 10; Report of the President's Commission (1996), 52–53.

103. *Human Rights Watch World Report 1993*, 228–48; one of the bombings came later, in 1996.

104. Aleksandr Askandarian, "Chernofobia," *Novoe vremia*, no. 32 (1996): 12–14; Michael Specter, "Another Trolley Bombing in Moscow Leaves 30 Hurt," *New York Times*, July 13, 1996.

105. *Country Reports*, 1995, 945.

106. *Konstitutsiia RF*, Articles 22–27; Komissia po pravam cheloveka, *Doklad*, 14–15, 30–37; Aleksandr Podrabinek, "Khochesh'zhit'? Sprosi razreshenie!" *Ekspress Khronika*, March 6, 1997, 1.

107. Local authorities use *propiski* to deny residence to members of minority groups, particularly persons from the Caucasus or Central Asia. They assessed daily fees to visit Moscow, and fees of five hundred times the monthly minimum wage for residents of Russia to purchase a permit, a thousand times for persons from within the Commonwealth of Independent States, and fifteen hundred times for persons from other countries. *Konstitutsiia RF*, Articles 22–27; Komissia po pravam cheloveka, *Doklad*, 6–15, 30–37.

108. Aleksandr Dzyublo, "V Rossii vmesto propiski vvoditsia registratsiia: Novaia formal'nost' ili polnaia svoboda?" *Izvestiia*, December 21, 1996, 1.

109. *Country Reports*, 1995, 12.

110. Komissiia po pravam cheloveka, *Doklad*, 6–13.

111. V. A. Tishkov, "Chto est' Rossiia? (perspektivy natsie-stroitel'st va)," *Voprosy filosofii*, no. 2, 1995, trans. as "What Is Russia? (Prospects of Nation-Building)" in *Russian Politics and Law* 34, no. 2 (1995): 5.

112. "Aggressive Nationalism Threatens Human Rights," *Human Rights in Russia*, Interlegal International Charitable Foundation, Moscow, June 1993, 1–2; Konstantin Pleshakov, "Krym: Kuda nas tolkaiut glupye nationalisty," *Novoe vremia*, no. 31 (1993): 4–6; threatening parliamentary resolution directed at Estonia: "O merakh b sviazi s narusheniem prav cheloveka na territorii Estonskoi Respubliki," *Vedomosti*, no. 28 (1993), item 1074, July 1, 1993; Peter Juviler, "Russia's Time of Troubles," *International Symposium 1992*, Tokyo, Japan, 1993; Igor Torbakov, "The 'Statists' and the Ideology of Russian Imperial Nationalism," *RFE/RL Report* 1, no. 49 (1992): 10–16.

113. Tishkov, "Chto est' Rossiia?" 10–27.

114. Graham Smith, "Russia and the Russians," in Graham Smith, ed., *The Nationalities Question in the Post-Soviet States* (New York: Longman, 1996), 47–48.

115. Leonty Byzov, "V predverii reform," *Rossiiskaia gazeta*, December 13, 1995.

116. Peter Juviler, "Human Rights in the Ex-Soviet Successor States: A Case of the Bends," *Nationality Papers* 20, no. 2 (1992): 15–24.

117. *The Ingush–Ossetian Conflict in the Prigorodnyi Region* (New York: Human Rights Watch/Helsinki, 1996), 9–17. The census of 1989 counted 956,879 Chechens and 237,438 Ingush, making up 71 percent of the inhabitants of the area, along with

23 percent Russian and 6 percent other nonindigenous residents. Marjorie Mandelstam Balzer, "Turmoil in Russia's Mini-Empire," *Perspective* (Boston University) 2, no. 3 (1992): 2–3, 7; demographics from Goskomstat SSSR, supplied by Prof. Robert Lewis.

118. *The Ingush–Ossetian Conflict in the Prigorodnyi Region*, 19–100; *Human Rights Watch World Report 1992*, 539–41; *Human Rights Watch World Report 1993*, 234; Vladimir Socor, "Moldova's Dniestr Ulcer," *RFE/RL Report* 2, no. 1 (1993): 12–16.

119. V. A. Fokin, "Severnaia Osetiia i Ingushetiia: Problemy i vozmozhnie resheniia," *Kentavr*, no. 3 (1995), 82–95, trans. as "North Ossetia and Ingushetia: Problems and Possible Solutions," in *Russian Politics and Law* 34, no. 4 (1996): 49–65.

120. Tishkov, "Chto Est' Rossiia?" 10–14.

121. Edward W. Walker, "The New Russian Constitution and the Future of the Russian Federation," *The Harriman Institute Forum* 5, no. 10 (1992): 1–16.

122. Balzer, "Turmoil in Russia's Mini-Empire," *Perspective* 2, no. 3 (1992): 2–3, 7.

123. Interview with Executive Secretary Oleg Rumyantsev of the RSFSR Constitutional Commission, "Natsional'naia politika: Poslednii shans vozrodit' edinuiu gosudarstvennost' Rossii," *Rossiiskaia gazeta*, January 15, 1992; talk by Mr. Rumyantsev, Freedom House, New York, January 24, 1992; *Konstitutsionnyi vestnik*, nos. 8, 9 (1991). Rumyantsev publicly scorned nationalist agitation within the federation as "tribalism." Sharlet, "The Prospects for Federalism," 119.

124. *Konstitutsiia RF*, Article 4.

125. Ibid., Article 5(3).

126. Sharlet, "The Prospects for Federalism," 119–23.

127. *Konstitutsiia RF*, Article 71; N. A. Mikhaleva, "Konstitutsionnye reformy v respublikakh-sub'ektakh Rossiiskoi Federatsii," *Gosudarstvo i pravo*, no. 4 (1995), 3–10, trans. as "Constitutional Reform in the Subjects of the Russian Federation," in *Russian Politics and Law*, vol. 34, no. 4, 66–79.

128. Tishkov, "Chto est' Rossiia? 16.

129. Lapidus and Walker, "Nationalism, Regionalism, and Federalism," 87–109; Scott A. Bruckner and David J. Kramer, "At Stake in Russia's Endless Elections," *Christian Science Monitor*, December 2, 1996, 18; Marshall Ingwerson, "Moscow's New Angst: Yeltsin Loses Power to the Hinterlands," ibid., November 27, 1996, 1, 7; Gleb Cherkasov and Vladimir Shpak, "Regional Elections: Everyone Is Celebrating Victory," *Sevodnia*, December 26, 1996, *CDPSP*, 48, no. 52 (1996), 4.

130. "Turmoil in Russia's Mini-Empire," 2. Of those voting in the Tatarstan referendum, 61.4 percent favored independence in a population of 48 percent Tatar, 43 percent Russian, and 9 percent other non-Tatar inhabitants. Ann Sheehy, "Tatarstan Asserts Its Sovereignty," *RFE/RL Report*, no. 14 (1992), 4.

131. *Postanovlenie Konstitutsionnogo Suda RSFSR, 13 marta, 1992*, officially stamped, typed text.

132. Appended to the amended 1978 constitution were: a treaty on the division of authority between governmental organs of the Russian Federation and those of 19 "sovereign republics," excluding Chechnya and Tatarstan (including a "protocol" on giving no less than 50 percent of seats in one legislative chamber of the Russian Federation to deputies from the constituent republics, autonomous oblasts, and autonomous *okrugs*); a similar treaty signed by representatives of 56 *krais* and oblasts and the cities of Moscow and St. Petersburg (with a protocol on implementing agreements over matters like control of natural resources, states of emergency); and a treaty signed by 12 autonomous oblasts and *okrugs*—all dated March 22, 1992. In addition was the instrument of ratification of the Congress of People's Deputies, April 10, 1992, in *Konstitutsiia Rossiiskoi Federatsii*, the 1978 constitution, amended,

1992. The Federation Treaty, signed by 18 autonomous republics, March 13, 1992, *Rossiiskaia gazeta*, March 18, 1992, in *CDSP* 44, no. 13 (1992): 15–16. Decree of the Congress of People's Deputies ratifying treaty, *Vedomosti*, 1992, no. 17, item 898.

133. Robert Sharlet, "The Prospects for Federalism," 115–27.

134. Tishkov, "Chto est' Rossiia?" 16–19.

135. Jack Matlock, panel discussion, Columbia University, December 8, 1995; Dmitry Kamyshev, "Chuvashia Assigns the Center a Problem on a Constitutional Theme," *Kommersant-Daily*, January 20, 1995, in *CDPSP* 47, no. 3 (1995): 16; "Nikolai Fyodorov: 'A Russian Bureaucrat—That's Who Will Bring Russia Down,'" *Trud*, January 18, 1995, in *CDPSP* 47, no. 3 (1995): 16–17.

136. Gail W. Lapidus and Edward W. Walker, "Nationalism, Regionalism, and Federalism: Center–Periphery Relations in Post-Communist Russia," in Gail W. Lapidus, ed., *The New Russia: Troubled Transformation* (Boulder, CO: Westview Press), 79–114.

137. "Decree of the President of the Russian Federation: 'On a Day of Concord and Reconciliation,'" *Rossiiskie vesti*, November 10, 1996, in *CDPSP* 48, no. 45 (1996): 5; "Holiday: Ivan Rodin, November 7 Is Celebrated in Russia," *Nezavisimaya gazeta*, November 10, 1996, in *CDPSP* 48, no. 45 (1996): 6.

Chapter 10. The Struggle Continues

1. Ludmilla Alexeyeva, lecture at meeting on "Human Rights Education in Russia," Moscow Province Advanced Educational Training Institute, December 15, 1995.

2. Katherine Young, "Growing a Democracy: Russia's Non-Profit Sector Takes Root," *Russian Life*, September 1996, 13.

3. Alexeyeva, lecture at meeting on "Human Rights Education in Russia."

4. Interview with Viktor Kogan-Yasny, head of the NGO "Za Chelovecheskoe Dostoinstvo" (For Human Dignity), Moscow, December 19, 1995.

5. Interview with Vladimir Rudnev, Moscow, December 15, 1996.

6. Alexeyeva, lecture at meeting on "Human Rights Education in Russia."

7. Interview with Ludmilla Alexeyeva, Moscow, December 18, 1995.

8. Alexeyeva, lecture at meeting on "Human Rights Education in Russia."

9. Moscow Helsinki Group, *Spravochnik pravozashchitnikh organizatsii SNG* (St. Petersburg: Norma, 1995), 3–79; I thank Ludmilla Thorne of Freedom House for the book.

10. Ibid., 5–9.

11. Interview with Natalia Taubina, Columbia University, New York, September 20, 1996.

12. A. Ya. Azarov, "Obuchenie Pravam Cheloveka: Rasmyshleniia i nektorie itogi," *Pedagogicheskii poisk*, no. 1–2 (1995), 1; *TACIS Democracy Programme Moscow: Project: Human Rights Education in Russia* (Moscow, 1995); meeting on "Human Rights Education in Russia," Moscow Province Advanced Educational Training Institute, December 15, 1996; interviews with Doctor of Laws Anatoly Azarov, director, project on "Human Rights Education in Russia," Moscow Regional Institute for Advanced Teacher Training, December 15 and 20, 1995.

13. Moscow Helsinki Group, *Spravochnik pravozashchitnikh organizatsii SNG*, 5, 8, 9, 19.

14. Ibid., 19, 22.

15. Interviews with Arseny Roginsky, President, "Memorial" (Historical-Enlight-

enment and Philanthropic Society), Yan Rachinsky, Co-President, Moscow Memorial, member of Council of the Human Rights Center of Memorial, Moscow, December 16, 1995.

16. The project of uncovering victims' fates goes on in Moscow, Ekaterinburg, Perm, Ryazan, Tula, Voronezh, Tomsk, and, outside Russia, in Georgia, Kyrgyzstan, and Ukraine. "Memorial" in Ekaterinburg runs a "Saturday Club of the Repressed." Meeting at "Memorial," Moscow, December 16, 1995, for kin and survivors of purge victims to mark the publication of two of three books in a series listing victims of purge-era executions who were shot and buried secretly in Donskoe and Vagan'kovskoe Monasteries (*Rasstrel'nye spiski: Vypusk 1. Donskoe kladbishche 1934–1940* [Moscow: Memorial, 1993, published in 1995]; *Rasstrel'nye spiski: Vypusk 2. Vagan'kovskoe kladbishche, 1926–1936* [Moscow: Memorial, 1995]). Information was assembled in the Central Archive of the Ministry of Security of the Russian Federation and is part of the large project of rehabilitation conducted by the archive since 1990 in accordance with the Edict of the Presidium of the USSR Supreme Soviet "On additional measures for restoring justice for the victims of repressions during the thirties and forties and beginning of the fifties" of January 16, 1989, and the law of the RSFSR, "On rehabilitation of victims of political repressions" of October 18, 1991 (ibid., 187). Panel of speakers, chaired by Arseny Roginsky, included Justice Anatoly Kononov of the Constitutional Court, Sergei Kovalyov, and Oleg Borisovich Mozokhin (archive worker in the Ministry of Security of the Russian Federation [MBRF]).

17. *Country Reports*, 1996, 993; Veronika Marchenko, *Takaia armiia . . . narusheniia prav cheloveka v voorzhennykh silakh* (New York: Freedom House, 1995); "Belaya kniga: Polozhenie s pravami cheloveka v vooruzhenykh silakh," Moscow, 1996; I thank Natalia Taubina for the book.

18. Aleksei Arbatov, talk at preelection meeting, Precinct No. 1, Moscow, December 15, 1995.

19. Moscow Helsinki Group, *Spravochnik pravozashchitnikh organizatsii SNG*, 29–67; Yury Dzhibladze (initiative group of the antiwar campaign of noncommercial organizations in Russia), "Tretii sektor protiv voiny"; "Obrashchenie obshchestvennykh organizatsii Rossii k prezidentu Rossiiskoi Federatsii, chlenam pravitel'stva RF, dputatam Federal'nogo Sobraniia RF," Moscow, February 1996.

20. Interview with Vladimir Ilyushenko, a leading research fellow in the Institute of Comparative Political Science and Problems of the Labor Movement of the Russian Academy of Sciences, and member, Amnesty and Pardon Committee under the President. Vladimir Ilyushenko, (coeditor with A. I. Zorin), *Vokrug Imeni Otsa Aleksandra* (Moscow: Obshchestvo "Kul'turnoe vozrozhdenie," 1993); comment in Z. A. Krakhmal'nikova, ed., *Russkaia ideia i evrei: Rokovoi spor—sbornik statei* (Moscow: Nauka, 1994), 233–37; note in *Mezhdunarodnyi forum "Fascism v Totalitarnom i Posttotalitarnom Obshchestve": Ideinye osnovy, sotsial'naya baza, politicheskaia aktivnost'. Bypusk 1 Voina v Chechne: Opastnost' totalitarizma. Materialy kruglogo stola* (Moscow: Institute Otkrytoe obshchestvo—Fonda Dzh. Sorosa Programma "Vostok-Vostok," 1995), 17–20; Vladimir Ilyushenko, "Vozdukh nenavisti," *Literaturnye novosti*, no. 17 (1993): 9; Irina A. Levinskaya, "The Churches in Russia amid Changes: The Russian Orthodox Church," paper presented at conference on "Human Rights Movements and Religious Organizations in Russia and Eastern Europe after 1985: The Search for New Identities," Columbia University, November 17, 1995.

21. Interview with Rachel Denber, Human Rights Watch/Helsinki, Moscow, December 19, 1995.

22. Prospectus, *Moscow Research Center for Human Rights*, Moscow, 1995. The NGOs include Soldiers' Mothers Committee of Russia (1989) and the Mothers' Rights

Foundation (1990); the Movement without Frontiers (1992); the Moscow Helsinki Group (1976); the Moscow Center for Prison Reform (1988), which publishes and does research on the subject, and runs a weekly radio program for prisoners (interview with Valery Abramkin, Director, Moscow Center for Prison Reform, Moscow, December 18, 1995); the Society for the Guardianship of Penitentiary Institutions (1992), offering help to prisoners and their relatives; the Independent Psychiatric Association (1989); the Right to Life and Human Dignity Association (1990), which opposes death penalty and torture and other governmental violations of the rights to life; the Society for the Defense of Convicted Businessmen and Economic Freedoms (1989); and the Association for the Protection of the Disabled (Moscow Branch, formed 1992). Among a half-dozen Center affiliates are: The Civic Forum Association (1992), a member of the European Civic Forum, concerned with interests of socially unprotected groups—refugees, orphans, disabled, servicemen; the Moscow Antifascist Center (1989), which opposes extremist movements; Omega Society (1992), which is an interethnic, interconfessional human rights charitable society with the purpose of heading off interethnic conflicts; and the Society for the Defense of Human Rights in Central Asia (1993), which joins activists from Central Asian republics engaged in the gathering and distribution of information on human rights violations there.

23. *Pravo cheloveka v Rossii: informatsionnaia set'*, no. 21 (1996): 37–38.

24. Sergei Smirnov, "Otchet o provedenii pervykh dvukh seminarov v ramkakh proekta rasshireniia informatsionnoi pravozshchitnoi seti, finansiruemykh Fondom 'Evrasia'" (grant No. M95-0524), *Prava cheloveka v Rossii: informatsionnaia set'*, no. 21 (1996): 37–43.

25. Ibid., 60–65.

26. Ibid., 6–7.

27. Ibid., 8–13.

28. Ibid., 14–15.

29. Ibid., 4–6.

30. Information on the Perm Center, here and in what follows, comes from Igor Averkiev, "Otchet o realizatsii 'Permskogo pravozhshchitnogo proekta' v period s 1 fevralia 1995 goda po 1 fevralia 1996 goda (subproekt Zashchitim prava cheloveka)," *Prava cheloveka v Rossii informatsionnaia set'*, no. 21 (1996): 12–27.

31. Averkiev, "Otchet," 14.

32. *Pravo cheloveka v Rossii: informatsionnyi set'*, no. 11 (1995): 14–23.

33. Averkiev, "Otchet," 16–18; quote on 17–18.

34. Ibid., 20.

35. Artem Fyodorov, "Kto zashchishchaet nashi prava?" *Ekpress-khronika*, May 24, 1996, 1.

36. Vladimir Kartashkin, chairman of the President's Human Rights Commission, letter to author, September 9, 1996.

37. Katherine Young, "Growing a Democracy: Russia's Non-Profit Sector Takes Root," *Russian Life*, September 1996, 13.

38. Ibid., 13.

39. Those signing the appeal included the Supreme Coordinating Center of the Religious Board of Russian Muslims, the Foundation for the Development of Moslem Peoples, the Islamic Congress of Russia, the Association for the Observance of Human Rights in Central Asia, the Union of Muslims of Russia, the Nur Movement, and the Islamic Cultural Center of Russia. "Appeal to the Religious Community, to the Russian and International Public," October 11, 1995, Moskovskii Issledovatel'skii Tsentr po Pravam Cheloveka, *Ezhemesiachnyi informatsionnyi biulleten'*, no. 14 (1995): 3.

40. Ibid., 29–30; quotes on 30.

41. Ibid., 31–32; quotes on 31, 32.

42. Ibid., 32–34, quote on 33.

43. Ibid., 33–34.

44. Mary Holland, "Nongovernmental Organizations," in *Human Rights and Legal Reform in the Russian Federation* (New York: Lawyers Committee for Human Rights, 1993), 110.

45. Moscow Helsinki Group, *Spravochnik pravozashchitnikh organizatsii SNG*, 68–77.

46. Alla Kazakina and Mary S. Holland, "The Law on Charitable Activities and Organizations: A Preliminary Assessment," *CIS Law Notes*, February 1996, 24–27.

47. Ibid., 24–27; Young, "Growing a Democracy," 13.

48. Interview with Natalia Taubina, Associate Director, Civil Society Fund, Columbia Human Rights Center retreat, Cornwall, CT, August 27, 1996.

49. Averkiev, "Otchet," 22.

50. Moscow Helsinki Group, *Spravochnik pravozashchitnikh organizatsii SNG*, 21–22.

51. *Pravo cheloveka v Rossii: informatsionnaia set'*, no. 21 (1996), 67.

52. Moscow Helsinki Group, *Spravochnik pravozashchitnikh organizatsii SNG*, 2, 6, 12–13, 43.

53. Natalia Taubina, "Otchet o Rabote Fonda "Za Grazhdanskoe Obshchestvo (iul'–sentiabr' 1995g)," *Moskovskii Issledovatel'skii Tsentr Po Pravam Cheloveka. Ezhemesiachnyi informatsionnyi biulleten'*, no. 14 (1995): 4–5.

54. Averkiev, "Otchet," 14.

55. The Supreme Coordinating Center of the Religious Board of Russian Moslems et al., "Appeal to the Religious Community, to the Russian and International Public," 33–34.

56. Young, "Growing a Democracy," 14.

57. Ibid., 15.

58. Y. Orlov, "Memorandum" for Secretary of State James Baker, February 20, 1991, courtesy Jeri Laber and Helsinki Watch.

59. See, e.g., Stephen White, Richard Rose, and Ian McAlister, *How Russia Votes* (Chatham, NJ: Chatham House Publishers, 1996), xi.

60. Aisle Mil'shtein, "Vouch i strakhi: Privichka v kotoryi raz okazalas' sil'nee progressa," *Novyi vremya*, no. 4 (1996): 15–16.

61. Mikhail Gorbachev, interview with Fred Coleman and Alan Cooperman, *U.S. News & World Report*, February 13, 1995, 65.

62. Max Weber, "Politics as a Vocation," in H. H. Gerth and C. Wright Mills, eds., *From Max Weber: Essays in Sociology* (London: Routledge & Kegan Paul, 1948), 128.

63. Interview with Knothole Taubina, Columbia University, New York, September 20, 1996.

64. Dmitry Likhachev, "O proshlom i budushchem Rossii, interview with Natalia Zhelnorova," *Argumenty i fakty*, October 23, 1995; trans. in *Russian Politics and Law* 34, no. 4 (1996): 85.

Selected Bibliography

Human Rights and Democratization

Caraley, Demetrios, ed. *Presidential and Parliamentary Democracies: Which Work Best?* Special issue of *Political Science Quarterly* 109, no. 3 (1994).

Center for the Study of Human Rights, Columbia University. *Twenty-Five Human Rights Documents*. New York, 1994.

Claude, Richard Pierre, and Burns H. Weston, eds. *Human Rights in the World Community: Issues and Action,* 146–56. 2d ed. Philadelphia: University of Pennsylvania Press, 1992.

Concluding Document of the Vienna Follow-Up Meeting. Washington, D.C.: U.S. Commission on Security and Cooperation in Europe, January 1989.

Dahl, Robert A. *A Preface to Democratic Theory.* Chicago: University of Chicago Press, 1956; Phoenix edition 1963.

Diamond, Larry, "Is the Third Wave Over?" *Journal of Democracy* 7, no. 3 (1996): 20–37.

Diamond, Larry, and Marc E. Plattner. *The Global Resurgence of Democracy.* 2d ed. Baltimore: The Johns Hopkins University Press, 1996.

Document of the Copenhagen Meeting of the Conference on the Human Dimension of the CSCE. Washington, D.C.: U.S. Commission on Security and Cooperation in Europe, June 1990.

Donnelly, Jack. *International Human Rights.* Boulder, CO: Westview Press, 1993.

Encyclopedia of Human Rights. 2d ed. New York: Taylor and Francis, 1996.

Fleron, Frederic J., Jr., and Erik P. Hoffmann. *Post-Communist Studies and Political Science: Methodology and Empirical Theory in Sovietology.* Boulder, CO: Westview Press, 1993.

Forsythe, David. *Human Rights in World Politics.* Lincoln: University of Nebraska Press, 1989.

Fox, Gregory H., "The Right to Political Participation in International Law." *Yale Journal of International Law* 17, no. 2 (1992): 539–607.

Greenberg, Douglas, Stanley N. Katz, Melanie Beth Oliviero, and Steven C. Wheatley. *Constitutionalism and Democracy: Transitions in the Contemporary World.* New York: Oxford University Press, 1993.

Henkin, Louis. *The Age of Rights.* New York: Columbia University Press, 1990.

Horowitz, Donald L. "Democracy in Divided Societies: The Challenge of Ethnic Conflict." *Journal of Democracy* 4, no. 4 (1993): 19–38.

Human Rights Violations in the United States. New York: Human Rights Watch and ACLU, 1994.

Huntington, Samuel. *The Third Wave: Democratization in the Late Twentieth Century.* Norman and London: University of Oklahoma Press, 1993.

Jowitt, Ken. *New World Disorder: The Leninist Extinction.* Berkeley: University of California Press, 1992.

Juviler, Peter. "Clearing a Path to the International Bill of Rights." In Kenneth Hunter and Timothy Mack, eds., *International Rights and Responsibilities for the Future,* 53–66. Westport: Praeger 1996.

Laqueur, Walter, and Barry Rubin. *The Human Reader.* 2d ed. New York: Meridian Books, 1990.

Linz, Juan, and Alfred Stepan. *Problems of Democratic Transition and Consolidation: Southern Europe, South America, and Post-Communist Europe.* Baltimore: The Johns Hopkins University Press, 1996.

Maier, Charles S. "Democracy and Its Discontents." *Foreign Affairs* 72, no. 4 (1994): 48–64.

Marks, Gary, and Larry Diamond, eds. *Reexamining Democracy: Essays in Honor of Seymour Martin Lipset.* Newbury Park, CA: Sage Publications, 1992.

O'Donnell, Guillermo, Philippe C. Schmitter, and Laurence Whitehead, eds. *Transitions from Authoritarian Rule.* Baltimore: The Johns Hopkins University Press, 1986.

Putnam, Robert D. *Making Democracy Work: Civic Traditions in Modern Italy.* Princeton, NJ: Princeton University Press, 1993.

Schoenbrod, David. *Power without Responsibility: How Congress Abuses the People through Delegation.* New Haven, CT: Yale University Press, 1993.

Sen, Amartya. "Individual Freedom as a Social Commitment." *New York Review of Books,* June 14, 1990, 49–54.

Steiner, Henry, and Philip Alston. *International Human Rights in Context: Law, Politics, Morals.* New York: Oxford University Press, 1996.

Weiss, Thomas G., David P. Forsythe, and Roger A. Coate. *The United Nations and Changing World Politics.* Boulder, CO: Westview Press, 1995.

World Conference on Human Rights, Vienna, Austria, June 1993. New York, UN DPI/ 1394-39399-August 1993-20M, 1993.

Tsarism's Ambiguous Legacy

Abramovitch, Raphael R. *The Soviet Revolution, 1917–1939.* New York: International Universities Press, 1962.

Billington, James H. *The Icon and the Axe: An Interpretive History of Russian Culture.* New York: Alfred A. Knopf, 1966.

Browder, Robert Paul, and Alexander F. Kerensky, eds. *The Provisional Government 1917: Documents.* 3 vols. Stanford, CA: Hoover Institution, 1961.

Crisp, Olga, and Linda Edmondson, eds. *Civil Rights in Imperial Russia.* Oxford: Clarendon Press, 1989.

Custine, Marquis de. *The Empire of the Czar: A Journey through Eternal Russia.* New York: Doubleday Anchor Books, 1989.

Deutscher, Isaac. *The Prophet Armed: Trotsky, 1879–1921.* New York: Oxford University Press, 1954.

Emmons, Terence, and Wayne S. Vucinich, eds. *The Zemstvo in Russia: An Experiment in Local Self-Government.* New York: Cambridge University Press, 1982.

Fischer, George. *Russian Liberalism: From Gentry to Intelligentsia.* Cambridge, MA: Harvard University Press, 1958.

Florinsky, Michael T. *Russia: A History and an Interpretation*. Vol. 2. New York: Macmillan, 1953.

Heuman, Susan. "Prerevolutionary New Thinking." In Peter Juviler and Bertram Gross, eds., with Vladimir Kartashkin and Elena Lukasheva, 69–93. *Human Rights for the 21st Century*. Armonk, NY: M. E. Sharpe, 1993.

Karpovich, Michael. *Imperial Russia, 1801–1917*. New York: Holt, Rinehart, and Winston, 1932; paperback reprint, 1961.

Kucherov, Samuel. *Courts, Trials, and Lawyers under the Last Three Tsars*. New York: Praeger, 1953.

Lincoln, C. Bruce. *The Great Reforms: Autocracy, Bureaucracy, and the Politics of Change in Imperial Russia*. Dekalb: Northern Illinois University Press, 1990.

Milyoukov, Paul. *Russia and Its Crisis*. Chicago: The University of Chicago Press, and London: T. Fisher Unwin, 1905.

Pares, Bernard. *A History of Russia*. Rev. ed. London: Jonathan Cape, 1947.

Pipes, Richard, ed. *The Russian Intelligentsia*. New York: Columbia University Press, 1961.

Raeff, Marc. *Understanding Imperial Russia*. New York: Columbia University Press, 1984.

Riasanovsky, Nicholas V. *A History of Russia*. 5th ed. New York/Oxford: Oxford University Press, 1993.

Schapiro, Leonard. *The Communist Party of the Soviet Union*. 2d ed. New York: Vintage Books, 1971.

Skripilev, Evgenii. "Individual Rights before October 1917: A Russian Perspective." In Peter Juviler and Bertram Gross, eds., with Vladimir Kartashin and Elena Lukasheva. *Human Rights for the 21st Century*. Armonk, NY: M. E. Sharpe, 1993.

Stavrou, Theofanis George, ed. *Russia under the Last Tsar*. Minneapolis: University of Minnesota Press, 1969.

Taranovski, Theodore, ed. *Reform in Modern Russian History: Progress or Cycle?* Washington, D.C./Cambridge: Woodrow Wilson Press and Cambridge University Press, 1995.

Weissman, Neil B. *Reform in Tsarist Russia: The State Bureaucracy and Local Government, 1900–1914*. New Brunswick, NJ: Rutgers University Press, 1981.

Wolfe, Bertram. *Three Who Made a Revolution*. New York: Delta, 1964.

Wortman, Richard E. *The Development of Russian Legal Consciousness*. Chicago: University of Chicago Press, 1976.

Soviet Communism: Political and Social Cleansing

Barry, Donald B., F. J. M. Feldbrugge, George Ginsburgs, and Peter B. Maggs, eds. *Soviet Law after Stalin. Part III: Soviet Institutions and the Administration of Law*. Alphen aan den Rijn, the Netherlands/Germantown, MD: Sijthoff and Noordhoff, 1979.

Berman, Harold J. *Justice in the U.S.S.R.: An Interpretation of Soviet Law*. Rev. ed. New York: Vintage, 1963.

Bialer, Seweryn. *The Soviet Paradox: External Expansion, Internal Decline*. New York: Alfred A. Knopf, 1986.

Brown, Archie, and Jack Gray. *Political Culture and Political Change in Communist States*. 2d ed. New York: Holmes and Meier, 1979.

Brzezinski, Zbigniew K. *The Soviet Bloc: Unity and Conflict*. Rev. ed. New York: Praeger, 1961.

Carrere D'Encausse, Helene. *Confiscated Power: How Soviet Russia Really Works.* New York: Harper & Row, 1980.

Chamberlin, W. H. *Russia's Iron Age.* London: Gerald Duckworth, 1935.

Cohen, Stephen F. *Bukharin and the Bolshevik Revolution: A Political Biography, 1888–1938.* New York: Alfred A. Knopf, 1973.

Conquest, Robert. *The Great Terror: A Reassessment.* New York: Oxford University Press, 1991.

———. *The Nation Killers: The Soviet Deportation of Nationalities.* New York: Macmillan, 1970.

Fainsod, Merle. *How Russia Is Ruled.* 2d ed. Cambridge, MA: Harvard University Press, 1963.

Garthoff, Raymond. *Detente and Confrontation: America–Soviet Relations from Nixon to Reagan.* Washington, D.C.: The Brookings Institution, 1985.

Geiger, H. Kent. *The Family in Soviet Russia.* Cambridge, MA: Harvard University Press, 1968.

Goldman, Wendy Z. *Women, the State, and Revolution: Soviet Family Policy and Social Life, 1917–1936.* New York and Cambridge: Cambridge University Press, 1993.

Hazard, John N. *Communists and Their Law: A Search for the Common Core of the Legal Systems of the Marxian Socialist States.* Chicago: Chicago University Press, 1969.

Juviler, Peter. "Contradictions of Revolution: Juvenile Crime and Rehabilitation." In Abbott Gleason, Peter Kennez, and Richard Stites, eds., *Bolshevik Culture: Experiment and Order in the Russian Revolution.* Bloomington: Indiana University Press, 1985.

———. "Mass Education and Justice in Soviet Courts: The Visiting Sessions." *Soviet Studies* 18, no. 4 (1967): 494–509.

———. *Revolutionary Law and Order: Politics and Social Change in the USSR.* New York: The Free Press, 1976.

———. "Soviet Marxism and Family Law." *Columbia Journal of Transnational Law* 23, no. 2 (1985): 385–400.

Juviler, Peter, and Henry Morton, eds. *Soviet Policy Making: Studies of Communism in Transition.* New York: Praeger, 1967.

Karklins, Rasma. *Ethnic Relations in the USSR.* Boston: Allen and Unwin, 1986.

Lewin, Moshe. *The Gorbachev Phenomenon.* 2d ed. Berkeley: University of California Press, 1990.

———. *Lenin's Last Struggle.* New York: Pantheon Books, 1968.

Luryi, Yuri I. *Soviet Family Law.* Buffalo, NY: William S. Hein and Co., 1980.

Luxemburg, Rosa. *The Russian Revolution and Leninism or Marxism.* Ed. Bertram D. Wolfe. Ann Arbor: University of Michigan Press, 1961.

Medvedev, Roy. *Let History Judge: The Origins and Consequences of Stalinism.* Rev. ed. New York: Columbia University Press, 1989.

Pipes, Richard. *The Formation of the Soviet Union.* Cambridge, MA: Harvard University Press, 1954.

Rywkin, Michael. *Moscow's Moslem Challenge: Soviet Central Asia.* Armonk, NY: M. E. Sharpe, 1982.

Rubinstein, Alvin Z., ed. *The Foreign Policy of the Soviet Union.* 3d ed. New York: Random House, 1972.

Russian Institute, Columbia University. *The Anti-Stalin Campaign and International Communism.* New York: Columbia University Press, 1956.

Schlesinger, Rudolf, ed. *The Family in the U.S.S.R.: Documents and Readings.* London: Routledge and Kegan Paul, 1949.

Treadgold, Donald W. *Twentieth Century Russia.* 8th ed. Boulder, CO: Westview Press, 1995.

Tucker, Robert C. *Stalin as Revolutionary, 1879–1929.* New York: W. W. Norton, 1973.
———. *Stalin in Power: The Revolution from Above, 1928–1941.* New York: W. W. Norton, 1990.
Ulam, Adam. *Stalin: The Man and His Era.* Expanded ed. Boston: Beacon Press, 1989.
Unger, Aryeh L. *Constitutional Development in the USSR: A Guide to the Soviet Constitutions.* New York: Pica Press, 1982.
Valkenier, Elizabeth. *The Soviet Union and the Third World: An Economic Bind.* New York: Praeger, 1983.
Voslensky, Mikhail. *Nomenklatura: The Soviet Ruling Class.* Preface by Milovan Djilas. Garden City, NY: Doubleday, 1984.
Wolfe, Bertram D., ed. *Khrushchev and Stalin's Ghost: Text, Background, and Meaning of Khrushchev's Secret Report to the Twentieth Congress on the Night of February 24–25, 1956.* New York: Praeger, 1957.

The Human Rights Struggle and Dissident Movements

Alexeyeva, Ludmilla. *Soviet Dissent: Movements for National, Religious, and Human Rights.* Middletown, CT: Wesleyan University Press, 1985.
Amalrik, Andrei. *Will the Soviet Union Survive until 1984?* New York: Harper & Row, 1970.
Avrich, Paul. *Kronstadt 1921.* Princeton, NJ: Princeton University Press, 1970.
Bloch, Sidney, and Peter Reddaway. *Psychiatric Terror: How Soviet Psychiatry Is Used to Suppress Dissent.* New York: Basic Books, 1977.
Brumberg, Abraham, ed. *In Quest of Justice: Protest and Dissent in the Soviet Union Today.* New York: Praeger, 1970.
Chalidze, Valery. *To Defend These Rights: Human Rights in the Soviet Union.* New York: Random House, 1974.
Chornovil, Vyacheslav. *The Chornovil Papers.* New York: McGraw-Hill, 1968.
Cohen, Stephen H., ed. *An End to Silence: Uncensored Opinion in the Soviet Union.* New York: Norton, 1982.
Grigorenko, Petro G. *The Grigorenko Papers: Writings by General P. G. Grigorenko and Documents in His Case.* Boulder, CO: Westview Press, 1973.
Hayward, Max, ed. *On Trial: The Soviet State versus "Abram Tertz" and "Nikolai Arzhak."* Rev. and enlarged ed. New York: Harper & Row, 1967.
Kaminskaya, Dina. *Final Judgment: My Life as a Soviet Defense Attorney.* New York: Simon and Schuster, 1982.
Litvinov, Pavel, comp., and Peter Reddaway, ed. *The Trial of the Four: The Case of Galanskov, Ginzburg, Dobrovolsky, and Lashkova.* New York: Viking Press, 1971.
Mamonova, Tatyana. *Zhenshchina i Rossiia: Al'manakh* (1979). Translated as *Women and Russia: Feminist Writings from the Soviet Union.* Boston: Beacon Press, 1984.
Marchenko, Anatoly. *My Testimony.* Introduction by Max Hayward. New York: Dutton, 1969.
Medvedev, Roy. *On Socialist Democracy.* New York: Alfred A. Knopf, 1975.
Meerson-Aksenov, Michael, and Boris Shragin, eds. *The Political, Social, and Religious Thought of Russian 'Samizdat'—An Anthology.* Belmont, MA: Nordland, 1977.
On Speaking Terms: An Unprecedented Human Rights Mission to the Soviet Union (January 25–31, 1988). Vienna: International Helsinki Federation for Human Rights, 1988.
Reddaway, Peter, ed. *Uncensored Russia: Protest and Dissent in the Soviet Union.* New York: American Heritage Press, 1972.

Rubenstein, Joshua. *Soviet Dissidents: Their Struggle for Human Rights.* 2d ed. Boston: Beacon Press, 1985.

Sakharov, Andrei D. *Sakharov Speaks.* New York: Vintage Books, 1974.

Shanor, Donald R. *Behind the Lines: The Private War against Soviet Censorship.* New York: St. Martin's Press, 1985.

Solzhenitsyn, Aleksandr I. *The Gulag Archipelago: An Experiment in Literary Investigation, 1918–1956.* 3 vols. New York: Harper and Row, 1974–78.

———. *Letter to the Soviet Leaders.* New York: Harper & Row, 1974.

Tertz, Abram [Andrei Sinyavsky]. *On Socialist Realism.* New York: Pantheon Books, 1960.

Tokes, Rudolf L., ed. *Dissent in the USSR: Politics, Ideology, and People.* Baltimore: The Johns Hopkins University Press, 1975.

Perestroika

Barry, Donald D., ed. *Toward the "Rule of Law" in Russia? Political and Legal Reforms in the Transition Period.* Armonk, NY: M. E. Sharpe, 1992.

Colton, Timothy. *Dilemmas of Reform in the Soviet Union.* 2d ed. New York: Council on Foreign Relations, 1986.

Goldman, Marshall I. *What Went Wrong with Perestroika.* 2d ed. New York: W. W. Norton, 1991.

Gorbachev, Mikhail. *Perestroika: New Thinking for Our Country and the World.* New York: Harper & Row, 1987.

Hajda, Lubomyr, and Mark Beissinger, eds. *The Nationalities Factor in Soviet Politics and Society.* Boulder, CO: Westview Press, 1990.

Hosking, Geoffrey. *The Awakening of the Soviet Union.* 2d ed. Cambridge, MA: Harvard University Press, 1991.

Huskey, Eugene. "Between Citizen and State: The Soviet Bar (*Advokatura*) under Gorbachev." *Columbia Journal of Transnational Law* 28, no. 1 (1990): 95–116.

Juviler, Peter. "Human Rights after Perestroika: Progress and Perils." *The Harriman Institute Forum* 4, no. 6 (1991): 1–10.

———. "Presidential Power and Presidential Character." *Soviet Union* 16, nos. 2–3 (1991): 245–55.

Juviler, Peter, and Hiroshi Kimura, eds. *Gorbachev's Reforms: U.S. and Japanese Assessments.* Hawthorne, NY: Aldine de Gruyter, 1988.

Korey, William. *The Promises We Keep: Human Rights, the Helsinki Process, and American Foreign Policy.* New York: St. Martin's Press, 1993.

McCauley, Mary. *Soviet Politics, 1917–1991.* New York: Oxford University Press, 1992.

Matlock, Jack F., Jr. *Autopsy on an Empire: The American Ambassador's Account of the Collapse of the Soviet Union.* New York: Random House, 1995.

Millar, James R., and Sharon L. Wolchik, eds. *The Social Legacy of Communism.* Cambridge and New York: Cambridge University Press, Woodrow Wilson Center Series, 1994.

Sakwa, Richard, *Russian Politics and Society.* New York: Routledge, 1993.

Human Rights Reports

Abramkin, Valery, Rachel Denber, Richard Schimpf, and Clare Hughes, eds. *In Search of a Solution: Crime, Criminal Policy, and Prison Facilities in the Former Soviet Union*. Moscow: Center for Prison Reform, 1996.

Amnesty International Report. New York. Annual.

Amnesty International. *Prisoners of Conscience in the USSR: Their Treatment and Condition*. 2d ed. London, 1980.

Anti-Semitic Propaganda: Evidence from Books, Press, and Radio. London: Institute for Jewish Affairs, 1978.

Country Reports on Human Rights Practices for [year]: Report Submitted to the Committee on International Relations, U.S. House of Representatives, and the Committee on Foreign Relations, U.S. Senate, by the Department of State. Washington, D.C.: U.S. Government Printing Office. Annual since 1977.

Freedom in the World: The Annual Survey of Political Rights and Civil Liberties. New York: Freedom House. Annual editions, since 1977.

Freedom Review, 28, no. 1 (1997). Issue on "1997 Freedom Around the World."

From Below: Independent Peace and Environmental Movements in Eastern Europe and the USSR. New York: Helsinki Watch, 1987.

Gitelman, Zvi. *The Jewish Religion in the USSR*. Synagogue Council of America, 1971.

Helsinki Watch. *New Citizenship Laws in the Republics of the Former USSR*. New York, April 15, 1992.

————. *Overview: Prisons and Jails in the Helsinki Countries*. New York, September 1991.

————. *Ten Years Later: Violations of the Helsinki Accords*. New York, 1985.

Human Rights Watch/Helsinki. *Russian Federation: A Review of the Compliance of the Russian Federation with Council of Europe Commitments and Other Human Rights Obligations on the First Anniversary of Its Accession to the Council of Europe*. New York: Human Rights Watch, 9, no. 3(D) (February 1997).

Human Rights Watch World Report. New York. Annual since 1982.

Lawyers Committee for Human Rights. *Critique: Review of the U.S. Department of State's Country Reports on Human Rights Practices for [year]*. New York. Annual since 1980.

Report of the President's Commission on Human Rights On the Observance of the Rights of Man and Citizen in the Russian Federation (1994–1995). Moscow, 1996.

Taylor, Telford, with Alan Dershowitz and George Fletcher. *Courts of Terror: Soviet Criminal Justice and Jewish Emigration*. New York: Vintage Books, 1976.

Democracy and Human Rights in the Post-Soviet States

Bremmer, Ian, and Ray Taras. *New States, New Politics: Building the Post-Soviet Nations*. 2d ed. New York: Cambridge University Press, 1996.

Colton, Timothy J., and Robert Legvold, eds. *After the Soviet Union: From Empire to Nations*. New York: W. W. Norton, 1992.

Dawisha, Karen, and Bruce Parrott. *Russia and the New States of Eurasia: The Politics of Upheaval*. Cambridge and New York: Cambridge University Press, 1994.

Gellner, Ernest. *Nations and Nationalism*. Ithaca, NY: Cornell University Press, 1983.

Gurr, Ted Robert, and Barbara Harff. *Ethnic Conflict in World Politics*. Boulder, CO: Westview Press, 1994.

Horowitz, Donald L. *Ethnic Groups in Conflict*. Berkeley: University of California Press, 1985.

Human Rights Watch. *Slaughter among Neighbors: The Political Origins of Communal Violence.* New Haven, CT: Yale University Press, 1995.

Hurst Hannum. *Autonomy, Sovereignty, and Self-Determination: The Accommodation of Conflicting Rights.* 2d ed. Philadelphia: University of Pennsylvania Press, 1996.

Lieven, Anatol. *The Baltic Revolution: Estonia, Latvia, Lithuania, and the Path to Independence.* 2d ed. New Haven, CT: Yale University Press, 1994.

Park, Andrus. "Ethnicity and Independence: The Case of Estonia in Comparative Perspective." *Europe-Asia Studies* 46, no. 1 (1994): 69–87.

Smith, Graham. *The Nationalities Question in the Post-Soviet States.* 2d ed. London and New York: Longman, 1996.

Zarycky, George. "Along Russia's Rim: The Challenges of Statehood." *Freedom Review* 27, no. 1 (1996): 34–43.

Human Rights and Democratization in Russia

Åslund, Anders. "The Russian Road to the Market." *Current History* 94, no. 594 (October 1995): 311–16.

Azhgikhina, Nadezhda. "Will Russia Become the Capital of World Feminism?" *Demokratizatsiia* 3, no. 3 (1995): 243–51.

Barry, Donald D. "Constitutional Politics: The Russian Constitutional Court as a New Kind of Institution." In George Ginsburgs, Alvin Z. Rubinstein, and Oles M. Smolansky, eds., *Russia and America.* Armonk, NY: M. E. Sharpe, 1993.

Bonner, Elena. "A Letter to Boris Nikolaevich Yeltsin," December 28, 1994. Trans. Catherine Fitzpatrick. *New York Review of Books,* February 2, 1995, 44.

The Constitution of the Russian Federation. Russian and English texts. Moscow: Iuridicheskaia Literatura, 1994.

Dakin, Mary I. "Women and Employment Policy in Contemporary Russia." *Demokratizatsiia* 3, no. 3 (1995): 252–61.

Feshbach, Murray. *Ecological Disaster: Cleaning Up the Hidden Legacy of the Soviet Regime.* New York: Twentieth Century Fund Press, 1995.

Foster, Frances H. "Freedom with Problems: The Russian *Judicial Chamber* on Mass Media." *The Parker School Journal of East European Law* 3, no. 2 (1996): 141–74.

Goldman, Marshall I. "Is This Any Way to Create a Market Economy?" *Current History* 94, no. 594 (October 1995): 305–10.

Hoffmann, Erik P. "Challenges to Viable Constitutionalism in Post-Soviet Russia." *The Harriman Review* 7, nos. 10–12 (November 1994): 19–56.

Holland, Mary. *Human Rights and Legal Reform in the Russian Federation.* New York: Lawyers Committee for Human Rights, 1993.

Karatnycky, Adrian. "Democracy and Despotism: Bipolarism Renewed?" *Freedom Review* 27, no. 1 (1996): 5–11.

Korkeakivi, Antti, "A Modern Day Czar? Presidential Power and Human Rights in the Russian Federation." *Journal of Constitutional Law in Eastern and Central Europe* 2, no. 76 (1996): 76–110.

Lapidus, Gail W., ed. *The New Russia: Troubled Transformation.* Boulder, CO: Westview Press, 1995.

McDaniel, Tim. *The Agony of the Russian Idea.* Princeton, NJ: Princeton University Press, 1997.

Petro, Nicolai N. *The Rebirth of Russian Democracy.* Cambridge, MA: Harvard University Press, 1995.

Posadskaya, Anastasia. *Women in Russia: A New Era in Russian Feminism.* London/New York: Verso, 1994.

Remnick, David, *Resurrection: The Struggle for a New Russia.* New York: Random House, 1997.

Shalin, Dmitri N., ed. *Russian Culture at the Crossroads.* Boulder, CO: Westview Press, 1996.

Sharlet, Robert. "Citizen and State under Gorbachev and Yeltsin." In Stephen White, Alex Pravda, and Zvi Gitelman, eds., *Developments in Russian and Post-Soviet Politics*, 109–28. Durham, NC: Duke University Press, 1994.

White, Stephen, Richard Rose, and Ian McAlister. *How Russia Votes.* Chatham, NJ: Chatham House Publishers, 1996.

"Women: Victims—or Agents of Change?" *Transition* 1, no. 16 (1995): 2–28.

Index

Ablova, Natalia, 103
Abramowitz, Raphael, 25
adapting human rights and democracy, x, xiv, 6–8, 10
Afanasyev, Yury, 48, 55
Afghanistan, 92, 96, 97, 100
agenda of struggle for human rights and democracy, 186–87
Akayev, Askar, 66, 79
Alexander I, 14–15, 20, 36
Alexander II, 15, 18, 20, 36, 44
Alexander III, 19
Alexandra, Tsarina, 19, 22
Alexis, Tsarevich, 22
Aliyev, Haidar, 89
Ametistov, Ernest, 54, 153
Andreeva, Nina, 51
Andropov, Yury A., xi, 34, 44
Applebaum, Barbara, viii
Argentina, 129
Aristotle, 5
Armenia, 40, 61, 62, 66, 67, 78, 83, 85–88, 90, 91, 101, 129, 170; Armenian National Movement, 86; and Azerbaijan, 86; constitution, 86; democracy, 86; economy, 85–86; independence, 85; Dashnak Party, 85–86; Nakhichevan Autonomous Oblast, 85; and Russia, 85; and Turkey, 85; civil rights, 87–88; "Dro" group, 87; European Union condemnation, 87; economic and social rights, 87; forced conscription, 88; International Covenant on Civil and Political Rights, 86; laws on presidency and parliament, 86; Metzamor Nuclear Power Station, 88; minority members' cultural life, 88; parliament, 86; political rights, 85–87; Radio Liberty, 87;

Soviet favoritism, 86; war over Nagorno-Karabakh Autonomous Oblast, 85, 88; women, 88 (*see also* Women's human rights and advocacy)
Åslund, Anders, 71
Astor, Lady, 31
authoritarianism, ix, xii–xiii, 2, 66, 79, 82–103, 108, 124, 128–30, 185; pseudo-democracies, 83–95, 185
Azarov, Anatoly, 259 n.12
Azerbaijan, 61, 62, 83, 85, 88–91, 92, 102, 129, 170–71; Azerbaijani Independence Party, 89; Caspian Sea oil, 88, 89, 91; civil rights, 89–91; coups, 89; economy, 91, ethnic cleansing by Armenians, 90; Islamic Party, 89; military prisoners, 91; and Moscow, 90–91, 102; Musavat Party, 89, 90; National Council, 89; OSCE/UN Joint Electoral Observation Commission, on censorship and electoral fraud, 90; pogroms, 61; parliament, 89; political prisoners, 90, 91; political rights, 89–91; Popular Front Party, 88–91; refugees and displaced persons, 89; Social Democratic Party, 89, 90; violations of humanitarian law, 89, 90; and U.S. Commission for Security and Cooperation in Europe, 90; Nagorno-Karabakh Autonomous Oblast (NKAO), 61, 89, 90, 102; wives and children mistreated in, 90; women, 91 (*see also* Women's human rights and advocacy)

Baltic states, xiii, 62, 66, 104–23; "Baltic Way" demonstration, 107; civil and political rights, 105; civil rights, 110–11; corruption and organized crime, 109, 110; Council of Europe, 108, 109; economic

Smirnov, Igor, 76
Smirnov, Willy, 50
Snegur, Mircea, 61, 74
Sobchak, Anatoly, 63, 137
Solinar', Vladimir, 75–76
Soskovets, Oleg, 143
South Africa, 41, 148
Soviet breakup, xii, 60–65, 70; belated
  agreement on "union of sovereign states,"
  62; coup attempt, 62–63; use of force in
  republics, 55–56, 61–62; separatism and,
  60–62, 63–65
Soviet Communism (1917–53), 25–34; repression and terror, 28, 29–30, 31, 33, 35;
  Constituent Assembly, 28; enserfment,
  31–32; economic and social rights, 30;
  inequality, 31; juveniles and homelessness,
  30; Kronstadt massacre, 29; legitimacy,
  32–33; minorities, 30, 33; minority deportations, 31; NEP, 30; peasants, 30; legal,
  political, and social "cleansing," viii, 27–
  28, 149; "revolution from above," 30–31;
  RSFSR (Russian Soviet Federated Socialist Republic), 29, 124; secret police, 29,
  32, 33; "socialism in one country," 30;
  "socialist realism," 33; Stalin cult, 33, 34–
  35, 42; women and family, 30, 32. See also
  Women's human rights and advocacy
Soviet Communism (1953–64): abolition
  of police and parallel courts, 34; anti-
  Stalin campaign, 34–35; campaign against
  religion and proselytizing, 36; discrimination, 36; due process rights, 36–37;
  "intensification of class struggle" rejected,
  34; limits of the thaw, 34–38; Novocherkassk killing, 37; political prisoners, 35;
  repression of dissent, 35, 36, 37
Soviet Communism (1964–85): creeping
  openness, 43–44; death penalty, 57; dissent and repression, 38–41; KGB (secret
  police), 38, 39, 63; Prague Spring, 38.
  See also Human rights champions and
  advocates
Soviet democratization (1985–90), 48–59;
  Afghan War, 48; Andreeva letter, 51;
  legalizing freedoms of assembly, association, expression and information, religion
  and proselytizing, and emigration, 54;
  legalizing civil liberties, 54–55; CPSU de-
  throned, 52–54; glasnost', 2, 47, 49, 51, 57;
  Gorbachev's ambivalence on democracy,

pluralism, and market reform, 53–55,
  64–65; censorship under Gorbachev, 56;
  Kommunist, 49; International Helsinki
  Federation, 50; new thinking on human
  rights, 49–50, 57; obstacles to economic
  reform, 59–60; old thinking, blunders,
  50–52; parliamentary-electoral reforms,
  53; parties and democratic inexperience,
  58–59, 65; Reagan visit to Moscow, 48,
  51, 52; pro-Yeltsin demonstration (March
  1991), 57–58; violating rights, 55–57;
  Yeltsin expelled from leadership, 51
Soviet regime, vii, xi, 25–26, 27, 45–46;
  creeping openness, xi, 3, 43–44; dependency and supremacy of law and rights,
  28–29, 38, 45, 49. See also Communist
  Party; Legacy; Lenin
Speransky, Mikhail, 14–15
Stalin, Joseph, vii, ix, xi, 11, 27, 28, 30–35,
  39, 41, 42, 51, 59–61, 70, 75, 78, 92, 96,
  105, 137, 139, 148, 162, 171, 185
Starr, Frederick, 44
Stepashin, Sergei, 131
Stolypin, Pyotr, 16, 21
successor states, xii
Suprynuk, Boris, 94
Szporluk, Roman, 139

Tajikistan, 83, 92, 95–97, 100, 102, 129;
  civil war, 96, 97; civil rights, 96–97; economy, 97; economic and social rights,
  97; ethnic makeup, 96; human rights
  NGOs and international monitoring, 97;
  Islamic fundamentalism, 95; OSCE, 97;
  parliament, 96; political rights, 96–97;
  humanitarian aid, 97; refugees, 96; Soviet
  and territorial, linguistic, ethnic, and clan
  manipulation and incitement, 96; United
  Nations, 97; women, 97
Taranovski, Theodore, 12
Ter-Petrossian, Levon, 86
Thorne, Ludmilla, 133
Tocqueville, Alexis de, 82, 103
totalitarianism, vii, 2, 187
Trotsky, Leon, 24, 25, 27, 30; on party, 28;
  warning against dictatorship, 17
Tumanov, Vladimir, 154
Turaniyazova, Asia, 99
Turkey, 85, 92, 102, 129
Turkmenistan, 83, 92, 95, 98–99, 102, 129;
  parliament, 98